PERFORMANCE FLYING

by DENNIS PAGEN

HANG GLIDING TECHNIQUES FOR INTERMEDIATE AND ADVANCED PILOTS

steppe eagle

ILLUSTRATIONS BY THE AUTHOR

PERFORMANCE FLYING

HANG GLIDING TECHNIQUES FOR INTERMEDIATE AND ADVANCED PILOTS

First Printing: April, 1993
Printed in the United States of America
1 2 3 4 5 6 7 8 9 10 11 12 13 14

Published by Dennis Pagen
P.O. Box 101, Mingoville, PA 16856

Books by the Author

Hang Gliding Flying Skills
Hang Gliding Techniques
Understanding the Sky
Powered Ultralight Training Course
Powered Ultralight Flying
Paragliding Flight
Vol Libre! (French Edition)
En Parapente! (French Edition)

ISBN 0-936310-11-1

ACKNOWLEDGEMENT

Any work of this volume necessarily involves the ideas and input of many people. In fact I am grateful to all the pilots with whom I have shared the sky for I have learned from each of them. I also wish to thank those who contributed. A "thank you" goes to Chris Arai, Tony Barton, Mark Bennett, Johnny Carr, Kari Castle, Peter Harvey, Nelson Howe, Judy Leden, Jim Lee, Mark Newland, Butch Peachy, John Pendry, and Al Whitesell for contributing personal stories, observations or tricks of their aerial trade. I am greatly indebted to John Heiney, Donnell Hewett, Jerry Forburger and Pete Lehman for inspiration from their published articles. John also provided an abundance of excellent photos.

Finally, I must make special mention of two wonderful pilots, Mark Bennett and my wife, Claire. Mark performed the monumental job of editing on short notice, under pressure—some of which took place while he was competing. His literary wisdom is greatly appreciated and this book is better for it. To Claire fell the tedious task of typesetting, composing, organizing, scheduling and polishing the entire work in progress. I'm sure I'm better for it.

Dennis Pagen
Sand Ridge, Pennsylvania
    (Spring, 1993)

PHOTO CREDITS

Front Cover   — Larry Tudor in a dramatic Sky — Courtesy of Wills Wing
Back Cover   — Nelson Howe explores the lift in Japan.
                 — John Heiney drags a finger in the drink.

Courtesy of Bright Star Design Team: Pages 252 and 290
Courtesy of Danny Howell: Page 291
Courtesy of Moyes Delta Gliders: Pages 110, 145, 264, 271, 321
Courtesy of Mountain High Equipment: Page 95
Courtesy of Pacific Airwave: Pages 251, 297, 319, 320 (left)
Courtesy of Wills Wing: Pages 63, 288, 302, 329

Kamron Blevins: Page 300
Peter Burghardt: Pages 43, 146, 147, 310
Pat Cameron: Page 237
Richard Cobb: Pages 193, 194
Chris Etherton: Page 111
John Heiney: Pages 33, 42, 47, 52, 104, 153, 168, 214, 220, 286, 288 (bottom), 294, 322,
Nelson Howe: Page 154
Jane Indik: Page 23

Jim Lee: Page 78
Michael Robertson: Page 269
R. Spark: Page 270
Angela Szareck: Pages 10, 74, 281
Courtesy of Sherri Thévenot: Page 274
Howard Trapenau: Page 311
Cliff Whitney: Pages 247, 272 (top left)
All the other photos by the author.

ABOUT THE AUTHOR

*D*ennis Pagen has been writing about sport aviation—hang gliding, paragliding and ultralights—since 1975. He has written eleven books and over 350 articles, all related to flying for fun. There doesn't seem to be an end to this activity, for as the sports continue to evolve, new techniques and experiences demand definition.

The author was raised in Port Huron, Michigan, and educated at Michigan State University where he majored in physics and electrical engineering. Upon graduation he decided to see more of the world than a tourist town and a bucolic college could offer. He moved to Boulder, Colorado for a year, then to San Francisco, California, then to Leysin, Switzerland after touring Europe.

Dennis spent three years in Switzerland teaching skiing and mathematics at the Leysin American School. By 1972 he had seen enough of Swiss splendor and headed east. His overland route took him from Europe to Asia through all the countries in between. After a year exploring the orient as far south as Bali and as far north as Japan, he crossed the Pacific to the U.S. west coast.

In California in the fall of 1973 he witnessed personal flight for the very first time. This was hang gliding. After settling in Pennsylvania and buying a glider, Dennis learned to soar the endless Appalachian ridges and decided to devote himself to mankind's age-old dream of free flight.

Dennis researched and wrote his first book, *Flying Conditions*, in 1975. Also, this year he was appointed to the United States Hang Gliding Association Board of Directors and has served on this board to the present time. During this tenure, Dennis wrote the USHGA Instructor's Manual and helped develop many of the training and rating programs. His further activity in hang gliding consists of designing gliders, instructing and running meets as well as competing. Dennis has won numerous Regional Competitions and the 1978 US National Championships. He continues to compete without too much embarrassment around the globe.

TABLE OF CONTENTS

PREFACE

*H*ang gliding is a sport that has opened up new vistas for humanity in general and each individual pilot in particular. We can be transported far beyond our earthly limits and land ecstatic from the aerial feats we have accomplished. Flying is a mood enhancer.

On the other hand, fear, boredom or the demands that hang gliding imposes on our time can leave us with the "Thrill is Gone" blues. There is no need to be humming such a song, however, for offered in this very book are remedies to dispel doubts, plans to renew excitement and methods to maximize your airtime while minimizing your effort.

Expert pilots from around the world have contributed their wisdom throughout this manual. With their help we have endeavored to create a guide for intermediate and advanced pilots who wish to better their own performance. Novice pilots will also find a wealth of useful information in these chapters, but a certain amount of understanding, skill and experience is assumed in our discussions.

In order to best use the vault of the sky as our playground, we must cover some flying theory. But the non-technically inclined reader will dance a jig of joy to know what most of our information is practical and easily understood. We have included an appendix for those who desire detailed analysis. We have used the measurements of pounds and feet throughout but include the metric system in graphs and other important places. Conversions to the metric system appear at the end of the Appendix.

The first six chapters speak to the pilot wishing to excel at his or her home site. The next three chapters address the question of going places on the wing while the final chapters illuminate special skills or special considerations. Although a logical learning order is followed throughout, the reader may turn to any chapter of immediate interest and still gain understanding.

It is our hope that pilots of all levels will discover nuggets of insight on each page to further their reach and enjoyment in flight. If you find yourself overly compelled by gravity when others are scratching to cloud base, or landing in the slough of despondency when others are reaching goal, then this book is your passport to performance.

CHAPTER 1

Perfecting
the Pilot

"Once you have flown...

Flying is a passion that compels each of us to spend time, effort and money in pursuit of excellence. While our definition of excellence may differ, our desire to become better pilots is universal. We dream of longer, higher, further flights and fantasize about feats of aerial prowess. We are Superman at heart.

Occasional reality checks remind us that we can't all be heros. We have limits imposed by lifestyles and mediocre genes. But most of us *can* improve our flying skills to a very satisfying level.

In this chapter we examine the first two elements of the flying regime—the pilot and exercising judgement—with a mind to review and improve each one. We will provide tips from the masters and establish an overall plan to facilitate our progress. Here we begin our quest for excellence in the air.

I - THE COMPLETE PILOT

Qualities of a superior pilot:
- *Vision*
- *Imagination*
- *Understanding*

Up in the boundless sky you are the captain of your fate. You have command of your safety and performance potential. If you've progressed this far we can assume that flying has captured your spirit and you are taking the necessary steps to become a model of safety, a paragon of skill. The path to success is not difficult (remember flying is fun!) but is best negotiated with *vision, imagination* and *understanding.*

THE GIFT OF INSIGHT

We need *vision* to see our goals and appreciate where elements of training or practice fit into the overall scheme of flying. Such foresight is what helps develop record setters and champions. How's this for a goal:

> **Hang Gliding Goal**
> Extend your personal records, set a site record, win a regional contest or place in a national contest without having a single accident.

MAKING THE SCENE

Imagination is a great asset to a motorless pilot. A natural pilot is one who can observe the scene, imagine where the lift will be and follow the best flight path into that scene. This process is either conscious or unconscious depending on the pilot's experience with the procedure and with the site. Imagination helps us develop the big picture and figure out the conditions at a given site on a given day.

A STORE OF LORE

The bird learns to fly. The logical progression:
- *1st flight*
- *1st high flight*
- *1st 360*
- *1st soaring*
- *1st thermal*
- *1st XC*
- *1st competition*

We develop *understanding* by reading, questioning, experiencing, pondering then starting the whole process all over. This book is one of the tools—be sure to use the others—in this process. Instructors, articles, top pilots and plenty of flying are part of the source you must draw on to improve and excel.

Understanding gives us the framework on which to base decisions. But you can't absorb everything at once. There are a thousand things to think about and an overload of decisions to make. With experience however, more and more of these matters get handled by your "automatic pilot" and you can make decisions further afield. Like a chess player you become familiar with given situations and extend your game many moves ahead.

THE INTERMEDIATE SYNDROME

"Swollen pride obscures judgement."

Perhaps you have heard of the term *intermediate syndrome*. A syndrome is simply a common symptom that we all share as imperfect humans. The intermediate syndrome in hang gliding refers to the tendency for pilots at the intermediate level to feel they are invincible and therefore to push their limits. This is a dangerous malady. It can kill.

Sure, after years of effort you've earned your place in the sky. You want to stretch your wings. You want to fly. However Icarus of legend tells the story how brashness or overenthusiasm will plunge us into the drink. It is the intermediate stage where this is most apt to happen.

A bold ego may prevent you from becoming a bald eagle.

How can you avoid being a victim of intermediate syndrome? Simply pause to "know thyself" as Plato instructed. Do you have a desire to outdo your fellow pilots? Do you push your limits constantly? Do you think accidents happen only to the other less natural pilots? Do you deny that you may

A pilot prepares to launch at Le Grand Colombier in France.

have the intermediate syndrome? Do you have an overactive ego? Has anyone suggested that you should slow down or exercise more caution?

If you answer yes to two or more of these questions then you should probably carefully assess your situation and entertain the possibility of putting more caution into your flying. Mind you, pilots tend to be strong-willed and confident creatures which means many of these symptoms come with the package. It's only when they get out of control that we have a problem.

To cure the problem, remind yourself that patience is a virtue. Do not diminish your flying goals, but move them further into the future. The mountains and wind will be providing lift long past your expected life span. Hang gliding is great fun at all levels, so take time to savor the experience level at which you are flying.

THE ADVANCED SYNDROME

We mustn't just pick on intermediate pilots. There are beginner and advanced syndromes as well. While intermediate pilots *think* they are good, true advanced pilots by definition *are* good. However, sometimes they become complacent or lackadaisical about their flying.

In my flying I have never blown a launch beyond the training hill scuffles (I'm knocking on wood as I write this). However, some years back a friend pointed out that my takeoff runs had slowed . Yes, I was displaying the syndrome by waltzing off launch because it came easy. I saw the light and since that time I have tried to always focus on producing a fast, clean takeoff. The confidence and experience that this practice has produced is very useful when I am confronted with a challenging launch situation.

To avoid the dreaded advanced syndrome, simply put your pride on the shelf for the moment and realize that even the birds sometimes screw up. Take stock of each phase of your flying. The main idea is to review every segment of flight, especially your equipment (do you preflight carefully?), takeoff and landing procedures. Make sure they are impeccable and you always leave a margin for error. Now take your pride back and continue to assure there is not a sign of syndrome anywhere near you. .

FEAR OF FLYING

Fear is a natural part of flying because it's a natural defense mechanism. You know by age one (two if you're slow) that it hurts to fall. That we can fall with our wings is obvious to anyone who has struggled at the training hill.

So a reasonable amount of fear can keep you safe by switching on the flashing red lights whenever challenging situations threaten your security. This can be useful to pilots for promoting good health and longevity. However, too much fear can be debilitating. Anyone who has been flying for a while can cite cases where a pilot rushed his or her learning, scared themselves with an accident or near miss, then found their progress slowed greatly by inordinate fear. Phrases like "lost their nerve" or "shell-shocked" are heard.

Use your natural fear to keep yourself flying safely. Here's how:

▶1. *Listen* when it speaks. Ignoring all fear is probably pathological. It's there to get your attention so apply step 2.

▶2. Quantify exactly why fear is present. Is the launch more challenging than you are used to? Are conditions more rigorous than normal? Are there unknowns in the situation (new glider, harness or landing field)? Pinpoint exactly what is causing your anxiety*, then:

▶3. Focus only on that matter after putting all other matters to rest (e.g. secure equipment, landing field in reach and of ample size, winds steady, etc).

* The Robertson Charts of Reliability (RCR) are a great tool for helping you categorize and assess your fears. They also teach judgement, an important part of this fear control process.

▶4. Determine whether or not your particular fear is reasonable. Are you biting off more than you can chew? is the basic question. Certainly in the course of learning we must constantly stretch our limits, but the stretch should be with baby rather than giant steps. For example, limit yourself to winds less than 5 mph stronger than those of your past experience up to 20 mph, then progress in smaller increments. Likewise a new launch or landing should have only one thing more difficult than you are used to, such as a flatter slope or smaller size and those changes should be incremental.

If you are taking too big a jump, it is reasonable to wait for another day, more experience. If the situation is only slightly more challenging, go to step 5.

▶5. Assuage your fear by logically assessing the situation. Carefully determine if what you intend to do is within your capabilities. Other pilots can give you valuable feedback here. This is especially true if they fly first to indicate launch clearance, smoothness of the air and so forth. Look for a balance between your great desire to fly and the necessity to add new experience gradually. If your decision is to fly, be assured that it is the right decision, recognize your fear as merely a watchdog, then fly with confidence. And you know what?... Conquering fear is a reward in itself that increases your post-flight sense of wellness.

▶6. The last step in this fear control process is to practice flying within your limits often. Don't try to outdo yourself on every aerial expedition. You'll find that fear will maintain a low profile if you spend time perfecting your skills at each stage of development.

Fear has been with us since we dropped out of the trees and started chasing mammoths, if not before. We have fears of heights, fears of the unknown, fears of failure among others that hover around the flying scene. They will always be with us when we rise to new challenges. However, learning and experience will eliminate most fear.

I remember when I first started soaring I became more fearful the higher I rose. Now I know that there's safety in altitude (the monsters lurk mostly down low) and glory in 10,000 foot gain.

If you fly long enough you will no longer feel any twinge of fear during a normal flight—we guarantee it. The problem then will be to maintain awareness of safety without a Jimminy Cricket of fear whispering in your ear (see the previously mentioned syndromes). So any fear you experience at this point is a temporary rite of passage. Use it to guide you to a high level of competence.

DECISIONS, DECISIONS _____

As we alluded earlier, upper level flying is fraught with decisions. The pilot that constantly makes wise decisions is the pilot that excels. An example of this point occurred in the 1990 East Coast Championships in Tennessee.

A short task to the north was called in a crosswind. Conditions were weak and pilots managed to stay in the air mainly by hanging out on the steep fingers that faced into the wind. About fifteen pilots were stuck on the last good finger with only about 500 feet over the ridge. One by one pilots topped out and peeled off to stretch for goal. They all landed short.

Nelson Howe had noticed a cloud approaching upwind. He waited while everyone left and was rewarded with an extra thousand feet and easily made goal. He also won the meet by virtue of this one decision on that one flight.

Your decisions may not have as dramatic an outcome as this (unless you decide very unwisely), but they can make the difference between a great flight and a short slide. Here's a brief course on improving your hang gliding decisions:

▶1. Be aware that you *are* making decisions. This isn't as obvious as it sounds. We aren't always paying mind to the fact that we constantly make choices in the air. At the level of sky ace these decisions are often automatic, but as a progressing pilot we need to be conscious that we have a choice to make when it comes time to make that choice.

Fear is a natural survival instinct. Make it an asset rather than a liability by:
1. Listening when it appears.
2. Quantifying exactly why it's there.
3. Focusing on the matter that causes it.
4. Determining whether it is legitimate.
5. Assuaging it by logical assessment.
6. Repeatedly practicing within your own limits.

Healthy decision-making:
1. Be aware when it's decision time.
2. Make expedient decisions.
3. Be flexible as you carry out your choice.
4. Learn from the outcome.
5. Exercise patience.
6. Err on the side of safety.

►2. Make your decision quickly with the best information at hand. Waiting too long to make a decision often means a missed opportunity. This doesn't mean make a hasty choice, but eliminate vacillation or wishy washiness from your decision process. Once you have made a decision, follow it through with confidence.

►3. Be flexible in the air to take advantage of new opportunities that arise as conditions or your position change. Your decision may have been a wrong one, but your new situation may present new decisions to make and you can make them correctly. A good decision maker is a good opportunist who quickly recognizes a good thing and takes advantage of good fortune.

►4. Learn from your mistakes *and* successes. This is the real key to successful decision making. Every decision has an outcome that can help you make choices in future similar situations. Tony Barton, one of the world's top pilots, keeps a notebook describing his mistakes and other observations. In recent years his notes must be few indeed as his decision making hass become notoriously excellent.

►5. Know when to be patient. This matter of patience is perhaps the hardest for most pilots to learn, especially in competition when other pilots are ahead. We'll learn more of this in later chapters.

►6. If you err, err on the side of safety. The whole matter of building confidence is extremely important to performance flying. If you make rash decisions that end up scaring you, your decision making ability will suffer. You will be more worried about each critical decision you make and you'll be less able to weigh all points objectively.

We approach decision making with the attitude that some of our choices will be wrong. However, making a wrong choice and learning from it is better than making no choice at all. Nothing ventured, no altitude gained. This applies when you're boating around at your home site or going for distance in a new sky.

JUDGING SPACE

Much of the decision making we face concerns putting ourselves in a particular place in three-dimensional space. This in turn requires that we can judge this space accurately.

The human eye cannot determine distances. Beyond ten or twenty feet, binocular triangulation doesn't work because the angles are so slight. We thus use secondary means which consist of relative size, relative motion, position relative to the horizon and changing texture. Because ground and trees viewed from aloft are not distinctive in terms of these four factors, we are hard put to visually judge altitudes or distances. For that reason we use tricks.

Flight plan: A constantly updated package of intentions.

✓ Judging Landings

The landing approach is probably the one element in our flying that takes the longest to learn. The secret to consistent landings, especially in smaller fields that we sometimes encounter as we gain experience is to learn patterns that can be used in any landing field and to judge angles. This matter is largely covered in our novice book *Hang Gliding Flying Skills*. Here we simply point out the idea with figure 1-1 on the next page. Our eyes are very good at estimating angles and a little practice leads to perfection.

✓ Judging Glides

We covered glide path judgement as well in the aforementioned book. For completeness we'll simply note that any point shorter than your glide path will appear to move down in your field of vision. Any point that you aren't going to reach will slowly rise in your view. The point you are gliding to will remain stationary.

To tell if you are going to clear a ridge , tree line or power line, watch the ground behind these obstructions. If you see more and more of this ground rising behind the obstruction,

Figure 1-1: Judging Angles

you have it made. If you see ground disappearing behind the obstruction you're not going to clear it and should exercise your alternate plan.

In the Sequatchie valley of Tennessee, competitions are often run on some very light days. Reflights are allowed so if a pilot doesn't get up after a couple tries the best strategy is to glide as far as possible—an act known as diving for distance. To the north a sloping promontory juts out over a mile away. It is desirable to cross this promontory as high up as possible. To do this without altering course it is a neat trick to watch the background beyond the promontory. Lower down on the promontory, the background appears to rise above the slope and higher up it appears to drop. Where the background remains stationary in relation to the promontory is the place to aim for the most efficient path.

✓ Judging a Flight Path

When flying in wind your ground path is very different from your heading direction (unless your are aimed parallel with the wind). To go from point to point most directly you must set up a crab angle. To do this automatically, look at the point you are trying to reach.

Draw an imaginary line on the ground with checkpoints and fly along this line as shown in figure 1-2. We cannot overemphasize the advantage of straight flying from point to point in terms of efficiency and performance. We return to this subject in later chapters.

✓ Judging your Position

At times—mostly in competition—you wish to know exactly where you are in the air. For example turn points and goals require you to be in a specific place. We learned in the early days when using manned pylons that pilots always think they are further ahead than they are. Practice determining right where you are by using a building, pole or other vertical structure which will indicate when you are right above it (see figure 1-3). Pinpointing exactly where you are above the terrain will prove useful for practical flying as we see next.

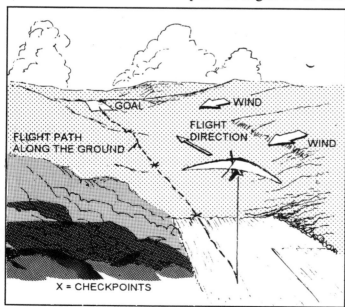

Figure 2-2: Ground Track Directing Flight

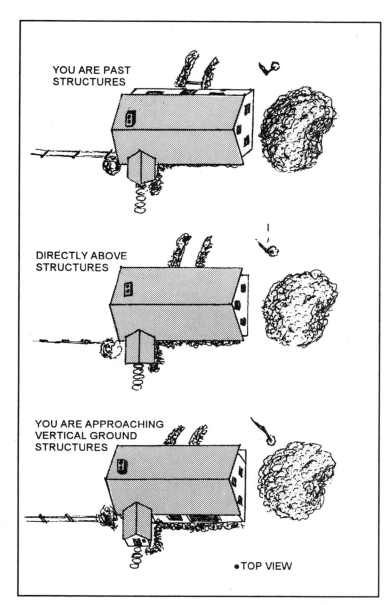

YOU ARE PAST STRUCTURES

DIRECTLY ABOVE STRUCTURES

YOU ARE APPROACHING VERTICAL GROUND STRUCTURES

• TOP VIEW

Figure 1-3: Determining your Position

SHADOW TALK

✔ Judging a Flying Distance

If you wish to know how far it is to a lift-indicating cloud, another pilot or across a gap, estimate your position on the ground then mentally measure off the distance to the ground position of the object you're trying to reach. With practice you can become very good at telling how far an aerial object is from you and how much altitude it will take to reach it. This process is very important when reaching for lift marked by a turning pilot, a cloud or a mountain formation.

After using this method for some time you'll notice that gliders usually appear further than they are. When following another glider along a course it is important to know this so you know at what point you are going to encounter the same lift or sink he or she displays.

✔ Judging a Glider's Height

There is a trick which lets us judge how high a glider is over launch. Every time you are soaring over gliders set up on takeoff or in the landing field, hold your arm at full length and note how far your thumb and forefinger must be spread to equal the apparent full span of a glider. Do this for specific heights—say 500, 1000 and 3000 feet—and you will soon be able to judge a glider's height with reasonable accuracy by measuring with your fingers. This method will let you know how high gliders are topping out before you launch and how much below you another glider enters your thermal. This is useful information for free flying as well as competition.

✔ Cloud Pictures

Cumulus type clouds are very important because they indicate lift. However, clouds present a problem because they can be any size so we can't get a fix on their precise distance. But a good trick is to judge their distance from *your* shadow to the *cloud* shadow along the ground. Figure 1-4 on the next page illustrates this matter. Note that your shadow won't be directly below you (except at high noon above the equator), but neither will the cloud shadow be below the cloud. The greater the difference in the relative height of you and the cloud, and the lower the sun is in the sky, the more this distance will be overestimated, but the error is not important.

Shadows can tell you more about clouds and position of other pilots than the real thing.

An alternate method is to judge the angle between you and your shadow then note the distance from your shadow to the point on the terrain you are directly above. Next note the cloud's shadow position and using the sun angle estimate the point on the ground the cloud is over. Finally, mentally measure the distance from your ground point to the cloud's ground point. These processes may seem complicated, but with practice they become clear and are essential to efficient cloud usage.

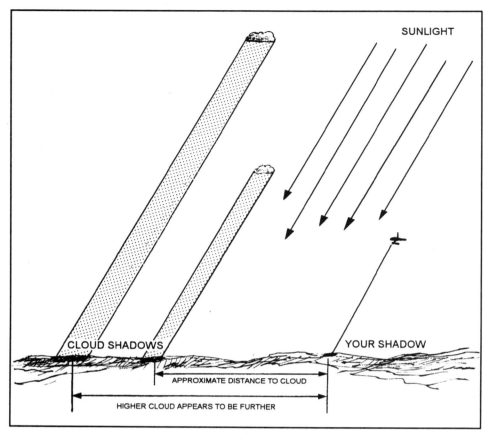

SUNLIGHT

CLOUD SHADOWS

YOUR SHADOW

APPROXIMATE DISTANCE TO CLOUD

HIGHER CLOUD APPEARS TO BE FURTHER

Figure 1-4: Judging Cloud Distances

Shadows can tell us more about clouds than just position. When you're moving through the air it is difficult to tell the cloud drift unless you look at the shadows. A bit of observation of cloud shadows moving over the ground will give the precise wind velocity at cloud level. This allows you to choose the best path for intercepting the cloud's lift. One note of caution: in light winds a building cloud can expand in all directions so your perception of the wind direction will depend on which side of the shadow you observe. For this reason always look at several sides of the cloud shadow in light winds. Also be aware that the wind at cloud level can be quite different from the wind at your level.

Shadows can also tell us the percentage of cloud cover, cloud size and rate of buildup.

Often, many clouds with vertical development seem to fill the sky, but shadows indicate plenty of sunny spots. Overdevelopment can block the sky and in such a case a sun spot on the ground may promise the last hope of lift.

One final technique is to use cloud shadows to watch the stages of cloud life. It is often difficult to watch cloud development without straining your neck, especially in traffic, but you can usually watch the shadows to see if a cloud is developing from a wisp or maintaining its form. In light clouds, shadows show a breakup long before the actual cloud does if you are high enough or close enough that you can't get a planform view of the cloud (see figure 1-5). Practice locating the specific shadows of individual clouds by noting the sun angle so you don't make a mistake and fly to the wrong one. We'll see the importance of clouds to performance flying in Chapter 5 and 8.

✓ *Your Projection*

Finding your own shadow is important for estimating distances as indicated above and also for noting your position in relation to other pilots (see the following section). But how do you pick out your vague shape among a bunch of moving umbras? The key is to note that your shadow *is the only one with a bright halo around it*. That doesn't mean that you are anointed by an archangel, it's just that you are in position to see the light reflected directly back to you as shown in figure 1-6. The other pilots are equally blessed.

As you get higher your shadow gets larger and more diffuse. Eventually you can't see any more shadow but your bright spot will remain for a couple thousand feet if you look carefully. Use the sun's angle to locate it to use for distance judging.

Shadows can tell us:
1. Cloud position
2. Cloud size
3. Percentage of cloud
4. Cloud vigor
5. Cloud drift

Figure 1-5: Cloud Shadow Clues

PILOT IS TOO HIGH TO SEE TOTAL CLOUD SHAPE

SHADOW ON THE GROUND CLEARLY SHOWS THE CLOUD SHAPE AND PROGRESS.

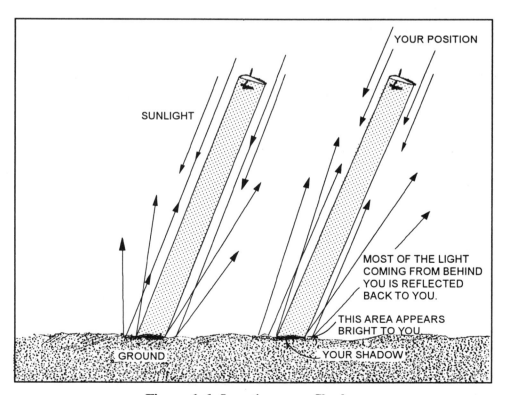

YOUR POSITION

SUNLIGHT

MOST OF THE LIGHT COMING FROM BEHIND YOU IS REFLECTED BACK TO YOU.

THIS AREA APPEARS BRIGHT TO YOU

GROUND

YOUR SHADOW

Figure 1-6: Locating your Shadow

THE OTHER PILOT

An observant and resourceful pilot will use all available information including that provided by the action of other gliders in the air. Even when other gliders are above you and out of sight, don't fret, but learn what you can from their shadows. Watch glider shadows to determine positions, climb rate and turning direction.

The shadow of another pilot will help you locate him or her. They will always be on a direct line from the shadow to the sun. If their shadow is larger than yours, they are higher. If your shadows do not meet you are in no danger of colliding. *Watch out for converging shadows!*

This pilot is above you because he appears above the horizon line.

✓ Positioning Clues

We can't overemphasize the importance of using the shadow of another pilot who is above you to help you center in a thermal as shown in figure 1-7. The higher they are compared to you, the more you have to account for the sun angle and the thermal drift. This can be tricky at first but becomes a great aid with practice. The size and change of their shadow lets you know how you're doing in comparison to them. All this shadow work is especially useful down low when you're scratching.

When you are near another pilot in a thermal it is best to be producing the same size and rate of turn. The problem is *it always looks like another pilot is turning outside or around you.* Note this well, for this is a common misconception. The only way to tell who has the tightest turning circle is to observe who catches up to whom. As figure 1-8 shows, the glider in the smaller circle will travel faster. This is a very important observation because it lets you know if another pilot is flying a different bank angle than you. If he or she is and their climb rate is better, adjust your circle accordingly. One note: most pilots fly too flat in thermal gaggles.

Other pilots can give you a good reference to your climb rate when they are at a distance as well, if you watch their position in relation to the horizon. Below the horizon it is difficult to tell

Watch other gliders for:
- *Signs of lift*
- *Position of thermals*
- *Climb rates*
- *Turning direction*
- *Speed*
- *Relative performance*
- *Circling radius*

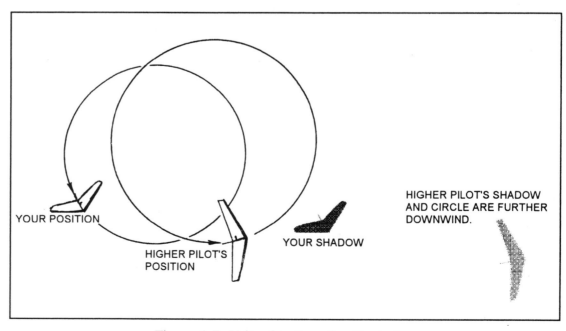

Figure 1-7: Using Shadows for Centering

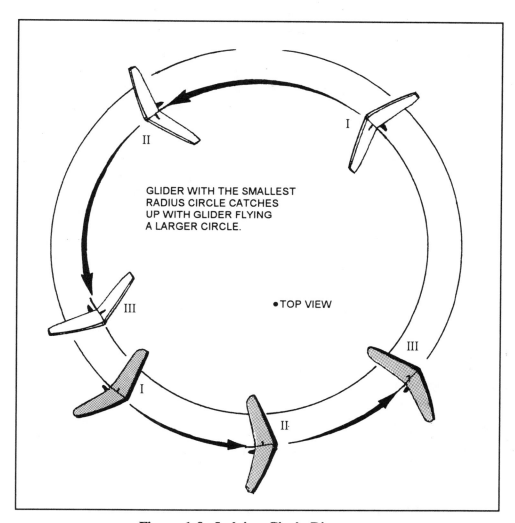

GLIDER WITH THE SMALLEST RADIUS CIRCLE CATCHES UP WITH GLIDER FLYING A LARGER CIRCLE.

•TOP VIEW

Figure 1-8: Judging Circle Diameters

another pilot's climb rate if you are also climbing, but with practice and careful observation you can learn to discern who's eking out the best climb.

In order to judge if you're higher than another glider, look at the horizon. If they appear to be above a distant horizon, they are higher. In many cases the horizon isn't so distant, so you have to estimate your height above the horizon as shown in figure 1-9.

The matter of glider height is important in situations where you are crossing a gap, unlandable

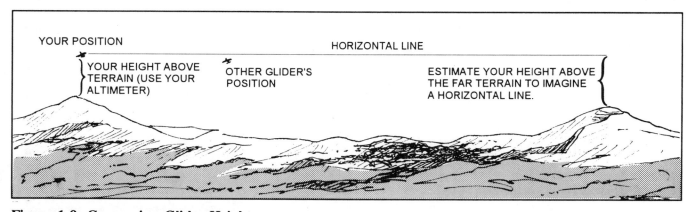

YOUR POSITION
HORIZONTAL LINE
YOUR HEIGHT ABOVE TERRAIN (USE YOUR ALTIMETER)
OTHER GLIDER'S POSITION
ESTIMATE YOUR HEIGHT ABOVE THE FAR TERRAIN TO IMAGINE A HORIZONTAL LINE.

Figure 1-9: Comparing Glider Heights

areas or cross-country flying in general for you can judge your expected results by a pilot preceding you.

✔ *Performance Clues*

One more thing you can learn from other pilots is your relative performance. If you are unsure of what speeds to fly between thermals, use other pilots as a guide. Even if they are inexperienced and you don't agree with their speed choice they give you information by indicating how much they are above or below you when you arrive at the lift. This is how you learn the important matter of maximizing thermal usage.

You can get a very good idea of your performance in climb and decision making in all phases of flight when flying with other pilots. We all do this when we try to top out at our local hill. However, one thermal or one flight will not tell your own or your glider's overall performance. Each day is different and various designs and wing loadings excel in different conditions. Be honest in your appraisals. It's amazing how many times two pilots will land and both confide that they got the highest and stayed on top. Well, optimism and confidence are useful attitudes in performance flying, but we need facts to know where our path of improvement lies.

II - JUDGING CONDITIONS

A major part of our exercise of judgment (or lack thereof) is in assessing conditions. Before we fling our body into space we better have a good idea what's happening in that space. While we are in the wild blue yonder we must know how to interpret signs to solve the three-dimensional puzzle. Good judgment is good health.

DANGERS

Hurricanes, tornados and thunderstorms are reminders of the awesome power in the atmosphere. In the course of learning to fly we must also learn to respect this power for the benefit of our great-grandchildren. The dangers in the air can be understood and predicted so we'll review them here.

✔ *High Winds*

Wind is a complicating factor in all aviation. When the wind velocity doubles, its force—which is directly related to its potential danger—increases fourfold. Obviously there is an upper limit to safe wind speeds. The safe upper limit is somewhat different for various skill levels, but in general no pilot can safely fly inland in winds much over 25 mph because of the limitations of weight shift control and penetration speeds. Here are guidelines to wind speed safety limits related to the chart in figure 1-10:

Safe Wind Limits
1. Do not fly coastal sites in winds over 30 mph. Coastal conditions tend to be stable and smooth, but even so higher winds can be dangerous.
2. Do not fly inland in winds over 20 mph with a slow gust factor of only a few mph.
3. In strong thermal conditions do not fly if *peak* wind is over 20 mph with 5 mph gusts or over 15 mph with 10 to 15 mph gusts.

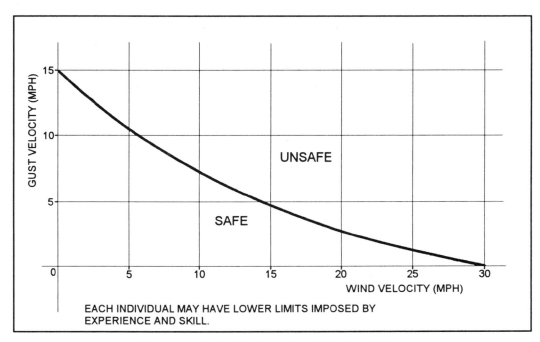

Figure 1-10: Guidelines for Safe Conditions

The daily wind velocity and gustiness usually changes as heating builds towards midday then diminishes in the evening. We expect the strongest conditions during and just after peak heating. Therefore early (before noon) launches will tolerate less wind since we know it will increase.

✓ Wind Indicators

Of course to make wind decisions we need to have an idea what the true wind is. Wind meters can give wind speed at launch (many new variometers incorporate airspeed indicators that measure wind speed). Every pilot should learn to feel the wind and guess its strength accurately. Practice with your wind speed indicator until you can *feel* your limits.

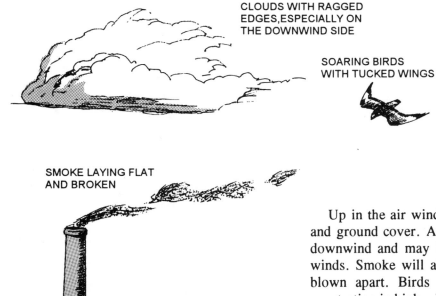

Up in the air wind indicators are clouds, smoke, birds and ground cover. As shown in figure 1-11, clouds slant downwind and may have a ragged appearance in higher winds. Smoke will also have a flatter angle and may be blown apart. Birds will pull their wings in for more penetration in high winds. When turkey vultures have their wings tucked, winds are generally too strong for hang gliders. Hawks tend to stay in the nest in such winds (they're smart) while swifts or swallows will fly in anything and are not reliable wind speed guides.

Ground cover moves with the winds. In the green parts of the world you can watch wind lines move up the mountains providing direction and speed information.

Figure 1-11: Higher Wind Indicators

Normally these wind lines (visible as the bottoms of leaves are turned up) don't begin until the wind is at least 12 mph. The stronger the wind the further down the mountain the motion will extend, and the more rapidly it will change as gusts move through. On the ground blowing dust, debris and waves in grass or crops indicate winds of at least 15 mph.

✓ Extreme turbulence

Our personal definition of extreme depends on point of view, of course, but we would all agree that turbulence that requires constant rapid corrections near the terrain can be dangerous, while it may be uncomfortable but quite safe aloft. Besides winds, thermals and shear conditions can also produce turbulence.

Dangerous conditions:
- *High winds*
- *Excessive turbulence*
- *Thunderstorms*

Pilots have been caught in shears, for example, when evening catabatic flow streams out of a canyon, but for the most part the associated turbulence is limited in extent and can be escaped. Thermal turbulence, on the other hand can be extensive and reach to ground level. The feel of thermals on the ground is changes in wind velocity. Thermals accompanying wind are worse. Use the guidelines given in the wind section to judge safety. Often the gusts imposed on the general wind speed are thermal induced.

When dust devils abound expect strong thermal turbulence. When they are drifting rapidly or are accompanied by generally blowing dust, then conditions are dangerous. Be aware that dust devils are different in different regions. Areas where ground cover is fine dust will exhibit more frequent dust devils (Chelan, Washington for example). Areas with coarser ground cover with large dust devils are producing stronger thermals. The conditions near such dust devils can be dangerous.

✓ Wave-Induced Rotors

Rotors occur behind obstructions and under waves as shown in figure 1-12. We already know enough not to fly tightly behind big, blocking objects (see *Hang Gliding Flying Skills*), but what about waves? Generally rotors from waves are less severe in lower terrain such as the Eastern USA, except in wind conditions stronger than you care to fly.

TYPICAL ROTOR CLOUD ORIENTED PERPENDICULARLY TO THE WIND, STATIONARY, WITH A SINUOUS, SLOWLY CHANGING OUTLINE.

WIND

MOUNTAIN FORMING ROTOR

Figure 1-12: Rotor Clouds

The low rolling hills of England often exhibit benign waves that have offered hang glider pilot over 10,000 ft gains. In higher mountains (over 3000 ft—1000 m) large and powerful rotors can exist. Generally these conditions accompany higher winds. A classic example of this is the Sierra wave that sets up in the Owens Valley and parts north in strong westerlies. When you see signs of waves in the big sky country (Alps, Rockies, Sierra, etc) it is wise to stay grounded. In less majestic terrain judge the wave safety by the wind on launch:

Maximum Wind in Waves
Limit your takeoff in wave conditions to a maximum of 15 mph wind speed since wind usually increases significantly aloft in waves.

Virga under a thunderstorm.

✔ *Thunderstorms*

Thunderstorms are the nemesis of pilots and their dangers are illustrated in figure 1-13. Judging them is worthy of a long discourse in itself. A chapter in *Understanding the Sky* is devoted to this subject. Read it and put the information in your judgement tool kit.

The big problem with thunderstorms is when they arise very rapidly or when they are imbedded. For example in Bassano, Italy seven pilots were sucked up into a rapidly building magnum storm and a few of them suffered severe consequences.

Thunderstorm clouds: When a cloud climbs high enough to turn the droplets to ice, the cloud becomes hazy. At this point expect a mature thunderstorm with lightning, precipitation and a dangerous gust front.

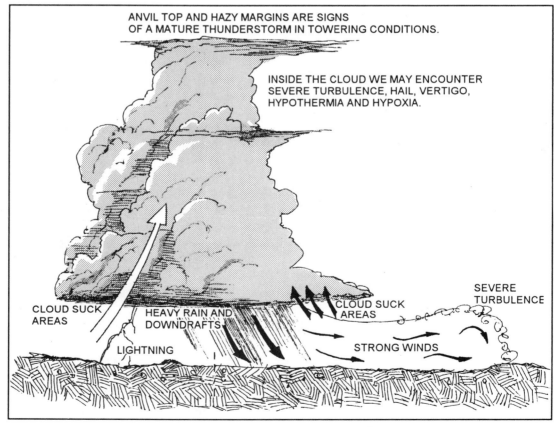

Figure 1-13: Thunderstorm Dangers

At the 1990 US Nationals in Dinosaur, Colorado several pilots were tumbled by thunderstorm-induced gust fronts. In midsummer 1992 at Telluride, Colorado two pilots were caught and injured in a surprise thunderstorm. My own most severe thunderstorm encounter occurred not with the massive cloud islands that we fly around in the Western USA, but in Arkansas when a mild imbedded thunderstorm dropped a gust front that met me in the landing area and planted me vertically.

The whole point of these testimonials is to indicate that thunderstorms can threaten anywhere and deserve respect. A common thread that runs through all these tales is that the signs of thunderstorms were present—either with cloud buildup or a weather report of possible thunderstorms. The victims missed these signs due to competition pressures, peer pressures, bad judgement, lack of understanding or inattention.

If we don't wish to avoid flying when a possibility of thunderstorms exists (many good days exhibit this possibility), we must learn the rules to thunderstorm judgement and fly accordingly.

WIND DIRECTION

A superior pilot is an observant pilot. He or she will know the wind direction as well as strength from the ground up to cloud base. Part of this knowledge comes from watching the signs and part from imagination. Ground indicators include flags, streamers, hanging clothes, smoke, dust, debris and moving vegetation. As mentioned earlier, wind lines up a mountain covered with trees give a good indication of direction as shown in figure 1-14. This is the best way to tell if the wind is crossing at launch (watch for turbulence) since launch slots channel the wind up and provide a false reading.

Figure 1-14: Wind Lines on Tree-Covered Mountain

Clouds are the best indicators in the air. Their orientation, slant and shadow drift tell the story. Sometimes only their general shape will belie the wind in light conditions as shown in figure 1-15. Thermaling gliders and birds can also indicate wind aloft by their drift but the latter usually remain within a few thousand feet of the ground in order to hunt lunch.

The reason we want to know winds aloft is to know the best direction for cross-country distance, routes to take to reach lift and the possibility of shears that indicate inversion layers, changing weather or convergence. All this information adds to your ability to find lift. Imagination comes in when you visualize how the wind changes with altitude and where lift could be drifting.

THESE CUMULUS CLOUDS ARE ROUNDED, BUT ELONGATED IN THE WIND DIRECTION.

Figure 1-15: Clouds Showing Wind Direction

LOOKING FOR LIFT

Judging the sky and terrain for lift is one key to success in the air. Of course we look for soaring birds (especially for circling ones) and cumulus clouds. But there are other, more subtle signs we must look for.

✓ Little Signs

Signs of soarability in order of reliance:
1. Soaring gliders
2. Soaring birds
3. Wind into launch
4. Thermal gusts
5. Cumulus clouds
6. Cloud streets
7. Good solar heating

Swifts and swallows mentioned previously tend to fly when it's soarable either because they have to work less or because the rising air is providing them free delivery service of succulent insects. Whenever you see these birds flitting back and forth across launch it is almost always soarable. They frequently inhabit thermals, not just ridge lift.

Changes in wind velocity on the ground—especially if sudden—indicate thermals (unless you're observing in the lee of a mountain). Vigorous brush or leave movement along a ridge or mountain can identify a passing thermal, although often it means faster, sinking air is coming down from aloft. In Chapter 6 we discuss when to launch in thermal conditions and other matters of advanced thermal judgement.

✓ Cloud Signs

A change in sky conditions often signifies a change in the lift patterns. A solid cloud bank moving toward you may cool the ground and suppress all thermals behind it, but at its leading edge it may exhibit convergence. It may produce a heat front or it may represent a wind shift. A sharp line of clearing often doesn't signify lift until some time has occurred for the ground to heat and thermals to generate.

The presence of cumulus clouds almost always indicates a better soaring day than a blue sky conditions. Clouds don't create the lift, of course, but they do imply a little bit of moisture in the air which helps instability. A blue day usually occurs under a high pressure system which means slowly sinking air (that's why it's blue). This air becomes more stable and weakens thermals.

Scattered lines or patches of cumulus—often flat—or stratus of a limited extent usually signifies convergence (see figure 1-16). Whether or not you can use it depends on how strong the convergence is and how low it extends. Very high clouds are generally not usable and are related to upper air disturbances. Lower clouds with better development are worth a try.

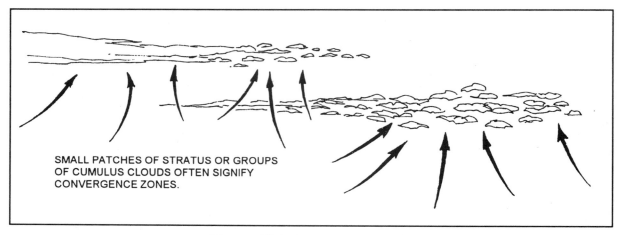

Figure 1-16: Convergence Signs

Weak convergences that promote thermals in their area occur often in the sky. Your chances of finding a thermal within the convergence area are much greater than elsewhere (see figure 1-17). Convergences and divergences due to pressure waves and air mass changes account for the variable blue holes and cloud areas on some days. The weather is often banded for a variety of reasons.

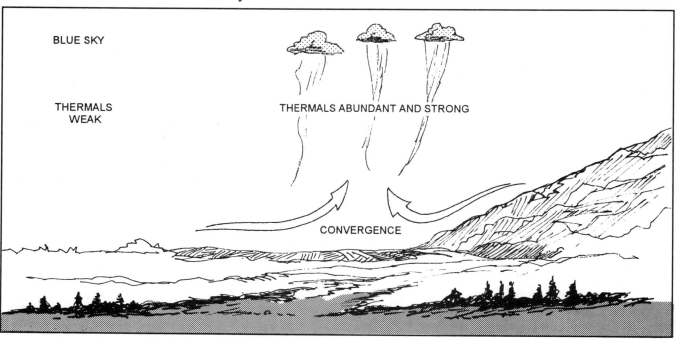

Figure 1-17: Convergence Promoting Thermals

Cloud streets, as in figure 1-18, are signs of lift, of course. The main matter of judgement here is how far we must go to reach them (and can we make it). We discuss this also in Chapter 8. If you are not versed in the mysteries of convergence and cloud streets, we refer you to *Understanding the Sky*. This book also contains heating charts and general information that indicates instability and soaring prospects.

✓ *Deciphering the Day*

The pilot who figures out the day as soon as possible is the pilot who excels. Figuring out the day involves observing all of the above factors and putting them together with past experience concerning what changes should occur. Every flying day ask yourself: Will cloud base rise?

Will conditions overdevelop? Will the wind shift? Is an inversion likely? Is it soarable yet?

The last question always perplexes many pilots, but in reality the only way to develop judgement on soarability in iffy conditions is to experiment by popping into the air. If you always wait until you're sure it's soarable in a fun-flying situation you'll sometimes sit on the hill while others get up and you won't develop light lift skills or judgement (in competition you must be more cautious). It's amazing how many pilots at large gatherings put down roots at launch when other pilots are out front thermaling. If they want a sure thing they should take up hog raising.

Judgement in conditions is a skill that takes time to learn. The best way to learn this skill is to get yourself out in the conditions once you have determined they are safe. Take notes mentally or otherwise to build up your store of knowledge on which to base your decisions.

Figure 1-18: Cloud Streets

III - FLYING STYLES OR POSITIONS

"Birds and Superman fly prone."
— Early prone pilot
"I'd rather watch the sky than the ground."
—Supine pilot

*M*ore than 99% of hang gliders pilots today fly prone (head forward on their stomach). This wasn't always the case; about half the early pilots flew seated. Seated or supine (reclining back as in an easy chair) is still a viable way to fly, especially for pilots with back troubles. Cross-country pilots like Bob Thompson of Arizona who flies great distances in the supine position prove this statement. Furthermore, many of the new class II gliders (fixed wings) are flown in the supine position.

For your interest we compare the advantages of both styles of flying:

THE PRONE POSITION _____

- Usually produces less drag if the pilot is oriented into the airstream.
- Easier on takeoff. Supine pilots fly below the basetube which means their harness risers are much looser when they hold the control bar during takeoff.
- Easier to see turn points, ground sources of thermals and lower pilots marking lift.

- More pitch travel. High wind penetration and diving for aerobatics is a bit more limited with a supine harness.

THE SUPINE POSITION

- More comfortable for long flights. This is the big advantage in flying supine and is significant with multiple-hour flights.
- Better crash protection. It is always better to simulate a lawn dart feet first than head first.
- More natural control and spatial judgement position. We grow up driving cars and bicycles in the seated position.
- Easier to watch cloud thermal markers and pilots overhead. This is especially important when flying X-C.

Perhaps the biggest difficulty with the supine position is in taking off. If the glider rests on the pilot's shoulders then it must rise a couple of feet to tighten the main risers at some point during the run. This transition affords less control in gusty conditions. At least one pilot solved this slight problem by fashioning a release that suspended him at prone height until after takeoff at which point he lowered himself to normal supine position.

In Chapter 4 we discuss harness adjustment.

SUMMARY

...you will walk the earth with your eyes turned skyward, for there you have been, and there you long to return."

Leonardo da Vinci

We have touched on much of the pertinent points that relate to personal development of a pilot. These points include dealing with attitude, ego, observation and judgement. We learn that a confident attitude helps in decision making. Ego must be controlled to maintain safety and aid progress. Many items demanding observation—from other pilots to conditions—have obvious importance to our learning and ability to make judgements. Judgement, whether of conditions or choosing a particular path is the essence of hang gliding. Indeed hang gliding has been said to be 90% judgement and 9% skill *. We constantly work on developing better judgement and recognize this is perhaps the supreme challenge of flying.

* Where is the other 3%? That's luck, but we make our own luck largely by exercising good judgement!

John Heiney and friend exploring the air.
Note the glory in the cloud below.

CHAPTER 2

The Art of Flying

If you carefully watch a sea gull you will get a lesson in precision soaring. These sleek birds constantly adjust their speed to play in the wafting air currents and extract every bit of lift or run from every bit of sink they encounter. They seem to do this with an innate sixth sense.

Soaring humans can develop this extra sense as well, through understanding and practice. In this chapter we polish the techniques that lend us the skills to achieve the performance flying we are pursuing. We'll learn to cure our bad habits, add new good ones and become more familiar with our glider's capabilities. Our goal is to rival the sea gulls soaring skills.

I - TECHNIQUE TOUCH-UP

*P*rogress beyond the training hill is often achieved through a process of osmosis where we gradually absorb the knowledge necessary to accomplish new feats. Since this learning is not generally programmed, we often miss something along the way. Thus we have a review.

TAKEOFFS FOR EXPERTS

We presume you are good at taking off. If not, some time at a training hill or with an instructor can not only save you injury but relax you on takeoff so much that you'll enjoy hang gliding more. Here are a few points to use as a mental checklist.

✓ *Holding the Control Bar*

Most of us are able to support the control bar on our shoulders and use our arms and hands to stabilize and control the glider during launch.

Launch procedure:
- *Hold the bar properly*
- *Verbally say "I'm hooked in" (you've already performed a hang check)*
- *Assess the conditions*
- *Pick up your glider when it looks good and lift it to do a hook in check*
- *As soon as the glider is steady, say "clear" (don't dally)*
- *Run with long strides and put as much energy into the system as possible.*

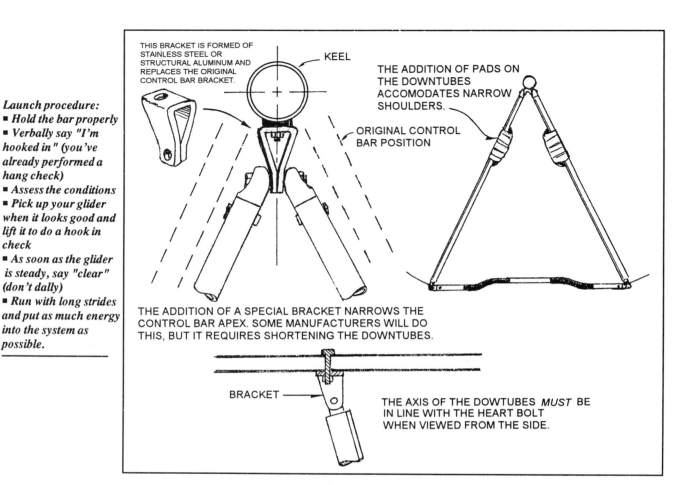

THIS BRACKET IS FORMED OF STAINLESS STEEL OR STRUCTURAL ALUMINUM AND REPLACES THE ORIGINAL CONTROL BAR BRACKET.

KEEL

THE ADDITION OF PADS ON THE DOWNTUBES ACCOMODATES NARROW SHOULDERS.

ORIGINAL CONTROL BAR POSITION

THE ADDITION OF A SPECIAL BRACKET NARROWS THE CONTROL BAR APEX. SOME MANUFACTURERS WILL DO THIS, BUT IT REQUIRES SHORTENING THE DOWNTUBES.

BRACKET

THE AXIS OF THE DOWTUBES *MUST* BE IN LINE WITH THE HEART BOLT WHEN VIEWED FROM THE SIDE.

Figure 2-1: Control Bar Alterations

THE ARMS ARE FIRMLY LOCKED AROUND THE DOWNTUBES.

Figure 2-2: The Grapevine Grasp

Smaller pilots have some trouble with this and various solutions such as adding pads at the top of the control bar or changing the upper bracket to narrow the apex (see figure 2-1) have been successful. The grip that proves most solid in any case is with the arms around the outside of the control bar and with the hands pointed downward (the grapevine grip) as shown in figure 2-2.

The reason we recommend this method for advanced pilots is that it provides more solid roll control in gusty conditions and is less conducive to pushing with the hands and popping the nose. The proof of the benefit of this launch style is that almost all competition pilots, with their need to perform quick takeoffs in sometimes less than ideal conditions, use the grapevine grip.

The alternate grip, the "beer can" grasp as shown in figure 2-3 has some uses and an advanced pilot should feel equally comfortable with it. Tandem flying, some forms of towing and very windy, wire assisted cliff launches often go better with the beer can grip.

✔ *Getting off*

Pilots unsure of their launching skills tend to linger on launch, waiting through good cycles only to put the glider back down and wait for another good cycle to come through.

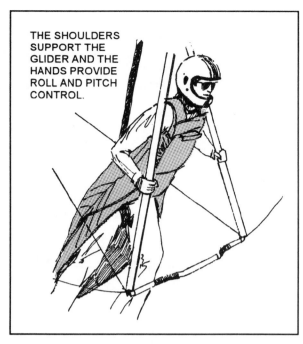

THE SHOULDERS SUPPORT THE GLIDER AND THE HANDS PROVIDE ROLL AND PITCH CONTROL.

Figure 2-3: The Bottle Grip

The problem is sometimes good cycles diminish in frequency or quality, excessive waiting increases anxiety and other pilots begin to add pressure—all of which doesn't help launch concentration.

The first step in breaking this cycle is to only pick the glider up if launch conditions look good. Once you do pick it up, set the pitch, level the wings, then go. Obviously you can't learn to do this in tricky conditions, so start by practice on calm or light days. Your goal should be to launch within 3 seconds of picking up your glider.

Continue this practice in gradually stronger conditions. Remember, pick the glider up only when conditions are good, balance, then run. If conditions deteriorate while you have the glider up, set it down. You only get tired and more tense (you can't relax when you're fighting gusts) holding your glider. Mind that we aren't suggesting you never wait for your glider to settle, but we are saying more often launch problems are compounded by a tentative approach than by hasty procedures.

➤ **Pro Tip**: In totally calm winds launching with VG full tight starts the glider lifting sooner.

✓ The Run

By now we shouldn't have to mention fledgling matters, but the fact is, pilots with good skills in the air sometimes retain poor launch habits. Bad runs and popping the nose of the glider up are the most common mistakes—they go hand in hand. Some competitors in the Owens Valley World Meet stuffed launches for this reason. Presumably the universally steep launches in some countries do not develop the skills necessary to handle the flat slope, high altitude Gunter launch in the Owens.

"A good aggressive launch technique translate to every launch situation."

We all know a gradually accelerating launch pushing with our shoulders to top speed is desirable. This means long strides, a relaxed grip and eyes ahead. If you aren't doing this (ask any other pilot and you'll find out) you need to change. The best way to effect this change is not necessarily to go to the training hill, but to go to flat ground, mark off a reasonable launch distance and practice moving your glider to top speed. If you can get your glider flying in no wind on the flat you will have the right technique. Transfer this on every launch every time regardless of the conditions and you will have flawless launches.

"Every pilot needs to perfect calm wind launches."

Even in high winds your launch should be an aggressive run attempt. It may take ten or more runs to learn such a launch run. You'll never climb the training hill that many times with your heavy glider unless you're a Neanderthal, so practice your launches in a landing area after a flight. If you ever blow a launch this practice is essential to regaining your confidence quickly.

Tony Barton launches a windy cliff in Tennessee

SOFT LANDINGS

"Nothing can ruin a good flight like a bad landing."

Some of us are great entertainers and provide much hilarity to groups of watching pilots as we whack in the landing area. But this behavior doesn't play well when you're on the road away from your own arena. The point is, when we begin to fly other sites, cross-country or high performance gliders our landings had better be darn near impeccable. Here are some points to help make them so.

✓ The Right Approach

High performance gliders demand a downwind, base and final (aircraft type) landing approach. We discuss why in a later section. In early training we provide a simplified version of this approach. Here we add 360° turns for a complete setup that is useful for tight fields and spot landing as well as everyday landings. Figure 2-4 shows the desirable setup. Lose altitude with 360s upwind of the landing spot. At the proper height—you know it from all your practice—enter the downwind-base-final pattern.

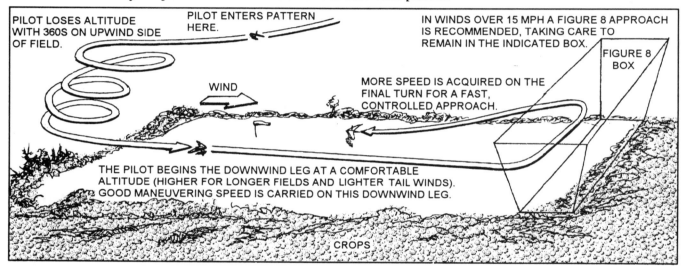

Figure 2-4: Advanced Landing Setup for Limited Fields

Other types of turns upwind of the target will have you losing sight of the target too long, may drift you too much toward the target and aren't as effective for achieving a precise altitude. Another benefit of this method is you can acquire lots of speed out of your last 360 that carries over into your downwind leg for good control.

Practice your 360s enough so you can lose a precise amount of altitude with each one. In stronger winds you may wish to fly upwind a bit to compensate for wind drift. Assess the situation after each 360. In winds over 15 mph use a figure 8 approach (in the box indicated) on the downwind side.

✓ The Final and Flare

Many pilots carry over a bad habit into their advanced flying: flying their final approach too slowly. You get away with this on a soft intermediate glider and much of the time on a high performance glider, but every so often turbulence will greet you on approach and addle your smooth style. If you are having problems with landings ask an experienced pilot to observe you to see if you are coming in too slowly. Coming in faster makes things happen quicker, but this isn't a problem as long as you have your setups in order so you don't have to make last minutes maneuvers.

Coming in too slowly can carry over to create a flare problem since a glider often stalls when it enter ground effect. Also, lack of speed doesn't allow the glider to climb during the

- 24 -

flare. Finally, coming in fast and gliding in ground effect gives you time to feel the glider and judge the flare timing.

Use a fast final to combat turbulence and wind gradient as well as provide reasonable flare speed.

Flare timing and the amount of flare are, of course, different with different wind conditions and are a bit more critical with advanced gliders. The key to a proper flare is to keep your eyes directly ahead, have a sensitive, relaxed grip on the downtubes, detect a change in the glider (a settling, sudden slowing and pitch pressure change), then push forward and up while at the same time reaching back with your feet. If flare timing is a personal problem, you *must* work it out at the raining hill with multiple flights. A couple of landings a week will not give you the repetitive trials you need to perfect your timing. One helpful hint is to remind yourself on final to *concentrate and relax.* Say it out loud until you do so automatically.

SPOT LANDING

Trying to hit a spot is good practice for precision landing control, but it's also often featured in fly-ins, friendly contests and as a prize giveaway at goals of some cross-country contests. It's nice to wow the crowd and be rewarded for your good habits.

The secret to consistent spot landing is not only entering final at the right place, but also being able to vary your glide distance. To find yourself in the right place, remember to judge *angles* to your spot as you proceed on your downwind leg. If trees or other obstructions surround your field you have to enter final higher and further from the spot, but the *angle* is the same.

There are essentially two ways to enter to control your glide path on final. The first is coming in high and changing drag by altering your stand-up position and speed. This is the safest method, but less accurate. An addition to this method, producing little stalls along the way, allows a more precise path control, but is not safe in all but the smoothest air and should not be attempted by anyone less than an expert (see figure 2-5). Kissing a stall near the ground may leave you smacking that ground.

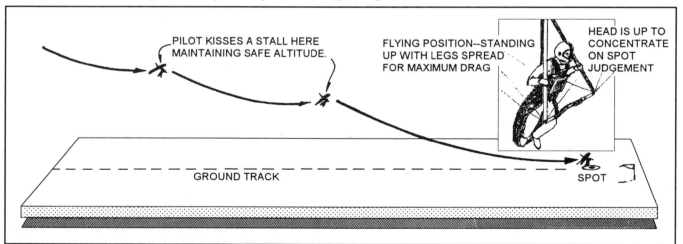

PILOT KISSES A STALL HERE MAINTAINING SAFE ALTITUDE.

FLYING POSITION--STANDING UP WITH LEGS SPREAD FOR MAXIMUM DRAG

HEAD IS UP TO CONCENTRATE ON SPOT JUDGEMENT

GROUND TRACK

SPOT

Figure 2-5: Losing Altitude on Final

The second method, favored by many, including long-time ace spot lander Steve Moyes, is to come in low and fast in ground effect. This technique, shown in figure 2-6, affords good directional control (lots of speed), penetrates you well into any wind (less wind near the surface) and allows you to vary your distance achieved quite a bit by climbing a little or dropping lower as you approach the target. You can acquire your extra speed with a diving turn onto final or pulling in—the former can be made more precisely with practice.

The drawbacks of this practice are: you fly very fast near the ground, things happen more rapidly and if you hit the ground you will hurt. Also in higher weeds or uneven terrain you lose sight of the spot.

With either method be sure to enter a direct line to the spot on the exit of your turn to final. Last minute direction changes can lose too much altitude. Small corrections for varying air can be made with slight nudges on the control bar. In any case, much practice is needed to form good spot judgement. It's not a bad idea to put a spot out every time you fly locally.

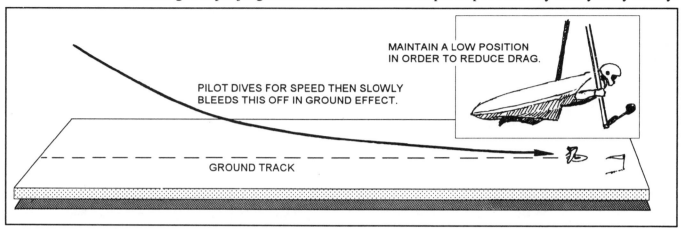

MAINTAIN A LOW POSITION IN ORDER TO REDUCE DRAG.

PILOT DIVES FOR SPEED THEN SLOWLY BLEEDS THIS OFF IN GROUND EFFECT.

GROUND TRACK

Figure 2-6: Fast Spot Approach

BAD HABITS

Breaking bad habits can be as difficult as trying to surf a microwave. Learn skills correctly in the first place.

Before we proceed to develop habits we should mention a few bad habits that occasionally appear at the hill. Each pilot can search his or her soul to see if they are guilty offenders.

BAD HABIT I - *Looking at the nose of your glider* when holding it up at takeoff. This is a common malady which serves to break your focus. You should be looking at the horizon, with your glider and your run path in your peripheral vision. On very rough or bushy terrain you may have to drop your vision a bit to aid in foot placement, but never raise it above the horizon.

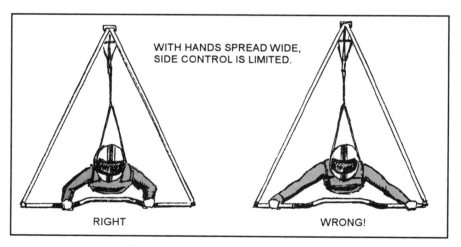

WITH HANDS SPREAD WIDE, SIDE CONTROL IS LIMITED.

RIGHT

WRONG!

Figure 2-7: Proper Hand Position

BAD HABIT II - *Standing at launch excessively*. We addressed this earlier. Launch confidence is the cure. Too much waiting at launch identifies you as a yam—that's a yellow launch potato.

BAD HABIT III - *Overwide grip on the control bar*. Various hand positions on the basetube are fine for relaxation but pilots who constantly use a very wide grip limit control action and strength.

Figure 2-7 shows the right and wrong ways. The wide grip is often a carry over from training.

BAD HABIT IV - *Staring at your variometer in traffic*. Sure, your vario gives you a lot of useful information, but would you stare at your speedometer on the avenue? Learn to interpret the *sound* of your vario and keep an eye on the other pilots.

BAD HABIT V - *Always thermaling in the same direction*. Most of us have a preference (see chapter 3), but when this preference turns into an obsession we are limiting ourselves.

"Bad habits are learned behavior. Any learned behavior can be unlearned."
Quote from behaviorist psychology

BAD HABIT VI - *Staying prone on final approach.* The prone position affords comfortable control and a lower center of gravity but is much more dangerous in case stray turbulence drops you to the ground. One hand down and one hand up is a good compromise in strong turbulence.

BAD HABIT VII - *Pumping the bar.* Some pilots do this in the air; some do it during landing flare. Random pumping on the bar when soaring disrupts your feel for the air texture. Certainly, constant adjustment is necessary to extract the most out of some thermals, but this is mostly roll control. Some pilots perform a tentative little push during landing to see if the glider is ready to flare, and that's OK, but repeated pumping is a poor excuse for an insufficient flare in the first place. By all means, don't pull the bar in once you've flared unless you are headed to the moon and flared way too high. Even then it is best to hold the bar out and take your medicine.

BAD HABIT VII - *Putting our landing gear in front of us during the landing flare.* This creates a problem: it puts weight forward and makes the flare less effective, usually resulting in a nose-in.

II - FLYING IN DIFFERENT CONDITION

*W*ith more skill, time and experience comes the opportunity or (misfortune) to fly in more demanding conditions. Such matters as flying in high winds, turbulence, rain, cloud suck and high altitude need our attention.

HIGH WIND ADVENTURES

We emphatically do not recommend flying in high winds. Strong winds only blow apart thermals and make flying a struggle rather than a dance of cooperation with the air. Sometimes, unfortunately, we are caught unawares by an increasing wind.

In high winds:
- *Stay well in front of a mountain*
- *Do not fly near the lee side of any solid*
- *Use an alternate landing field if necessary*
- *Do not flare Significantly*
- *Turn your glider or push on your front cables until help arrives.*

Techniques for handling high wind consist first of proper positioning. Do not drift back over the top of a mountain (unless extremely high in a thermal) and in general stay well in front of the crest. Remember, you'll have less penetration in high winds. Avoid flying any where near the downwind side of obstructions. This may necessitate using an alternate landing field that is more open than the primary one. Do not turn downwind except when very high and with the landing field downwind of you—you might not make it back otherwise.

To reach a distant landing field or other goal in high winds the shortest path is *a direct line.* In other words do not think you'll come out higher by heading upwind or crosswind first unless you're expecting some lift or are trying to avoid sink or higher winds caused by a venturi. If you encounter lift in a crosswind, fly directly upwind in it to get "ahead of the game." Resume the proper crab when lift dies. You must fly at the proper speed as well. This is faster than your best glide speed in order to achieve the best glide path in a head wind. Crosswinds are a bit like head winds in that they slow you down (you have to crab) so you need to increase speed. The exact speed to fly in any condition is the subject of speeds-to-fly covered in Chapter 7.

HIGH WIND LANDINGS

✓ *The Approach*

Landing is the main complication in high winds. Expect ruffled air near the ground. To handle this, a semi-prone position as shown in figure 2-8 is recommended. In this position you have better roll control than when standing and better crash protection than when prone.

KEEPING ONE HAND ON BASETUBE ALLOWS QUICK CONTROL.

Figure 2-8: Turbulent Landing Position

When nearing the ground on final you may have to keep the control bar pulled in considerably. Your normal approach should be fast enough to handle winds up to 20 mph. In higher winds more pull-in is required. Some pilots have found themselves flying backwards until very near the ground, but don't give up, wind almost always diminishes below your maximum reasonable speed close to the ground due to wind gradient.

✓ *The Flare*

In winds above 15 mph not much flare is required. Just a slight easing out of the bar stops your vertical descent. In winds over 20 mph no flare should be used, simply walk along as you touch down after rounding out.

In very strong winds you may have to fly the control bar to the ground, then hold the uprights with the nose slightly down until help arrives (see figure 2-9). An alternate method is to stand on the control bar while pushing forward on the front cables (see figure 2-10).

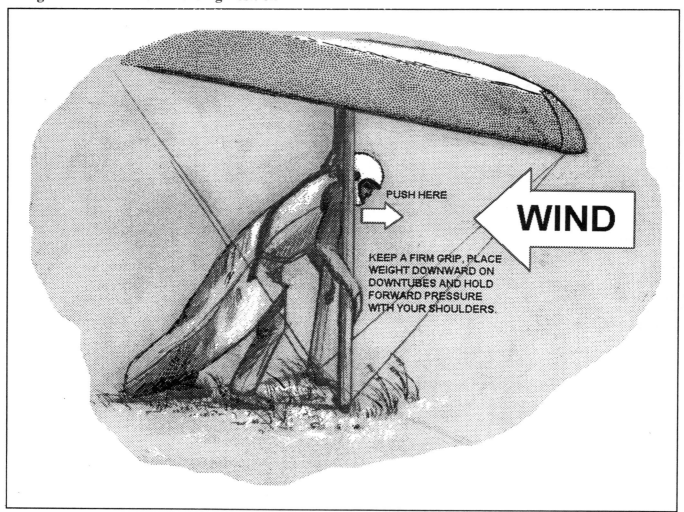

PUSH HERE

WIND

KEEP A FIRM GRIP, PLACE WEIGHT DOWNWARD ON DOWNTUBES AND HOLD FORWARD PRESSURE WITH YOUR SHOULDERS.

Figure 2-9: Holding a Glider in High Winds

Figure 2-10: Alternate Holding Method

Don't let the nose up or matters will get really exciting. If no help is available, rotate your glider slowly while keeping the upwind moving wing low. Eventually you can set the tail on the ground with the wind quartering from behind as shown in figure 2-11.

Pilots sensitive to the air currents prefer more moderate winds so they can cooperate with the air.

In the 1992 Pre-World Meet many pilots landed at goal at Luning, Nevada. The wind was a smooth 30 mph on the flat pan, and not enough assistance was available. Pilots were unable to unhook and had to stand with their gliders for long periods until help came. Those gliders who quartered their gliders were free to get out of their harness and coats in 100° heat!

Once you are unhooked you can move your glider to the breakdown area by walking backwards and pulling it with the front cables (let it fly). Another method is to let it fly while you are behind the control bar. If it climbs, pull down on the downtubes.

TURBULENCE TRIBULATIONS

Turbulent designations:

WORSE
| Textured
| Rowdy
| Rodeo
| Roller coaster
| Heart stopping
▼ Life threatening

by acclamation

None of us likes rodeo air unless it signals a rocket thermal that propels us to dizzying heights. This is not the case many times. In fact turbulence is often a pilot's greatest fear.

✓ *Turbulence Limits*

Handling turbulence is mainly a matter of producing quick positive control movements and maintaining ample airspeed. The sooner you make these controls, the less severe the turbulence feels. Turbulence is a normal part of the air's characteristics and after time you learn what turbulence level is acceptable in terms of safety and what amount of bashing around is too much for fun and profitable flying.

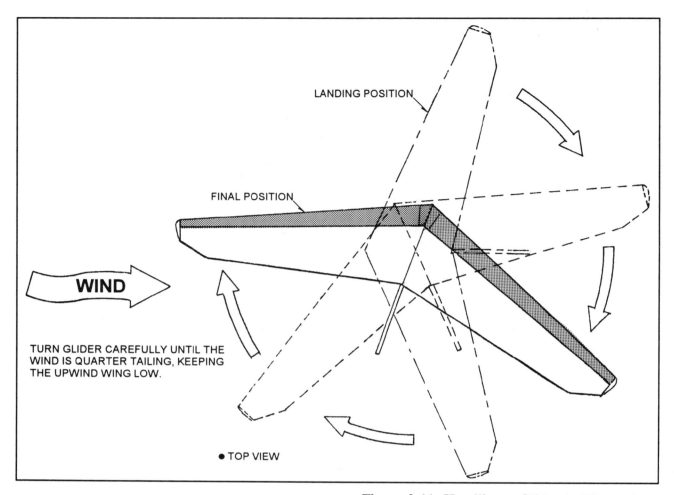

WIND

TURN GLIDER CAREFULLY UNTIL THE
WIND IS QUARTER TAILING, KEEPING
THE UPWIND WING LOW.

LANDING POSITION

FINAL POSITION

● TOP VIEW

Figure 2-11: Handling a Glider in High Winds

It should be noted that with experience you may learn to appreciate moderate turbulence as part of the excitement of the ride, similar to windsurfing or jet skiing in waves rather than the dull, flat surface of an undisturbed lake.

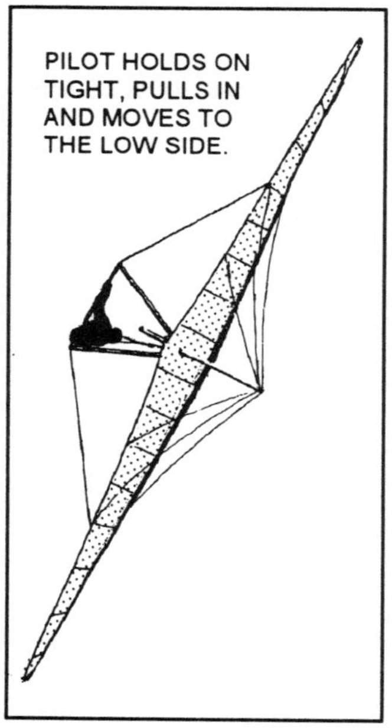

The limits of safe turbulence occur when our quick control actions do not serve to keep us on an even keel or we start getting frequent slack side wires and harness mains.

On a strong west day in the Owens Valley in july 1992, some fifteen pilots flew from Horseshoe Meadows to find body slamming turbulence. One pilot hit the keel with her back and found her base bar bent permanently upwards by the pull of her arms. All pilots promptly went out to land in such unfriendly conditions except one who flew the length of the Sierra and was found two days later under a crashed glider.

The lesson is to get down and out of severe turbulence if possible. Sometimes you can't.

I once landed behind 200 feet high foothills after loosing the lift at Clinch Mountain, Tennessee. As I neared the ground I was tossed out of control and flung into a wingover, ending up in a tree. Since that time (1977) I have resolved to never fly behind such obstructions in soaring winds.

✔ *Tumbling Blues*

Up in the sky thermal induced turbulence can sometimes alter your immediate flight plan dramatically. A severe sledgehammer thermal can create a hard roll, sometimes past 90° as shown in figure 2-12.

In this situation you should pull in to fly fast and stay on the low side of the

PILOT HOLDS ON
TIGHT, PULLS IN
AND MOVES TO
THE LOW SIDE.

**Figure 2-12: Rolling
past 90° in Turbulence**

control bar. The Result will be a split S which is similar to a "wingover"* without the initial climb. If you go to the high side of the bar you may end up upside down.

In severe, glider tumbling turbulence as in figure 2-13, the safest technique is to hold the bar in to chest level possibly with both arms wrapped around the base tube. The faster you go the higher the pitch stability forces (as well as roll forces) so the less likely you are to tumble, but the greater the turbulence induced G loading will be. *Therefore , the best control and assurance against tumbling is with the bar in chest position (from 30 to 35 mph).* Be cautious of pulling the bar in too rapidly if you start going over the falls for this action can over-rotate you. If possible you should have ample speed *before* you hit the tumbling turbulence.

Handling turbulence:
- *Maintain good control speed*
- *Maintain extra speed in rowdy thermals*
- *Remain centered in thermal when circling*
- *Gain speed before exiting thermal*
- *Make quick control corrections*
EXCEPT:
- *In a tumbling situation do not pull in rapidly but hold bar firmly at chest*
- *Move to the low side of the control bar once you get rolled past 90°.*

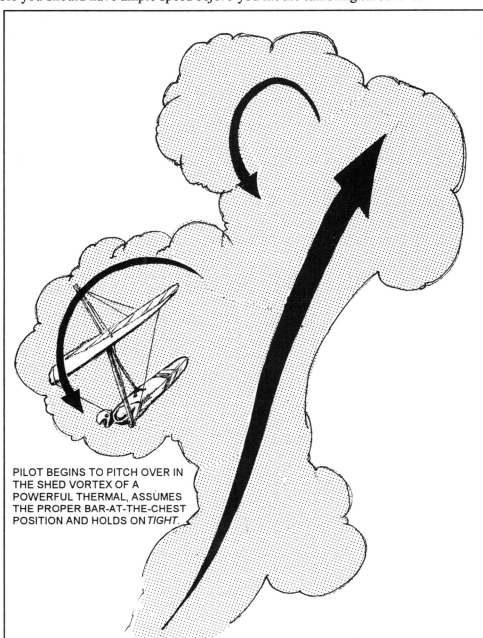

PILOT BEGINS TO PITCH OVER IN THE SHED VORTEX OF A POWERFUL THERMAL, ASSUMES THE PROPER BAR-AT-THE-CHEST POSITION AND HOLDS ON *TIGHT*.

Figure 2-13: Control in Tumbling Turbulence

* What is known as a wingover in hang gliding is not a true wingover and is sometimes called a rollover.

Most personal accounts of tumbling (from Bruce Goldsmith, Kari Castle, Glen Volk, Tim Arai, Al Whitesell, Butch Peachy, for example) express a sudden unavoidable upset before the pilot could react. After the tumble is the only time they had to regain control, wet their pants, check for damage and deploy a chute if necessary (remember: when in doubt, whip it out). However, if you have reaction time in any tumbling situation your best bet is to move *to one side of the control bar*. This prevents you from ending up on your back and is the best argument we've heard for practicing wingovers.

Sometimes even moderate thermals can present a problem. I witnessed one pilot several hundred feet below me in a moderately turbulent thermal go upside down and deploy nylon. He landed unscathed as his canopy lowered him into the trees. Upon later questioning it was apparent that he was pushing way out when he hit the turbulent edge of the thermal.

The moral: stay centered in a thermal, maintain ample control speed and pull on extra speed when exiting exciting thermals.

Pro Tip: Experienced pilots bank steeply in rowdy thermals because the extra speed provides control and a greater pitch stability margin.

The last word on turbulence: avoid high winds, especially when they're laden with strong thermals, and lee side situations and your rough encounters should remain mild to moderate.

WINGING IN THE RAIN

You never get caught without your umbrella when hang gliding, but you may find that little solace when rain coats your wings. Rain, hail, snow and sleet occasionally greet us in the air, especially during winter flying or when skirting overdevelopment. The only real problem (besides loss of visibility if you wear glasses) is that a coating of water can change your glider's behavior. If water beads up on your upper surface and specifically on your leading edge, pitch pressures and stall behavior will change.

Usually you'll find the glider will trim faster (the base bar will be further back), the stall will occur at higher speed and it will be more abrupt. As a result you will not get as good a sink rate and landing will be more complicated.

Rain beads on a leading edge.

When landing with a rain coated glider, try shaking the glider hard in the air or diving fast to remove water before you reach final approach. On final keep your speed up, be extremely sensitive to the first sign of stall, then flare aggressively. The flare will occur at a faster flying speed than you are used to —don't try to slow to normal speed or you'll be eating mud—but you shouldn't over-climb since the glider the glider will stall sooner. Be ready to run.

Water on your wing will make the glider act as if it is suddenly smaller. The reason for this is beads of water disrupt the flow along the upper surface.

Snow, if it is cold enough, doesn't have this effect (in fact snow is fun to fly in for you can watch the streamlines around the wing) while sleet does. All-Mylar gliders are the worse in these conditions because the water beads up over the entire surface. Gliders with smooth Mylar leading edges are the next worse. Gliders with bumpy Mylar (scrim cloth) leading edges aren't affected nearly as much.

I once flew a Formula on a demo flight when it began to rain. About ten other high performance gliders with Mylar leading edges lost the lift as their sink rate deteriorated. The Formula, however, didn't notice the rain for its Dacron leading edges just soaked up the water so airflow wasn't disrupted. Imagine my surprise (and their chagrin) when I continued soaring as the other pilots struggled with sluggish gliders in the landing area.

Taking off with a soaked glider can be an exercise in running. Not only will the glider be heavier, but it will be tail heavy as well (more soaked area behind the CG). In addition, if the leading edge is Mylar and beaded with water you may not get in the air. The solution is to sacrifice a shirt and wipe off the leading edge. Heavy dew or fog can have similar effects. In any case be ready to run extra with a soggy wing.

THE THREAT AND DREAD OF CLOUD SUCK

Cloud suck is a descriptive and appropriate term for the strong, widespread lift that develops beneath certain clouds. The situations where this occurs are in moist, unstable conditions or under thunderstorms. An overdeveloping sky commonly exhibits cloud suck because it is the abundance of moisture in the air that leads to overdevelopment and moist air rises readily.

We have experienced cloud suck under a solid cloud street (no individual cumulus, just long, long clouds), under individual building cumulus, under a solid overcast sky (weak widespread cloud suck) and under the bench of a thunderstorm. Some of these situations are potentially dangerous, some not. The danger is not the lift of course, but getting sucked up into the cloud. We investigate cloud flying in Chapter 6.

Pilot launches with towering storm in the background requiring vigilance.

The most terrifying minutes I have spent on a hang glider was during a one-on-one competition in Guatemala when my opponent and I were sucked into a cloud that formed immediately after launch. He was only about two wingspans away from me when we entered the cloud and I could barely see my wing tip. Fortunately we did not collide but I came out of the cloud a bit disoriented behind the top and barely squeaked through a gap in the trees to the front of the mountain.

Despite the horror stories and the title of this section, cloud suck isn't necessarily dangerous if you understand and prepare for it. Here are the signs:

▶ 1. When you are under a building cloud or overdevelopment, expect cloud suck within 2000 feet of cloud base in desert conditions or 1000 feet in greener areas.

▶ 2. Darker, larger clouds are more apt to exhibit cloud suck, darker areas are more apt to be sucking.

▶ 3. If thermals begin to smooth out or get stronger within the above limits of cloud base, expect cloud suck. Multiple cores going up (other gliders and birds indicate this) within these limits are signs of cloud suck, especially if these cores merge.

Finally, if lift remains above 500 FPM (feet per minute), especially if in a broad area , as you reach these limits you should expect cloud suck.

To be sure, good thermals often have multiple cores and good climb rates all the way to cloud base. The worrisome cloud suck occurs when the lift is so widespread that you can't easily escape it before you enter the cloud.

Figure 2-14 shows how to handle cloud suck depending on conditions. If the cloud is small enough when you detect cloud suck and you wish to continue climbing, move to the front (upwind side) of the cloud. This allows you to pull out to blue sky if need be. If you are flying cross-country downwind you can head to the downwind side of the cloud, but be cautioned that thunderstorms spread more rapidly at their downwind edge.

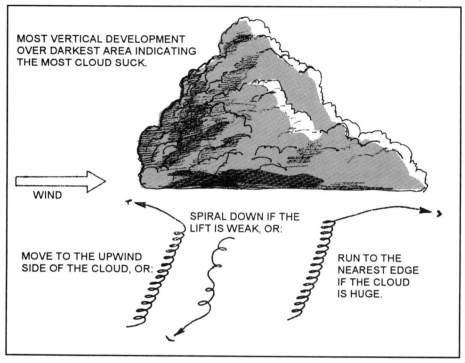

MOST VERTICAL DEVELOPMENT OVER DARKEST AREA INDICATING THE MOST CLOUD SUCK.

WIND

SPIRAL DOWN IF THE LIFT IS WEAK, OR:

MOVE TO THE UPWIND SIDE OF THE CLOUD, OR:

RUN TO THE NEAREST EDGE IF THE CLOUD IS HUGE.

Figure 2-14: Escaping Cloud Suck

In 1987 US Nationals, Tony Barton was working weak lift in a blue sky low on a task north of the Owens Valley. He saw a cloud begin to form above him and the lift improved. As he got higher he noticed the cloud building and spreading. He expected cloud suck and headed on course. The lift spread out with the cloud faster than he could fly away even though he left well below base. Eventually rain and lightning caught him and put him on the ground.

Tony experienced sparks, fear and loathing from the charged air despite the fact he recognized the dangers and left early. Perhaps an upwind or crosswind escape route away from goal would have put him out of range of the storm.

LOSING ALTITUDE

If cloud suck lift is widespread but below 500 FPM you can escape it by spiraling down. The greatest average sink rate you can sustain over a long period of time is only 500 to 700 FPM, so turning is not the way to deal with lift greater than 500 FPM.

To perform your greatest sink rate you must do *diving* (slipping turns).Pull in at least to your waist and move to one side of the bar. The glider will dive and turn. As soon as G forces build up the glider is entering a spiral turn not a slip (see Chapter 3) and the descent rate slows. At this point reverse your turn—remain pulled in and shift your weight to the other side—and a slip to the other side will occur (see figure 2-15). Typically you can perform two to three 360s per side.

When you wish to stop these turns go to the high side to level the wings and fight the nose-up tendency to slow down gradually. Very high forces can result if you let the bar out at any time in the maneuver.

Turning with high G forces can be disorienting. You can build up your tolerance to the disorientation with practice. We suggest you practice this maneuver up high to familiarize yourself with your limits long before you need to use it. While you're at it check your altimeter against your watch to see what average sink rate you can sustain.

ESCAPING CLOUD SUCK STORMS

At times we blunder into great lift that gets too good. Spiraling down ends up being a spiral up. This can occur anytime when thunderstorms are building, but occasionally with large fair-weather cumulus as well. When lift is strong and the cloud is large we must run from it.

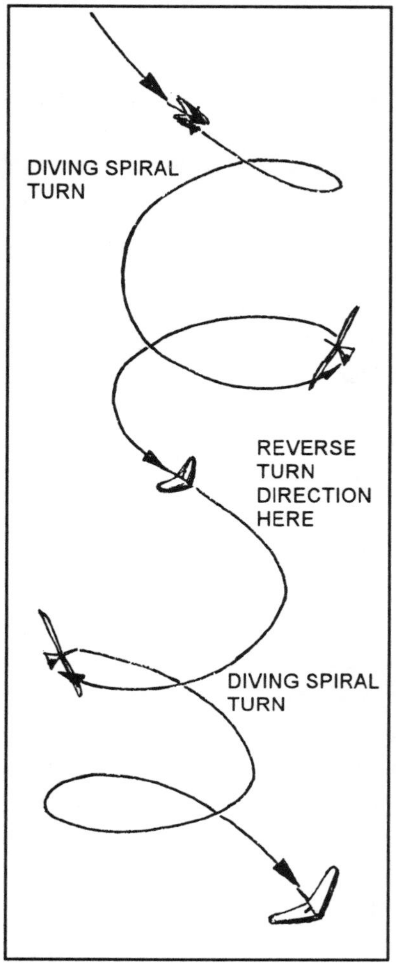

Dive toward the closest edge of the cloud. If thunderstorms are expected it is wise to head for the closest edge in the crosswind direction as shown in figure 2-16. Downwind a gust front can extend for 10 miles or more while the upwind side exhibits the most lift. Your dive should be at least fast enough to maintain zero climb. In very strong lift the dive should be a full-blown bar-stuffing race with tucked knees if necessary (see figure 2-17).

At the 1990 Pre-World Meet in Brazil I raced beneath the bench of a huge thunderstorm with the bar at my waist and maintained a steady 5,000 feet ground clearance for 22 miles before I ran clear of the storm.

Even with a screaming dive it is possible to get sucked up. As soon as you reach wispy air in this case, slow down gradually to about best glide and try to fly as straight and still as possible. The reason for this sudden change of tactic is that once you are in the cloud it can become turbulent and turn you. If you are diving you will swing around and lose all sense of direction. Any attempt at correction in this situation will only serve to create high forces and confuse you more.

This is an important point proven by many pilots. We summarize below:

> **Escaping a cloud**
> When sucked up into a cloud immediately fly slowly straight and level. You will eventually come out the side of the cloud. A compass can help only if you fly straight. Before you enter the cloud, check its shadow to estimate its extent and where you may end up. Good luck.

Figure 2-15: Losing Altitude with Slips and Spirals

Escaping suck:
1. Spiral down if lift is 500 FPM or less.
2. Move to front edge of cloud if still well above or cloud small.
3. Dive to nearest edge if you are very near cloud.
4. Once in cloud slow up to maintain equilibrium and fly outside of cloud.

Do not throw your parachute in a thunderstorm. It will only serve to carry you up faster.

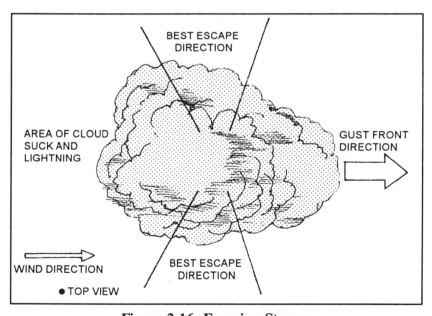

Figure 2-16: Escaping Storms

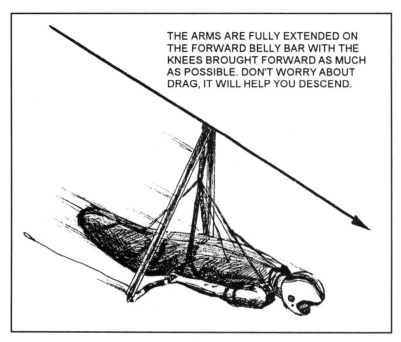

THE ARMS ARE FULLY EXTENDED ON THE FORWARD BELLY BAR WITH THE KNEES BROUGHT FORWARD AS MUCH AS POSSIBLE. DON'T WORRY ABOUT DRAG, IT WILL HELP YOU DESCEND.

Figure 2-17: Diving from Cloud Suck

Thunderstorms are special because they build rapidly, spread rapidly and present hazards beyond mere blind flying such as lightning, hail and strong winds. We should note that if we have to escape a thunderstorm *it is better to outrun it* than try to land when it is dumping rain or virga*, for this is a sign of a possible gust front. Often it is advisable to use the lift at the edge of a thunderstorm to gain enough altitude to get away from the storm rather than leave the area low.

The dangers of thunderstorms were summarized previously in figure 1-13. If you get caught by surprise or choose to play with thunderstorms you had better know how to judge them (see *Understanding the Sky*).

One Spanish pilot was sucked higher and higher into a thunderstorm with no relief. He climbed into his control bar, unhooked and free-fell. When he appeared below the cloud he deployed his parachute and floated to safety. This is not an exercise for the faint at heart!

FLYING AT ALTITUDE

The higher we go the thinner the air becomes. The question often arises as to what effect this has on our performance. We can look at the change in air density and get an exact value from equations, but the density doesn't always vary the same as we go higher due to changes in lapse rates (temperature profile of the air) and pressure systems. Thus we use a general rule of thumb for soaring conditions.

> **Performance at Altitude**
> All speeds increase 2%
> for every 1,000 feet we gain.

This rule has interesting results. It means that both horizontal and vertical velocities increase the same amount so that glide ratios (including maximum glide) at each bar position remain the same as shown in figure 1-13. The difference is we follow these glide paths at a faster rate. Changing altitude is essentially** the same as changing wing loading. For example, a 1,000 ft increase in altitude has the same effect as adding 4 to 5.5 lbs (depending on your starting weight) to your body.

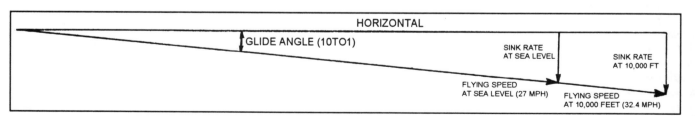

HORIZONTAL

GLIDE ANGLE (10 TO 1)

SINK RATE AT SEA LEVEL

SINK RATE AT 10,000 FT

FLYING SPEED AT SEA LEVEL (27 MPH)

FLYING SPEED AT 10,000 FEET (32.4 MPH)

Figure 2-18: Speed Changes with Altitude

* Virga is a veil of rain falling from a cloud and drying before it reaches the ground (see photo in Chapter 1).

** It isn't quite true due to Reynolds Number effects—see Chapter 12.

Have you ever wondered what it would be like to fly as a heavy weight? To find out go fly at Telluride, Colorado with its 12,000 plus foot launch. If you take off at 18 mph at sea level you'll take off at nearly 22.5 mph at Telluride. That's as if you added 60 lbs to your body! Mind you, achieving this extra speed only requires another step or two, but obviously a good launch technique is in order in this air. Landing has the same requirements, of course.

When we investigate speeds-to-fly and cross-country flying in later chapters we will return to this subject.

ESCAPING AIRCRAFT

The volume of air that shrouds our blue planet seems to be getting smaller. That's because there's more humans taking to the sky. Bigger planes need more elbow room and us little guys get elbowed off to the side. We try to remain in uncontrolled airspace, but even there we occasionally encounter the "heavy iron".

The danger to airplanes we present is nil if they see us. Whether it is a jet or a Cessna, you *want* them to see you so they can maneuver around you for a midair with any airplane would leave you in dire straits. To that end 360s or S turns will flash the best signal of your presence as long as the aircraft is far enough away to react. If you appear to be on a collision course, a spiral dive is the best way to displace yourself and become visible. Flying away from an aircraft makes you nearly invisible. Be aware that power pilots spend much of their time looking at instruments, especially around airports. It is up to you to see and avoid.

In contested air-space we lose due to our light weight and lightweight political clout.

Even if a collision isn't imminent, an aircraft presents danger because of wake turbulence. A clean sailplane is not much of a problem. A small airplane won't necessarily knock you out of the sky, but it will seriously rock you. A large transport can tear your glider apart. A helicopter can do equal damage and slam you to the ground. Helicopter pilots, while some of the most highly trained, seem to be oblivious of their wake turbulence. The early champion and hang gliding pioneer, Bob Wills, was killed by a helicopter wake, and former World Champion Rex Miller was slammed into the trees by a helicopter flying over to check him out.

Wake from aircraft descends slowly (fast with a helicopter) and drifts with the wind. In stable conditions it can linger for up to 5 minutes. To avoid wake turbulence, simply remain above the flight path or fly away from it if possible. Often an aircraft will pass in front of you and you can't fly back into the mountain. The best bet in this case is to fly parallel to the airplane path to give the wake time to dissipate. Be sure to avoid flying within a couple hundred vertical feet of where a helicopter has *been* if you don't want to get shredded and pounded.

III - STRETCHING OUR WINGS

We are aspiring birds at heart. To achieve our dreams of free flight we must become integrated with our wings just like a bird. This is not an abstract concept, but a realistic goal whereby we know our glider's behavior so well we react instantly to each nuance in the air with correct direct action.

FEELINGS IN THE AIR

To reach this goal we will practice some relaxation and awareness stunts. First find a lot of clear airspace and try controlling your glider by different methods. Try it one handed.

Try soaring on the uprights. Try flying with your hands behind you on the rear cables. Notice the roll and pitch pressures in each of these configurations.

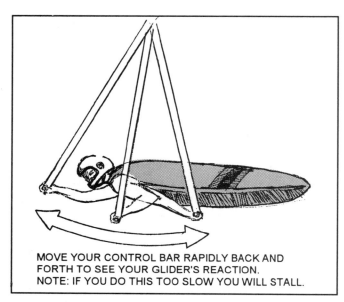

MOVE YOUR CONTROL BAR RAPIDLY BACK AND
FORTH TO SEE YOUR GLIDER'S REACTION.
NOTE: IF YOU DO THIS TOO SLOW YOU WILL STALL.

Figure 2-19: Testing Pitch Dampening

Next try the fast and slow regime to feel the pitch pressures. Especially try stalling your glider (slowly) both straight ahead and at various angles of bank (we'll do more of this in chapter 3). In the same practice try initiating turns at various speeds with various amounts of control force. The object is to implant into your mind your glider's reaction to all inputs.

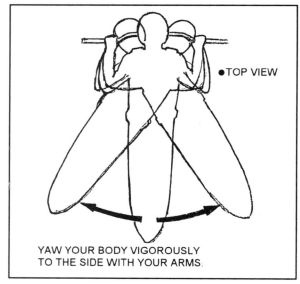

• TOP VIEW

YAW YOUR BODY VIGOROUSLY
TO THE SIDE WITH YOUR ARMS.

Figure 2-20: Testing Yaw Reaction

We must all learn our glider's response to all combinations of roll, pitch and yaw.

Now we have some fun. Move your base bar well back and forward in one second cycles as shown in figure 2-19. Next move it from side to side at a similar speed. Combine the two for a circular motion. What did you find? The aerial flexibility of your glider allowed it to remain tracking straight. In fact, if you do this in light lift you will find you will not lose any net altitude. You can try slowing these cycles down to find the limits of your glider's reaction.

Finally try putting strong yaw controls into the glider by rapidly twisting your body (see figure 2-20). Notice how the glider yaws and corrects but creates a small roll. This action will have its uses when turning.

The whole object of all these gyrations and exercises is to make you feel at home on your glider. This feeling then in turn builds confidence and precision control for those graceful arcs and demanding patches of elusive lift.

USING YOUR GLIDER'S SPEEDS

To maximize your efficiency you need to know your glider's "sweet spots" or cardinal speeds. These are the speeds or bar positions, if you will, where certain maximum performance parameters exist *in still air*. We list them for review in ascending order on the side bar.

We can add trim speed to this list, but this is a speed you can adjust while the other speeds are essentially determined by glider design and your wing loading.

For best thermaling performance we recommend your trim speed be set at minimum sink. Most gliders come from the factory adjusted a little fast for safety reasons so check every new glider you fly.

Cardinal Speeds
Stall speed
Minimum sink speed
Best glide speed
Best maneuvering speed
V$_{NE}$—Speed never to exceed
(Figure 2-21 shows their
approximate relation).

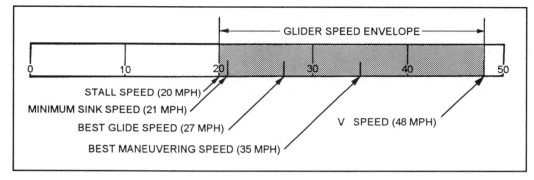

Figure 2-21: Cardinal Speeds

Many of us do not fly with airspeed indicators because we develop a pretty good feel for airspeed on our windblown faces. However, more and more pilots are flying with varios that include airspeed in their system. This is helpful for speed-to-fly techniques.

Airspeed indicators

Airspeed indicators are good reference points, but they don't tell the truth. To begin, the air under a glider is slowed considerably from the true airspeed while at the same time it is accelerated on the top of the wing. At the base tube where many instruments are located, this can be 5 mph or more at slow speeds. This error is smaller the faster you go.

In addition, misalignment with the airstream which changes with angle of attack and is deflected by the pilot and control bar can introduce errors. Finally, density changes as you go higher mean your true airspeed is again faster than that indicated (the error is approximately 2% per 1,000 feet).

We aren't too concerned with these sources of error if we are using an airspeed indicator to register stall speed, minimum sink speed and best glide speed, for we're only interes-

ted in a relative number. Once we find a speed—say minimum sink— it should register the same every time, even at different air densities, as long as the same airspeed indicator setup is used. The reason for this is that just as our wings go faster at higher altitudes (less density) to create the needed lift force, so too does the airspeed indicator need to go faster to register the same airspeed. It works out that an airspeed indicator will read the same at every set angle of attack—min. sink in our example—no matter what the altitude.

Propeller type airspeed indicators are designed to read true airspeed. However, friction in the system will prevent this, but they are more true than other types and thus the stall speed they indicate changes with air density (altitude).

✔ *Stall and Minimum Sink Speed*

Stall occurs about as slowly as you can go. On some wings you can still maintain control after the wing starts to stall but your sink rate is increasing. We call this "mush mode" or mushing.

Minimum sink will occur just before the wing begins to stall. One manufacturer puts a tuft of yarn on their gliders to help identify this point (the yarn begins to fluctuate and blow forward at stall). You can do this with any glider but you must use multiple tufts since you don't know for sure where stall will first appear (usually in the center 2/3 of mid-span as illustrated in Chapter 12). The tufts must be on the upper surface—you can see them through the sail on a sunny day.

Without tufts you can find minimum sink fairly easily by slowing down in light ridge lift, maintaining straight flight and watching your vario and altimeter or better yet, another pilot beside you. When you are going as slowly as you can go without a wing "sticking" and the

> Minimum sink occurs at the same bar position and airspeed no matter what the air is doing.

altimeter or your fellow pilot shows you that you've achieved your best possible altitude, you have arrived at minimum sink. Mark this bar position and know it well for use in straight flight.

✓ Best Glide Speed

As you know, best glide speed gives us our best glide ratio over the ground in still air. In moving air our best glide path is found at a different speed which is the subject of Chapter 7 (speeds-to-fly). Theoretically, best glide speed is 1.3 times minimum sink speed. This is in the ball park which means around 6 mph faster than minimum sink speed.

Several trials from a hill one hundred to three hundred feet high can help you pinpoint where best glide is on your glider. Fly in calm conditions and hold one speed with each flight to see which speed gets you furthest. Most inexperienced pilots fly too slowly to achieve best glide.

An alternate way to find best glide is to fly with a friend away from a high mountain (out of lift) in calm air. While your friend holds a steady speed, change yours to fly a little faster and slower to see which speed gives you the best glide maintained in relation to your friend. One or two trials like this should teach you where the best glide bar position is. Memorize it.

✓ Best Maneuvering Speed and VNE

The faster you go, the easier your glider turns, up to a point. If you go too fast in turbulence, gust-induced loads stress your glider and may jerk your wings up and down. There is a best maneuvering speed for each glider which is a compromise between too slow and too fast. This speed is generally 5 to 10 mph faster than best glide speed or 30 to 35 mph (bar from chest to waist). Use it for landing setup and maintaining equilibrium in strong turbulence.

The velocity-never-to-exceed speed (VNE) is the maximum velocity for which a certified glider has been tested. Pilots do exceed these speeds, especially during aerobatics. At one time it was thought impossible to break a hang glider by pulling positive G forces because the glider would deform and off-load. We now know that gliders with tighter sails and longer spans can be broken with severe diving and pushing out maneuvers as pilots have discovered much to their disappointment. However, for the most part modern gliders are strong enough to handle any positive load they encounter, be it from gusts or maneuvers. But you should know that the faster you fly the closer you can come to your glider's stress limits. Your glider has been tested for the VNE speed. Beyond that you're on your own.

GOING FAST

Every pilot should know how to fly their glider in a bar-to-the-knees all-out dive. This is necessary to escape thunderstorms as mentioned previously, but also to get out of venturis and penetrate unexpected high winds.

It's not hard to pull in the bar, but there are two considerations. First, we want to remain streamlined. Forward bar pressure tends to rock us upward as shown in figure 2-22, creating drag which doesn't help our penetration. A shifting center of gravity harness can prevent this. If you don't have one of these harnesses, push yourself all the way forward with your toes and rock your head down as far as you can *before* you pull in. Usually friction on your Shoulder-to-leg rope will keep you down as shown before.

The second matter is oscillations. Some gliders become less stable at high speed and begin roll oscillations when disturbed. You may have to slow and start over if they occur. We discuss this in a later section. In any case, learn to fly your glider fast, long before you need it so something like oscillations or overwhelming pitch pressures don't limit this important safety valve.

PRACTICING TECHNIQUES

Whenever you are high above your same ol'site in the same ho-hum conditions you have an ideal opportunity to hone your skills and judgement. After all, what do you learn from just hanging around? Here are some suggestions as to what you can do to achieve enlightenment

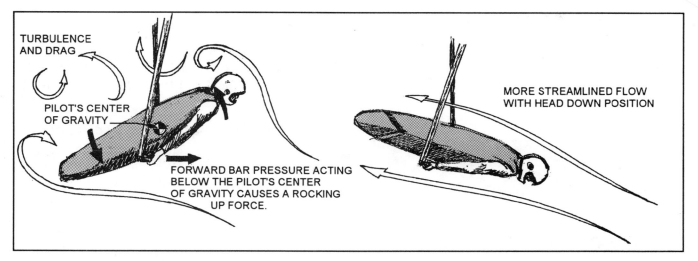

Figure 2-22: Proper High Speed Position

(which in our case means get higher more often).

• *Set a goal in front of the mountain which you try to reach, then return to soar.* Do this multiple times in one flight, each time setting the goal further. Trying this with other pilots to see who can succeed first is great fun and good competition training.

• *Set a goal along a ridge or mountain to reach and return as in the preceding exercise.*

• *Buzz down to launch level then see if you can become top pilot.* Again do this more than once and challenge your buddies to join you.

• *Race your flying fellows to cloud base.*

• *Practice making all thermaling 360s the opposite to your preferred side.* See if you can climb with other pilots. If not, keep doing this exercise every day until you can. As a corollary to this, practice setting your landings up with turns to your "bad" side. Is that uncomfortable? Then you have something to practice.

• *Practice figuring out the day as soon as possible* by noting sizes of thermals, drift, sources, inversion level, changes in thermal direction, cloud base, etc. You'll be surprised at how being aware of these factors as soon as possible will put you on top.

• *Most importantly, practice flying to clouds* either by meeting them out front or intercepting them along the mountain. Learn to judge where you'll encounter their lift and how far away you can be and still reach it. It is amazing how this simple practice will get you to cloud base while other gliders are floundering low elsewhere.

• Other matters to try involve familiarizing ourselves with our gliders which we discussed earlier in the section FEELINGS IN THE AIR.

"Practice makes perfect" or at least perfectly able.

INTRODUCING HIGH PERFORMANCE GLIDERS

At some stage in your flying career you may wish to transition to what is known as a high performance glider (in our usage this will mean a glider with close to maximum performance available).

To make this step you should be aware of the differences between a "blade wing" and your old reliable rag. We'll categorize these as setup, takeoff, handling and landing differences. Setup is generally obvious; you have more battens to stuff, more weight to truck and more to preflight.

✓ Takeoff

Takeoff is not much more difficult in a hi-per glider except loose side cables with typical variable geometry (VG) gliders require extra care in levelling the wings. Also extra weight makes holding the glider up and accelerating it a bit more difficult. On the other hand, a tight double surface glider may begin to lift sooner than older, looser gliders. A good running launch habit will overcome any added difficulty in any case. Here's a trick: launching with your VG 1/3 to 1/2 on will not hurt handling too much and will take a lot of slack out of those sagging side cables.

A high performance glider planform.

High performance gliders generally are:
1. Heavier
2. More complicated
3. Provide less side to side feedback on launch
4. Less solid in pitch
5. Less responsive in roll (except at high speed)
6. More critical in the landing phase...
than intermediate gliders.

Landing a high performance glider...
1. Requires more planning ahead
2. Requires more runout room
3. Requires a faster final for control
4. Requires a more precise flare timing...
than an intermediate glider.

✓ Handling — Controlling Oscillations

High performance gliders with a VG system have variable handling. With the VG off, many of them handle like intermediate wings. One big difference is pitch pressures. Advanced gliders are designed to have very light pitch pressures. A common mistake pilots make when flying these gliders for the first time is subconsciously looking for pitch pressure and diving them excessively. This error is often compounded by roll oscillations (Dutch roll) that can border on wingovers and lose much altitude. Pilots have died from this tragedy of errors.

The best way to prevent oscillations is to proceed away from the hill and slow the glider up to just above stall. Keeping a little VG on will help as well. We have seen this over-control occur on several different designs so we repeat:

To Prevent Oscillations on a First Flight
Adjust to trim immediately after takeoff. Slowing down and making very small inputs will stop over-control oscillations.

Oscillations can occur beyond the first flight with some gliders. The problem is the pilot applies too much input too late. The whole matter is cured with proper timing that comes with practice. With such twitchy gliders you'll learn to apply a roll correction then release it *before* the glider reacts. If you wait until the glider starts rolling with your input, it will roll past level and on to an opposite bank angle.

To Prevent Oscillations
Make your roll corrections of short duration and of small movement.

With a VG 1/2 to full on a hi-per glider becomes more like a semi than an aircraft in handling. The idea is to have great straight ahead performance at the expense of handling. In Chapter 3 we'll see how to turn stiffer gliders and we'll explore using a VG system in Chapter 6.

✓ Landing

When you consider moving up to a hi-per glider your landing skills will gain much attention. Advanced gliders:

▶ 1. Are slower to respond to turns (they are tighter and spannier), so you need to plan ahead more and maintain more clearance from obstructions. Thus, figure 8 approaches are no longer advisable except in stronger winds or with huge landing fields. The standard downwind, base and final approach is best for landing (see previous figure 2-4).

►2. Glide further and thus require more run out room. Speeding up a hi-per glider isn't nearly as effective for bringing it down as with an intermediate glider.

►3. Have a more specific flare window. A hi-per glider carries more speed retention and will climb higher if you flare too early. Flaring too late will result in a more severe nose-in since the stall is a bit more abrupt in a hi-per glider. Landing isn't outrageously difficult in an advanced glider, it just requires more attention than with more loosely strung wings.

SUMMARY

We work on basics in any endeavor so that we can add to them to get to more complex achievements. In this chapter we reviewed some of the situations such as taking off, landing, challenging conditions and new gliders that can prove to be lingering problems to advancing pilots. It is our hope that every pilot will have these matters well in hand before moving too quickly to the more complex and demanding material that comes later. We can't be that sea gull's rival until we earn our primaries.

A pilot thermals high above the flatlands of Florida

CHAPTER 3

Maximizing Turns

One of the most important technique we must investigate in order to prepare for advanced flying is efficient turning. Turning a glider efficiently is where much of the skills comes that separates the auks from the hawks. An auk is a rather feeble flyer while a hawk is nimble and resourceful in the air. We rise to salute the hawks among us.

To maximize turns we usually want to change directions with a minimum loss of altitude or produce the best turn to exploit a particular thermal core. However, at times we use turns for applications such as losing altitude, gaining speed or performing maneuvers. We'll investigate all of these species of turns as we prepare for advanced flying.

I - EFFECTIVE COORDINATED TURNS

To eke out every bit of lift from a passing thermal or minimize loss when jockeying around on a ridge, we must perfect our turns. Listen to John Pendry, former World Champion and multiple winner of the European Championships: *"To excel we must fly as efficiently as we can at all times, especially in turns."* Flying efficiently in turns means producing the coordinated kind.

COORDINATED TURNS

A class I hang glider turns with weight shift. There is no rudder to help pull it around, the automatic yaw stability of the glider must take effect. Our main job as pilots is to control roll (bar to the side) and pitch (bar forward and back). Let us look briefly at this action.

✔ How it Turns

*"One good turn
deserves another."
— One of the tenets
of western thought*

In figure 3-1 we see the rear view of a glider banked or rolled to the left by the side control of the pilot. The simple side control creates an imbalance of force as shown in the upper drawing and the glider wants to move sideways (side slip). However, if we add forward pitch control we increase lift to create an arc in our flight path. This curving flight path results in an apparent centrifugal* force swinging our body to the outside of the turn to reestablish the balance of forces and produce a coordinated turn (right drawing).

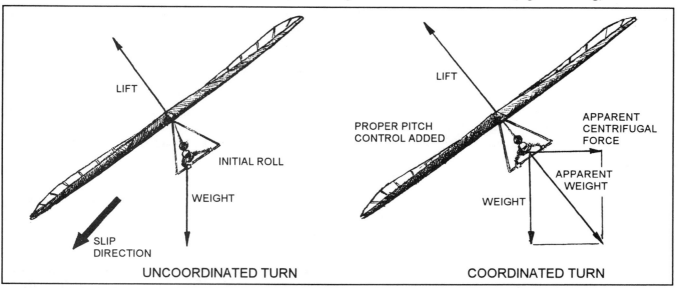

Figure 3-1: Difference in Slipping and Coordinated Turns

*Coordinated turns
produce the least
altitude loss.*

We can learn several things from this short description. First, since we need some forward pitch control to coordinate our turn, we should not be flying right at stall as we initiate our roll. Second, as our turn coordinates and centrifugal force builds up, our body usually becomes centered on the bar. Third, there is a specific ideal pitch for each bank angle.

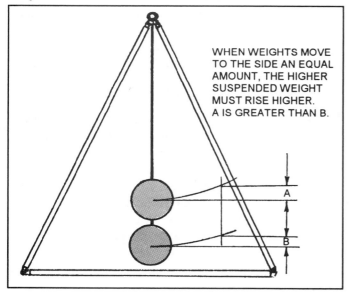

Figure 3-2: Hang Position Effect on Roll Forces

✔ Roll Control

To roll our glider we shift our weight to one side. The effort this takes depends on five things:
- The flexibility of our glider
- Our hanging height
- The glider's lag in response
- Our wing loading
- The glider's roll stability

An aeroelastic glider is one that flexes as it moves through the air. If your glider flexes rather than plows air it will be easier to roll. For response lag and roll stability, see below.

Our hanging height dictates roll forces because the lower we are with respect to the glider, the more leverage we have and the less we have to lift ourselves for a given sideways deflection (see figure 3-2). The reason for kingpost hang points is to effectively increase our hang length. Hanging too low creates comfort problems so a compromise is necessary.

*In reality the force is directed inward and called centripetal force. Due to our body's inertia it feels as if it is being pulled outward and the effect is popularly know as centrifugal force even though no centrifugal force exists.

However, we can generally state: the lower you hang, the lighter the control forces.

Wing loading means how heavy we are on our glider. Invariably, the higher our wing loading the easier our glider will turn.

➤ **Pro Tip:** You may note that your glider turns easier in lift and is less responsive in sink. The reason for this is that increasing lift simulates an increased wing loading while sudden sink decreases our wing loading. This has great importance when we are trying to negotiate the varying lift and sink in thermals.

We should note that the qualities that contribute to good roll handling do not necessarily promote good overall performance. In particular, loose gliders will not usually have outstanding glide performance, especially at higher speeds.

✓ *Roll Response*

It is possible to have a glider with light roll pressures and yet a slow roll response. Some intermediate gliders behave in this manner. Conversely, we have flown high performance gliders with higher roll forces but quick response. The point we are expressing is that roll *responce* and roll *forces* are two different things. We must be aware of this when discussing the relative handling merits of various gliders.

The ideal handling glider is one that reacts immediately to every input and requires very light roll forces. Many high performance gliders fit this description with their variable geometry (VG) systems loose, but few if any do so when the VG is strung tight as a violin. It should be apparent that good roll control is essential for effective use of thermals and VG settings have a lot to say about how our turns go. We discuss VG settings more in Chapter 6.

One final point to put in the memory bank: The only way to truly tell the handling of a glider is to fly it in thermals. Calm or smooth air only allows you to try reversing turns, which is one test of handling, but it doesn't tell you how quick a reaction you'll get when a wing gets lifted at slow speeds.

For ease in turn control we want:
- *Flexible (loose) glider*
- *Good yaw stability*
- *Lower hang*
- *Higher wing loading.*

Roll response:
How quickly a glider reacts to a roll input.
Roll forces:
How hard it is to move a given distance on the bar.

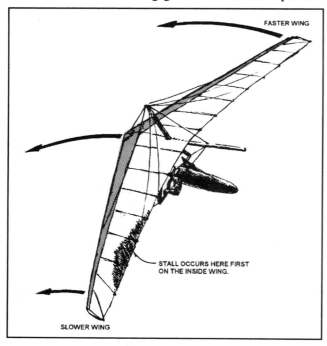

FASTER WING

STALL OCCURS HERE FIRST ON THE INSIDE WING.

SLOWER WING

Figure 3-3: Stall on Inside Wing Limits Turns

✓ *Pitch Control*

The proper speeds to fly in thermal conditions are dealt in detail in later chapters. The main point is that we will be flying faster in the inter-thermal sink and the near-thermal turbulence. Thus, when we encounter lift we have good speed to initiate a roll and push out to establish a coordinated turn. In the next part we address techniques for turning when flying near stall speed. Here we consider that every turn is made with ample entry speed.

From our early learning we know that the proper amount of pushout for any set bank angle is that which establishes an airspeed that neither speeds up or slows down (see *Hang Gliding Flying Skills*). The airspeed that is established will be equivalent to our minimum sink angle of attack at the point on our inside wing where stall will occur first (see figure 3-3). More pushout control will stall us and less will allow the glider to pick up speed as it begins to dive.

Each glider design and wing loading requires a different amount of pitch control in banks, but you can become very familiar with your glider so that you find the sweet spot every time while monitoring airspeed for changes wrought by the fickle winds. The bar position and force will usually be different for slowest speed in a bank than when level, and the airspeed will be higher. The reason for all these points is that the centrifugal force adds to the apparent weight of you and the glider (we call such an addition G forces) which changes stall speed and increases forces. Another factor is that with a curving flight path your wing tips meet the air at a higher angle of attack and produce more up force that must be offset with more pushout.

There is one ideal pitch setting for a coordinated turn at every bank angle.

✓ Pitch and Roll Together

The airspeed at a given bar position in a turn is not the same as in level flight.

The point of all the above discussion is to get you to think about how to produce a coordinated turn all the way from first initiation to an established steady-state circle. Ideally your roll control is accompanied by your pitch control following in phase. As figure 3-4 shows, the control movement is a smooth transition ending up with a coordinated turn at the desired bank angle (solid line). Waiting too long to perform the pitch control results in the dashed line path and some slipping in the early part of the turn. This is the meaning of a sloppy turn.

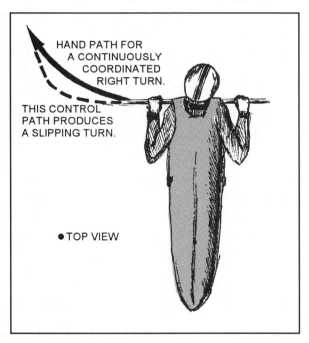

Figure 3-4: Turn Control Pattern

A pilot coordinates a left turn. Note the loose VG and absence of any high siding.

At times we misjudge our turn control and push out too much or not enough for the bank we've invested in our glider. Varying air currents may also serve to prove our touch imperfect.

Turns in thermals often require constant adjustments to maintain flight at minimum sink in various banks in varying air.

In any case, if we are threatening a stall we can pull in to speed up , or roll more to bank steeper. If we begin to dive (slip) we can push out to slow up or flatten out our bank. The steeper the bank, the more pushout required so we can cure a speed problem either by adjusting pushout or bank.

The preceding point should be very well understood for thermaling efficiently most often requires constant adjustments in this manner to accommodate moving cores and surges in upward flow. Often the difference in a so-so pilot and aerial artist is the ability to make these subtle adjustments perfectly.

✓ Turn Preferences

While we are on the subject of maximizing turns we should mention the all-too-common *turn preference syndrome*. Most of us have a direction to which we prefer to turn. There may be several reasons for this bias: our strongest arm is better at pushing on the high side, our dominant eye prefers to lead or our divided brain processes the input from one side better. Whatever the reason, right handers generally prefer to turn left and left handers, right. Since right handers dominate humanity, many meets require all left turns within a certain distance of launch for traffic reasons. This is probably not a good thing for it discriminates against left handers, but most importantly it reinforces the tendency in the majority of pilots to only scratch while turning in one direction.

At any rate, the consummate pilot will be equally adept at working lift or setting up landings in both directions. If this doesn't describe your talents, we suggest the following exercises:

▶1- When fun-flying make *all* thermaling turns to the side opposite to that of your preference.

▶2- Mount your vario in the middle of your base bar or better yet on the opposite downtube to your preferred direction until your habit is cured.

▶3- Starting with wide open landing fields, consciously set up landings using turns to your bad side. Try this in smaller and smaller fields until your prejudice is gone.

Turning one way exclusively can stretch a glider asymmetrically so that it always becomes easier to turn in the same direction. Also, in many situations, such a crossing winds, a run one way down the ridge, a thermal placed to one side or an established gaggle, the turn direction is dictated by the situation. If you are uncomfortable with this direction you will not perform to the max. One worthy goal for all pilots is to acquire airborne ambidexterity.

An expert pilot is equally adept at turns in both directions.

In the 1990 US Nationals the near-launch turn direction was altered daily. One pilot was so habituated that the right turn days left him helpless and hopeless. His solution was to damn the tide and turn left despite the rules. He braved the confused, tangled gaggles he caused and suffered the shouted expletives from the wide-eyed pilots he passed, while persisting in his wayward ways. After a warning and a repetition of this antisocial behavior he was emphatically requested to leave. His departure was duly applauded by all the remaining reasonable pilots whose own safety and pleasure was enhanced.

The adverse yaw effect is less the faster you go.

ADVERSE YAW

Adverse means contrary and when a glider yaws opposite to the intended direction it is exhibiting adverse yaw. This undesirable trait is known as *perverse* yaw to some designers. All high performance gliders produce adverse yaw to some degree.

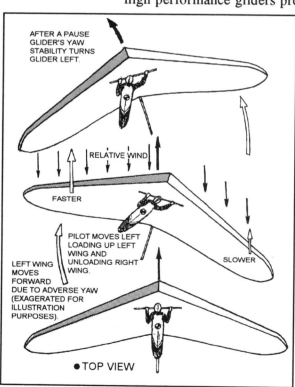

AFTER A PAUSE GLIDER'S YAW STABILITY TURNS GLIDER LEFT.

RELATIVE WIND

FASTER

PILOT MOVES LEFT LOADING UP LEFT WING AND UNLOADING RIGHT WING.

LEFT WING MOVES FORWARD DUE TO ADVERSE YAW (EXAGERATED FOR ILLUSTRATION PURPOSES).

SLOWER

● TOP VIEW

Figure 3-5: The Cause of Adverse Yaw

Adverse yaw in a weight-shift glider occurs when you move your body to one side, thereby loading up that wing and unloading the other. Changing loading in this manner causes the heavier loaded wing to fly faster and the lighter loaded wing to slow down. As a result the glider yaws away from the turn as shown in figure 3-5. This is perverse.

Once adverse yaw happens, the glider is flying somewhat sideways so the natural yaw stability can take over and bring the glider around to turn properly with the correct yaw as shown in the top illustration.

Adverse yaw is worse the slower you are going and the tighter your glider is strung whether from tightening the tips, tightening the VG or both. Adverse yaw causes the lag in glider response we mentioned earlier and may result in more strength required when turning since you have to hold a side control longer before you get a response. Adverse yaw is usually responsible for the "sticky wing" experience.

To minimize adverse yaw, enter your turns faster. It may be necessary to pull on extra speed when trying to battle turbulence and turn in feisty thermals. We recommend higher speeds (good maneuvering speed) when setting up landing so you have good glider response with little adverse yaw.

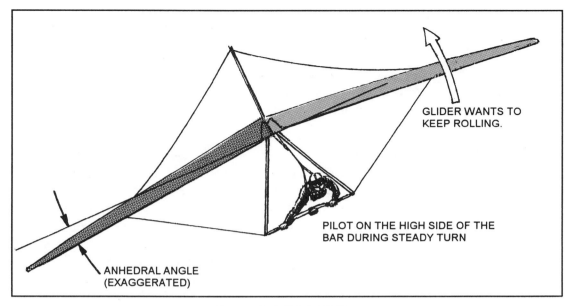

GLIDER WANTS TO KEEP ROLLING.

PILOT ON THE HIGH SIDE OF THE BAR DURING STEADY TURN

ANHEDRAL ANGLE (EXAGGERATED)

Figure 3-6: High-Siding

HIGH SIDING

With a glider in a bank there is a high side and a low side. Many high performance gliders require the pilot to remain on the high side of center during a turn to keep the glider from overbanking. The reason for this is that tight gliders with heavy cloth and lots of double surface tend to be stiff so designers give them anhedral* to help them initiate a turn.

Once in the turn the glider wants to keep banking so you have to move to the high side of the bar to maintain equilibrium (see figure 3-6).

Tightening a VG tends to make a glider need more high siding since opening the nose angle produces more anhedral in the frame. Also lighter pilots are more likely to have to high side a given glider since less weight on a glider creates less dihedral (more anhedral) due to sail twist.

High siding results in more continuous effort but is not all bad. In fact, a glider that requires high siding can turn a given circle radius with a lesser bank angle (all other matters being equal) than one with a centered pilot. The reason for this is the glider with the pilot on the high side has a center of mass that traces a larger circle so doesn't have to bank as much to offset centrifugal force as shown in figure 3-7. This effect is only significant with bank angles below about 30°, for the steeper thr bank, the less high siding required.

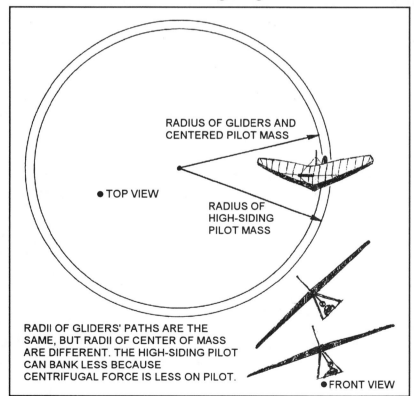

RADIUS OF GLIDERS AND CENTERED PILOT MASS

• TOP VIEW

RADIUS OF HIGH-SIDING PILOT MASS

RADII OF GLIDERS' PATHS ARE THE SAME, BUT RADII OF CENTER OF MASS ARE DIFFERENT. THE HIGH-SIDING PILOT CAN BANK LESS BECAUSE CENTRIFUGAL FORCE IS LESS ON PILOT.

• FRONT VIEW

Figure 3-7: Turning more Efficient when High-Siding

* Anhedral is an angling down of the wings from the center to tip.

II - TURN VARIATIONS

*A*long with our classic coordinated turn we sometimes have the need to vary our turn controls to deal with cantankerous gliders or challenging situations. Let's review the matter to supply ourselves with as many tricks as possible.

THE VG IN TURNS

We have already briefly mentioned the effects of VG setting on handling in Chapter II. Here we'll make a generality that you can use as a starting point to experiment with your glider to wring out maximum performance. In a turn, *the steeper the bank, the less VG should be applied.*

The reasoning behind this statement is that at steeper banks the inside wing is limiting how much you can slow down. If it is allowed to wash out (twist) with a looser VG setting you can slow down more and get a better sink rate. On the other hand, in flatter turns with some VG added you get better overall performance with a tighter sail. Also some high siding may be needed. Finally, in very large, flat turns with little or no turbulence a tight VG setting will bring out your best sink rate.

When conditions are choppy or thermals vigorous, little or no VG may be necessary to keep you cored.

"Keeping a tight VG can result in a lockout in a thermal which will lose you more altitude than you'll ever gain with the slight advantage of a tighter VG."

— Rick Duncan, 1987 World Champion

You'll have to find for yourself the ideal VG setting for your glider in various conditions.

FLAT TURNS—YAW TURNS

We hear a lot about flat turns, but the fact is, the rules of nature say to get a turn you have to bank. There are ways however to tweak a glider around so that bank is minimized.

A *flat turn* is best produced by flying very slowly (near minimum sink), creating a small but abrupt side control along with a yawing of the body as shown in figure 3-8. This is called a *yaw turn*. The yaw inertia of your body is 1/4 to 1/3 that of your glider and will help rotate you wings so adverse yaw doesn't occur and minimum bank is needed.

If you overdo this yaw input or get too slow, your inside wing will stall and you'll lose altitude as you regain speed.

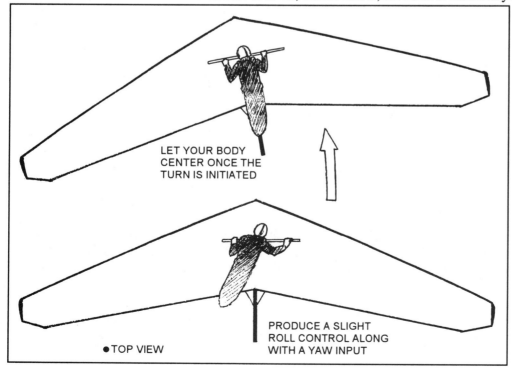

LET YOUR BODY CENTER ONCE THE TURN IS INITIATED

PRODUCE A SLIGHT ROLL CONTROL ALONG WITH A YAW INPUT

•TOP VIEW

Figure 3-8: Flat Turning

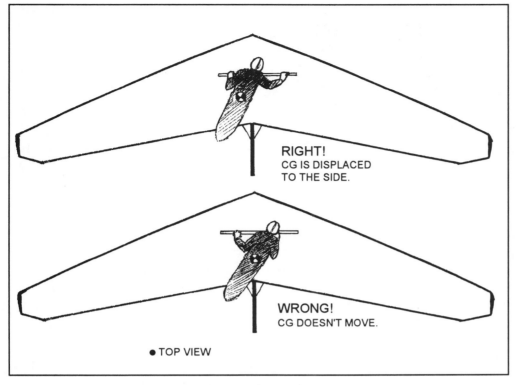

Figure 3-9: Turn Control

RIGHT!
CG IS DISPLACED
TO THE SIDE.

WRONG!
CG DOESN'T MOVE.

● TOP VIEW

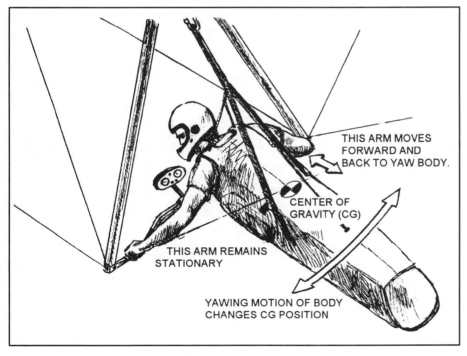

THIS ARM MOVES
FORWARD AND
BACK TO YAW BODY.

CENTER OF
GRAVITY (CG)

THIS ARM REMAINS
STATIONARY

YAWING MOTION OF BODY
CHANGES CG POSITION

Figure 3-10: Yaw Control During a Turn

This is, of course, inefficient so you must practice this maneuver (both directions please) until you can do it with exactitude.

Yes, we know your early instructor drilled into your hypothalamus the phobia of yawing your body during turn control. That's because beginners often just rotate their body without actually shifting weight. What we're doing here is both rotating (yawing) our body and shifting weight as shown in figure 3-9.

The right control method is to move your center of gravity to the side and is a vigorous roll and yaw control. Note that you can vary the relative amounts of roll and yaw with this control for different effects. Try it.

You may also use a yaw input at higher banks and higher speeds. In fact, it combines well with high siding by keeping the low arm fairly stationary and extending or retracting the upper arm to produce more or less yaw and roll control as shown in figure 3-10. Notice how a yawing of the body also induces a roll control in this case since the body's center of gravity (at the hips) is moved to the side as you yaw. When thermalling a yaw turn can help kick a quick 90° addition to your heading to help you avoid sink or follow a core.

PUNCH TURNS

Another way to fool your glider into obeying your wishes is to produce a *punch turn*. To do this perform, a roll control then punch the bar forward and back in a rapid movement as seen in figure 3-11. The result will be a quick roll response on the part of your recalcitrant glider.

- 51 -

THE PILOT MOVES TO THE SIDE FOR ROLL CONTROL NORMALLY THEN APPLIES A QUICK PITCH PUNCH AS SHOWN BY THE ARROW.

Figure 3-11: Punch Turn

The amount of the punch should be a few inches up to a foot.

You can use this technique to wake up a glider that refuses to roll into a thermal after you've moved to the side or to nudge it around into a tighter turn. It is especially effective when flying slowly either straight ahead or in a turn. You will need to practice punch turns a bit to see how much pitch to punch for different bank angles, speeds and gliders. Sometimes you have to follow a punch by a hard high side to keep the glider from overbanking.

Not all gliders respond to punch turns. Gliders with curved tips generally will not do so, but they respond well to yaw turns. You can try a quick yaw control in this case. Gliders with large flexible tips respond best to punch turns. In any case you should try combinations of yaw and punch turns to see what works for your machine in all situations.

PITCHING A TURN

A variation of a punch turn results when you are in an established bank and you wish to tighten the turn. Assuming you're flying close to a stall in a thermal for best climb rate, any more pushout may put you over the edge. However a brief smooth pushout along with a

Pitch control is the secret of versatile turns.

move to the low side of the bar will tighten the turn and prevent the stall. This is followed quickly by a pull-in and a high side to reestablish the proper bank and airspeed.

Use this maneuver to follow an elusive thermal core, to center quickly or to turn inside another pilot swinging wide in a thermal. If you have an occasion to watch Larry Tudor working up in a crowd you will see a textbook example of this technique.

DIVING TURNS

A *diving turn* can also be called a *fast turn*. This form of turn is performed by initiating a roll control and not pushing out in pitch enough to slow the glider to minimum sink. If you are just barely faster than minimum sink your glider will gradually pick up speed. If you roll hard and don't push out at all the effect will be a heady dive.

If you pull in then move to the side as in figure 3-12 you'll fall and yaw in an exciting but controllable turn. If you roll hard first then pull in the initial part of the turn will be less predictable in heading but you'll end up going as fast as in the previous controls.

A Wills Wing Sport exhibiting the ease of handling characteristic of modern advanced intermediate gliders.

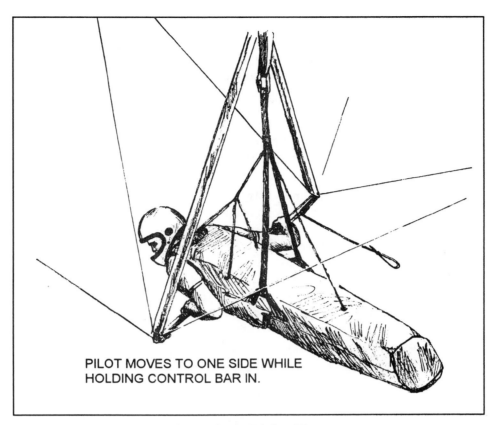

Figure 3-12: Diving Turn

> PILOT MOVES TO ONE SIDE WHILE
> HOLDING CONTROL BAR IN.

You'll also lose more altitude. This last form of diving turn begins with a slip (see below). We saw an application for these turns in Chapter 2 under the section LOSING ALTITUDE.

All pilots should be very familiar with their glider in diving mode. You never know when you may want to impress a crowd. More seriously, we already saw how diving turns can get us down from moderate cloud suck and we'll see in Chapter 6 how to use diving turns for squeezing into tight landing fields.

III - SPECIAL TURNS

*A*viation has a list of S turns: slips, spirals, skids, stalls and spins. We'll briefly consider each to complete our understanding.

SLIPS

Moving to the side of our control bar and pulling in results in our glider falling to the low side in an uncoordinated or slipping turn. As this quick descent occurs the natural yaw stability will bring the nose around until we are performing a turning slipping dive. Eventually pitch stability also comes into play and our slip becomes a spiral. The slip lasts for 1/2 to one revolution depending on how much we're pulled in. Figure 3-13 illustrates the progression of a slip turning into a spiral.

SPIRAL TURNS

A spiral is a tight diving coordinated turn. Since it is so tight and coordinated, high G forces build up and may cause you discomfort or disorientation (see Chapter 13). Figure 3-13 shows how a spiral naturally ensues from a slip. It is impossible to maintain a slip on a weight shift hang glider—it always evolves into a spiral. The longer you do maintain a slip, the tighter and more dangerous will be the spiral. The high Gs in a spiral can stretch your sail as much as aerobatics.

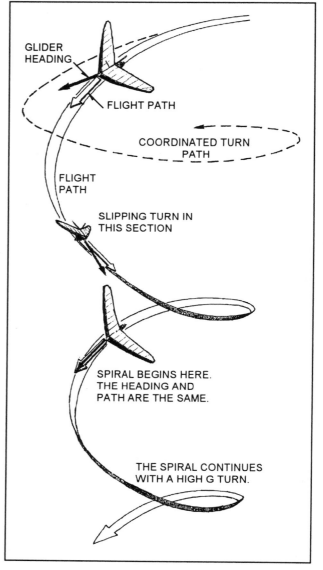

To exit a spiral, simply make the opposite roll control (move to the high side). Some heavy roll forces may be felt since you "weigh" more under the pull of centrifugal force. Response should be quick however. As you begin to level out, *keep the control bar in at least to your waist, then let the speed bleed off gradually.* This is to prevent a whip stall or excessive loading on your glider.

Spirals can be entered inadvertently during a loss of horizon reference in clouds. The consequences in this case can be severe especially if the spiral continues for very long. You can build up your experience with spirals safely by entering them from gentle slips held until G forces build up to a reasonable level.

Figure 3-13: Spiral Turn

SKIDS

While a slip is a falling to the inside of a turn, a skid is sliding to the outside of a turn. Skids on a hang glider occur only during yawing, are short lived and thus of little importance. We mention them here to inform those pilots familiar with other forms of aviation that they can ignore skids when flying by tug and struggle (weight shift).

STALL TURNS

A stalled turn isn't really a thing of beauty and profit, but a mistake. A stalled turn occurs for exactly the opposite reason as a slipping turn: you push out too much. We mention it here to understand the result of your heavy handedness.

Generally it's easier to stall in a flatter turn than a steeper since a steeper turn requires more pushout anyway. Also, there is a greater difference in airspeed between our left and right wings in a flat turn so we get a more problematical asymmetrical stall.

When we stall in a turn the inside wing will gain sudden willful and contrary manners. It will slow and drop, disrupting our precise circle and efficient flying. The quickest way to recover is to pull in a little and move toward the low side of the control bar to follow the turn. How much remedial action you must take depends on how badly the stall developed. In any case if you move to the high side of the bar to try to level the wings you may worsen the stall. Any roll control is ineffective until you lower the angle of attack by pulling in.

Stalled turns are a good thing to practice in both directions at various bank angles. This practice renders you quick as a mongoose to detect and remedy stall that can happen in turbulent thermals.

SPINS

A spin is a stalled turn that comes home to stay. The dynamics of a spin are somewhat complicated involving centrifugal force and gyroscopic effect as well as pitch, roll and yaw factors. However, we can understand it as a continuous turn around a stalled wing. The axis of the turn is closer than that of a coordinated turn and may indeed be within the wing itself in a severe spin/stall (see figure 3-14).

Spins do not readily occur on a hang glider because of our wing's washout (twist) and low moment of inertia. A severe stall on one wing usually results in a turn of about 90° and a rapid pitch down and recovery. While spins are a major concern with general aviation, flex-wing hang glider of current design are immune to this potentially dangerous occurrence. Aerobatics pilots perform spins with special and deliberate effort.

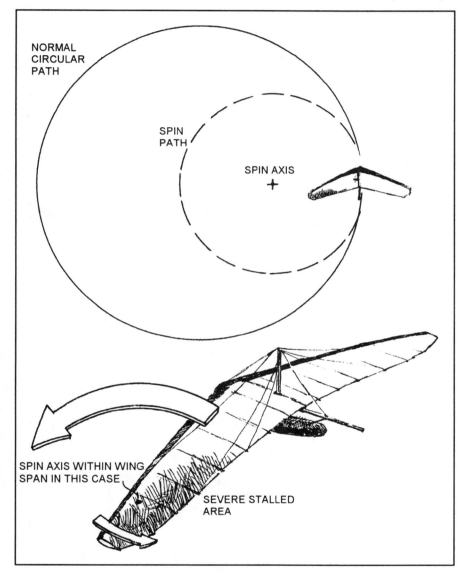

Earlier hang gliders were more prone to spin because of their narrow tapered tips or limited washout through a fixed tip spar. I witnessed one pilot enter a slow 360 about 100 feet up and proceeded to slow until a spin caught him by surprise. He rapidly screwed his way to the ground and pancaked in a flurry of dust, debris and glider shards. He shook himself off with newfound awe for the immutable laws of nature.

Figure 3-14: Spinning Turn

IV - TURN EFFECTS

At this point we finish our discussion of turns with a look at some of the factors that govern how our gliders perform in a turn. The idea is to learn how we can coax the maximum performance from our personal wings.

TURNING RADIUS

When you were too young to consider hang gliding you probably fulfilled your needs for the feelings of flying freely with playground swings, merry-go-rounds and slides. From that early experience you are most likely to be quite familiar with G forces and the fact that the faster you move in a curving path and the tighter the path is, the more the force builds up.

This same law, first articulated by Sir Isaac Newton, the guy with an affinity for apples, not figs, applies to hang gliders in the air. It turns out that the more we bank, the smaller the circle we cut through the air and the faster we go, building up the Gs. In *Hang Gliding Flying Skills* we provide chart of G loading and stall speed at various bank angles. We note here that in a coordinated turn the loading increases to :1.4 Gs in a 45° bank, 2 Gs in a 60° bank, over 3 Gs in a 70° bank and to infinity in a 90° bank (you can't perform a coordinated continuous 90° banked turn for you disappear into a black hole at infinite Gs).

The steeper the bank in a coordinated turn, the higher the stall speed, G loading, rate of sink and rate of heading change.

From this little knowledge we can actually define the turning radius of your glider at any angle of bank. All we need to know is our stall speed and the bank angle. The math, physics and other stressful disciplines relating to turn radii are discussed in the Appendix. Here we will give examples.

In figure 3-15 we illustrate the case for a glider with a 20 mph stall speed. As our bank goes up so does our wing loading and thus our stall speed. Taking this all into account we find the turn radius, time for a full 360 and stall speed at various bank angles in the table below:

TURNS			
Bank Angle	**Turn Radius**	**Time for One 360**	**Stall Speed in Turn**
20°	78.6 FT	16.3 SEC	20.6 MPH
30°	53.8 FT	10.7 SEC	21.5 MPH
45°	38.0 FT	6.9 SEC	23.8 MPH
60°	31.0 FT	4.7 SEC	28.3 MPH

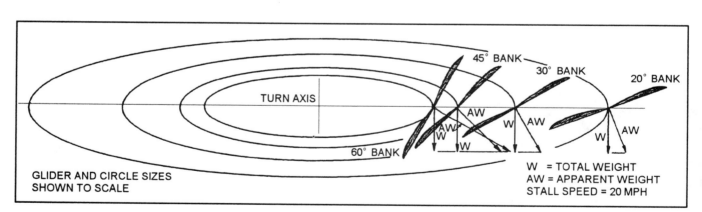

Figure 3-15: Turn Factors

From this chart we can deduce some useful information about thermals. Since we typically thermal at about 30° bank in a good thermal we see the core must be over 100 feet in diameter. If we were flying straight through this thermal at an interthermal speed of say 30 mph, we would pass it in 2.3 seconds. Of course, the thermal would be larger than its core, but we can get a feel for the size of thermals necessary for our enjoyment.

A 45° bank is fairly steep and only used for the strongest thermals. It requires a core of at least 75 feet and we'll pass through this in 1.7 seconds at 30 mph. Such small cores must be caught quickly and dealt with handily.

As a side note to this discussion, if a certain amount of turning is required (not in lift) the least altitude will be lost in a 45° bank. Shallower bank results in slower sinking, but more time is required to complete the turn. If a steeper turn is used the time of completion goes down, but the sink rate increases dramatically. Because of the time necessary to roll in and out of a steeper turn, this rule is not strictly valid until about 270° of turn is required. Such information is useful only in fun competitions requiring maneuvers, for when turning in lift the optimum bank angle depends on the thermal profile as we see in a later section.

WING LOADING

Using ballast or getting fat increases our wing loading. What does this do to our turning radius? From before you'll note that we only needed our stall speed and bank angle to figure turn radius. Weight didn't come into play. However, changing wing loading does change our stall speed, so we can make the statement in the side bar.

Increased wing loading increases turn radius or sink rate in a turn.

As we shall see below, increasing our bank angle increases our sink rate, so a heavier pilot either sinks faster in a turn or must produce a larger circle thereby missing some better lift in the thermal core. Heavyweights need not despair however, for *wing loading* is the secret and you can simply use a larger glider. In addition, the better handling that a higher wing loading affords can often make up for any sink rate deficiency as you negotiate turbulent cores with more agility.

Wing Loading Effects on Turns
- Increased wing loading increases our turn radius and stall speed at a given bank angle.
- If another glider has a lighter wing loading we will have to bank our glider more steeply to get the same radius turn.

For your information, figure 3-16 shows a graph of a glider's turn radius at various bank angles with a 20 mph straight ahead stall speed.

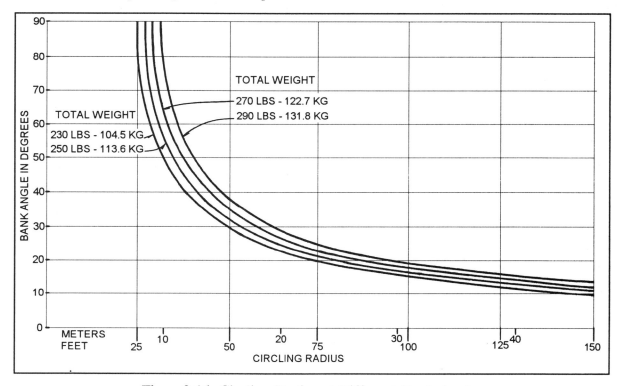

Figure 3-16: Circling Radius at Different Bank Angles

The wing loading is assumed to be 1.6 (250 lbs divided by 155 square feet). Also shown are the radii curves at various other wing loadings. For example, we can see that adding 20 pounds increases our 30° turn radius by over 4 feet or 8%.

TURN POLARS

In Chapter 7 we learn all about polars. These are simply performance maps that graph our sink rate at various flying speeds. It turns out that we can produce such a graph at any bank angle and this known as a *turn polar*.

Figure 3-17 shows typical turn polars at selected bank angles for a modern hang glider. The main point to observe is that the sink rate increases dramatically the more steeply we bank. Also we should note that the highest point on each curve is the best (lowest) sink rate and slowest speed we can fly for that bank angle and it represents the most efficient turn.

We can combine the graphs of figures 3-16 and 3-17 into a more meaningful graph to display the turning radius at each angle of bank and flying speed. This is shown in figure 3-18. Note

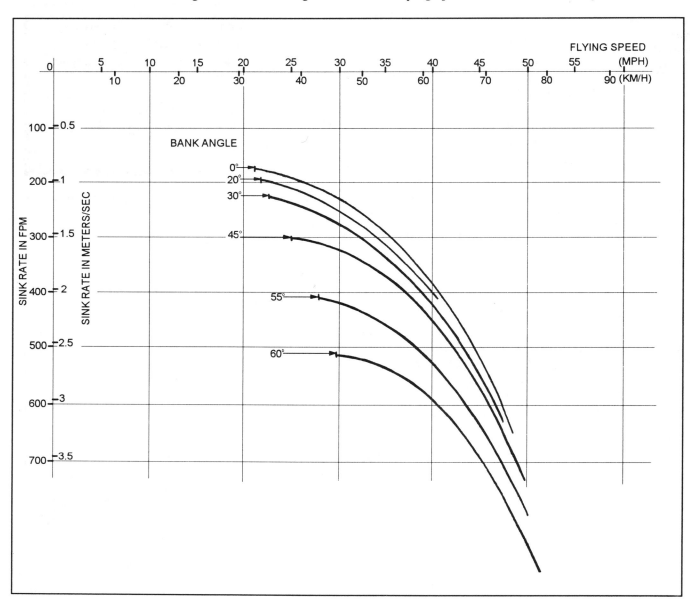

Figure 3-17: Hang Glider Turn Polars

that the steeper the bank, the smaller the turning radius and the greater the sink rate.

If we draw a line through the most efficient points corresponding to figure 3-17, we have the dashed curve shown. We call this our *circling polar*. It is interesting to see how the sink rate of our best possible turns increases rapidly as we tighten the bank.

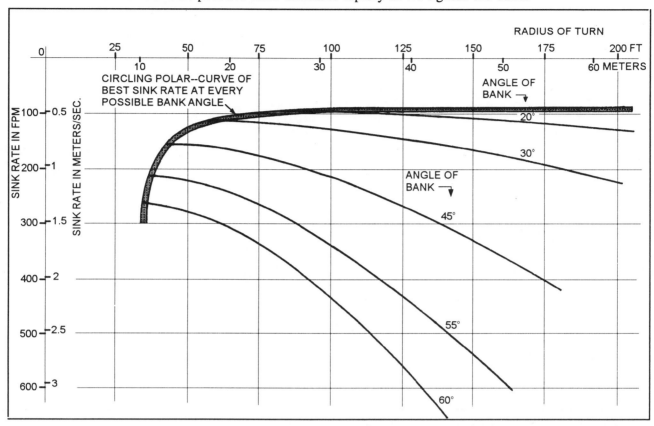

Figure 3-18: Circling Polar

TURNING IN THERMALS

The most useful thing we can glean from circling polars is how to peak our performance in a thermal. To see this we model the cross section of a thermal as in figure 3-19. This model is based on the ideal of several researchers. Below this thermal model we place our circling polar on the same radius and lift (or sink) scale as the thermal. Next we combine the lift of the thermal with the sink of our glider to get the curve displaying our climb at each angle of bank as shown. It should be immediately clear that for the thermal shown the greatest climb rate occurs at a turn radius of 62 feet corresponding to a bank angle of 28 degrees.

✓ Thermal Variations

From the above illustration it should be clear that:

Each thermal profile has an optimum bank angle for best climb for a given

This bank angle depends on the glider's circling polar (which depends on its sink rate and stall speed) and the distribution of lift in the thermal. In figure 3-20 we show three thermal types:

▶1. a weak thermal   ▶2. a wide thermal and   ▶3. a narrow, strong thermal.

Our circling polar and the combination curve for each thermal type are shown.

Notice that with the weak thermal we barely have much climb at a moderate bank angle. If we flatten out to reduce our sink rate we circle too wide to find the lift. If we tighten up

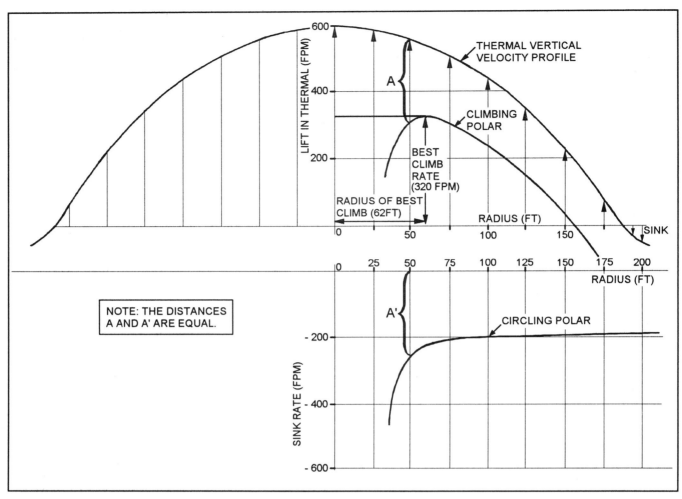

Figure 3-19: Finding Best Climb in a Thermal

to find better lift, we sink too fast and fail to climb.

With the wide thermal, our circle is large and our bank is less than 30°. Errors in bank angle or circling radius are not penalized nearly as much as in the previous case.

Finally, the strong, tight thermal, typical of desert conditions, demands a steep bank and small circle to max it out. Our climb rate falls off fairly rapidly if we choose more or less bank than optimum. In general, the majority of pilots bank too shallow in most thermals rather than too steeply.

✓ Wing Loading Effects

Our final comparison shows what happens in a thermal at different wing loadings as in figure 3-21. Here we see an idealized thermal and three circling polars based on different wing loadings as shown (25 lbs between each). This can be due to different pilot weights, different glider sizes or the carrying of ballast.

It is clear from the figure that the lightest loaded glider can get a better climb rate not only by possessing a better sink rate but also by producing a smaller circle at any given bank angle and thus remaining in stronger lift. The diameters, bank angles, sink rates and time to complete one 360 is shown for each glider in the figure. Note that the lightest loaded glider takes the longest to circle even though its circular path is the shortest.

The effect we see here takes place no matter what the type of thermal (unless the pilot is too light to control the glider). However, the thermal depicted is fairly wide and shallow. A tighter thermal makes a larger difference in the ideal circles of the different wing loadings. So we see a lighter wing loading improves climb rate in all thermals, but, of course, slows progress between thermals.

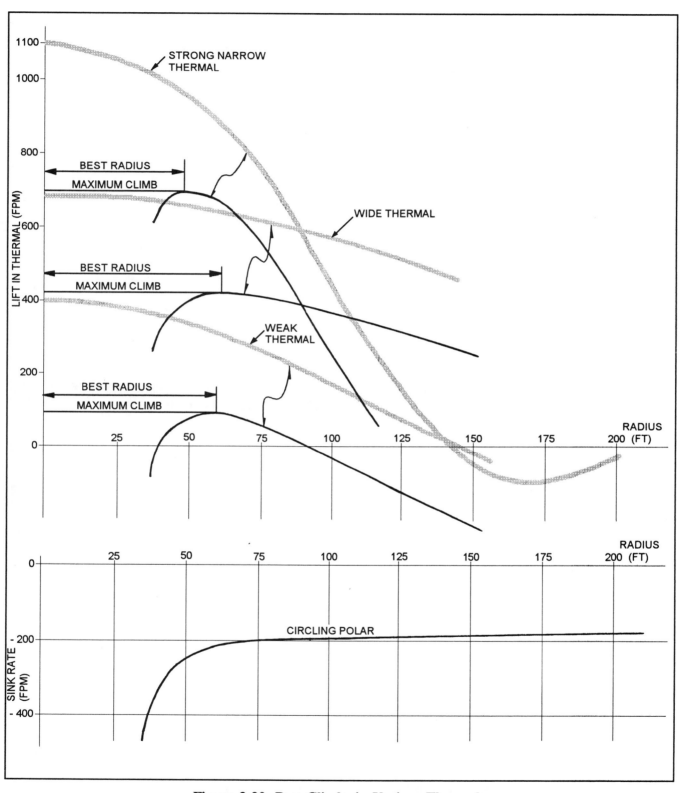

Figure 3-20: Best Climbs in Various Thermals

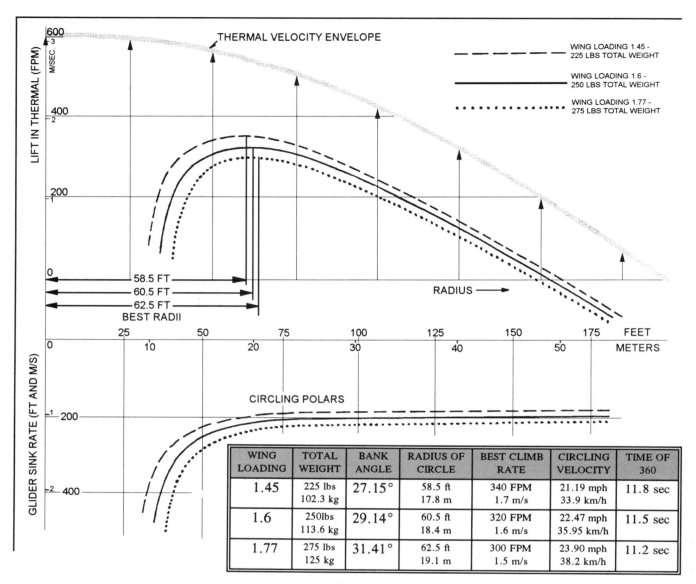

WING LOADING	TOTAL WEIGHT	BANK ANGLE	RADIUS OF CIRCLE	BEST CLIMB RATE	CIRCLING VELOCITY	TIME OF 360
1.45	225 lbs 102.3 kg	27.15°	58.5 ft 17.8 m	340 FPM 1.7 m/s	21.19 mph 33.9 km/h	11.8 sec
1.6	250lbs 113.6 kg	29.14°	60.5 ft 18.4 m	320 FPM 1.6 m/s	22.47 mph 35.95 km/h	11.5 sec
1.77	275 lbs 125 kg	31.41°	62.5 ft 19.1 m	300 FPM 1.5 m/s	23.90 mph 38.2 km/h	11.2 sec

Figure 3-21: Wing Loading Effects on Thermal Climbs

We cannot draw such clever graphs in the air, especially since we really don't know the true lift profile of a thermal we invade. However, with the insight these diagrams provide we know we should search for the best bank angle and turn radius for the best climb. An efficient pilot does this quickly using feeling, vario output and visual clues from other pilots.

SUMMARY

Turns are a fact of life in aviation. In our particular niche of the realm of flight, we spend as much as 1/4 to 1/2 our time turning in thermals when on a cross-country jaunt. It is clear that we must learn to make our circles efficient.

Various types of turns are available to the pilot in need. Tricks exist for seducing a glider into turning when it has another agenda. Other control variations produce maneuvers that may be useful or prove dangerous depending on the situation. Every advanced pilot should be well-versed in the performance and applications of these turn permutations.

Finally we should be aware that wing loading affects turn performance by improving handling but increasing sink rate at any given bank angle. This has implications in thermal flying, especially if thermals are weak or small.

Effective turning, once mastered, is the raw material for legends fir it leads to thermaling ability that puts you on top and takes you leagues away. We must strive constantly for graceful economy in motion and accurate arcs.

A clean high performance glider and harness.

CHAPTER

Wings and Things

Pilots tend to form rather personal relationships with their wings. Generally this relationship is one of close attachment, although at times doubts, fears and downright hatred can occur when lift turns to sink. The emotional and monetary expense we undergo to fly freely would seem to dictate that we choose and maintain our equipment carefully.

In this chapter we look at equipment with an eye toward maximizing its performance. We'll also describe how to select, care for and respect the limits of the components that make up our flying outfit. Becoming one with our wings is our intended goal.

I - THE HANG GLIDER BUYERS GUIDE

The most important item in our hangar is our glider. It is most complex, most wonderful and most expensive. If we expect to get our money's worth we should take care in selecting the right wing for our peculiar needs.

JUST YOUR TYPE

There are many great gliders on the market—new and used. Sometimes one speaks to you like a puppy in a store window and you just have to take it home. Other times you're undecided. Here are some helpful hints to ease the agonizing process of *what glider to buy*.

✔ Locating a Wing

Let us assume you are looking for a high performance glider. If you have the bucks to buy new, it's time to contact some dealers for demos. If not start scouring the want ads. In either case the preferred approach is as follows in order of desirability:

- ▶1- Fly the glider you hope to buy.
- ▶2- Fly a demo glider of the model you want.
- ▶3- Watch another pilot demonstrate it.
- ▶4- Visually inspect the glider for condition.
- ▶5- Buy from a reputable dealer or manufacturer sight unseen.
- ▶6- Buy from another pilot (with whom you've established a rapport) sight unseen.
- ▶7- Buy it over the phone. *Caveat emptor* which loosely translated means: Good luck!

✔ What to Look for

To buy the glider designed for you, you must consider the following:

Qualities to Look for in a Glider

1. Size of glider	6. Hardware design	11. Dealer availability
2. General condition	7. Resale value	12. Manuf. reputation
3. Performance Potential	8. Glider weight	13. Color pattern
4. Longevity of sail	9. Glider balance	14. Delivery time
5. Service for parts	10. Ease of setup	15. Unique design

These items are roughly in order of importance and we cover them briefly.

▶1. The right size glider for you depends on your all-up weight, of course, but also the type of conditions you fly in. Punchy desert air favors smaller gliders while green areas indicate a larger size. Generally manufacturer's recommendations along with the opinion of local expert pilots and dealers can help you here.

▶2. If you are buying used, the condition of the glider is of utmost importance. Age means nothing. Airtime means everything. Stretch and stress, sunlight and setup all take their toll on a glider's sail to reduce its store of performance and its longevity. Fifty hours in the high desert with its grit and UV bombardment is equivalent to 100 hours in soft green areas with gentle blue thermals. Take a moment to reflect on the type of pilot selling the glider and you'll have a clue to its condition.

▶3. Performance—that's why most of us buy a new set of wings. However, how do we know we are getting better performance? Competition results and manufacturers' blurbs do not tell the story, for great competitors can make almost any glider shine and some luck is involved in competition. Also, very popular gliders will do better in competition over the long run because more pilots flying them give more chances of finishing in the top ten. Furthermore, gliders of the same model often exhibit different performance due to some perverse law of craftsmanship. All manufacturers when plied with a few drinks on a deserted island about to erupt will admit to this.

Even though most modern gliders are similar in overall performance, there *is* variation in some of the different aspects of performance. For instance, some designs do handle better than others, some are a little faster at the same wing loading, some are noted for climbing ability and some for glide. Most of these differences are due to the designers' choices in where to make compromises (see Chapter 12).

With all these extenuating circumstances, what can we do? Again fly the glider and see if it works for you in your conditions. Another ideal suggestion is to go to meets either as a competitor or a free flyer to see how different gliders do next to you in general. Don't be

Glider performance gradually diminishes after about 100 hours.

overawed by the one that wins, and be sure to make allowances for gliders over or under represented. Talk to competitors and see what they like (or dislike) about their glider. Take note or make a check list if you really want to be serious about selecting the best glider for your needs. Remember, handling is part of performance and is at least as important as pure performance in many situations.

►4. The sail is what wears out first in most gliders. If you are buying a new glider be aware that the heavier the sailcloth, the longer it will last. Also heavier sail material can contribute to performance but may hurt handling. Unless you are committed to competition you should avoid an all-Mylar sail as this material doesn't last as long as regular Dacron material. Later we'll discuss specific sail cloths.

►5. The occasional need for parts due to little peccadilloes is a greater concern for some pilots than others. In any case, easy access to replacement downtubes and other elements either from the manufacturer or dealer should be a part of your decision making process.

►6. Every manufacturer has their own list of gimmicks and gadgets to connect the various parts of their gliders. Sometimes the flashiest looking stuff is not the strongest or most functional. For example, one manufacturer's new hardware looked good but bent at the control bar corner. Another's side cable tang didn't allow the cable to fold during storage which stressed the cable at its Nico press fitting—a potentially dangerous situation.

Besides these little details, look for a glider that sets up with a rear pull back. Such a device, along with quick replaceable downtubes and simple hardware fittings are becoming a standard in the industry because they make sense.

►7. to 14. These items are mostly personal preference and don't necessarily result in better performance or more enjoyment. Resale value is important if you turn gliders over or your money tree dies. Glider weight comes into play especially if you have some carrying to do at your local aerial playground. Poor static balance can make a glider feel heavier on the ground in setup conditions. However, slight tail heaviness can help prevent nose-ins. A good quick setup allows you more choice of launch window in a crowd. You may like a particular dealer and want to get the brand he or she markets. Finally, uniqueness means you go for a design different from what's popular in your area simply because, after all, pilots are independent individuals.

✓ *Inspection of Used Gliders*

If you intend to buy a used glider here is a guideline of what to inspect:

►1. *Look at all tubes for straightness and inspect for dents.* The crossbar is particularly vulnerable to dents. The leading edges' outboard section are most likely to be bent. It's often hard to tell this with the sail on, but if the glider flies straight they should be OK. Don't forget the keel and downtubes. Any bends in the downtubes are a sign that the glider has been nosed in. A bent base bar is also a sign of possible whack abuse although wheels on a base bar will often bend it. Note: Refer to Chapter XII for how to inspect graphite tubes.

►2. *Inspect all cables for kinks, abrasions and broken strands.* Look with a detective's eye at the ends of Nico fittings, especially at the bottom of the side cable as shown in figure 4-1. This part experiences a rough life during fold up. If cable thimbles have been elongated the cables have been subjected to a force of 300 – 400 lbs (135 – 180 kg) and should be renewed. Finding damage in tubes or cables is not cause to reject a glider, but parts will have to be replaced and the price should reflect this fact.

►3. *Look for corroded bolts and fittings.* Such corrosion is

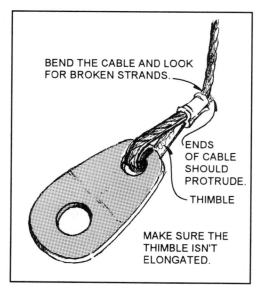

BEND THE CABLE AND LOOK FOR BROKEN STRANDS.

ENDS OF CABLE SHOULD PROTRUDE.

THIMBLE

MAKE SURE THE THIMBLE ISN'T ELONGATED.

Figure 4-1: Inspecting Cables

generally a sign of poor care and although little parts can be replaced, corrosion may also have crept into the tubes. Do you really want an unknown entity strapped to your back at a grand over?

▶4. *The sail requires thorough inspection.* Look for tears, abrasions and blown batten pockets. Tears near the trailing edge must be repaired. Small rips in the leading edge are unsightly but of little consequence. Blown (ripped out) batten pocket are a real pain during setup and must be repaired. To do this you must crawl inside the sail and sew on a patch (see *Hang Gliding Flying Skills* for care and repair instructions). The alternative is to remove the sail and ship it to a repair loft—a lot more hassle and expense.

It's a rare glider that hasn't been bonked, biffed, whacked or wanged—all of which stretches the sail.

Look for signs of stretch in the trailing edge, especially near the tips. These signs are a folded down edge or loose material. When you test fly, go fast and see if you detect flutter in the sail. Any flapping is the sound of performance flying away. Finally inspect the nose cone and leading edge. These areas tell you a lot about whether the glider has been pounded or not. Hard nose-ins stretch sails. Let the price you pay reflect the glider's history of care and airtime.

TEST FLYING

If you get a chance to buy a prospective buy, don't just boat around, but put the glider through its paces. The following list is the minimum you should do, assuming you're competent on the glider and you have enough altitude in the bank.

Test Flight Elements

Score Card

1 2 3 4 5 6 7 8 9 10

1. Ease of takeoff	A loose tank	I—I—I—I—I—I—I—I—I—I	A tight feather
2. Handling with loose VG	A lag with drag	I—I—I—I—I—I—I—I—I—I	Power steering
3. Handling with half and full VG	Impossible!	I—I—I—I—I—I—I—I—I—I	Steerable with more power
4. Sink rate in straight flight	A rock	I—I—I—I—I—I—I—I—I—I	A cloud
5. Thermal climb	In the rocks	I—I—I—I—I—I—I—I—I—I	In the clouds
6. Fast speeds (VG loose and tight)	Slow and wanging	I—I—I—I—I—I—I—I—I—I	Stable and blazing
7. Stalls	Gut wrenching breaks	I—I—I—I—I—I—I—I—I—I	Gentle nudges
8. Landing Characteristics	Needs an aircraft carrier arrester	I—I—I—I—I—I—I—I—I—I	Lands itself

Obviously you may need an hour in the air or several flights to evaluate all these items.

Ease of takeoff is an important factor in reducing the anxiety of any flight. Ask yourself: "Are the side cables extremely slack? If so will I be comfortable taking off with some VG pulled to tighten them? Is the static balance OK? Is the glider so heavy it takes an extra couple steps to get it moving? Score it accordingly.

Handling should be experienced in all VG settings. Many pilots forget that to exploit the full potential performance of a glider they must use the full range of the VG system. If you are new to a VG system, use it cautiously on your test flights, but use it. Check for handling by making flat turns, steep turns, reversing turns and thermal turns. The latter lets you know the most about how the glider will handle in the real world. Remember, high siding may not be what you're used to but is a fact of life with many high performance gliders.

Pro Tip: Most demo gliders are tuned for handling since that's what sells gliders and helps thermaling while it hurts higher speed performance.

Sink rate can be tested by comparison with other gliders in the air (see below). Likewise, thermal climb is only meaningful in comparison with others. Keep in mind wing loading factors when you make these evaluations.

Fast speed capability is important on any glider. You need it to escape high wind and cloud suck as well as race to goal. Can you fly fast without oscillating? Too much pitch pressure can result in fatigue on long, fast glides.

Gentle stalls should be tried with plenty of clearance to make sure the glider has no undue surprises. You might try them in turns as well to see how the glider will react when you are thermaling on the edge of efficiency.

Landing characteristics are the secret love of many pilots. We can all use a glider that *slows* down and settles *like* down. Large VG movements, large gliders and loose sails all lead to easy landing traits, but the latter two items may compromise performance.

Once you've tested these items, tally up their scores and compare them with other gliders you have tried. Notice that we didn't mention glide ratio or overall performance. That's because such testing requires the cooperation of another pilot as we see next.

II - PREENING YOUR WINGS

Once you get a personal glider to have and to hold, you must care for it if you expect it to sever the fetters of gravity and fling you to the heights. We deal with maintenance and repair in *Hang Gliding Flying Skills*. Here we learn about performance and handling perfection.

PERFORMANCE TESTING

Your constant flying companions are the best yardstick of the performance of a new wing.

You can use all your flight instruments, stop watches, laser beams, wind tunnels, global positioners, mojos and magic wands and you will have a hard time finding out your true performance. That doesn't matter really, for we're interested in relative performance—how one glider does compared to another. This is easy to test, by any pilot, without a single dial face to study.

✓ Sink Rate

As mentioned, test your pure (straight ahead) sink rate by seeing how you stack up against other pilots in plain vanilla ridge lift (no thermals mixed in). Also note your forward speed in relation to other gliders at minimum sink. If you are moving faster, it's possible that you won't be able to thermal as well because you can't slow down as much. A best minimum sink occurring at a fast speed may hurt in thermals but will help when ridge running, especially when hurrying against other competitors or the limits of daylight.

✓ Thermal Climb

This performance factor can only be tested with other gliders near you in the same thermal. Both the pilot and the glider are responsible for overall performance in thermals. It takes many such comparisons of climb rate to truly know your climb potential. Also you may find that you excel in one type of thermal (weak and flat, for instance) and fall off in another (small and tight, perhaps). Try to evaluate whether your technique or the glider is responsible for your performance. If you don't know, don't worry, for the real question is *what a particular glider can do for you.*

With all these sink rate comparisons it is most enlightening to fly with a known entity. That is a pilot whom you join often in the air. Your height of climb in comparison to him or her will let you know if you've improved your lot when you try a different glider.

✓ Glide Performance

We are really interested in a glider's performance over its entire speed range. This is easy to find out with a cooperative friend. On a soarable day or on the way out to landing, fly side-to-side in a straight line. If one pilot is above the other, an S turn should be made until both pilots are even (see figure 4-2).

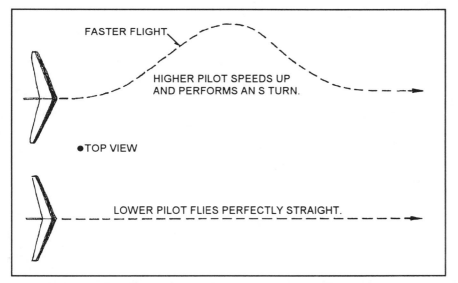

Figure 4-2: Equalizing Gliders for Performance Testing

Set a given speed and hold it for at least 10 seconds. The glider that remains highest has the better performance at that speed. Next get even again and go to a faster speed. Hold the speed 10 seconds and compare. Repeat this all the way to top speed for a true test of how your glider stacks up against another.

It is best to perform this test in smooth conditions. Radios help but aren't essential as long as both pilots know they should start out even and *remain even* in forward position. If one falls back it's not a true comparison. Hand signals can be used to initiate a test. Be aware that wing loading is a factor in these glide tests and you may find that the lighter loaded pilot gets a better sink rate while the heavier gets better glides at speed.

TUNING FOR HANDLING

In *Hang Gliding Flying Skills* we discuss how to trim a glider for the proper speed. One of the first things to check when trying to improve handling is that the glider flies hands off somewhere between stall and a couple miles per hour faster than minimum sink. Personally, we prefer minimum sink speed.

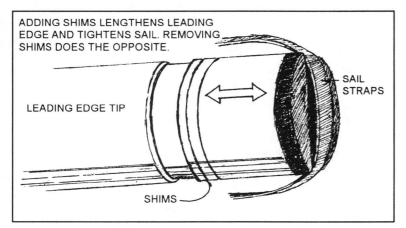

Figure 4-3: Altering Sail Tightness

✓ Your Tuning Tricks

Once your glider is in trim, there are essentially only two things you can do to achieve easier handling: loosen the tip tension and loosen the batten ties.

Most gliders have shims or some other device at the ends of the leading edges to alter sail tightness (see figure 4-3). The tighter the sail is pulled, the less washout it has, the better it performs (up to a point) and the stiffer it becomes. If you loosen the leading edges too much the glider becomes mushy and performs horribly. Consult your manufacturer's info for the limits of this adjustment. Usually removing all the shims is the lower limit.

Inboard batten ties should be looser than tip batten ties. Tighter inboard batten tension does not help performance but hurts handling. More outboard batten tension does help performance somewhat while it hurts handling. Batten and sail tension adjustments go partially hand in hand. Loosening the tip tension more than 1/8 inch should be accompanied by loosening the batten tension, especially if your glider has a tip batten that plugs into the leading edge.

When you make changes to the batten ties, mark them with a ball point pen so you can return to the original setting if necessary. Since batten ties are double loops, 1/4 inch change in the knot will change the overall tension 1/8 inch which is a reasonable first adjustment (see figure 4-4).

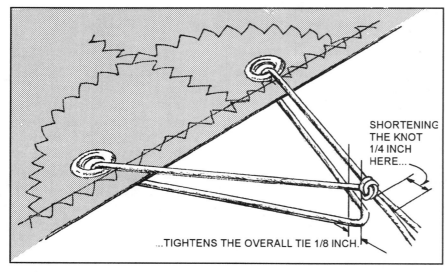

SHORTENING THE KNOT 1/4 INCH HERE...

...TIGHTENS THE OVERALL TIE 1/8 INCH.

Figure 4-4: Adjusting Batten Ties

Handling and performance are at opposite ends of the tuning scale.

Better handl-ing	*Better perfor-mance*
Looser	*Tighter*

Wing loading changes:
A heavier pilot bows and twists a glider more. The glider will trim slower and have more dihedral making it more roll stable.
A lighter pilot will trim faster and have less dihedral making the glider more apt to fall off on a wing and more difficult to roll out of a turn.

✓ Other Handling Factors

Other handling adjustments can be made by a trained professional. Sometimes the stop position of a VG system is made to be altered and has a looser setting. A retrofit kingpost hang, different reflex bridles or side cables length or even a new batten pattern may be available for your glider if the manufacturer continued development. All these items affect handling.

Other matters that relate to handling that you probably can't do anything about are the length of crossbar restraint, the presence of a keel pocket on older gliders and heavy cloth or airframe. In particular, very short crossbar restraints do not allow the airframe flexibility conducive to light handling.

Pro Tip: The better grip you have on the bar, the less you have to grasp, which relieves fatigue, increases sensitivity and eases handling. If your bar is uncoated, we recommend bathtub anti-skid tape (soft, gray tape). If you have slippery bar mits, run a few beads of silicone caulking on the surface where they grip the bar.

✓ Wing Loading and Handling

We all know that a heavier pilot on a glider gets better handling in general because of more weight to shift and slightly faster flying speeds. What isn't widely known is that change in weight also changes the dihedral balance of a glider because the tips bow more and the sail washes out more. Gliders are made for one ideal weight range and if you're very light on a glider you may find it wants to overbank and you may have to high side too much. Conversely, if you are at the upper limit you may create too much dihedral and have more trouble initiating a turn into a thermal (usually heavier weight will mask this problem).

Very light pilots may want to investigate the possibility of getting slightly longer side cables made for their glider. Another option is an extension on the base tube. This latter change is the easiest to engineer for testing whether or not a permanent change is desirable.

Up to a one inch increase or 1/2 inch per side cable addition is reasonable. Such an alteration will usually require an adjustment to reflex bridles as well (see your owner's manual) to bring their settings back to manufacturer's specifications, for as leading edges are adjusted up and down, effective reflex bridle lengths change. Only an experienced shop can make such changes. Note that manufacturers do not offer such options because they need to maintain inventory standards and they are reluctant to recommend this as a solution.

✓ Pitch Pressures

We can count pitch control as part of handling. Generally, there is not much you can do to affect pitch pressures other than making sure the glider is in proper trim and changing your VG setting (pitch pressures tend to be lighter at tighter settings). However, if your glider seems to have different pitch pressure than others of the same design, you may wish to compare battens or measure bridles. I have personally had a glider with a batten profile that was too flat which exhibited arm rubberizing positive pitch at fast speeds. Updating the battens cured the problem. Another glider needed the reflex bridles lowered to improve both roll and pitch control. A kingpost hang system lightens pitch pressure, but such a system must be incorporated in the original design.

WORKING OUT A TURN

Flying a glider with an innate turn is like raising a juvenile delinquent. It will go straight when you supervise it, but once you relax your guard it takes a turn for the worse.

Sometimes a glider says "left" when you say "right." It has a noticeable nagging turn. High performance gliders in particular are susceptible to slight imbalances from one side to the other because they are strung so tightly. Here are the known causes of turns:

> **Causes of Turns in a Weight-Shift Glider**
>
> 1. One sail tighter than the other.
> 2. The entire sail shifted to one side.
> 3. An asymmetrical sail due to manufacturing or stretching.
> 4. Battens tighter on one side.
> 5. Battens cambered more on one side.
> 6. Different degree of twist in the sail mounting.
> 7. Fatigue or a slight bend in one leading edge.
> 8. Different tubing wall thickness in leading edges.
> 9. Reflex bridles or defined tips set differently from side to side.
> 10. Trailing edge string too tight on one side.
> 11. Mylar folded on one side.
> 12. Foreign objects in the leading edge pocket.
> 13. Gremlins from hell.

The above list is ordered from the most to least common (except for lucky 13 that pops up everywhere).

✓ Turn Tendencies

Two tubes from the same batch can be as different as apples and apples—similar but not exactly the same.

When you notice a turn or dropping of a wing on landing, make sure it's repeatable and note the direction. The classic case is when a turn in flight occurs in one direction but the opposite side wing drops on landing as shown in figure 4-5. The reason for this is that one side has less twist in the sail so it performs better and the glider turns away from that side, but during the landing flare it stalls first due to the lesser twist. In this situation the first six items in our list should be looked at for a cure. Note: Usually only a landing flare indicates an asymmetrical stall since that's the only time you can safely produce such a severe stall in the outboard area.

Sometimes a turn is only indicated by an easier roll in one direction. Hands off it flies straight, but turning one way is a cinch while the opposite turn requires coaxing. This may be caused by the first six items, but items 7 and 8 should be checked as well. The only way to do this is to remove the leading edges, sight them for straightness and compare their flexibility.

To sight the tube hold it vertical to remove the natural bow due to its own weight and turn it in your hand, looking for wobble. Another method is to use a flat surface of sufficient length and roll the tube looking for wobble.

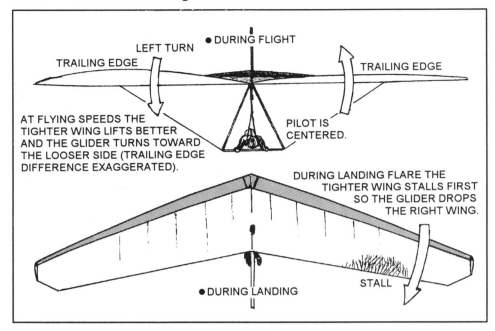

Figure 4-5: Turning and Dropping Wings

To check the flex, put the front end under a table, support the tube at the crossbar junction and hang about 20 lbs on the other end (see figure 4-6). Do this with both leading edges exactly together to see if they match up. If they don't one is weaker than the other. If the tube is perfectly straight it may have been fatigued or it has a different wall thickness. It is the nature of drawn aluminum tubing that the tolerance of dimensions results in walls of as much as 10% variation. Some manufacturers try to match up tubes of the same thickness, but this isn't always done. If your leading edges don't bow the same you'll have to replace one—we suggest the more flexible one.

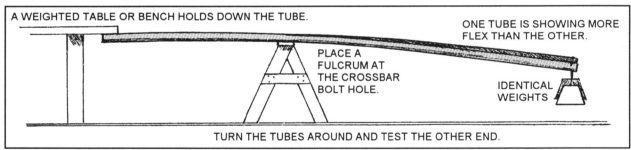

Figure 4-6: Testing Tubing Flex

Finding the source of a turn can be as frustrating as fishing in a wishing well, as even manufacturers have discovered.

CAUTION: Removing the leading edge involves two or more bolts, cables and end fittings. The side cables are particularly confusing to reinstall. Make a drawing before you undo them and set the glider up to check it for proper configuration *before* you fly. It helps to get things right if you spread the wings somewhat to straighten the cables.

Occasionally a glider will turn to one side in flight and stall to the same side on landing. This perverse behavior is usually caused by and can be cured by batten camber adjustment. The glider will turn towards the less cambered side and stall on that wing first as well.

✔ *Troubleshooting*

The first thing to do when you detect a turn is to check all battens for symmetry by matching up left and right. Next, stand at the nose of your glider and adjust it up or down so the trailing edge of the glider just disappears behind the high camber point of the sail as shown in figure 4-7. Check for symmetry. Also sight the leading edges to see if they appear to flex evenly (this is not easy to detect). Finally, have someone hold the glider level while you sight from tip to tip for an equal position. Perform all these eyeball tests with the glider on level ground so sail shift doesn't give a misreading.

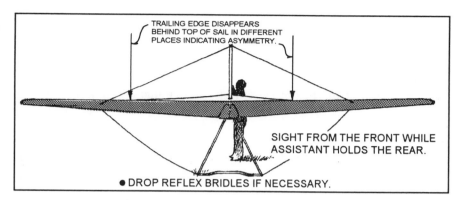

Figure 4-7: Checking Sail Symmetry

If you detect an imbalance, first measure bridle lengths to make sure they're the same and check the sail attachment at the tips to verify it is twisted the same amount. If things are satisfactory to this point, go down the list of causes and try to eliminate each one. If nothing asymmetrical is found, you'll have to make asymmetrical adjustments. Here's what to try:

First consult your owner's manual, for different gliders are more responsive to particular adjustments. Stalls are sensitive to tip tension, tip twist and batten cambering. Turns are also sensitive to these items. At high speeds turns are usually due to misaligned defined tips or mismatched reflex bridles.

A true gremlin was involved with a new glider that we were asked to straighten out. Sighting made it clear that there was an imbalance, for one outboard trailing edge was higher than the other. Measuring the length of reflex bridles, side cables, tubes and our patience demonstrated nothing out of sorts. Finally it was discovered that the glider had the outboard right leading edge in upside down, tilting the tip wand downward. Details such as this are posers.

A more bizarre occurrence happened to another manufacturer who test flew a glider and sent it out in perfect condition. The customer complained of a turn and the glider was checked thoroughly yet no asymmetry was found. Still the turn existed. Finally, after dismounting the sail the culprit was found: a spare downtube was discovered stuffed in the leading edge pocket! The customer had stowed it in there as a spare on a flying safari. At least he would have been prepared for a bad landing.

✔ Tip Tension and Twist

When you adjust tip tension with shims or ties, do it about 1/4 inch at a time. As little as 1/8 inch can be noticeable. Tighten the tip on the side the glider turns towards, to make it fly better, or loosen the opposite side, depending on whether you want more performance or more handling (generally tightening is better since many turns arise due to a sail stretch). If you are working on an asymmetrical stall, tighten the side that doesn't stall.

When adjusting wing twist at the mounting point, do so in increments of 5 to 10 degrees (see figure 4-8). Twist a wing up if it's stalling and up if the glider turns away from the side in question. Alternately you can twist the opposite wing down.

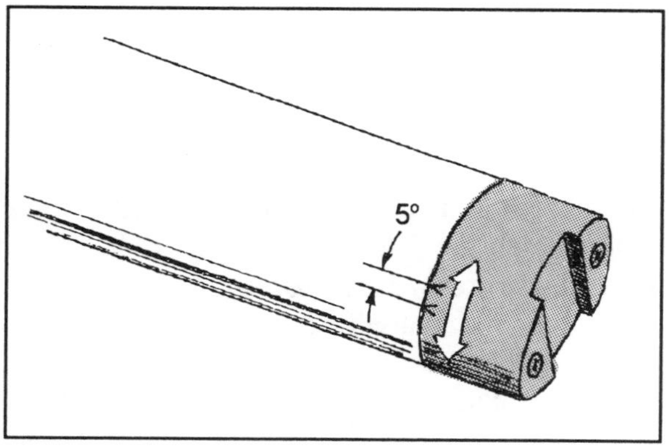

Figure 4-8: Adjusting Tip Twist

✔ Batten Camber

If you use batten camber to adjust out a turn, bend only the 1st two or three battens. Add

Glider dropping a wing on landing due to right wing stalling first.

camber (curve) to the side the glider turns towards or the side on which it stalls. At the same time remove an equal amount of camber from the opposite side. Figure 4-9 illustrates the common tuning techniques and their effects.

Once you have made a small tuning change, take a test flight in mild conditions to see if you've improved matters. It could be you need a little more tweaking or you've made things go the other way. In that case rethink what you did and make the proper adjustment.

Pro Tip: Always take notes concerning what changes you make for things can get confusing and you may have to start at the beginning. Mark the original settings before you start.

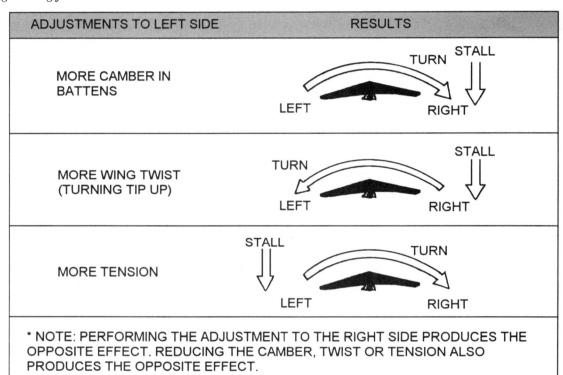

Figure 4-9: Tuning Summary

PERFORMANCE TUNING

To maintain performance true your battens:
1. After every nose-in or dropped control bar
2. After a flight in windy conditions
3. Every 25 hours
4. Before every competition

Much of performance tuning is the opposite of tuning for handling. In other words, you tighten the leading edges, tighten the battens and tighten the VG system if possible. The penalty is, of course, poorer handling. Tightening these items is a matter of diminishing returns. At some point your handling is degraded so much that anything you gain in straight line performance is lost in thermals as you are slow to center in a thermal core, you lock out and miss the small nuances. Also, curved tip gliders actually end up with a looser trailing edge if they are tightened too much.

In general, tightening a glider helps most in glides between thermals. Each pilot has to experiment with what works best with his or her flying style and wing loading.

Other things you can do are minor or not recommended. Perhaps the best thing possible is closing up the kingpost hole with a neoprene arrangement that velcros around the kingpost as shown in figure 4-10. This device blocks the air escaping from the hole—a nasty bit of drag—and protects the hang straps from UV degradation for kingpost hang setups.

Some competition pilots strip the plastic off their cables for less drag. The cables will have about 20% less drag in this case, but that is a small amount of the total. The drawbacks of this action are the fact bare wires will turn your sail black if they get wet and they can slice your arm or parachute bridle like a cheese cutter in a mishap. If you do bare your cables, do not do so to the ones that surround you—the lower front to rear cables.

Pilots in the past have been known to lower their reflex bridles and change the shape of their battens in hopes of improving performance. Manufacturers cringe at this thought for it makes the glider less stable generally and certainly uncertified. Lowering bridles for performance gain is generally useless: most gliders manufactured do not have bridles which engage except at negative angles of attack—well outside normal flight mode. All that is gained is a more tumble-prone machine. Several pilots have found out the hard way that altering their battens can invite disaster. The truth is, modern gliders have had a lot of airfoil work with sophisticated computer programs and it is highly doubtful that you will be able to improve on what the manufacturer deems best for performance and safety.

Performance is the elusive grail for which we all strive for, but in fact a pilot on any modern high performance glider will make much more of a difference improving techniques and tactics than is possible by tweaking the glider.

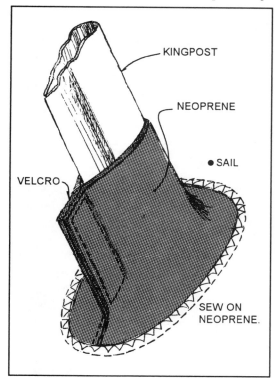

Figure 4-10: Closing the Kingpost Hole

REMOVING SAIL WRINKLES

If you look along your leading edge you will see a beautiful compound curve. The sail maker's trick is to take a basically flat material and create a three-dimensional shape. Craftsmanship and voodoo are involved. Sometimes it is almost impossible to fit a sail and wrinkles are the evidence.

If your sail exhibits wrinkles you can try to remove them. You have two avenues of recourse: tightening the battens and tightening the sail. To begin, make sure the wrinkles appear in the air (let an observant friend get above you) and not just on the ground. Ground wrinkles only matter when you are selling the glider to a perfectionist.

Perfecting sail cleanliness with rib and leading edge tension is a subtle balancing act between art and science.

Locate the wrinkles. If they appear in the midspan on the upper surface just behind the leading edge (very common) they are caused by an imperfect leading edge cut called a *luff* curve. The only thing you can try is tightening the battens in that area. If that doesn't work, try tightening the leading edges to pull twist out and change the sail shape.

Wrinkles in the tip area can be cured by tightening the tip battens. Sometimes adding a little batten camber helps, but this should not be done without the manufacturer's approval. Occasionally too tight leading edges will create tip wrinkles that can be alleviated by removing shims. All this tightening will adversely affect handling, so you have to decide how much to do. If your wrinkles are permanent, take solace for small ripples don't seem to hurt performance to any noticeable extent.

Designing and fabricating a sail is a work of art and craftsmanship that requires much consideration of material selection and orientation of weave as well as the deft application of tucks, darts and seams.

In these high-tech times many types of sail cloth are available for use on gliders. We have the sailboat industry to thank for this state of affairs. Here is a general review of material types to help you select a sail structure and be conversant out on the hill.

✔ Different Materials

Before we begin we should define our terms. *Dacron* is a trade name owned by the Dupont company and it refers to polyester fibers. Woven Dacron is the material from which most of our sails and loud leisure suits are made. *Mylar* is also polyester but it is made in solid sheets or a thin film. *Kevlar* is made from aramid fibers and has more strength with less stretch than Dacron. *Spectra* (known as Dyneema in Europe) is a fiber that has properties between that of Dacron and Kevlar and is used occasionally in hang straps. Carbon fibers are also used in hang gliding, but their brittleness precludes using them in sails.

✔ Cloth Variations

Leading edges require the stiffest cloth, while the trailing edge is next, followed by the main body then the undersurface (see figure 4-11). Leading edges may have a bumpy texture which is known as *scrim* cloth. This material is almost bullet proof and is what we recommend. It is made by bonding Mylar to a coarse open Dacron weave. The resulting bumps may cause a bit extra drag at high speeds, but also seem to allow a higher angle of attack (and thus better sink) by activating the air's boundary layer. Scrim cloth may delaminate a bit after long exposure to sunlight, but this is a cosmetic not a strength problem.

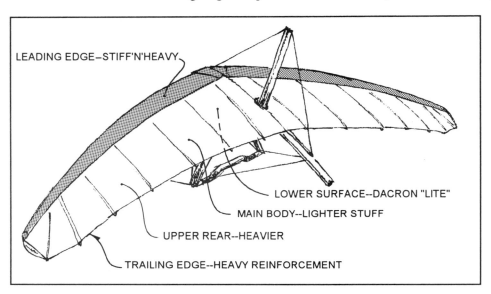

LEADING EDGE–STIFF'N'HEAVY

LOWER SURFACE--DACRON "LITE"

MAIN BODY--LIGHTER STUFF

UPPER REAR--HEAVIER

TRAILING EDGE--HEAVY REINFORCEMENT

Figure 4-11: Sailcloth Weights

Other leading edge materials include a solid Mylar cloth and heavy close-weave Dacron. The Mylar is especially susceptible to the effects of rain on the sail. It should be noted that too heavy a leading edge material prevents it from stretching and thereby tightening the trailing edge.

Trailing edges receive different treatment sometimes. A few manufacturers have tried a Kevlar band or broad Mylar strip in that area. Others use as much as 5 ounce* Dacron in the trailing edge construction. In general the heavier the sailcloth the better performance and the longer it will maintain its good performance but the tougher the handling. All-Mylar upper surfaces are common enough on competition gliders, but be warned that they won't last as long as regular Dacron.

The main body of the sail—between the leading and trailing edges—is sometimes made of a lighter material than the rear. This is for handling purposes and to let the sail seat well over the cambered airfoil.

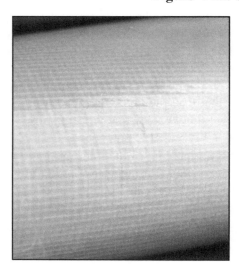

Close up of a scrim cloth leading edge.

* The weight of material is a general measure of thickness and refers to its actual weight per square yard.

Lower surfaces are made of the lightest material for handling. They tend to be of 3.8 ounce Dacron or even less.

Different material suppliers make different weights and types of cloth so manufacturers sometimes change sail material depending on availability. The important thing to do when you are choosing sail material is to ask the manufacturer what is available and what are the benefits of each choice. Material is always changing, and a particular type offered today may be obsolete tomorrow. Find out what will suit your needs before you buy.

➤ **Pro Tip**: The string you often see in a trailing edge is a safety device in case of rips and should be left loose at the center unless you owner's manual instructs you to tighten it if flutter appears.

III - THE HARNESS

The second most important piece of equipment in our flying ensemble is that which enshrouds our body and weds us to our glider—the harness. Here we review the use and benefits of different high performance harness types available today.

POD HARNESS TYPES

A totally enclosed harness is known as a pod harness. Such a design makes sense: it is warmer, more comfortable, easier to take off and land and more streamlined than other options. Their only drawback is a bit more bulk and sometimes weight.

A modern pod harness. Note the low drag profile.

The first pod-type harness in the USA was the bulletman inspired by Rich Pfeiffer while working at Wills Wing. This harness had long battens to make it rigid. Later designs were totally soft with a few more lines. The CG 1000 by Jay Gianforte was the first successful design with a single low-drag support line. Jay invented the back plate and center of gravity systems that make these harnesses practical. These types of pod harnesses can offer minimal drag and are now convenient to use with front entry systems.

New designs are again incorporating longitudinal battens with separated main straps routing to the side of the hips. The advantage of these changes are lighter weight and ease of landing (see PODS IN FLIGHT below). One other design that demands mention provides the lowest drag of all: Jim Lee's fiberglass pod. It is a rigid airfoil with clam doors for takeoff and landing. It is a bit bulkier in storage, but it obviously provides superior performance.

CHOOSING A POD

The three items to look for when contemplating are *strength, comfort* and *ease of use.* Strength varies according to the care of a designer.

We once saw a European harness separate at the back board. The pilot was left hanging on the control bar. He fortunately was able to drop into a river and said goodby to his glider.

Look for continuous webbing used in the harness body. Also make sure that thick thread (type 5) is used on the main webbing connections. You should be able to free-fall and deploy a chute in your harness—you may have to.

The right pod for you depends upon your needs. If you mainly fly for recreation, get a regular pod from a reputable company. They are most convenient and easiest to land. Only if you are an avid competition pilot should you consider the more advanced designs. The reason for this is they are a bit more challenging to land.

Jim Lee's composite competition harness.

If you are buying used, getting a right fit is very important. One of the highlights of a full-body harness is comfort and this is not realized if you have a poor fit. Dangle around in a harness you intend to fly or better yet, take an hour flight. You should feel no pressure points and should land wanting to fork over hard cash. Be sure to check a used harness for wear on the main straps, lines, zipper and boot area and adjust the price accordingly if anything needs replacing.

The length of the leg straps is important on a harness. If they are too long the harness will let you drop too far when you stand to land making it difficult to flare fully. With adjustable leg straps you should snug them and fix them so they don't change. If the harness you choose does not have adjustable leg straps you must have it altered if they are too loose.

HARNESS OPTIONS

A pod harness is the way to fly for performance and comfort. The only problem is deciding which pod to fly.

Whether you are buying used or new you should look for options on the harness. Rule 1: the more storage space the better, unless a lot of extra pouches are on the outside of the harness adding drag. A large inside pouch for your glider cover, pads and harness bag is a necessity, especially with today's well-padded, amply covered gliders. Zippered pouches above and below a chest mounted parachute are also mighty convenient.

Ballast bags are advisable if you plan to compete in the big air. An oxygen pouch is also required if you plan to get high. A radio pouch with an external antenna and microphone may be added or you can attach the radio to your shoulder strap. Finally you should consider storage space for water when out exploiting the desert air. Colors and design options are left to your vanity or aesthetic sense.

Pro Tip: We highly recommend you mount your parachute system on your chest. Such a shock absorber has prevented many injuries in accidental belly landings.

USING A POD HARNESS

✓ Taking Off

Keep your shoe laces tucked in your shoes or they may join your zipper.

The launch-in-a-pod is easy since the harness is behind you and your legs are free to churn gravel. Once in the air you stick your feet in and zip, you're a human bean in a pod. On first glance you may find it difficult to find the foot port, but as long as your boot isn't floppy, when you bend a knee your foot is in the right place.

Two types of leg opening exist—the slot and the barn door as shown in figure 4-12. The slot system feels a bit restrictive on your legs at first but doesn't seem to cause problems on launch. Its benefit is that the boot is held up off the ground somewhat by your legs separating the slot. Also, the slot is almost closed once your feet are in the boot.

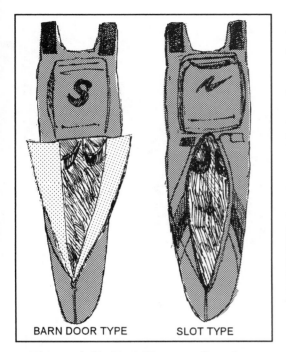

Figure 4-12: Pod Harness Openings

BARN DOOR TYPE   SLOT TYPE

The door system allows more freedom on the ground and a better run when landing downwind, but the doors add some drag until they're zipped up.

Once in the air you need to get zipped. However, you don't have to do it right away. We suggest waiting for a moment of peace before you attempt closure. Nothing is worse than watching a gyrating pilot fiddling with his harness close to launch. If you have a door type harness you can put the doors behind each leg if you have a drag phobia. You should learn to locate your opening and closing tabs by feel. With a bit of practice you can put your hand on them automatically.

➤ **Pro Tip:** Raise your butt as you zip up to take weight off the zipper and reduce its stress.

My pod's zipper would stop at the same place above my knees every time on the first pull. I would leave it there in traffic and close it later as the sky opened up. Eventually this wore the zipper so that on one memorable competition flight the whole thing separated shortly after takeoff. Imagine my joy at flying for four hours up to freezing temperatures with an open boot. On another occasion my shoe lace dangled in the zipper and jammed it. I could neither open or close it beyond my shin and had to land on one foot!

✓ Adjusting a Pod

For problem-free use: Silicon your zipper regularly.

The most important thing to consider about a pod in mid-flight is its adjustment. If you're going to fly a streamlined harness you should aim into the streamlines. Too many pilots hang with their feet too low and create excess drag. Figure 4-13 shows the right and wrong hang. The reason for the bad angle of hang is *hang strap length*. Many pilots think that shoulder line adjustment determines hang position, but as figure 4-14 shows, shoulder lines can only limit your range of angles while raising the mains raises the hips. If you are too low at the hang points you can never tilt down enough to get streamlined.

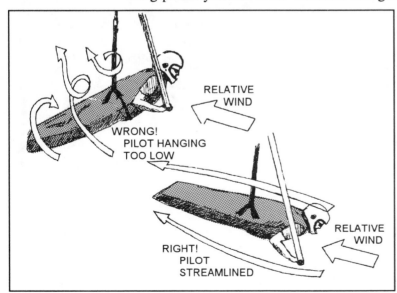

Figure 4-13: Proper Prone Position

RELATIVE WIND

WRONG! PILOT HANGING TOO LOW

RIGHT! PILOT STREAMLINED

RELATIVE WIND

To adjust a pod harness, always make sure your *hips* are several inches above the base tube. Since your shoulders can be rotated up and down, it doesn't make sense to put your parachute over the bar and have it clear by a fist and consider the problem solved.

A pod harness must have the main risers attached behind your body's center of gravity (CG) so that you remain in prone position hands off the bar. If this is not the case you need to move your body forward if possible (adjustable shoulder straps) or get a new harness. You can't fly with pleasure and finesse if you are continuously rocking up.

✓ Landing in a Pod

Landings in recreational pods are easy. The only thing to remember is to unzip *at least 500 feet above the ground.* You never know when a zipper may jam. Most pods have their zipper on strips of Velcro to be opened in emergencies but this is very difficult to do and you're guaranteed to fail unless you attempt it early.

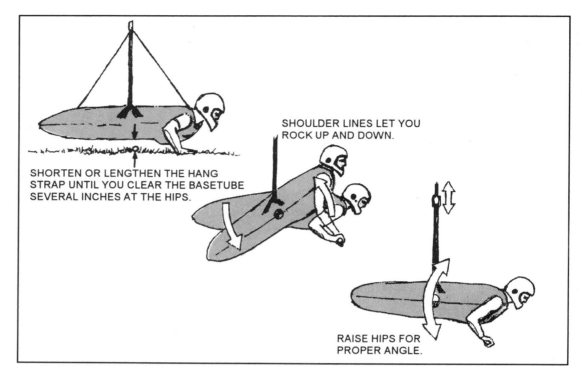

Figure 4-14: Adjusting Hang Position

One pilot in the rare air of Telluride, Colorado found he couldn't unzip his pod. This discovery was made while he was low to the ground so he decided to land pogo stick style. The problem was he flared early, stalled big time and came down head first to conk himself cold.

In such an emergency we recommend:

Landing an Unzipped Pod
Find the smoothest landing surface and aim into the wind. Get as low as you can in ground effect and remain in the prone position with your legs slightly down. Keep your hands on the base tube but put your thumbs on top and gradually slow to near stall. Then push out more to mush with the bar only inches off the ground. Land on your belly and let go of the basetube if a nose-in occurs.

The reason the above method works is you experience more ground effect when you bring the glider lower and you relieve the glider of some weight as you drag the ground, thus you are slowed more than normal. Furthermore, you can slow as much as possible since you don't need energy to climb to upright height. To see how the procedure works, watch novice pilots at a hill—they frequently use belly landing gear.

One-strap harnesses are more difficult to land because they tilt you downward since the strap comes from your back which means your body's CG is below the attachment point shown in figure 4-15. As a result, to get vertical for flare you have to hold yourself upright which reduces your sensitivity to your glider's feedback. A sliding mechanism in the harness can help relieve some of this pressure but doesn't eliminate it. There is a transition period as you learn to land with these harnesses, but most pilots have no lingering problems and the reduced drag is worth it if you compete.

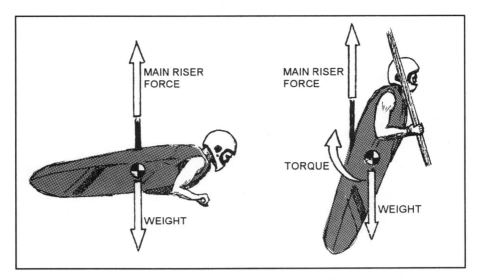

Figure 4-15: Downward Tilting Force Due to Rear Attachment

HARNESS CARE

We can state the easy steps to harness care in few words: Keep it clean, store it out of heat and moisture and apply silicone to the zipper every 20 flights. Most harnesses are made from nylon, a polyamide material that is strong, stretchy and vulnerable to ultraviolet degradation. You can clean it with mild detergent and warm water (remove the parachute!) and dry out of the sun.

Pro Tip: Getting a harness wet will make it shrink—you may find yours too small after it is cleaned. The best bet is to clean only dirty spots with a sponge. If you expect to be caught in rain occasionally we suggest getting a harness that's an inch or two larger.

Safety Tip: Place your harness in the shade of your glider when it lies ready for use.

Keep your harness in the bag or in the shade as much as possible to avoid tanning. Suntanned harnesses may look good but they're weaker. Spray-on UV protection can help, but may cause the harness to pick up dirt. Experiment with a small spot. Silicone spray on the zipper can help avoid many post-launch or pre-landing stress syndromes.

IV - INSTRUMENTS

*W*e can easily spend as much as a third of the cost of a new glider on instruments. It should be apparent that some thought should go into their selection not only because we have to ransom our next of kin to afford them (we've already mortgaged the house for our glider) but also because they can enhance our performance. We covered variometer basics in *Hang Gliding Flying Skills* and speak about vario uses in later chapters. Here let us learn more about how they do their magic.

VARIOMETER FEATURES

Variometers are essential items for soaring pilots although we encourage all pilots to learn to thermal without their vario as well, to improve their senses and reduce their reliability on batteries. You can get as many features as you wish to as long as your bankroll is plump. Essential items are a visual scale and an audio signal. Desirable additions include dual vario scales, digital altimeter and a clock. A speed-to-fly ring (see Chapter 7) and a barograph memory are icing on the cake.

All effective vario have an audio signal, for surely you need to be watching other gliders in traffic. This signal should be chopped or raised in pitch increasingly as climb rate climbs. Sink signal threshold should be adjustable. Another important item is a climb rate averager. This feature comes in handy when using speed-to-fly rings and lets you know the true worth of a thermal. Modern barograph varios allow you to print out a record of your flight to serve as a log book, a conversation piece or a record attempt documentation. Expect to pay heartily for this feature.

Ideally you should be able to dial in the amount of sensitivity you desire. A very sensitive vario with no lag is perfect for very light conditions but may be bothersome in turbulence. Most plots get used to the lag in their varios and are able to judge when to turn in relation to their vario sound. We prefer as little lag as possible but other respected pilots like a lag to filter out transient tugs of lift.

All these goodies come in a variety of packages. No one vario flight deck combines all the ideal features. Look for one that has the most items to suit your needs and wallet thickness. A nice low-drag durable cover is also an attraction. Finally, make sure the instrument has an easy, secure and versatile mounting system.

VARIOMETER VARIATIONS

Older variometers came in two principle varieties:

    1. *Flask-type* varios that measure the mass of air escaping from a given capacity, or

    2. *Diaphragm-type* that measure the change in size of an "aneroid" enclosure.

These designs are still available, they work fine and are the cheapest varios you can find. However, new variometers incorporate electronic magic to do much more than report rate-of-

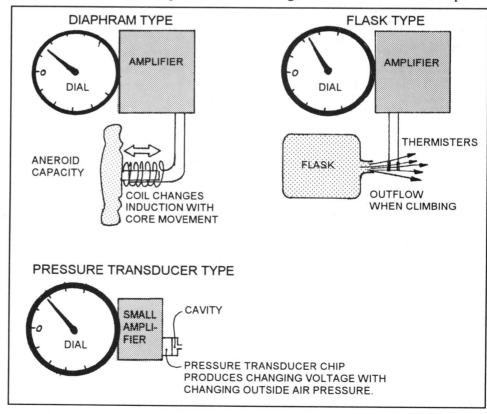

Figure 4-16: Modern Vario Types

climb. These new *electronic variometers* use a pressure sensitive chip (pressure transducer) to measure air pressure changes and thus rate of climb and altitude in as little as a few inches (10 cm) of climb. The schematics in figure 4-16 illustrate these vario types.

✔ *Total Energy Compensation*

Since a variometer simply notes the rate of change in air pressure, it will tell you when you are going up or down, even if it is due to your changing speeds. If you slow down very fast your vario indicates climb, usually with a lag (try some speed changes on a smooth day to get a feel for this). The problem arises when you are flying fast between thermals and slow down when you detect lift. If you slow as quickly as is desirable you create a *stick thermal* (a term from aviation, since old airplanes were controlled by a stick) that masks the real thermal so you don't know what's actually there until the glider's speed settles down. By then you may have already lost altitude because the pop was in fact "fools lift" and you circled in sink.

A cluster of typical hang gliding instruments.

The solution to this problem is to use a *total energy compensated vario (TE vario)*. By total energy we mean the sum of kinetic (moving) energy and potential (due to height) energy. Such a vario will only register an up signal if we increase our total energy. That is, if we climb due to pushout only, we are simply trading kinetic energy for potential energy and the vario doesn't indicate a climb. On the other hand, if some lift was added to our climb as we slow down, we get a reading.

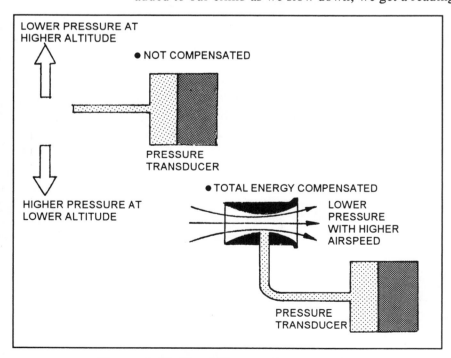

Figure 4-17: Total Energy Compensation

It may seem difficult to separate the energy in our wing without some weird relativistic hocus-pocus, but the solution is quite simple and therefore elegant. We make use of the fact that the (dynamic) pressure of the air increases with the square of the velocity. Furthermore, our sink rate increases pretty much with the square of our flying velocity (especially at lower speeds). Therefore, if we have some device to measure the air's dynamic pressure and hook this up to our vario's detection of change in pressure due to change in altitude we can compensate for the amount of altitude change due to altering our glider's speed.

Figure 4-17 illustrates how this is performed in a vario. We have a schematic showing a venturi that creates more negative pressure the faster we fly. Thus if we enter a dive, for example, more negative pressure makes the pressure sensor feel as if it were getting higher even though we are falling. The effect of higher pressure due to descent and lower pressure due to faster air moving through the venturi cancel each other out. When we push out the opposite effect takes place.

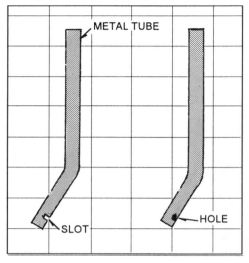

Figure 4-18: Total Energy Probes

The venturi is similar to the one in your carburetor. Other types of probes can be used to compensate for total energy as well and they are known as Nicks tubes or Braunschweig tubes depending on their arrangements of holes and slots. These tubes are shown in figure 4-18 and are quite sensitive to placement of the probe and the holes in it.

In the past, total energy wasn't used much in hang gliding because of the poor speed retention of our slow wings. However, modern gliders are sleeker and more likely to produce stick thermals. TE compensation is now popular with cross-country pilots. Examples of TE varios are the Ball designs which uses a venturi compensator and the Lindsay Ruddock which uses a Braunschweig tube.

✓ Netto Compensation

As we fly at different speeds our glider produces different amounts of sink. We have to mentally compensate for our glider's sink rate to get an idea as to what the air is doing. If we could totally cancel out our glider's contribution to the sink we would have a reading of the air's "net" sink or lift. We could map the lift patterns in the air.

Such a device exists for sailplanes and is called a *netto variometer*. Its working is incredibly simple since it consists of a pitot tube* (an open tube pointing directly into the airstream) connected by a thin capillary tube to the variometer capacity. However, this device is not readily adaptable to electronic (pressure transducer) variometer and as yet is not available for hang gliders.

VARIOMETER ERRORS _____

Calibrating a variometer is performed in an evacuation chamber that lowers pressure at a given rate. Forget trying to test yours in an elevator for building pressures create false readings. Flask-type variometers show the greatest error at altitude because their reading is based on the mass of the air escaping from the flask. This mass is less at altitude. The error can be as much as 30% (too low a reading) at 10,000 feet as shown in figure 4-19.

Diaphragm-type and electronic type varios are inherently error free, although variations can occur due to errors in the circuit. Comparing vario readings when climbing with a friend will point this out. Variometer errors are not of great consequence in general as long as you are aware of your vario type and its error potential *unless* you are using a speed ring which we explain in Chapter 7.

ALTIMETERS _____

An altimeter is a necessary piece of equipment for a cross-country pilot and of great comfort

_____

* A pitot tube is a tube facing the airstream to detect dynamic (moving) air pressure.

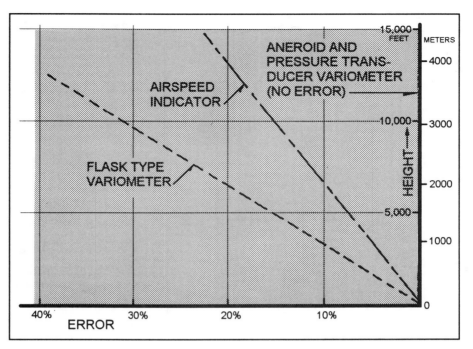

Figure 4-19: Instrument Error

to any type of pilot. We have come a long way since the early days of mountain climbing dial altimeters that would barely let us know if we gained fifty feet. Now we have digital devices that register as accurately as one foot intervals.

Most electronic variometers come equipped with a digital altimeters (or two). The reason is, the same sensor provides the data for absolute altitude (altimeter) and rate of change of altitude (variometer). Two altimeters let you display height above the ground or takeoff as well as height above sea level. The former is useful when soaring a small local hill while the latter is essential when flying around other air traffic or at high altitudes. We suggest buying an electronic altimeter/variometer combination if you don't have either one for the convenience, accuracy and ultimately lower cost involved.

✓ Altimeter Errors

All altimeters are erroneous if only because they must be made to a standard. They sense pressure change but the pressure change with altitude is linear only in the lower 10,000 feet and it is quite different from one day to the next. Therefore a Standard Atmosphere (see *Understanding the Sky* for an explanation and values of Standard Atmosphere) has been adopted that lets instrument makers off the hook and lets aircraft fliers all lie the same amount. Generally, in thermaling conditions our altimeters read low since they are calibrated to read the Standard Atmosphere value of lapse rate which is 3.5°F (2°C) drop of temperature per 1000 feet. Thermals cool off more than that, resulting in denser (simulating lower) air. The expected textbook error is shown in figure 4-20 for heights above takeoff assuming you set your altimeter correctly at takeoff. In the real world this chart won't be exactly correct because the air doesn't necessarily cool off uniformly aloft.

Other errors are rampant in hang glider altimeters as can be told by comparing readings with fellow pilots or checking your altimeter with topographic maps. These errors do not prove too problematical unless you use the altimeter for final glide calculations (see Chapter 7).

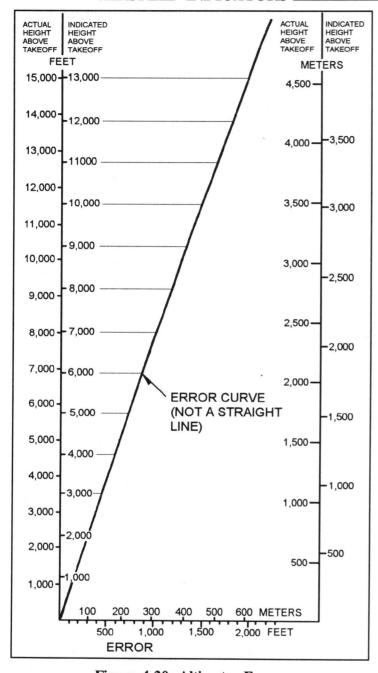

Figure 4-20: Altimeter Errors

Only recently have hang glider pilots begun to use airspeed indicators to any great degree. That's because when we need airspeed control most—in thermals, on landing or scratching close— we need to be watching the hard stuff (trees, other gliders, the terrain) not an instrument. We get very good airspeed feedback from our bar position and the airstream. However, speed-to-fly techniques use airspeed to produce the best flight in terms of distance or speed in varying conditions. Using these techniques has sparked a new interest in airspeed indicators.

✓ Airspeed Types

Several types of airspeed sensors exist. A venturi is a sensor of airspeed as is a total energy probe or a pitot tube mentioned earlier. However, all these airspeed sensors are sensitive to fluctuations and do not read true airspeed (as we go higher they read low in the less dense air). The most reliable airspeed probe is the little ducted fan illustrated in figure 4-21 for it is not affected by air density.

These fans can be made very accurate, but they are not sensitive due to the inertia of the vanes. Also, in comparison tests with multiple instruments their readings vary by as much as 10 mph due to frictional effects. Take their word with a grain of salt.

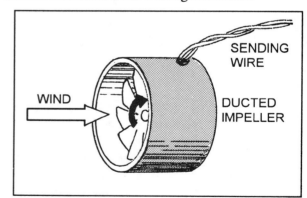

Figure 4-21: Ducted Fan Impeller

At altitude, an impeller or fan type airspeed probe reads true airspeed except for the effects of friction. This will have implications in speeds-to-fly as we shall see.

We recommend an airspeed indicator integrated with an electronic altimeter and vario package. Examples of these are the Ball instrument deck and the ergonomic Flytec design.

OTHER INSTRUMENTS

✓ Flight Computers

Not quite a reality as of this writing but certainly needed is a flight computer-instrument package that will automatically display speeds-to-fly and final glide heights. They have been used in sailplanes for some time and will be here eventually through trickle down technology.

✓ Thermal Detectors

Several versions of thermal detectors are available based on the supposition that a thermal is warmer than its surroundings. These devices seem to work best closer to the ground where any temperature differences are likely to be most marked. At best they can tell you where the thermal is when you are within range and check your centering performance. At worst they are an annoyance, squeaking at every passing patch of warm turbulence.

✓ Global Positioning Systems (GPS)

These are mainly navigation devices using satellite triangulation. However, they are so accurate (within 30 feet) and sensitive (to a movement of a few centimeters) that they can be used as altimeters, variometers and airspeed indicators. A truly complete instrument system will be a GPS that replaces all of these instruments and combines the functions of a flight computer as well.

✓ Turn and Bank Indicator

At least one such instrument is available for hang gliders. It uses tiny battery powered gyros to tell when you're turning. Its main purpose is to keep you from losing your equilibrium in a cloud. Having tried such an instrument where it is legal, I will attest to its effectiveness.

✓ Compass

Many cross-country pilots fly with a compass. The type to use is a *heading compass* which has a dial or ball floating in a fluid (similar to those sold for cars) as shown in figure 4-22. These work when they're tilted somewhat and are easy to read.

Compasses are prone to many errors. The biggest problem with hang gliding is when you start turning the compass doesn't exactly follow your heading. If you ever expect to use a compass when caught in a cloud, lower your expectations and read the sections on cloud flying in Chapter 2 and 6. General compass use for navigating appears in Chapter 8.

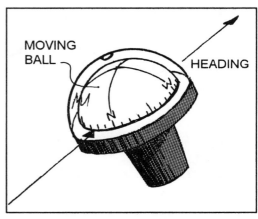

Figure 4-22: Heading Compass

V - PARACHUTES

𝒫arachutes have become an integral part of our flying gear. They have saved lives and will save more.

In the 1992 Preworld Meet, two pilots had a midair several hundred feet above launch. As they spun down together, first one then the other whipped out his chute. It was a beautiful sight to see both pilots floating down into the canyon essentially safe.

In the 1984 US Nationals a Japanese pilot was attempting aerobatics for the first time. He stalled and entered a series of repeated tumbles. After about 10 complete flips, centrifugal force pulled his parachute out and he too was spared a much more serious fate. Need we say more?

PARACHUTE PARTS

We should be conversant with the parts of a parachute so we can discuss them readily. A basic parachute is shown in figure 4-23. Here we see the main elements as the canopy, the shroud lines and the bridle. The top of the canopy is called the apex, the bottom the skirt and each panel is called a gore. Cut-outs may exist on some models which let air escape, thereby moving the chute forward and increasing stability (unstable parachutes have a habit of oscillating).

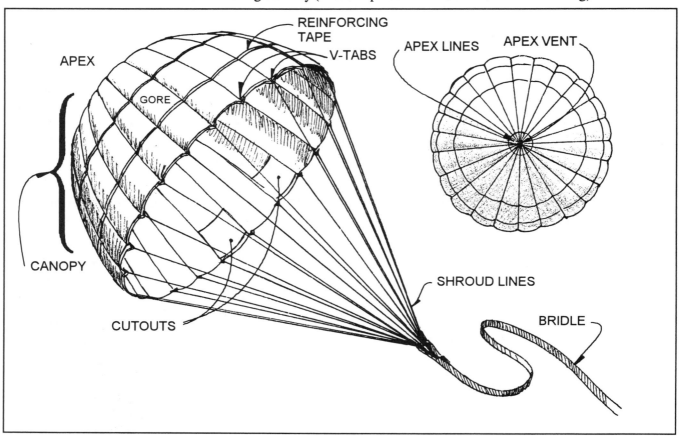

Figure 4-23: Parachute Nomenclature

PARACHUTE PERFORMANCE

There are several types of parachutes available for hang gliding, and we review them here:

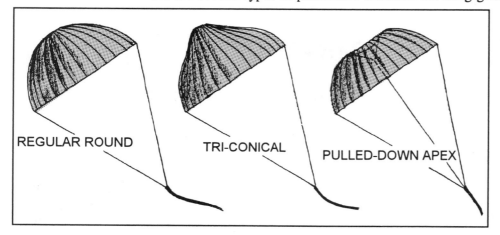

Figure 4-24: Parachute Types

REGULAR ROUND - This is the basic folded hanky as shown in figure 4-24. It has a relatively fast descent rate, a moderate opening time, good reliability, moderate stability, large packed bulk and lowest cost.

TRICONICAL - This type has shaped gores so the canopy itself is not semi-circular but breast-shaped for more drag. It has a slower descent rate, a moderate opening time, good reliability, the best stability. reasonable packed bulk (it can be of smaller diameter than the round type) and greater cost.

PULLED-DOWN APEX (PDA) - This parachute design pulls the center of the canopy down which broadens out the skirt for more drag compared to the previous types. It can thus be made much smaller. It has the slowest descent rate, the fastest opening time, the least reliability, the worst stability, the smallest bulk and the most cost.

In weighing these factors, we recommend either the tri-conical or the PDA design. The PDA will weigh less than 2 pounds while the triconical will be 3 or more pounds for the same payload. There are ardent advocates of both types, although PDA chutes are becoming more popular.

PARACHUTE SIZING

Because parachutes come in different types, sizes are mostly given in number of gores. The chart below summarizes the results of tests that have been made on hang gliding parachutes.

TYPE	SIZE	PAYLOAD	DESCENT RATE	EQUIVALENT JUMPING HEIGHT
PDA	20 GORE	250 lbs	19.5 FPS	5.9 FT
PDA	22 GORE	350 lbs	19.4 FPS	5.9 FT
PDA	24 GORE	450 lbs	20.5 FPS	6.6 FT

Triconical chutes of the same load rating get a similar sink rate but are larger. Look at the equivalent jumping height and imagine jumping from these heights into rocks, ruts or a tree. Note: There should always be one line per gore. Make sure your parachute has a minimum of 20 lines.

THE BRIDLE

The parachute bridle or leader connects you via your harness to the parachute shroud lines. It must be strong enough to absorb shock, resistant enough to prevent cutting on the cables and long enough to clear the wing. We recommend a solid one inch nylon webbing (type 18 or type 24 good for 6,000 lbs) at least 20 feet long for a bridle. Kevlar bridles do not stretch enough to relieve the load of a fast opening. If your bridle is too long, opening time will be increased.

Your bridle is susceptible to ultraviolet rays. Make sure it is *always* covered when mounted on your harness. Use a rubber band (a short section of bicycle inner tube works great) to keep the parachute bridle located properly on the carabiner. Finally we recommend installing a swivel on your bridle so that a twisting parachute doesn't wind up the lines.

DELIVERY SYSTEMS

The choice is hand deployment or rocket delivery. There is no doubt that rockets can increase speed of deployment and even reliability in situations where entanglement occurs. This reliability will only be realized however if the rocket deployment system is attached properly (errors have been made) and the system is maintained. Currently both chemical and compressed air rockets are available.

Parachutes have saved many lives without seeing the light of day. A chest mount protects vital organs—think about it.

Two warnings: Be sure your rocket can not catch on a side cable. This has occurred and is very dangerous close to the ground if you auger in. Also be sure your parachute is mounted on your chest and you can hand-deploy it if the rocket malfunctions. A parachute on your chest allows you to throw it with either hand (think of a broken arm) and protects vital organs if you flop on a rock or stump.

PARACHUTE PACKING

Various manuals and experts advise repacking a chute every 90 days to six months. Whichever is correct, we can be sure that we do not repack our canopies often enough unless we know how to do it ourselves. It is in the interest of safety, with the understanding that each parachute packs a little differently, that we offer this packing guide. There are several ways to pack a hang gliding parachute. We present a popular way here that has proved to be reliable. Use your manual and expert help along with these steps until you can do it yourself.

✓ Packing Steps (non-PDA)

Caution: Before opening your parachute, draw your system on paper so that you can duplicate the closing system.

▶1. Select a large clean floor or long bench (outside on a tarp in the shade will work), gather a few large books for weights and some bungees or rope to stretch the parachute.

▶2. Gather the apex loops in order and hook them to a bungee (figure 4-25). Hook the bridle to another bungee (or rope) so the parachute is stretched.

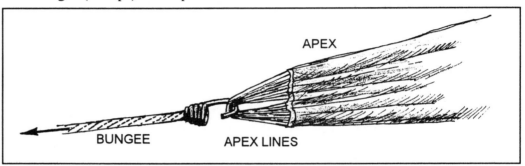

APEX

BUNGEE   APEX LINES

Figure 4-25: Holding Apex Lines

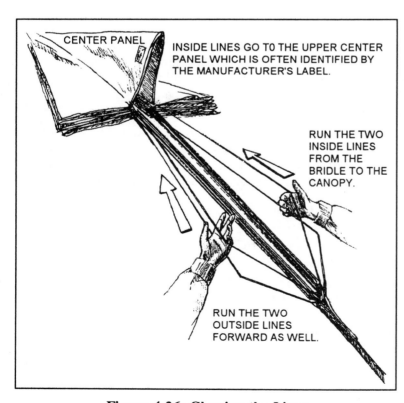

CENTER PANEL

INSIDE LINES GO TO THE UPPER CENTER PANEL WHICH IS OFTEN IDENTIFIED BY THE MANUFACTURER'S LABEL.

RUN THE TWO INSIDE LINES FROM THE BRIDLE TO THE CANOPY.

RUN THE TWO OUTSIDE LINES FORWARD AS WELL.

Figure 4-26: Clearing the Lines

▶3. Find the innermost two lines from the bridle end and run them toward the canopy to make sure every line is straight (figure 4-26). If some lines are crossed, the bridle has passed through the lines and must be corrected. Caution: this can be like working a jigsaw puzzle, so hold onto the lines you pass the bridle under so you can reverse what you do if necessary.

▶4. Once the lines are clear, separate half the panels on one side and half on the other. The top panels should be connected to your inside two lines and the bottom panels to your outside lines (figure 4-26).

▶5. Flake the canopy by flopping all the panels to one side then pulling a panel across—one at a time—and arranging it neatly (figure 4-27). Make sure all the canopy material of each panel is pulled out of the lines.

▶6. Now flop the other half of the panels across to the other side and repeat the process. Count the panels as you go and make sure you have the same number on each side. If not, move one over.

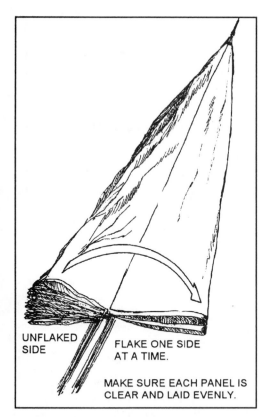

Figure 4-27: Flaking the Canopy

UNFLAKED SIDE

FLAKE ONE SIDE AT A TIME.

MAKE SURE EACH PANEL IS CLEAR AND LAID EVENLY.

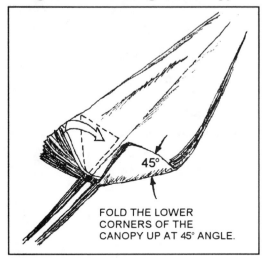

Figure 4-29: Forty-Five the Skirt

45°

FOLD THE LOWER CORNERS OF THE CANOPY UP AT 45° ANGLE.

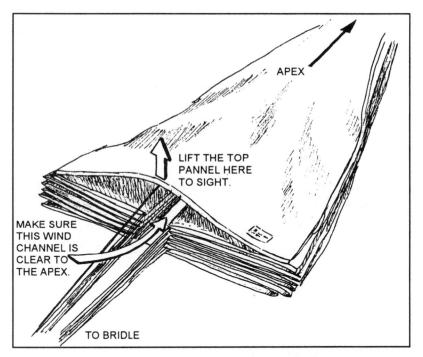

Figure 4-28: Check Inside Canopy

APEX

LIFT THE TOP PANNEL HERE TO SIGHT.

MAKE SURE THIS WIND CHANNEL IS CLEAR TO THE APEX.

TO BRIDLE

▶7. Once this is complete, separate the lines (left and right) a bit in the center and lift the top material to check for a clear wind channel up the center (figure 4-28).

▶8. Now 45° the skirt to avoid a large bulk at the skirt when the folding is complete (figure 4-29).

▶9. Fold the canopy lengthwise in thirds then in half again (figure 4-30).

▶10. Weight the canopy down with books to hold it and put a rubber band around the apex lines at the top to help inflation (figure 4-31).

▶11. Finish by S folding the canopy into the deployment bag (figure 4-32).

▶12. Close the bag with the shroud lines in the elastic loops to hold the bag shut (figure 4-33). Note: Different bags use different arrangements. Also, if your deployment bag is a flat bib you should only fold the canopy in thirds (step 9) and S fold it flat on the bib (figure 4-34).

▶13. Put your parachute in the harness container with the bridle S folded at the bottom. Close the container and kneel on the parachute to get the air out (do this only once). Rub your hand hard along the Velcro closures to fasten them tightly. Now secure the container top with pins on the handle of the container bag that insert into little bungees to hold the container securely closed. If you don't have these pins installed, get them from a dealer immediately or you will be in danger of an accidental deployment.

▶14. Finally, don your harness and hang from a strap to check your parachute security. Flop down a couple times and wriggle around vigorously to make sure the parachute doesn't pop out. Once everything is secure, go find some safe air and fly with such care that you never need to flash nylon.

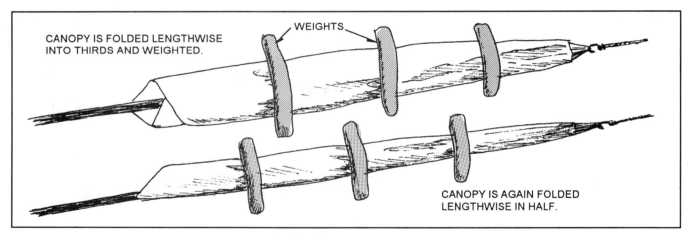

Figure 4-30: Folding and Weighting the Canopy

CANOPY IS FOLDED LENGTHWISE INTO THIRDS AND WEIGHTED.

WEIGHTS

CANOPY IS AGAIN FOLDED LENGTHWISE IN HALF.

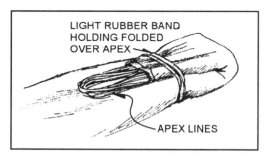

LIGHT RUBBER BAND HOLDING FOLDED OVER APEX

APEX LINES

Figure 4-31: Closing the Apex

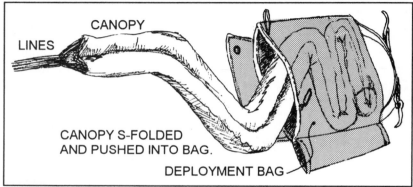

CANOPY

LINES

CANOPY S-FOLDED AND PUSHED INTO BAG.

DEPLOYMENT BAG

Figure 4-32: S-Folding the Canopy

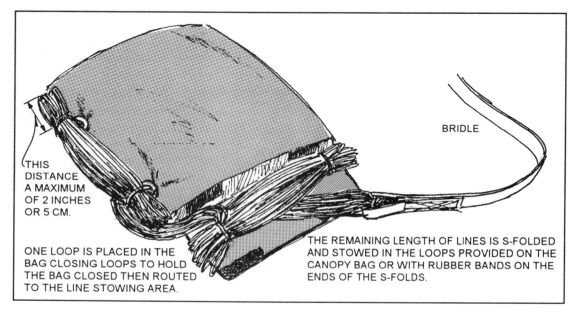

THIS DISTANCE A MAXIMUM OF 2 INCHES OR 5 CM.

BRIDLE

ONE LOOP IS PLACED IN THE BAG CLOSING LOOPS TO HOLD THE BAG CLOSED THEN ROUTED TO THE LINE STOWING AREA.

THE REMAINING LENGTH OF LINES IS S-FOLDED AND STOWED IN THE LOOPS PROVIDED ON THE CANOPY BAG OR WITH RUBBER BANDS ON THE ENDS OF THE S-FOLDS.

Figure 4-33: Stowing the Lines

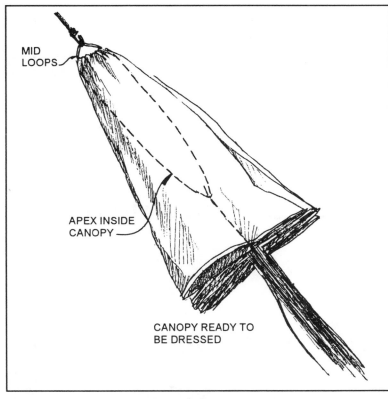

MID LOOPS

APEX INSIDE CANOPY

CANOPY READY TO BE DRESSED

Figure 4-35: Packing a Pulled-Down Apex

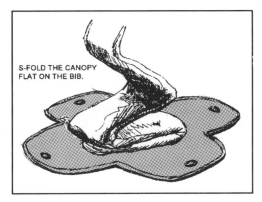

S-FOLD THE CANOPY FLAT ON THE BIB.

Figure 4-34: Bib Container Packing

✓ *Pulled Down Apex*

▶1. Locate the loops midway down the canopy and tie them together consecutively with a line. Pull the apex down through the canopy and tie off this mid-loop line to stretch the canopy (figure 4-35).

▶2. Follow the steps above from step 3. When flaking the canopy, have an assistant at the top inserting an arm in each gore to straighten the upper part of the canopy. After flaking, proceed as above.

Pro Tip: Each time you repack your parachute practice throwing it in as realistic a situation as possible (hang in a control bar). Then air it out for at least 24 hours before repacking.

PARACHUTE USE

We hope you never do. But just in case, it's smart to practice deployment every time you repack. Try to simulate a real emergency as much as possible for some valuable insights. Here is an outline of deployment steps.

Using your parachute for a cushion is like using your sail for a table cloth. Don't expect it to work well for its intended use once it has done double duty.

Throwing a chute

1. Don't hesitate. It's better to use it than loose it.
2. Look at the handle (with a rocket deployment *pull* the handle and go to step 7).
3. *Reach* for the handle.
4. Extract the chute by pushing down away from your chest (any other direction is more difficult).
5. *Look* for an opening in the wreckage.
6. *Throw* it mightily in the direction of the turn.
7. Pull it back and rethrow it if it hasn't extended the bridle. Jerk it hard if the bridle has extended but the bag remains closed.
8. Once deployed, stand on the base tube and let the glider take the landing shock if possible. The emergency isn't over until you're safely on the ground.
9. If hostile terrain awaits you, try to steer by moving on the glider.
10. If high winds are carrying you be ready to cut the bridle with a hook knife.
11. Once you're safely on the ground send your parachute manufacturer a bouquet of flowers and details of your deployment so they can improve their product.

PARACHUTE CARE

Parachutes are made of nylon for the stretch, strength and flex properties of this synthetic material. Nylon is very sensitive to ultraviolet rays, so keep it out of sunlight. Also avoid dampness for mold thrives on nylon. To clean your chute use a very mild soap and warm water. Rinse it thoroughly and let it dry just as thoroughly in the shade (inside preferably) any time it is wet. Don't sit on it (!) for such compression can make the canopy reluctant to deploy. Keep your parachute out of the hot sun as much as possible and never transport it in a car trunk next to a hot exhaust or in a pickup bed above a hot catalytic converter.

VI - MISCELLANEOUS EQUIPMENT

Other sundry items are important to our safe and effective flying. Here is a list for the well-outfitted pilot.

Radios:

- *Let you share the flying experience in real time.*
- *Bring help in emergencies.*
- *Get you a retrieve in an out landing.*
- *Turn you into a broadcasting blabbermouth if you're not careful.*

FULL-FACED HELMET

These helmets are becoming more popular because they have tremendous advantages. The Kevlar ones are lighter than older helmets, they provide more peripheral vision (important in traffic and looking for thermal signs aloft) and more protection. The drawbacks? You can't see your parachute as easily, your perception of wind noise is altered, you can't kiss your honey goodby and you can't expectorate (spit) or play a harmonica aloft. In our opinion the benefits far outweigh the drawbacks and they can save you a whopping dental bill.

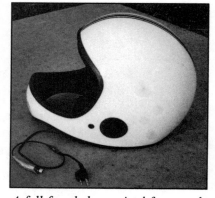

A full-face helmet wired for sound.

RADIO

Radios have become so common in hang gliding that we almost don't need to mention them. FM radios are the only way to go. They have caught on with the public so we highly advise you to get your license which allows you to find your own clear channel. Upgrade this license and you can use your radio like a phone anywhere you land as long as a repeater is within range. We suggest buying the more versatile (and expensive) type if you can afford it for they extend your capabilities tremendously. Other pilots or dealers can show you brands and prices.

Additions to your radio that are well worthwhile are the use of an in-harness coaxial antenna and a finger push-to-talk extension. The former expands your range considerably and the latter when used with a mouthpiece allows you to talk without taking your hand off the bar. Contact your radio buff fellow pilots to find out how to wire these setups. Also you may wish to keep a whip or telescoping antenna in your harness to put on for more range once you are on the ground. Finally, a spare battery pack preferably accessible in flight, is a wise adjunct to your radio. Note: Vox activated microphones (VOX) systems are taboo because they turn on with wind noise and allow a jabbering pilot to jam up the channels

Rechargeable nicad batteries need special treatment. They must be totally discharged occasionally or they take on a memory and will never receive a full charge. As a result they only work for half an hour or so. Every once and a

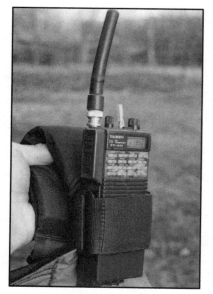

A typical two meter FM transceiver ideal for hang gliding.

while you should give them a "deep discharge". To do this turn on your radio for 10 hours or more after giving the batteries a full charge. Give the batteries another full charge and repeat the discharge process. After a couple treatments like this your batteries should be back to normal. You can discharge your batteries quickly after a flight for a nighttime recharge by turning the squelch all the way down and the volume all the way up. A recharger that fits in your car cigarette lighter is a necessity if you are traveling.

OXYGEN

When flying in the high desert you'll need oxygen or you'll jeopardize your fun and safety. Various systems are available and we suggest you call a reputable company to see what they offer. There are many tank sizes to choose from and several delivery systems. Generally you need one liter per minute at 18,000 feet and less at lower altitudes (Chapter 13 considers medical factors) so judge your capacity accordingly. Tanks are made of steel, aluminum or carbon fibers. Their weight and prices vary accordingly. An oxygen system isn't cheap, but should last a long time with proper care.

Oxygen use will keep you warmer, improve your vision and sharpen your decision-making at altitude.

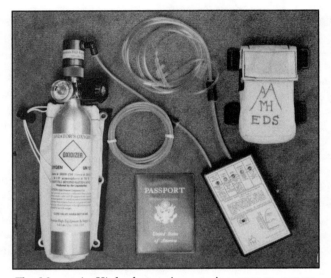

The Mountain High electronic metering oxygen system.

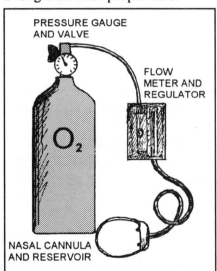

Figure 4-36: Oxygen System

You should get a pressure gauge on your tank and a regulator to adjust the oxygen flow. An electronic metering device is available from Mountain High Equipment which deliver the precise amount you need at every altitude. You may use a mouth tube or a nasal cannula and reservoir arrangement to save oxygen. All tubing should be designated oxygen safe. These items are shown in figure 4-36 in a typical setup.

Medical oxygen is especially filtered and is expensive. Most pilots use oxygen purchased from welding shops for a low price plus a deposit for the canister. This has proven safe over the years. However, filling your own oxygen requires some care. A slow fill is necessary to keep heat from building up in the process. Also, care to avoid overfilling is mandatory. These tanks can become lethal missiles if they break a nozzle. CAUTION: Never use oxygen near an open flame (cigarette or pilot light) and never use any type of petroleum lubricant on oxygen fittings as it will burst into flames when exposed to the gas. That goes for sun-tan lotion on you hands as well.

OTHER GEAR

Here are a few more items recommended or necessary for safety and performance.

STEEL CARABINER - These should come standard on harnesses, but they don't, so you should

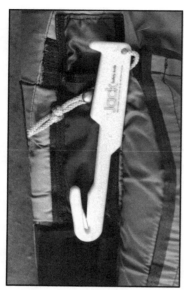

A hook knife is a necessary safety device when flying over water or towing.

The standard steel carabiner.

get one. Sure, aluminum is lighter, but it doesn't stand up as well shock loads and can be damaged if it receives a sharp blow. Wise rock climbers replace their aluminum carabiners if they drop them. A steel 'biner is a great confidence builder and stops the dangerous practice of using two carabiners (imagine unhooking in high winds with two 'biners).

HOOK KNIVES - Hook knives come to us from parachuting and they have great use for emergency situations. They are made to hook webbing or lines and cut them efficiently. Some uses include cutting away from your hang straps when landing in a tree, water or power lines (yes, it's been done), cutting out from a harness or cutting a parachute bridle when you are going for a drag in high winds.

SMOKE BOMBS - When you fly into strange country in unknown or L&V (light and variable) winds, a smoke bomb gives you that extra little bit of security. They come as tiny canisters that attach to your downtube or harness. When you pull them off and drop them they spew orange smoke that drifts with the wind for a minute or so. Get them from most any hang gliding shop and be sure to retrieve the spent canisters.

MAP HOLDER - Cross-country pilots need to know where they are going (or intend to go) which requires a map and thus a holder. You can make one out of clear plastic and Velcro or tape, or you can buy one ready-made. Ask your dealer.

CAMERAS - Cameras are necessary for photographing turn points in competition (at least until we get recording GPS systems that will record our position) and fun to use otherwise. We cover their role in competition in Chapter 10 and fun photography in *Hang Gliding Flying Skills*.

SUMMARY

We have covered the spectrum of hang gliding equipment from gliders to incidentals. The choosing and using, caring and wearing of our flying "stuff" is as much a part of flying lore as skills and techniques. The main point to understand is that hang gliding is an *individual* sport and each *individual* must select the right glider and harness suited to his or her unique needs.

When your equipment is working for you, nothing can be finer. You become one with your wings and truly climb to the top of the world. Once you reach this pinnacle maintain the high by maintaining your high gear.

Excelling in Thermals

Achieving your first thermal flight is a rite of passage equivalent to getting your first kiss, your first car and your first... well, never mind. It seems as if a light turns on that first time which illuminates the whole process and from that time onward we are changed individuals. Mind you, we're a bit sloppy and inefficient when we begin to thermal, but our enthusiasm for getting high in warm air bubbles is unbounded.

With time and practice we get better. However, that there is always room for improvement is in evidence almost every day a group of pilots are out flying. There is always one pilot on top. Generally this is due to superior thermaling skills. We propose here to give you the key to unlock those skills within your own store of lore and experience. This is the first step toward cross-country and competition flying. The top pilot might as well be you.

I - EFFICIENT THERMALING

Effective thermaling doesn't just mean coring skills, but finding the lift and avoiding the sink as well!

By the time we have reached the intermediate level we have no doubt wrestled with many a thermal. Each one had its unique characteristics and potential lift. Our goal is to fly all types of thermals effectively and extract every possible hair of altitude.

ENTERING A THERMAL

When we encounter a thermal we have to make two quick decisions: is it big enough to turn in and which direction do I turn? The answer to these questions depends on a number of factors and the right decision can make a big difference. Many times we have been flying with other pilots, felt a nudge of lift, tried to turn in it and ended up losing more than the others who continued on. We probably can never totally eliminate this floundering in "fool's lift", but we can reduce its rate of successfully baiting us.

✔ When to Thermal

In Chapter 3 we saw that different bank angles produce different circling radii as well as different sink rates. The tighter we circle, the greater our sink rate so a smaller thermal needs to be stronger than a large one to make it worth our while. Figure 5-1 is the graph of the thermal size vs strength needed for zero sink on an average hang glider (wing loading 1.6).

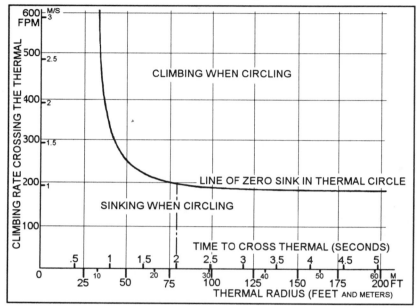

Figure 5-1: Judging Thermal Strength

We must learn to judge thermal strength and size to know when to 360 and when to merely slow down in lift.

More important is the *time* it takes us to cross a given size thermal which lets us judge its size. The time scale shown in the figure is for a moderate 27 mph flying speed. We are assuming light conditions here so we are not stuffing the bar between thermals. As an example, from the graph we can see that if we register 200 FPM for 2 seconds when going straight we can circle and find zero sink. It is apparent from the figure that lift lasting less than about one second (when flying at this speed) is too small for profitable circling.

Of course thermals vary in strength across their width and we may not be heading directly across their center. But this illustration helps you to picture the situation in your mind. *The important thing is to develop an internal sense of how much strength for how long is necessary for a profitable 360.* You can begin to learn this judgement by counting seconds as you enter a thermal and see how many seconds of straight flight are needed for different strength thermals.

Another thing to help you in this decision making is past success on the day. Thermals are remarkably similar in a given period of a few hours and what you found with the last one in terms of thermal strength, size and surrounding sink will probably relate to the next one.

✔ In Strong Thermals

The above discussion applies in weak or scratchy conditions. In stronger lift we often reject the weak stuff so the question is how strong is strong enough. This again is answered by your immediate past experience (the last thermal strength) and your understanding of how thermal strength increases with the day's progress to typically peak at 2:30 PM (local sun time) and dwindle thereafter (a complete discussion of thermal lifestyles appears in our weather book, *Understanding the Sky*). If you're flying to get high the absolute strength is less important than if you're racing for distance. However, as we see later, only the strongest thermals reach the highest.

Flying fast to find thermals should only be done if the thermals are very strong, other gliders (or birds) are marking them or, obvious ground sources exist. The reason for this is the faster we go, the less sensitive we are to the true nature of a thermal when we run over it. As explained in Chapters 4 and 7, a total energy variometer can solve this problem and allow us to fly an efficient speed-to-fly.

➤ **Pro Tip**: On days with small or elusive thermals, waiting to judge the size of a thermal will lose it. You must turn steeply at the first sign of lift and settle into the core immediately.

✓ *Turn Direction*

Some pilots have no decision to make here for they always turn in the same direction. This is not desirable, of course, for it is inefficient in some conditions. Given an ideal ambidextrous pilot, here are the rules:

Turning Direction Rules
1. Turn toward the direction of the lifted wing, or:
2. Turn away from the ridge when turning low.
3. Turn into the wind when close to the terrain.
4. Turn in the same direction as others already in the thermal.

We assume that we enter a thermal slightly off center most of the time. If so, one wing will be in more lift as shown in figure 5-2. To immerse ourselves in that better lift we turn toward it; that is, to the lifting side.

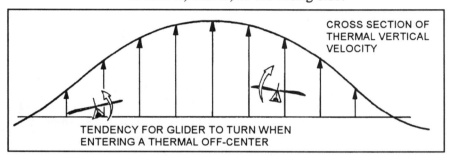

Figure 5-2: Turn Caused by Entering a Thermal

It should be clear that sensitivity to your glider is important in light thermals or when you are on the nether edge of a thermal. Gripping the bar too tightly can eliminate this sensitivity . (Of course a tight grip in a rugged thermal may be necessary for control.)

Again, you must develop a sixth sense as to which direction to turn. When you get really good this will happen almost automatically—you'll feel lift and turn in the appropriate direction before you are conscious of a decision.

This flying by automatic pilot is like reaching a transcendental plateau where your body takes care of the physical demands and your mind is free to contemplate other matters like where's the next thermal. There is nothing mystical about this process for it is merely a culmination of lots of practice and letting your right brain do what it does best: consult the subconscious and think in patterns. All expert pilots enter this thought mode.

"To utilize lift effectively a pilot must be able to look ahead and make decisions while thermaling."

— Chris Arai, U.S. World Team Member

Sometimes a strong thermal serves notice of its presence with a jolt on one wing that turns you handily from it. Modern technique dictates that you gain airspeed and turn into the thermal directly. A 270° turn to come around the other way invariably wastes time and altitude.

Always turn towards the lifted wing, event if you get locked out.

Often you will be tempted to change your thermaling direction, especially if you begin circling to your "poor" side. Generally, you should resist this temptation, for frequently you lose altitude if not the thermal altogether. If a core is off to one side, we suggest you shift your circle over, as described in the next section, rather than reversing your circle. That said, we will state that reversing your circling direction can be a faster way to core an elusive thermal than waiting a full 270° to shift over to a core beside you. In fact expert pilots do this frequently in conditions with bubbly cores (out of traffic, of course). However, judging where the core is takes some practice and until you develop that judgement it's best to be a one-way winger.

Pro Tip: In windy conditions thermal cores are further from the thermal border in the upwind and downwind direction.

CENTERING IN A THERMAL

The pilot flying for efficiency must learn to center quickly and accurately. Figure 5-3 shows how this is done with the shading indicating stronger lift. Pilot I enters the thermal from the side, feels the left wing lift, slows down and banks to the left at point A. He or she finds the core is strong so tightens the turn to maximize climb rate.

Imagine where a thermal is at all times for a good connection.

Pilot II enters the thermal through the center, feels no lifted wing so waits for about a 2 seconds count and turns left at B. He records diminishing lift so continues his circle around to open it up at C after 270° then tighten it again when the lift increases at D. He essentially ends up in the same circle as pilot I, but it took him longer. He could have been more efficient if he had produced a tight circle (steeper bank) immediately at B.

These two examples point out the two principle methods of centering in a thermal: the *270° correction method* and the *varying lift method*.

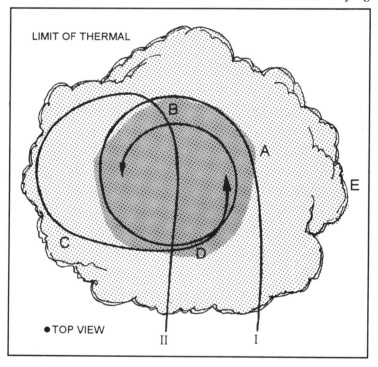

LIMIT OF THERMAL

●TOP VIEW

II   I

Figure 5-3: 270° Method of Thermal-Centering

✓ *The 270° Correction*

Pilots learning to core will find the 270° method easiest to perfect. To use this method mark the point in your circle where the best lift was encountered by noting some object on the terrain as point E in figure 5-3. Now when you come around your circle to aim at this mark 270° later, open your circle up (point D). Hold the lesser bank for a second or so then tighten back up to continue your original circle size. Note how the circle has been shifted toward the core.

You should apply this correction repeatedly until you are perfectly centered—the vario reads the same all the way around. Also be aware that as thermals move around you should continue to correct. With practice you should be able to center in the core with only one 360 by learning to judge how much to open up your circle at the 270° point.

✓ *The Varying Lift Method*

The 270° method is slower than the varying lift method. In this latter case we follow the general philosophy of banking steeper to tighten our circle when lift diminishes and opening our circle when lift increases as shown in figure 5-4. However, lag in vario report and glider response requires that we anticipate these changes in lift rather than wait for them to occur.

With this method we apply timing according to the type of thermals the day is offering. Tight thermals warrant right-now response which means we tighten our turn as soon as we feel increasing lift for if we wait for decreasing lift to alter our turn it will be too late. Also, a glider responds better in increasing lift than it does in diminishing lift or sink. Broader thermals let us pause a second or two to note the best lift then turn around it. Ideally this method settles you into the core with your very first circle which is only possible if you judge the core size accurately and turn at the right time.

Accomplished pilots use both methods with equal skill. Most of the time these thermal centering techniques take place unconsciously. Only erratic thermals require their full attention in order to continuously stay in the best lift to squeeze out the best climb. This thermal centering skill is, in fact, one of the main attributes of aerial experts. Until you reach this plateau, the important thing is to feel the lift variations with your body, listen to what your vario is saying and form a mental picture of where lift lies.

From the above discussion we can form a game plan for centering in thermals:

Centering is not a one-time affair—we constantly consider adjusting our circle in all thermals.

Thermal Centering
1. Center first with a steeper turn *then* adjust to the most efficient speed and bank angle.
2. Turn to the side of the better lift as soon as you detect it in smaller thermals.
3. If you do not experience uniform lift throughout your circle, tighten the circle as soon as lift diminishes, then open it when lift increases. Alternately, open your circle momentarily 270° past the point of best lift.
4. If lift is narrow, turbulent or increases, tighten your turning radius (most beginning thermal pilots use too little bank).
5. Continuously adjust your bank angle and speed to maintain the highest climb rate on your vario.
6. Experiment to find out control timing for different shots of lift.

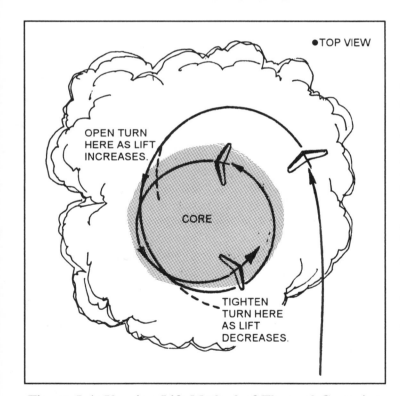

Figure 5-4: Varying Lift Method of Thermal Centering

To maximize your use of a tricky thermal, constantly remind yourself to concentrate.

✓ How much Bank Angle

The question often arises "how much to bank in a thermal?" The answer, of course, depends on the size and strength of the thermal. As we saw in Chapter 3, each thermal has a specific bank angle for a particular glider and pilot combination. So we can only be vigilant to bank the amount that provides the best climb as indicated by our vario and our performance compared to fellow climbers of the feathered or Dacroned ilk.

Generally, we use a 20° to 40° bank in 90% of all thermals encountered on this planet. Greater bank angles are used only for desert boomers strong enough to carry up Gila monsters and pack rats. Banks less than 20° are for those convergence zones or evening thermals that are mere warps in the airflow. In any case it's better to star out with too much than too little bank for control and quick centering.

✓ Difficult Thermals

Weak, small, elusive, drifting and multiple-core thermals all present special problems. When they are small or hard to find the best technique is to bank steeply as soon as lift is detected. This requires a certain amount of initial speed for adequate glider response. Nelson Howe is a master at just this practice and he uses it frequently in tricky conditions to great success.

Weak thermals can be those that offer less than zero sink rate to 100 FPM or so. If they are wide they should be flown with a minimum bank angle at minimum speed. If they are small we must bank tighter. At some point they will be too small to remain inside and still

Catching a narrow or small thermal requires a quick, steep bank.

climb. When this is the case we change tactics and perform a wider circle so that 2/3 or 3/4 of the circle is in lift. We may get a net climb in this manner.

Elusive and drifting cores are a result of wind or variations in thermal strength as pulses of lift pump upward. The way to handle such "movable feasts" is to *constantly be aware of the necessity to center.*

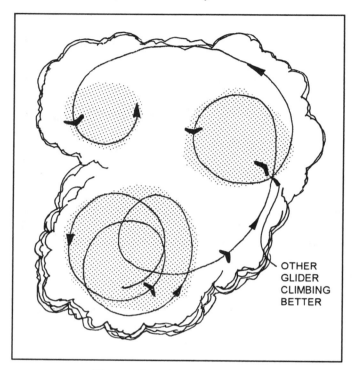

Figure 5-5: Multiple Cores

Multiple cores present a problem: which one do you work? If other gliders are around marking other cores you can watch them to see who climbs best. Be warned that occasionally you'll leave a reasonable core to go to a better climb and not find anything! This will have you spouting language saltier than whale tears.

If you know multiple cores are common on a given day, you might explore around a bit before committing to one particular core. However, any reasonable climb should be utilized if it's within 70% of the expected maximum, for the altitude you lose searching will be hard to make up with a better climb unless much altitude is to be gained.

Sometimes multiple cores turn on and off so it pays to center in one for a while then widen your turn to take in a better a better nearly one, then move again. Usually you can't do this unless other gliders or birds are showing you the lift (see figure 5-5). In any case you should use the same centering techniques when you find a core. The secret to success here is careful observation of other pilots and an awareness of how long a given core pumps.

✓ *Thermal Changes*

A thermal typically changes behavior as it rises. Near the ground a general inflow occurs as the thermal picks up warm surrounding air and consolidates as shown in figure 5-6. Later most of the currents are vertical, then higher still, if you rise near the top, outward flow and possibly turbulence are encountered. The size also changes generally, with the higher part of the thermal being wider.

What all this means is that the thermal is easier to center in the column area (unless it is not fully formed) and becomes more difficult at the very top. The outward flow at the top of a thermal may require a steeper bank angle, but its wider extent may alter this necessity. The main thing to understand is that the top of a thermal may be choppy and all your concentration is needed to stay in the best lift. Often if you fall out of the thermal at this point you can come back to the core and climb back to the glider that are bouncing around at the thermal ceiling, but this isn't always the case. It's better to stay on track.

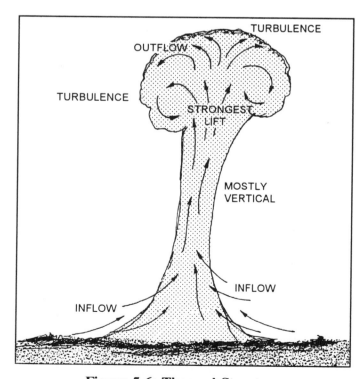

Figure 5-6: Thermal Structure

USING YOUR SENSES

Your feeling and hearing and sight are what tell you where the thermal is. You should *feel* the pitch and G changes that varying lift produces. You should *hear* your vario sing its song of varying climb. You should *see* where you are in the thermal to help you orient your circle alterations. Don't neglect the sense of smell either. I have used farm odors, chemical smells, factory fumes and the reek of a garbage dump to stay with a thermal.

In Brazil the best thing you can do is use a coffee thermal in season. The worst thing happened to me: A dead horse festered for days in a field that I always seemed to reach low on the initial glide from the launch of Govenador Valadores during the 1990 Pre-World Meet. This "dead horse thermal" saved me several times and kept me well informed of its location as it snaked upwards. Had I been a vulture I would have been in heaven, but as it was I experienced waves of disgust and relief when I topped.

Another trick that I learned from Nick Kennedy that truly works is tossing a length of toilet paper overboard when you enter a thermal. This paper climbs at about the same rate as a glider and tends to remain in the core (it doesn't have to circle). Some pilots take off with several pieces rolled and ready for use in a feisty core. Use biodegradable stuff only, please.

Sometimes natural debris is carried aloft to show your thermal core. I once gained 3,000 feet along with scores of dried corn leaves that climbed from the field below. Incidently, they out-thermaled me.

USING YOUR VARIO

You can learn to thermal effectively without a vario especially down low. We suggest turning your instrument off occasionally to better train your sense of feeling. Mounting your vario in the center of your base tube is also recommended so it is easier to see at all times.

With a vario in operation you should learn to work with the lag. A delay of a second or so is not a problem as long as you know when to time the turn. An instant vario usually requires a wait before you turn into a thermal while a slower one demands a turn when it sounds.

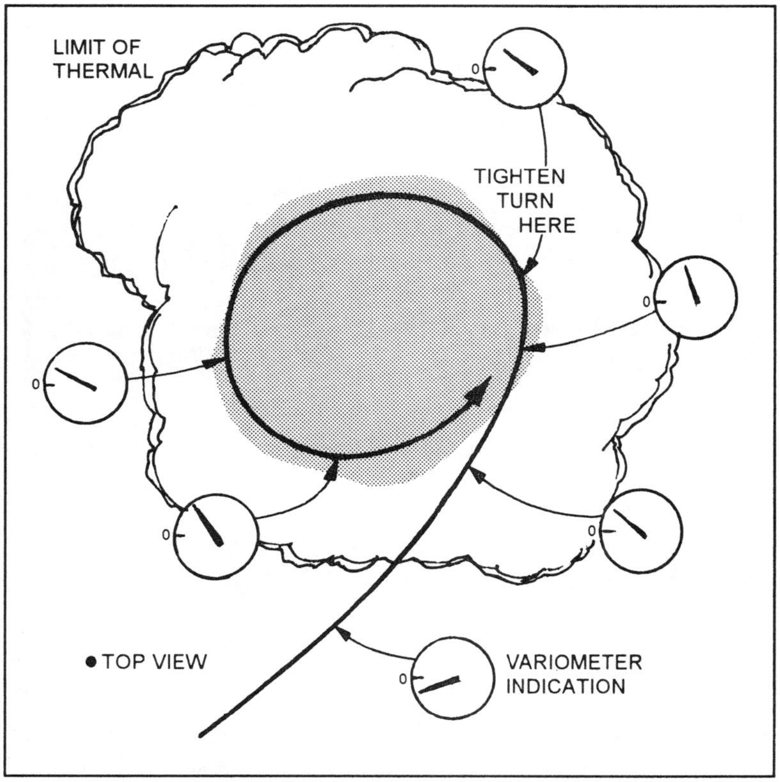

Ideally your vario varies its sound enough so you can tell the difference in as little as 50 FPM change in climb. This allows you to concentrate on coring efficiently by monitoring the sound for the best area of lift. Use your vario to map the lift profile as shown in figure 5-7.

Also you can experiment with changing bank angles to find the best climb. Remember, as we saw in Chapter 3 there is one ideal bank for the current thermal lift. We must be aware that the thermal nature can change and so should our bank angle. We should make continuous adjustments if necessary to maximize climb rate.

When in doubt, bank more steeply. You can always level out. If you bank too flat you take the risk of falling out of the thermal or encountering turbulence at the edges of a rowdy bubble. In general, stronger thermals

Figure 5-7: Mapping a Thermal

are more narrow, but you'll know until you bank steeply in them.

"In the majority of places, cores are small. Most pilots turn too flat and wide and are more likely to be spat out of a thermal."
— Judy Leden, 1989 Women's World Champion and Record holder

PRACTICE MAKES PERFECT _____

Practicing the wrong thing makes you good at the wrong thing!

Nothing could be more pleasing than the prospect of practicing thermaling. But that doesn't just mean soaring 'til you're sore. Floating around on the top floor doesn't necessarily teach you effective thermaling—it teaches you how to stay on the top of a thermal. That's a fine skill to acquire, but it is not of much help for cross-country flying. We need to learn to find cores lower down and use their ride as efficiently as possible. To do this we recommend losing altitude then trying to climb to the top of the stack as fast as you can. Do this repeatedly on a day you're confined to the local pasture. When losing altitude don't just spiral down (unless your fans are on launch), but use this chance to venture away from the given lift to look for other possibilities. Your knowledge of your local site will be the better for it.

Joie Perreault thermaling up under a forming cumulus at Inspiration Point, Utah

When you are going about the business of training yourself to be a better pilot perhaps it's best to explain to others what you are doing. Mark Bennett tells the story about testing the Comet-2 prototype. The test pilots were repeatedly flying out of the lift, getting as low as they dared and thermaling back up through other pilots orbiting at the thermal tops. Two weeks later the factory received a call from a distraught dealer who was having trouble generating excitement about the new glider. It seems that a couple of pilots from the dealer's area had been visiting the test site and went home bragging how they stayed on top of the factory pilots in their new supership at their own backyard!

Here it will serve to summarize the most important points for using thermals effectively.

Thermaling with Sensitivity
1. *Visualize* where the thermal is by forming a mental picture based on your vario readings and feeling.
2. *Feel* for little nuances that tell you where the lift is best or how it is changing.
3. *Concentrate* as you are climbing in an elusive thermal to stay with the wandering lift.

II - FINDING AND DETECTING THERMALS

The air's freight is thermals. Some days the lower atmosphere is loaded with lift and other days we would ransom our soul to feel a puff. Not even an eagle can find lift when there is none, but we can all become more bird-like in our ability to locate lift by being more knowledgeable and more aware.

Seek and surely you'll find is the key phrase in the quest for thermals. Unfortunately we can't see them, only their effects. We form a general plan:

> ### Thermal Guides
> 1. When below about 1/3 of the way to cloud base we use mostly ground sources to locate thermals.
> 2. When above 2/3 to cloud base we use clouds to point out lift.
> 3. In the middle third we use a combination of surface and cloud indicators.

The best vario is another pilot.

Of course, we should always use birds and other pilots at any level. In fact, *there is no vario as good as another pilot.* If that other pilot happens to have a radio and willingly transmits climb rate, you have an almost certain *gimme.*

✓ *Ground Sources*

We have learned that thermals spring from good sources of surface heating. Concrete, dry plowed fields, dry crop fields and desert areas are particularly productive. Local sources of heat such as fires and factory stocks also provide or promote thermals.

Locations with a sharp change in temperature are also surprisingly good generators. These are, for example, the edges of a forest, riverbanks, lake shores, the borders of towns, the edge of snow fields, roads, ridges and cloud shadows.

Pro Tip: When heading out to land, take a detour over possible thermal generators to see if your guesses are correct. You'll be rewarded with more knowledge. When boating on a ridge, park yourself downwind of an expected generator and see how often it releases heat.

To find thermals look for hills, warm ground and temperature contrast.

Damp areas such as irrigated farmland and swamps are generally poor thermal sources. However, large areas of water may develop thermals if the water is shallow and nearby dry areas do not exist. We would think that sand and rocks would create great thermals, but sand has a low heat content and is generally not a good source. On the other hand, rock outcroppings have a great storage of heat. The problem is they take so long to heat up. Consequently they are a good thermal source later in the day and into the evening. Trees, sheltered valleys and sometimes water can be evening sources as well as they release their heat more gradually, especially in light winds.

✓ *The Sunshine Game*

The sun is our engine. Indeed, when the sun leaves we can generally figure we have an engine failure although with ridge lift and residual heat some hope remains. For the most part, however, we depend on sunny areas for thermal production.

Slopes that face the sun are best. If the slope is bare, so much the better. Slopes slanting away from the sun are the worst, especially if they are on the lee side. Slopes that face the sun on the lee (downwind side) can be surprisingly good sources of thermals in light winds for the hill shelters the air mass and lets it heat for a longer period of time.

When clouds abound, patches of sun and shade move across the ground. If the movement is very slow, we look for the sunny areas to be much better sources of lift. If the movement is rapid (say 10 mph or more) the lift will develop over typical sources and triggers. In any case we'll see below that the lift is often better under the clouds rather than in the sunny blue.

✓ *Thermal Triggers*

Thermal triggers are spots on the terrain likely to send up thermals. We deal with these extensively in *Understanding the Sky.* Here we summarize: The best thermal triggers are hills for they initiate an updraft when ground wind encounters them. Other vertical structures such as cliffs, buildings and tree lines can do the same.

When exploiting such triggers, the secret is to remain downwind of the source. The downwind side of fields, tree lines and hills are the places of most likely thermal triggering as shown in figure 5-8.

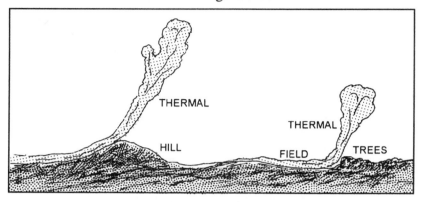

Figure 5-8: Thermal Triggers

I stood on launch at Flynn's in the Owens Valley and watched Rich Pfeiffer sinking out. He observed the changing wind sock in the landing area and constantly positioned himself downwind of a small hill near the field. He was so low we could see his shadow on the ground when he finally found weak lift that turned on to power him up to 14,000 feet. The rest of us were heartily encouraged to take off.

A general upslope to the terrain is better than a flat or downslope in relation to the wind as Brad Koji, 1992 U.S. National Champion once pointed out (see figure 5-9). Anything that raises the air can be thought of as a potential thermal trigger. Convergence zones behind an isolated peak at the interface of different air masses are especially good thermal generators.

Hills and mountains are often thermal fountains.

High ground is almost always better for producing thermals than surrounding lower areas. Of course the low area may harbor volumes of heated air sheltered from the wind, but when it releases it invariably runs up a hill or mountain if such a bump is nearby. The more undifferentiated terrain and air, the more subtle the triggers will be. On the flat desert, a difference in ground cover, a slight rise or even a telephone pole or tower can serve as a thermal trigger.

Figure 5-9: Thermal Production

We often make analogies to help visualize thermal triggering: Imagine the terrain turned upside down as a cave roof. Wherever you expect water to drip from such a ceiling (the hanging points) is where we are most likely to find thermals. Warm air tend to remain on the surface unless something triggers it. This is just like the water suspended on the cave ceiling. If you touch it with your finger it suddenly streams down, taking water in from the surrounding area. Your finger "trigger" initiates the flow just as a trigger on the ground does.

Thermal triggers:
- *Hills*
- *Vertical structures*
- *Hot spots*

Disturbances on the ground and residual gusts in the air can trigger thermals. Sailplanes have been known to swoop the ground to trigger a thermal with their wake, climb back up and blithely circle in the thermal they initiated.

In 1986 I had a driver run up and down the highway in my chase vehicle in Chelan, Washington when I was getting low. Sure enough a thermal released and I was once again on my way. The flying site at Hyner View, Pennsylvania has a railroad track arcing along its base. The regular run of the Pennsylvania Central Line releases a thermal right on schedule!

DUST DEVILS

These short-lived but spectacular denizens of the desert are signs of early thermals. They arise when the air is super heated and a thermal accelerates upward bringing slowly rotating air together in a tight swirl. They are sure indicators of thermals, but are not without dangers. We discuss flying in dust devils in the next chapter and details of their behavior appear in our weather book.

HAZE DOMES

In the eastern United States and much of Europe thermal soaring conditions are brought about by the passage of cold fronts, the arrival of cool air and subsequent thermal bubbling. This weather

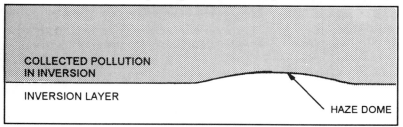

COLLECTED POLLUTION IN INVERSION

INVERSION LAYER

HAZE DOME

Figure 5-10: Haze Dome

takes place under a high pressure system with a gradually lowering inversion layer. Thermals rise to this layer and stop, carrying ground pollution, particulates and moisture. We can often see this inversion layer as a yellowish-brown line on the horizon.

When we are aloft we can also see thermals intruding into the inversion. They lift the layer and produce a haze dome as shown in figure 5-10. Blue blocking sunglasses are particularly helpful in detecting these haze domes. Fly to them as you would to a cumulus cloud and revel in the lift you find while others wonder what sort of voodoo you practice to have such luck.

CLOUD INDICATORS

If there is only one idea you acquire from this book, it should be: *go for the clouds*. We can't emphasize this enough, for "where there's clouds there's lift" is a universal rule. Of course, the lift may be too high, too weak or too far gone for you to use, but with this rule in mind you can start using clouds more effectively.

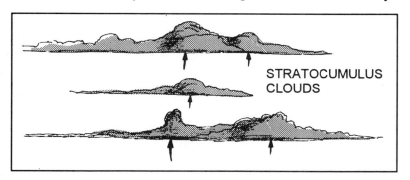

STRATOCUMULUS CLOUDS

Figure 5-11: Lift Under Vertical Cloud Development

Fair weather clouds are our fair-weather friends.

Not all clouds are created equal. Naturally we like the cumulus type as an indicator of thermal lift. However, even stratus (layer type) clouds are created by lifting air and as long as they don't cover the whole sky they can indicate a large area of generally upwelling air that promotes thermal production.

Often the sky conditions are banded with lines of clouds. These can be cloud streets, convergence zones, waves or large scale impulses in the air mass. Whichever the case, more lift is found under the clouds otherwise. Figure 5-11 shows mixed stratus and cumulus clouds (stratocumulus) and how lift is likely to be best under the most vertical development. These types of cloud often appear in general widespread lifting such as near a warm front or when the air is moist so cumulus clouds spread out rather than dry and disappear.

USING CUMULUS CLOUDS

Single cumulus clouds—fair-weather cumulus—are our best ally in the battle to stay aloft. Typically, the sky is one eighth to one quarter covered with clouds on a good cumulus day as shown in figure 5-12. However, only a third of them are active as indicated. Therefore it is imperative that we learn to judge the nature of clouds. In order to do this we must understand their formation and dissolution cycle.

Figure 5-13 pictures how a thermal gradually climbs to the condensation level (dew point) and begins to form a cloud with light wisps. The wisps soon develop into puffs that come together to form a solid base that expands upward and outward. Eventually the thermal feed diminishes and the cloud looses its base definition, finally turning to sink as the cloud dries and cools the air. The sinking air continues for a period after the last vestiges of cloud have disappeared.

Once we can envision cumulus cloud cycles, we can look at specifics to best use the clouds. It is most important to recognize:

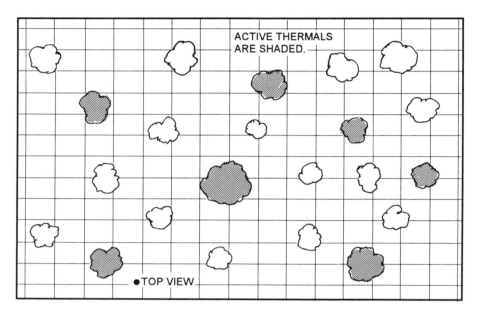

Figure 5-12: Cloud Cover on a Good Day

To Read Clouds Note:
☐ Cycle length
☐ state of development
☐ Areas of best lift

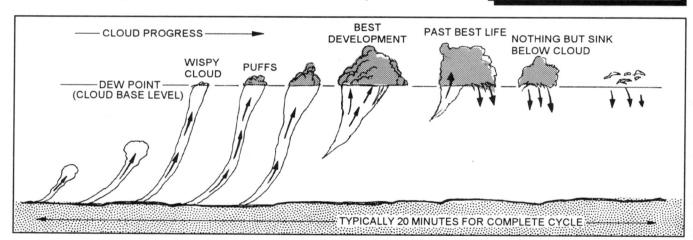

Figure 5-13: Thermal Cloud Cycle

✓ Cloud Cycle Length

Clouds typically have a life cycle of around twenty minutes but can be much shorter lived if thermals are short in weak heating. The cycle can also be much longer if thermals are tall columns or the air is moist. Longer cycles mean you have more time to reach a cloud and find it still working. Longer cycles let you plan farther afield to more distant clouds.

Observing the day as you fly or set up is the best way to get an idea of *cycle length*. However, sometimes you won't know this until you try a few clouds. On short cycle days you must go only for the young clouds or wisps for the others are already dead. The sooner you figure this out, the less time you'll waste floundering in roiled air where a thermal has been.

Pro Tip: As you circle in a thermal watch nearby clouds each time you come around to get a time lapse effect showing their development. This will let you judge the best cloud to head for next.

✓ Cloud Development

The longer the clouds last, the more options you have.

There are many keys to a cloud's *state of development*. These include the shape of the cloud, the growth of the tops, the sharpness of outline, the shape of the base and the color. A building cloud is usually narrower at the top than the bottom (see figure 5-13). When we are high or near cloud base we look at the body of the cloud. Nelson Howe advocates looking at the tops for nice cauliflower shapes, sharp outline and growth. When the edges get misty it's a sign of drying and a reduction in growth.

When we are lower it's best to look at the cloud bases. Flat, dark bottoms with sharp edges are the best bet for active clouds. If you see a concave (upward) base drop everything you're doing and immediately join the cloud—it's overachieving. The concave form is caused by air entering the cloud that is warmer air (and thus more buoyant) than usual. Also, if you see vertical wisps below a dark base go to them for they indicate moister air than normal and are equally extra buoyant.

When you are chasing your tail in a thermal don't forget to check the outside world.

Scraps of cloud around the base are possibly remnants of an older cloud that is being rejuvenated by a new thermal, but most often they are signs of a dying cloud as shown in figure 5-13. Any thermal found under such a cloud is likely to be weak.

Cloud color can change subtly and provide clues to its imminent demise. When a cloud begins to dry the smallest droplets disappear first altering the way the cloud diffuses light. Older clouds are often described as "dirty" with a brownish or yellowish tinge.

✓ Finding the Best Lift

The larger the cloud and the higher its development the better the thermals feeding it. A large cloud may have several areas of lift. The area of darkest base and highest vertical development will exhibit the best lift as shown by the arrows in figure 5-14.

In a wind, especially one increasing with altitude, the best lift is usually on the upwind 1/3 of the cloud since the thermals enter the cloud which then drifts downwind as it dissipates. Sometimes the lift is enhanced on the sun side of the cloud for the sun heats the air directly because visible light is absorbed once cloud droplets form.

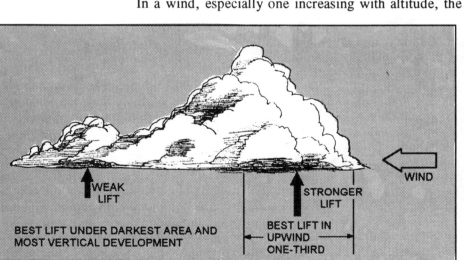

WEAK LIFT

STRONGER LIFT

WIND

BEST LIFT UNDER DARKEST AREA AND MOST VERTICAL DEVELOPMENT

BEST LIFT IN ← UPWIND → ONE-THIRD

Figure 5-14: Best Lift Under a Cloud

Pro Tip: Once you find the area of a cloud that works, go to the same place in other clouds on the same day for the atmospheric conditions that determine the nature of the first cloud will probably carry over to subsequent ones.

✓ Steady-State Clouds

Sometimes sources of plentiful thermals feed a cumulus cloud almost continuously so that the cumulus cloud above it is there as long as thermal production lasts through the day. Even in wind the cloud can appear to be stationary and constant for it always gets replenished on its upwind side while it erodes on the downwind side.

The most likely place for a steady-state cumulus cloud to dwell is above a mountain standing shoulders above the surrounding peaks, or over an isolated cone-shaped mountain. Such features attract warm air from all around them and channel it up their sides for an almost steady updraft to cloud base above their tops. An example of such and abundant lift source adorned practically every day with a steady-state "cap" cloud is Black Mountain in the Owens Valley. One word of warning: because such thermal sources so greedily suck up all available warm air they can, they often suppress thermals for miles around. It is wise to approach such sources with enough altitude to reach the lift above them for often it's impossible to know which side of the mountain is working lower down.

✓ Drifting Clouds — Multiple Thermals

Clouds do not suck thermals off the ground, but they seem to indicate where thermals prefer to rise. We can see this when clouds cross a valley. They often begin to die when they approach a ridge or mountain then rejuvenate as they are fed anew by thermals riding up the ridge. It seems that thermals pass easiest where other thermals have been.

Often you can sit in ridge lift and wait for a drifting cloud to arrive. When it does you find a thermal under it that will take you to cloud base almost as if the cloud was dragging the thermal along. The fact is, in greener areas with a lesser store of heated air next to the ground, it takes several thermals to form a cloud. We should expect cyclic lift production in these areas and judge our positioning accordingly.

✓ Additional Considerations

When using clouds, we can learn a lot about their drift, position, size and cyclic nature from observing their shadows as explained in Chapter 1. Distance to a cloud is particularly hard to discern, so locating its shadow helps answer the "can I make it?" question.

We must be especially wary of the possible growth of cumulus clouds to thunderstorm proportions. Read the techniques for escaping thunderstorms in Chapter 2 of this book and the chapter on thunderstorm judging in *Understanding the Sky*.

A Moyes XS plays in a sky full of beautiful flat-bottomed cumulus clouds

Next we should mention the presence of thermals between the areas of clouds. If you encounter one in the sky where cumulus clouds are scattered, chances are this is a great thermal for it is going to build a new cloud as the older ones die. This is especially true if clouds are of short duration. On the other hand, if clouds are aligned in streets, along a ridge or under waves, thermals between the clouds are almost invariably suppressed and have little chance of turning into boomers.

In any case we ideally want to go to clouds just starting out in life. Unfortunately this may be hard to do for often single thermals produce initial wisps that promise a lot and deliver nothing. In fact, it is extremely difficult to distinguish beginning clouds from dissolving clumps. If we've invested a lot of altitude in getting to these non-productive clouds we can be most disenchanted. OK, downright furious.

Unless you observe wisps becoming more substantial and turning into reliable clouds on a regular basis, it's better to limit your long glides to more developed clouds. A conservative approach finds us gliding only to visible clouds and preferring smaller clouds with a well-defined base rather than larger, older clouds.

BIRDS AND OTHER PILOTS

Observation yields clues to possible elevation.

We have mentioned others in the air. Other pilots including those in sailplanes and paragliders identify thermals. Sailplanes in particular are useful because their range allows them to explore a vast expanse of sky. If they aren't going anywhere in particular they will often play in your thermal then race ahead to show you the next one. We issue a general note of thanks to all sailplane pilots who not only have occasionally offered us "saves", but have pioneered many of the techniques hang glider pilots use. One reminder: a sailplane has a better sink rate but must circle wider. Don't try to duplicate its circle; find the core somewhere within it.

A view of forming and dissipating clouds of low vertical development in Colorado

When you see other hang glider or paraglider pilots thermaling, be aware of differences in efficiency. If you know the pilot is better than you and the climb doesn't look all that great, perhaps you'd better stay put. On the other hand, if you are better at thermaling (you know when to bank up in a core) you should expect a better climb rate. In Chapter 6 we learn how to best work into a gaggle and in Chapter 8 we see how to "read" a gaggle for indications concerning the nature of thermals.

Birds are good indicators of thermals because they find everything. The type of bird is somewhat important. Hawks are better thermal markers than turkey vultures because the hawk's climb rate is less than the turkey vulture's. My favorite thermal marker is the black vulture because it has about the same sink rate as a hang glider and is *always* in the best core. However, use judgement:

> *"Birds in a vertical gaggle are a good sign of lift. Birds in a large group are merely milling about eying a succulent carcass."*
> — Chris Arai, U.S. World Team member

Swallows and swifts, as mentioned earlier, fly in the best lift because that's where insects are carried aloft. Even though they flap, they linger in the thermals—the best thermals.

Birds are our mentors...but in nesting season they may become tormentors.

Birds of prey are often territorial. Sometimes when you join them in a thermal they become disgruntled, and showing superior performance, they climb above you and attack. Usually only the larger birds actually carry through with air strikes and fortunately they tend to hit the leading edges where they expect to do the most damage—after all we are simply overgrown gaudy eagles—but actually do the least. However, they can rip your leading edge, and if you don't want to sustain damage it's best to leave a thermal or area inhabited by such a cranky bird.

Once in Australia I heard sounds like children playing when I was thermaling. My error was soon rudely pointed out to me when my glider thumped under the attack of a screaming wedge-tailed eagle (similar to a golden). He had ripped other gliders in the area, so after another near miss I decided it best to preserve the pristine leading edge of my borrowed glider and resolved to head for a more hospitable neighborhood. Before I could do this the eagle dove at my right wing. I dodged mightily with a vigorous left turn which caused my right wing to rise and smack the eagle. He did two loops and a flutter before he recovered then gently rose to my altitude. I swear he gave me the most surprised look ever registered on a bird, then peeled off to nurse his pride. I went on to thermal in peace and no other pilot had a problem with him at the site.

Often a thermal offers hints to its presence through an increase in sink or turbulence. Figure 5-15 shows how sink is typically greatest around a thermal and lessens elsewhere. Also turbulence around the thermal border tends to be characteristically vigorous in an otherwise fairly smooth sky.

There are exceptions to this, of course, for sometimes turbulence lingers after the useful lift has departed and we are left to deal with the garbage. Also, dollops of sink can develop that aren't near a particular thermal and sucker us into searching. Many a time we can remember our vario pinned to the bottom of the scale while we waited with mounting despair for the sink to end and a booming thermal to sweep us upward. Often it does, but sometimes our despair turns to disgust as we are left groveling low and out of luck.

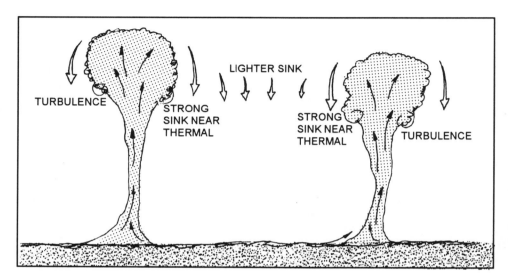

Figure 5-15: Thermal Clues

There is some judgement involved with this hand that nature deals us, for we can learn to sense the sink and turbulence to a certain extent. Usually the sink near a thermal changes in character as we progress. That is, it gets worse then gets better. Learn this nature yourself by carefully observing what happens as you approach a thermal. Sink between streets (whether they are visible or not) or some other more or less organized condition tends to be longer lasting than that around a thermal. The turbulence that announces a good thermal usually has as much up gusts as down gusts and is short-lived. If you encounter lasting turbulence you probably missed the thermal and might as well move on.

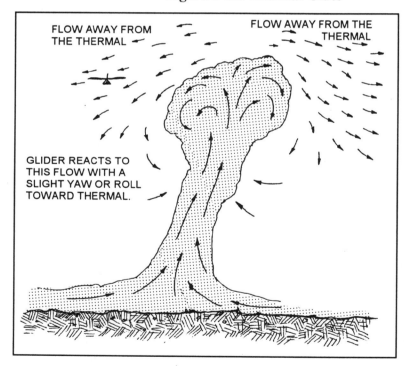

Figure 5-16: Flow Around a Thermal

In lighter thermal conditions and further away from the thermal there may be a subtle clue that expert pilots use to locate thermals. When a thermal rises it bulldozes air above it out of the way. This air moves horizontally as the thermal passes and it is possible to pick up the message of this disturbance field (see figure 5-16). Small changes in glider balance are the most noticeable effects in this case. With practice and awareness it may be possible to detect thermals further and further away with this method.

Thermal turbulence is a welcome sign of thermals... but sometimes it only signifies where thermals have been

Nonuniform thermals may be moving, broken or multiple. Moving thermals often occur in hilly terrain where different patches of warm air feed at different times to a single thermal thereby altering the thermal with their momentum (see figure 5-17). Multiple cores can result from this action as well. The thermals near Govenador Valadores in the Brazil meet series presented some of the most shifty lift in multiple cores that pilots had ever encountered.

✓ *Shredded Lift*

Broken thermals may consist of little snorts of lift or severe shots that last for several 360s. These conditions often occur when higher winds on the ground break up the smooth thermal feed. Sometimes the thermal is broken because you missed the bus and are on the train of residual turbulence beneath a limited thermal. Occasionally if you persevere in the confused lift you will be greeted by another thermal coming up or your lumpy air will organize into a cohesive core. At times when you rise to the top of a thermal you experience broken lift that can be hard to work. Often a thermal will break apart when it enters an inversion layer.

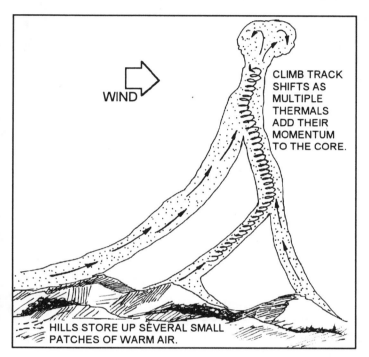

Figure 5-17: Moving Thermals

✓ *Finding the Missing Core*

Whatever the cause of nonuniform thermals, when you lose the core you have to refind it. In light winds the best way to do this is to widen your circle and go into search mode. The instant you hit a burst of lift tighten up and stay with it. At times in a shifting thermal we oval our circle in one direction when the lift diminishes to see if it moved in that direction (see figure 5-18). If not we resume the original circle then try another direction. If we try to make a large hunt circle in this case we may lose the original core that is still working.

In windy conditions, as we will see below, thermals tilt and we often fall out the back. In such conditions, heading into the wind reunites us with the core. Close to the terrain (below 200 feet) where the wind gradient is strongest, the thermal may leave us behind so stretching our circle downwind keeps us centered. The biggest mistake beginners make is underestimating thermal drift. Sometimes thermals are next to impossible to find even though other pilots are climbing in them. This can make you curse fate or take up bowling where the object of your desire doesn't move. In this case the thermal is almost invariably so narrow that you pass it by or has such a short core you're out of luck. The only thing to do here after you've tried a reasonable search pattern is to move on and hope that someone is keeping score so you get the break next time.

When a thermal reaches an inversion layer it often meets up with contrary winds in the inversion. Before you launch if you note cloud drift direction with respect to

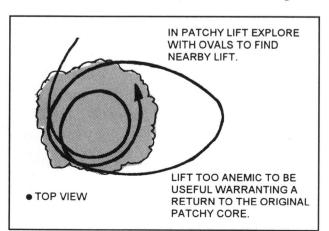

Figure 5-18: Searching for Light Lift

Snaky thermals require great concentration to catch and ride to their upper stories.

ground winds you can get an idea of the way the wind will shear a thermal in an inversion layer. Then when the thermal break apart search for them in the downwind direction of the upper winds (the cloud drift direction). You'll be amazed at how this increases your percentage of found thermals.

We summarizes these ideas here:

Finding a Thermal

1. In moving thermals, explore by making ovals in different directions when lift diminishes.
2. In broken thermals explore by widening your circles then tightening up when you find a burst of lift.
3. In windy conditions search upwind or downwind for a lost core. Thermals are often oval shaped in wind with multiple cores so the upwind and downwind directions are always the best choice. Look in the cloud drift direction for a thermal lost in a shear or inversion.

Only the best cores punch through an inversion layer if any do at all.

III - THERMAL TYPES

Thermal can be bubbles or columns and everything in between, depending on the warm air supply.

$\mathcal{I}$f thermal were all uniform repetition blobs we would all be flying the same glider design and probably be jaded after a few years. Thankfully, every day exhibits thermals of a different character: some mean, some gentle, some big and bounteous, some narrow and stingy with lift. Here we see how to handle all these types.

BUBBLE OR COLUMN?

The long-standing debate concerning the true nature of a thermal is meaningless, for clearly thermals come in all varieties from the merest puff to separate bubbles to columns that last for many minutes and extend to heaven like Jacob's ladder (see figure 5-19). This matter depends on several factors, principle among them being the supply of warm air at the surface available to feed the thermal. Things like the size of heated areas, the angle of the sun, the cloud cover, the wind on the ground and the strength of downdrafts are what determines how much warm air accumulates to emerge as a thermal.

✓ Recognition of Thermal Types

The main point is to recognize the given characteristics of the day's thermals in order to best exploit them. If thermals are tall columns you can expect to find lift well under a cloud or another circling pilot. On the other hand if thermals are short orders we can't

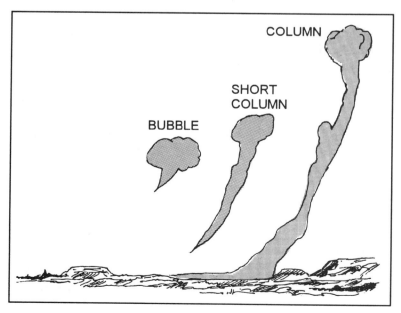

Figure 5-19: Thermal Types

expect to find them useful more than a few hundred feet below another flyer. Most of us have many stories how we flew directly under another pilot and watched a vigorous climb while we were left gnashing our teeth. Once in a while we can recall when the tables have been turned and we climbed a glory in a little bubbles while others suffered directly below.

"You must know whether the day's thermals are bubbles or columns before you dive to them."
— Peter Harvey, British World Team member

Short bubbles can carry us high if we can climb to their top and remain there. However, they must be suitably vigorous. Usually we end up gaining a thousand feet or so then have to look for another. It takes several thermals to step up to cloud base. If the thermals are too rare we lose too much in between them and never achieve great heights.

✓ House Thermals

Most sites have a house thermal—a local semi-reliable source of lift. More blessed sites have a thermal that pumps more or less continuously which is appropriately known as the "service elevator." This usually occurs when rocks or some other well heated surface is surrounded by green—trees or brush—so a circulation is set up, constantly feeding air to be boiled by the baking rocks. Lift of this sort is likely to be rowdy down low because of the unsteady flow, and light higher up. Sometimes such house thermals are cyclic and can be returned to with reliance once you figure out the timing. Watch other gliders in the air to see how frequent and how long a known a house thermal is working on a particular day. Sometimes a house thermal exists near launch and you can learn the timing of its cycles *before* you fly by its effect on takeoff wind. In any case exploring the timing of house thermal cycles is important practice which you should endeavor to do every chance you get on those stay-at-home days.

THERMALS IN WIND

Thermals are hot air balloons that respond to the whims of the air currents. But we also must realize that they have mass and therefore inertia so they cannot react immediately to the changes in the air (see side bar).

This mass is much more than most people realize and a moderate size thermal can weigh hundreds of tons. As a result we often find thermals drifting much slower than the wind speed if they are rising into faster moving air. Thermals tend to carry the velocity they acquired from be-

> *If we are thermaling with a circle of 60 foot radius, the thermal must be at least 120 feet across. This gives a total volume according to the formula for the volume of a sphere, $V = 4/3 \pi r^3$ of $7,238,229 ft^3$. Air weighs .0766 pounds per cubic foot at sea level, so our thermal weighs 554,243 lbs or 277 tons!*

low, so on rare occasions you may even experience them drifting a bit upwind. Many of us have been soaring in strong winds only to find thermals that essentially carry us straight up or drift much less than expected due to their inertia. When a thermal drifts very differently from the ambient air, the upwind side often exhibits the best lift.

There are several common forms thermals can take in wind and we review them here.

✓ Constant Source Thermals

When thermals arise from a trigger and are fed continuously they will become a tilted column in wind as shown in figure 5-20. The thermal shown does not quite achieve the profile of the increasing wind as it climbs.

Such a tilted column may be hard to relate to a ground source or a cloud destination unless

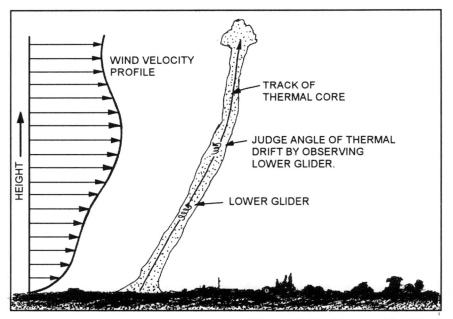

Figure 5-20: Thermal in Wind

some indicator such as other gliders or smoke at different altitudes give you clues as to what the column tilt looks like, as shown in the figure. Once you identify the general tilt angle you can usually rely on this to indicate the placement of other thermals upwind of a cloud or downwind of a ground source until conditions change. Remember, the stronger the thermal is, the less it will be tilted in a given wind profile.

✓ Drifting Thermal Source

Over open, undifferentiated terrain a heated layer at the surface may exist which becomes turbulent in wind and releases thermals randomly. These thermals drift with the wind and show very little tilt because their source moves along with them as shown in figure 5-21. In this case thermaling is about the same as in no wind although you are drifting.

✓ Pulsing Thermal Source

A fixed ground source can give off pulses of thermals if the supply of warm air is limited. This results in a series of drifting thermal bubbles with limited vertical development as shown in figure 5-22. Here each individual thermal acts like the case above. You may miss the tail of one thermal but you can often get the next one lower down as you glide towards the ground source.

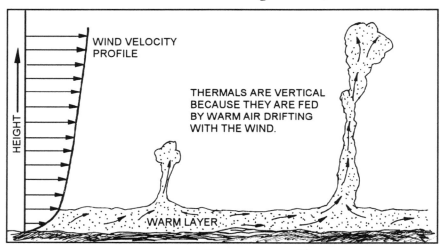

Figure 5-21: Drifting Thermal Source

✓ Using Drifting Thermals

A tilted column thermal (figure 5-20) can often be very difficult to stay in, especially if the tilt angle changes for since you climb slower than the thermal, your angle of climb is always more shallow than that of the thermal. Thus you fall out the rear or bottom as shown in figure 5-23. To remain in such a thermal you must occasionally lengthen the upwind portion of your circle. Again listening to your senses can help you make adjustments to stay in the core.

Very close to the terrain we often have a tendency to lose a drifting thermal by not drifting back enough, especially if landing

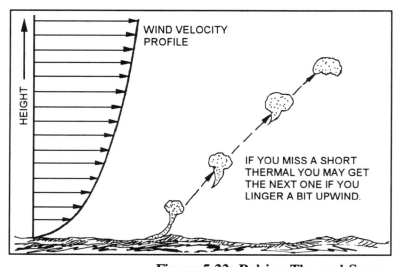

Figure 5-22: Pulsing Thermal Source

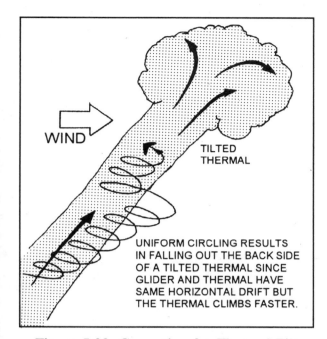

Figure 5-23: Correcting for Thermal Tilt

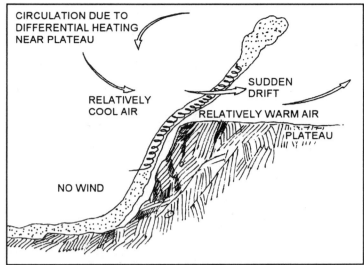

Figure 5-24: Thermal Drift Near a Plateau

possibilities are awful downwind. It takes much experience to know when you can reliably drift back with a thermal and be sure to get up when failure to do so means certain landing amongst the crocodiles and alligators.

Thermals often accelerate downwind once they crest a plateau. I have experienced this at the southwest face in Henson Gap in Tennessee, at Dinosaur, Colorado and at St Hilaire in France. If you aren't ready for this you can loose the thermal as I have. If you *are* ready you may stay with it while it invigorates from the heated air on the plateau as I have also done. Figure 5-24 indicates how a thermal often reacts in the circulation setup at a plateau edge.

CLOUD STREETS / THERMAL STREETS

That thermals often organize in long lines is well-known to the soaring community. The cause of this can be a ground source in wind, a mountain chain or more importantly a condition in the air where an inversion layer limits thermal heights and promotes a circulation creating lines of sink and lift. The latter are true *thermal streets*. When they produce clouds they are known as *cloud streets*.

Of equal importance with a cloud street is the sink street in between the lift streets.

We go into the details of using cloud streets in Cross-Country Flying (Chapter 8). Here we will mention that the time you enter in logbook depends on staying with the line of clouds or lift more when street conditions occur than in a sky with random thermals. The reason for this is that massive sink exists between the streets. The cause and nature of streets are covered in our companion book *Understanding the Sky*.

BLUE THERMALS

A typical blue thermal is shown in figure 5-25. What you see is not what you get, for although you see nothing, sometimes blue thermals—those that occur without producing clouds—are quite vigorous. The reasons blue thermals occur are extreme dryness of the air or more commonly an inversion layer putting a lid on the thermals lower than the condensation level. We explain this matter in this chapter.

Note that blue thermals are not the same as blue holes. The latter occur in the midst of a cloudy sky and is a particularly dismal place to be since it is usually caused by widespread sinking air. With blue thermals lift is generally of moderate strength (it can be strong in

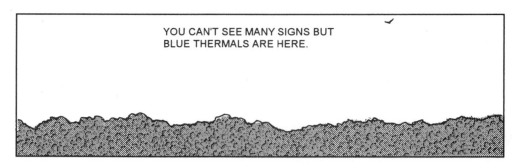

Figure 5-25: Blue Thermals

desert areas, mind you) and distributed as it is when cumulus clouds are present.

It is of course more difficult to locate thermals when you are high with no cloud clues. However, there are the traditional clues to the location of blue thermals:

Finding a Blue Thermal

1. Look for areas that produce thermals on cloudy days.
2. Look for obvious trigger points.
3. Look for visible signs of thermal triggering (moving smoke, trees, grass, dust or debris).
4. Judge the areas that should build up the most surface heat.
5. Judge the possible thermal tilt.
6. Look for circling birds or gliders.
7. Look for haze domes.
8. Expect streeting and search upwind or downwind from your last thermal.

CONVECTIVE BARRIERS AND THERMAL WAVES

We saw above how ponderous a healthy thermal can be. Often as it rises in a wind the thermal deflects the wind so that lift on the upwind side occurs as shown in figure 5-26. Pilots have been known to climb up the *outside* of a cloud in this case much like using slope lift. More often than this barrier lift occurs, however, is the presence of shots of drier air from a different part of a mountain moving up beside the cloud to form a base at higher level. Using this lift requires circling unless the clouds are in a line. I have observed this phenomenon in North Carolina, California, Greece and Brazil above a mountain and in France near a sea breeze front.

A line of thermals rising into a stable layer can create a barrier that produces waves downwind, much like a mountain. These waves will promote other thermals downwind that line up *across* the wind. This can be very baffling to pilots unaware of such an occurrence. The areas of sink in between these lines can be as disheartening as those between true thermal streets.

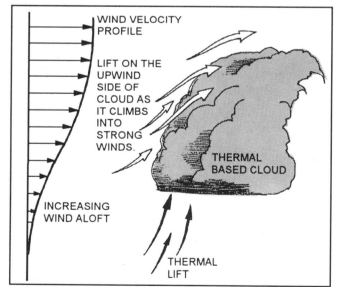

Figure 5-26: Lift From a Convective Barrier

THERMALS IN THE SHADE

When the skies are overcast we often think of clearing out the garage rather than clearing our

Cloud streets in Pennsylvania.

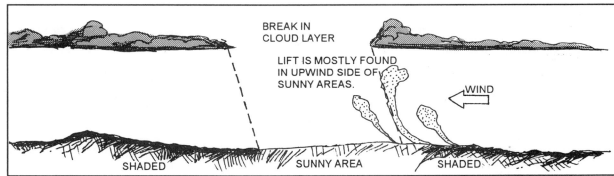

Figure 5-27: Thermals in a Mostly Cloudy Sky

turns, but sometimes thermals are lusty beneath a cloud cover. This is often the case when cool moist air moves over warmer ground. The place to find thermals in these conditions is above known triggers and under dark areas of the clouds. The darker areas correspond to thicker clouds indicating thermal feed.

If breaks occur in the clouds we head for the light like moths. In this case we should search on the *upwind* side of the patch as this is the area heated longest as shown in figure 5-27.

IV - THERMAL THEORY

*I*t is well to gain plenty of experience in thermals. This activity helps our reactions, our sensitivity, our overall thermal skills. However, it also is useful to understand how thermals behave on a more theoretical level as well in order to better fathom what we feel as we go wheeling off into the blue.

THERMAL BEHAVIOR

Most of us know that thermals begin as warm pools of air at ground level that buoy upward like a bubble because they are less dense than the surrounding air. The thermal will keep on rising as long as its cooling due to expansion isn't as fast as the rate of cooling of the surrounding air.

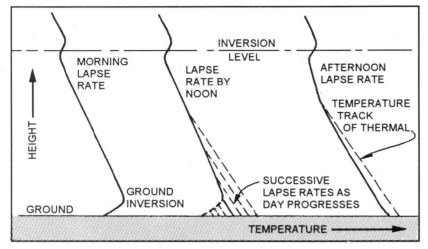

Figure 5-28: Typical Lapse Rates

Since a rising thermal cools at a fairly uniform rate (5.5°F per 1,000 ft) we can say that as long as the surrounding air cools more than that rate the thermal will continue to climb. We call this air's temperature profile the *lapse rate*.

Typical lapse rates are shown in figure 5-28. In the left graph we see a ground inversion (the temperature gets warmer with height) that gradually disappears as the sun heats the ground. Higher up we see an inversion that may eventually stop the thermals. Understanding these terms allows us to discuss thermal behavior (see our weather book for a better understanding of thermal production).

✓ Buoyancy

Thermal buoyancy which determines how fast it rises is itself determined by the height of any inversion present and the rate at which heat is supplied to the surface. The intensity of sunshine and surface type are what determine the heat supply rate.

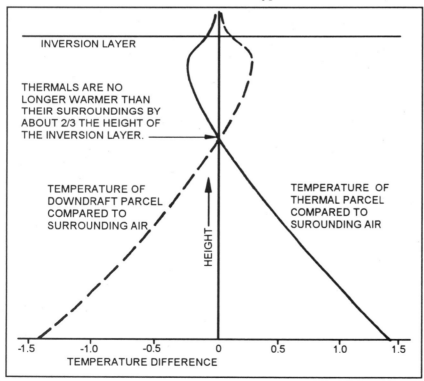

Figure 5-29: Typical Profile of Thermal Buoyancy With an Inversion

We can generalize to say that the higher the inversion layer and the faster heat is supplied, the stronger the thermals. Note that strong thermals exist in desert areas with high inversions. Use this rule of thumb to predict thermal strengths.

In figure 5-29 we see how the buoyancy changes with height for both updrafts and downdrafts (negative buoyancy occurs when a parcel of air is cooler than the surrounding air). The maximum buoyancy is near the ground for both because this is where the temperature differences are the greatest. By the time the thermal is 2/3 of the way to the inversion layer it has lost all buoyancy and becomes cooler than the surrounding air. However, its impressing inertia keeps it rising until drag can slow it down. Note how small the thermal temperature increase is compared to that of the surrounding air (0.15 degrees centigrade).

✓ Thermal Strengths, Spacing and Duration

Thermal buoyancy often comes more from additional humidity in the thermal than warmer temperature. More humid air is lighter.

From experience and theory we know that thermals are spaced about 2½ times their maximum height as shown in figure 5-30. Also, the higher we go the more spread out they are but the stronger and larger they tend to be. The total updraft that comprises a thermal is typically 50% larger in diameter at the top of the thermal than when it first organized at the bottom. Thus a 200 foot thermal near the ground will be 300 feet in diameter at cloud base.

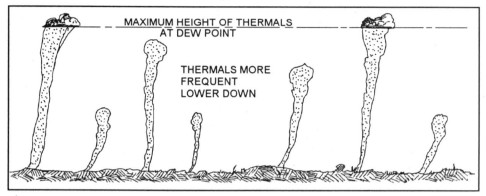

Figure 5-30: Thermal Spacing

In an ideal situation we can imagine how much altitude we will loose between thermals. Assuming we get an 8 to 1 glide in the sinking air, with a cloud base at 16,000 feet we would loose 3,125 feet gliding to another thermal 2½ times the cloud base height away. With a 6,000 foot cloud base we would loose 1,875 feet between thermals and 938 feet with a 3,000 foot base. Of course, lower down even with a high cloud base thermals are more frequent. On the other hand we may miss the next nearest thermal and terrain effects greatly alter the sink and lift patterns. Even so, experience over open terrain seems to confirm these numbers.

The average life of a thermal appears to be close to the amount of time it takes it to climb to inversion level. Thus if the inversion is at 6,000 ft, and the thermal rate of rise 800 FPM, the duration of the thermal will be about 7.5 minutes. Of course, all this thermal won't necessarily be usable by a soaring pilot, but this gives a rough idea of thermal duration.

✓ Up and Down Velocity

Although the average buoyancy is greatest near the ground, thermals gain cohesiveness as they rise and promote the core at the expense of the border areas. Thus the climb rates we experience are different from the buoyancy profile. Figure 5-31 shows a typical *climb rate profile*. Here we see a maximum climb rate at about 2/3 of the way up to the maximum thermal height. After this point the negative buoyancy slows the thermal down.

The case shown is with blue thermals. If good hearty cumulus clouds top the thermals then climb rates max out much nearer cloud base. The extent of vertical development determines how high this maximum occurs. Indeed, with towering Cus we may encounter powerful cloud suck right near the cloud.

The better the clouds appear, the better the lift higher aloft.

The maximum downdraft velocities are found close to the ground. There is no reduction of negative buoyancy as a downdraft approaches the ground like there is a reduction of thermal buoyancy as it nears cloud base. We can see this from the temperature profile in figure 5-29. This fact points out the desirability to stay high when flying cross-country.

Another general rule that is very useful when traveling from thermal to thermal is that the average rate of sink is 20% that of the thermal climb strengths. To see how the numbers work with this rule , imagine we climb an average of 400 FPM in thermals of the day. The true thermal strength is then about 600 FPM if we consider we sink about 200 FPM while

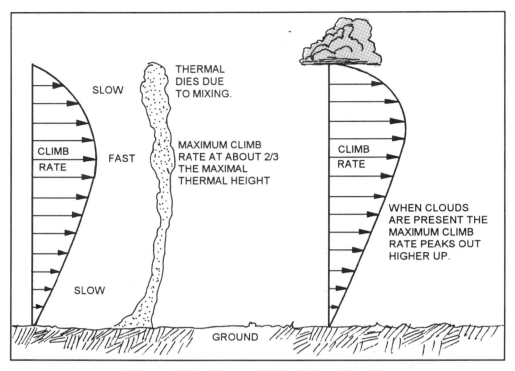

Figure 5-31: Thermal Climb Rate Profile

thermaling. Twenty percent of 600 FPM is 120 FPM which is the average sink we should encounter. If we fly our ideal speed (see Chapter 7) in this amount of sink we get a glider sink rate of 240 FPM for an overall indicated sink of 360 FPM.

The following chart provides the expected indicated sink rate we should see between thermals with various indicated climb rates:

Inter-Thermal Sink					
Climb Rate in Thermal (FPM)	Indicated Sink Rate (FPM)			Climb Rate in Thermal (FPM)	Indicated Sink Rate (FPM)
100	295			600	420
200	320			800	470
300	335			1000	530
400	360				580
	390				650

From the chart we should note that below about 350 FPM climb rates our sinking between thermals is *greater* than our climb rate. Naturally this chart represents an ideal and nature refuses to be so predictable. We'll often see exceptions to these numbers between streets or in blue holes where we would ransom our firstborn for merely 20% sink.

THERMAL DISTRIBUTION

Thermals seem to come in herds. Where there's one there is often two, three and more. Researchers in Australia and elsewhere have found that regular cells of circulation set up over the undifferentiated desert with thermals gathering at the corners where these cells meet. In most places the ground heating is more complicated so thermal distribution is probably

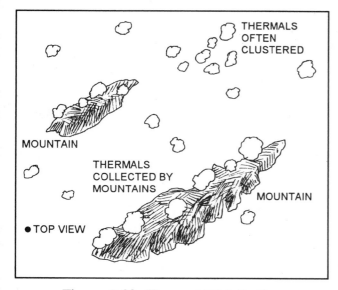

Figure 5-32: Thermal Distribution

complicated as well. Figure 5-32 shows a hypothetical model of thermal distribution affected by two mountains which exhibit the best thermals. In more wind this model would be somewhat altered and indeed the cells would change to streets if an inversion layer was present.

It should be clear that along with the areas of lift are broad areas of sink. In fact they tend to be of greater expanse than the lifting areas, but the lift is generally stronger. If you find yourself stuck in one of these sink areas without a cloud to beckon you it's best to head to the high ground, known triggers or fly 90° to the wind in hopes of going across a narrow sink trough.

✓ *Banded Weather*

We have mentioned banded weather before and it consists of anything from streets to waves to impulses in the air mass to local convergence. The main thing to understand is that generally the bands of clouds are more likely to be areas of thermals than the blue areas. This is true despite the fact that blue areas may be getting more sun unless the cloud areas are so widespread they block the sun for a long time.

✓ *Thermal Shapes*

There have been many studies done of thermals and most researchers have come to the

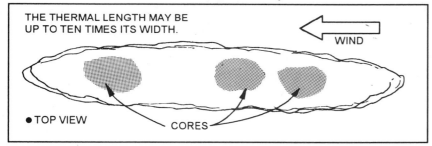

Figure 5-33: Thermal Planform in Wind

conclusion that the planform of thermals in wind are oval-shaped with a length up to 10 times the width. As we see in figure 5-33, several cores may exist in such a thermal and a hang glider is fully capable of remaining in one core. However, it should be apparent that an upwind or downwind search is most likely to produce additional lift.

THERMALS WEST

The West and the East of the United States have entirely different weather and entirely different thermal production. We include all desert areas (Australia, South Africa, southern Europe) in this discussion of the West and all green areas (northern Europe, Japan) in the discussion of the East.

In the West the dry conditions and abundant solar heating almost always produce "hard core" thermals. They are strong, narrow and long lived. Since there is rarely an inversion in the desert the thermals rise to the dew point (condensation) level which is typically 16,000 to 24,000 feet since the air is so dry.

Desert thermals are generally:
- *Strong*
- *Narrow*
- *Long-lasting*
- *Single-cored*
- *Quite high-reaching*

The only times that the thermals aren't vigorous are when haze, dust, smoke, smog or moisture cause stability since the sun heats these particles in the air, thus distributing heat throughout. A sea breeze acts the same way, bringing stable air from the sea inward and suppressing thermals in normally good areas. Near the oceans sea breeze fronts can produce strong thermals at their leading edge as they plow inland. Behind the front thermals are small, punchy and not too abundant.

Because fronts do not visit desert areas on a regular basis (one of the reasons they are deserts), air masses tend to linger for days, weeks or even months on end. This can result in the buildup of haze and various layering effects as thermals distribute heat aloft. In these resident air masses local effects are predominant with upslope winds and valley breezes dictating much of the thermal patterns.

Another important characteristic of desert thermals is the frequent production of dust devils as thermals lift off in super heated air. These dust devils are a sign of a good lapse rate, at least in the lower reaches, and usually signify the early presence of a vigorous thermal. We discuss dust devil flying in the next chapter.

The final point to note about Western thermals is their habit of exhibiting tight cores. This requires steeper bank angles for efficient climbing compared to the fat thermals of moist areas.

THERMALS EAST

The East is characterized by a greener, moister countryside. More clouds are present and thermals are on the average milder, often wider and not as tall as in the West. Typical cloud base in the East is from 5,000 to 10,000 feet. the lower height of thermals is caused by a lower dew point level which in turn is caused by more moisture and the presence of inversions.

✓ Inversion Layers

Moist areas thermals are generally:
- *Weaker*
- *Wider*
- *Short-lasting*
- *Multiple-cored*
- *Of lower extent*

To understand inversions we must realize that air is heated as it sinks. This is because it is compressed due to the higher pressure at lower levels. Under a high pressure system the air continually sinks at a slow rate—several inches per minute. As we can see in figure 5-34, the upper air warms as it sinks while the lower air moves out of the way, thus retaining its temperature profile. As a result an inversion layer is formed because the air is warmed aloft more than below. Thermals are stopped at the inversion layer because the warmer air in the inversion no longer remains cooler than the rising thermal.

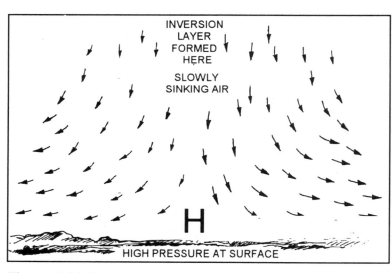

Figure 5-34: Inversion Formed in High Pressure Conditions

When a thermal reaches an inversion layer it is quickly slowed and becomes disorganized. We generally feels this as a sudden diminishing of lift with the addition of turbulence. Sometimes a nice friendly thermal turns ugly at the inversion for such layers are often accompanied by wind shear. Our only hope of punching through an inversion is to find the strongest core available and ride it through all the bucking turbulence—often for hundreds of feet—until it reorganizes. Sometimes we can do this and then remain above the inversion in abundant lift while others struggle below in weak thermals.

Occasionally several inversion layers can exist, usually being caused by the previous day's thermals carrying heat to a given level aloft. In such a case there is often one level between inversions where lift is strongest and he or she who remains there is happiest.

✓ Daily Changes

In most parts of the East the passage of warm and cold fronts occur on a regular basis. Warm fronts bring warm, southerly breezes, humid air and mediocre thermals (as well as imbedded thunderstorms). Cold fronts bring clear air, a cool air mass and generally good thermal conditions. The air mass behind the front is high pressure dominated and thus sinks a bit which dries out most widespread clouds. Thermals press upward through this sinking air and form fair-weather cumulus.

All days behind a cold front are not created equal. The gradual lowering of the inversion layer and the raising of the condensation level as the air mass dries and warms combine to make changes. Let us see what they are in an ideal model.

Figure 5-35 shows how a band of clear air may exist in the strong subsiding air behind the cold front. This may be followed by thermals and the buildup of clouds if considerable moisture remains from the frontal passage. The first day after the front goes through (Day I in the figure), a fairly low cloud base appears but there are high cloud tops as the inversion layer is high. The lapse rate below indicates the high inversion. Some rain may fall if the clouds build into thunderstorms.

High pressure systems bring gradually more stable conditions unless the inversion level lowers to near the ground.

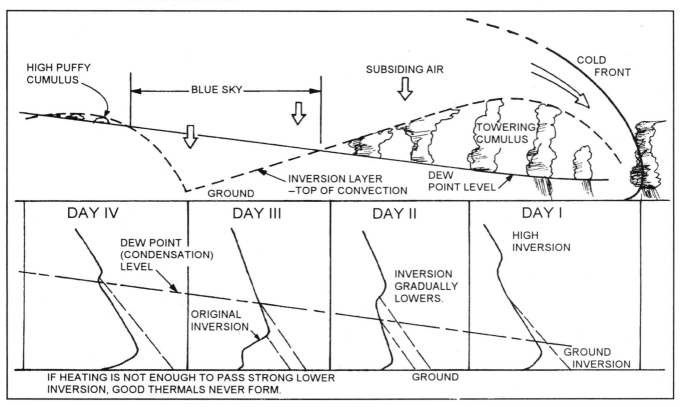

Figure 5-35: Post-Cold Front Conditions

Day II often shows a drying trend with lesser cloud buildup and higher bases. Some spreading of thermal clouds may occur (stratocumulus) as the inversion layer puts a lid on the tops if moisture is adequate. The lapse rate shows a raising dew point and lowering inversion.

Day III may bring a radical change. Here the inversion has lowered below the condensation level and thermals may never rise high enough to form clouds. These are the blue thermal days. The lower thermal heights indicate that conditions do not portend memorable thermals. If the inversion sinks too low, thermals may never develop even with strong heating and pilots are left sitting in their harnesses scratching their heads.

On day IV another major change is apparent. Here the inversion has nearly reached the ground so that the surface heating warms the air and eliminates the inversion as if it was a typical nighttime ground inversion. As the lapse rate indicates, thermals develop and reach a high altitude. These days are the ones that exhibit only light stirrings in the morning then suddenly turn on with cranking thermals in a matter of minutes, while most unstable days show a gradual buildup of thermals to the mid-afternoon peak.

On such a day the thermal height rises rapidly and may meet a new inversion high aloft. This condition continues with a gradually lowering inversion if the high is still active until the next front arrives.

The scenario we have painted is of course just a model. In real life the speed of the front and movement of the pressure system can greatly alter the progression of events. The whole process may take as little as two days or as many as eight. Then too, a trailing secondary front can come bashing through and spoil the whole party. The point is to understand how the overall system works so you can begin to see why different days exhibit different conditions. Eventually with observation and experience you can predict the day's thermal complexion.

SUMMARY

There are at least two ways to gain enlightenment: The most well-known is to sit on a mountain, eat grubs, contemplate your navel and wait for a satori. Another is to sit on a mountain, eat a sandwich, contemplate cloud base and wait for a cycle. We prefer the latter for such a form of enlightenment renders a feast for your senses with unbounded vistas and untold pathways through the heavens. In any event, if the cycle and subsequent enlightenment fails to appear we can always revert to navel contemplation. Forget the grubs.

Thermal soaring has that sort of mystique. We are almost performing an escape from mundane existence as we ride invisible currents to a lofty plane. The limits, the rules and indeed the burdens of the earth seem to depart from us as we enter Never-Never Land in the sky. But magic must be earned to be successful. Only with practice and learning will we be truly able to break our bonds and rise above the natural limits seemingly at will.

There are two facts of thermal exploitation we must perfect: finding thermals and coring them most effectively. The lore has been presented. It's up to you to put it to use in an enlightening manner.

A pilot takes off near Laragne, a prime cross-country site in France.

CHAPTER 6

Advanced Techniques

Advanced skills today are different from those of yesteryear. This is partially due to equipment improvements which require more input from the pilot as they provide more options. In addition techniques have evolved over the years for pilots have experimented out of boredom or necessity. A case in point is the practice of downwind, uphill landings. In this chapter we reap the benefit from these years of improvement.

Learning advanced skills requires that we proceed with caution and judgement. This is because some of the matters we will consider will be closer to our personal limits than those we have previously discussed. It is important for each pilot to exercise judgement when deciding whether or not to add a new practice to his or her repertoire of tricks. Any one of these items will not make you a great pilot. But their sum total provides the background to become a *consummate* pilot.

I - TRICKY LAUNCHES

We are not advanced pilots until we acquire advanced judgement.

*L*et us begin advancing our abilities with the practice that initiates our flights: launching. We covered many forms of launching in *Hang Gliding Flying Skills*. These include crosswind, tail wind, turbulent, flat, calm and windy cliff launches. If you are not well-versed and experienced at these launch variations you should review them now.

As Butch Peachy, US World Team member and winner of the 1992 US League Meet says, *"if you can't take off in tricky conditions you will miss many good thermals."* What this means is not that you should risk staving in on launch but that your launch skills should be impeccable. Here are a few tips to add to those in our novice bag of tricks.

In gusty, turbulent conditions very often launch windows are short, leaving you as nervous as a new nudist. The problem is you don't always know exactly how long the relatively stable periods are. For this reason we recommend the procedures in the box below:

The first step is to let you feel the variations in the air to understand how shifty conditions are. If you can't get 3 seconds of steady flow then you probably don't have a long enough cycle to launch safely.

"He who hesitates is lost."

We recommend putting the glider down, especially when the air is knocking it around, to keep your arms fresh and reduce mental stress. It doesn't help your concentration when you are fighting a live glider. It is always easier to level the wings with the base tube on the ground.

> **Gusty Wind Launch**
> 1. Pick up the glider and hold it to see if you can keep it stable for a *minimum* of 3 seconds.
> 2. Put it down and rest your arms.
> 3. When the wind socks appear steady, pick up the glider and begin running as soon as the wings are level. Do a fast takeoff for control.
> 4. If a wing lifts as you are about to run put the glider down and level it.

Too many pilots wait too long to begin their run. As they wait the glider gets out of whack, they struggle, tire, delay and often miss the cycle. *Pick the glider up, pause (less than one second) and run if the wings are level.* You can even begin your run before you are standing fully erect as long as you sense full glider balance. Keep the nose down to reach top speed for control.

Versatility in holding style provides versatility in launching.

It usually helps to tighten your VG system part way in gusty conditions to take up some side cable slack. But remember you may need good handling immediately after launch so don't overdo it.

✓ Cliff Launches

On windy cliff-type launches the glider often tends to be sucked off the cliff due to the necessary nose-down-into-the-wind attitude. Often this requires a helper on the *tail* cables holding you back. The problem is that the nose-down position puts the base bar at your shins and the glider may feel as if it wants to nose down.

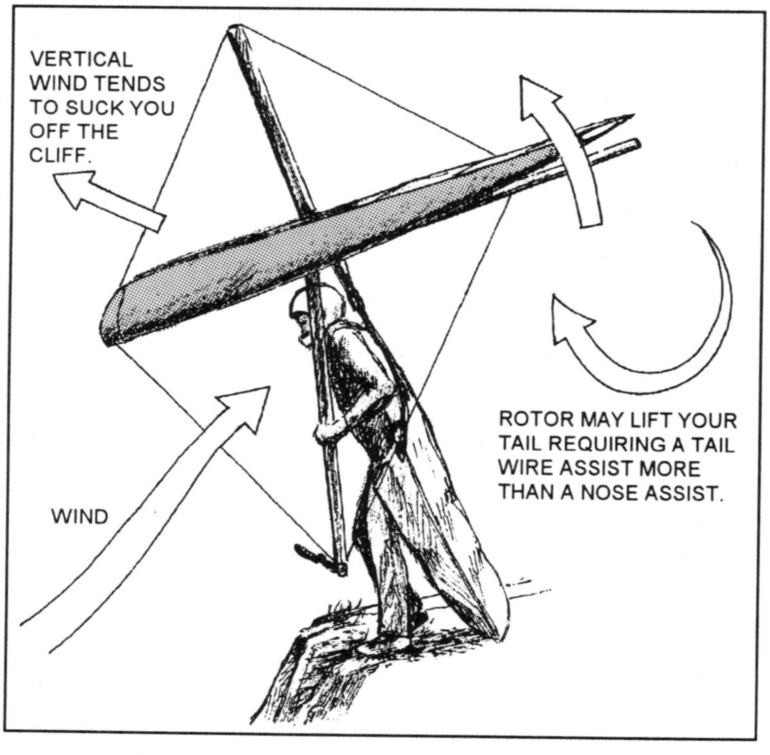

VERTICAL WIND TENDS TO SUCK YOU OFF THE CLIFF.

WIND

ROTOR MAY LIFT YOUR TAIL REQUIRING A TAIL WIRE ASSIST MORE THAN A NOSE ASSIST.

Figure 6-1: Cliff Launches

Two items may help you here. First, this is one place where we recommend the "pistol" or "beer can" grip on the downtubes. This allows you to be back away from the downtubes somewhat as shown in figure 6-1. The severe nose-down attitude shown is not unrealistic in some situations and makes it difficult to wrap your arms around the downtubes. Second, if you feel the base tube pushing back against your chins with a greater nose-down attitude than you are used to, be assured that as soon as you start moving the nose will lift in the rising air.

In the 1988 US Nationals in Tennessee we launched from the southwest cliff at Henson Gap in winds over 20 mph. A full seven man wire crew was needed to get pilots off safely due to cliff edge suck. Every launch was perfect in the smooth conditions.

SELF-LAUNCHING IN WIND

Sooner or later as you get better it will be your turn to launch last. By that time you will probably have used up all your friends as drivers and you'll have to self-launch. Some pilots are sure to arrive first and set up first so they are spared this fate, but such a trick is not fair to fellow pilots since *someone* must be last.

Self-launching safely depends on much the same techniques as the previous section with a few additions. First we must figure out how to get the glider to the launch position by ourselves, then we must hook in and do a hang check.

A steep launch at St Hilaire near Grenoble, France

✓ The Hang Check

If at all possible, I prefer to hook in and check myself *before* I move my glider. This allows me to lie down to feel the lines and avoids a tricky hookup at launch. If it isn't possible to hook up first, it is necessary to level the glider (we're assuming windy conditions), hook up then do a walk-through while still holding the glider level with the front cables. In gusty conditions this is difficult. I have been turned upside down twice trying this feat. Such a fate isn't dangerous but you can damage your glider and your image.

✓ Walking to Launch

Assuming we have checked conditions and they are as lulled as they get, we move the glider by turning it directly into the wind and carrying it with the nose level or somewhat down. Do not let the glider lift or one wing may loop around. In gusty slots you may have to pick the glider up quickly, move forward a few yards then set it down to level it. Out in the wind you might have to inch it forward by moving one side of the base tube then the other forward a bit at a time.

Sometimes you might have to step through the bar, push on the front cables and hold the uprights as a gust of strong wind passes through (see figure 6-2). Remember, you are vulnerable if you are hooked in for where that glider goes you are sure to follow. If you can't 'walk the glider straight into the wind, keep the upwind wing close to the ground to prevent a flipover.

✓ Taking to the Air

Once you are in launch position you should take great care to keep the nose down

Figure 6-2: Self Launching - Holding the Glider in a Gust

until you're ready to hoist the glider. Are you sure you've hooked in? Check the streamers, pick the glider up, pause (less than a second) and run.

The real secret to self-launching is perfect ground handling and learning to read smooth launch cycles by watching trees, brush and streamers as well as feeling your glider *before* you pick it up. These are important skills for every launch, but when self-launching it is best to avoid too many ups and downs of the glider.

LAUNCHING IN CYCLES

Soaring forecasts, sometimes available at meets, provide time of first thermal triggering. If it is well past this time and conditions are still light, it's time to consider finding the best cycle in town and riding it. When we speak of launching in cycles we really refer to two things. The first is a safe launch condition. The second is a soarable situation. They do not necessarily occur at the same time.

The secret of cycles is timing. We call them cycles because they repeat changes in wind conditions. Such cycles are usually due to the timing of heating effects and are somewhat regular. There may be large scale cycles and small scale cycles appearing together. For example, the overall wind may increase from a minimum to a maximum over the period of a half hour as a street migrates past while short term lulls and peaks may appear every few minutes as individual thermals move through.

✓ Safe Launch Cycles

Getting off safely depends on watching the cycles to see how long reasonable conditions last. When this is figured out, the wisest thing to do is *launch at the beginning of a safe cycle*. If wind is quickly switching direction, launch as soon as the streamers are showing straight in as long as the good direction has been lasting for more than a few seconds. If dust devils are moving through the area, do not launch when the wind is calm for that usually means a thermal is gathering steam and will soon lift off. Entering a dust devil immediately after launch is treacherous.

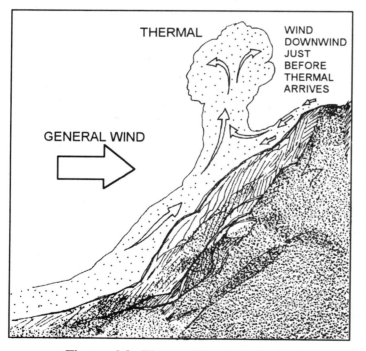

GENERAL WIND

THERMAL

WIND DOWNWIND JUST BEFORE THERMAL ARRIVES

Figure 6-3: Thermal Launch Cycles

✓ Lift Cycles

Getting off in a good time to capture lift is again a matter of good timing and an art in itself. As we said before the best indicators of lift are other gliders. Once they begin climbing out front it's time to launch. The further they are away the sooner you must go. We have witnessed countless pilots sit on launch through soarable cycles because they were waiting for something better—perhaps a sign from God. If gliders are staying up or climbing get off the hill. If gliders are slowly coming down sit tight and wait for the next cycle. Swallows and soaring birds passing by in front of launch let you know when it's time to go as well.

When thermals are moving through on a cyclic basis the ideal time to launch is just before they reach you so that you can be clear of the hill when they hit. This may not be possible if turbulence, crosswind or downwind exists outside of the thermal. In this case launch just as the thermal arrives and the flow steadies for the best chance to soar. In areas of strong thermals the air often gets quiet or trickles downhill when a thermal is building out in front (see figure 6-3). Launching in such periods requires a good slope and excellent launch technique but often rewards us with the best lift.

II - USING LIFT

*T*here are many sources of lift that we utilize on the highway to heaven. We have explored ridge lift in *Hang Gliding Flying Skills* and thermal lift in the previous chapter. In this part we will investigate how to combine these effects and use other types of lift.

THERMALS ON A RIDGE OR HILL

Often thermals on lower ridges or hills in green areas do not have enough power or frequency to sustain your flight. However, a little bit of wind into the hill or an upslope breeze due to heating make soaring possible and thermals are like the surprise in the Cracker Jack box. Using them effectively is our interest.

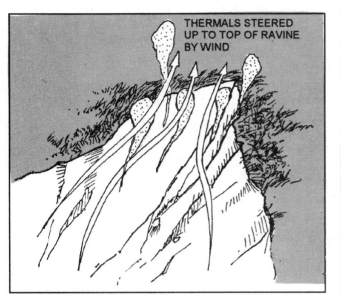

Figure 6-4: Thermals Guided by Terrain

We know that hills and ridges are thermal collectors. In general, if we remain at the top of a hill or along a ridge long enough we should blunder into a thermal.

This was my idea exactly on a cross-country flight in Pennsylvania when I lost 4,000 feet crossing a wide valley. I ended up at Tuscarora Mountain and instead of flying over the back with the 2,000 feet I had between my base tube and the ground, I veered left along the ridge. Not much wind was blowing so I continued to sink, but with only 1,000 feet left after a couple miles up the ridge, bam! a thermal hit my wing and I cranked into a climb. I clung to that core for several grand and was once again on my way.

✓ Where to Find Thermals

The location of thermals on a ridge has parallels to the problem over open country. Ground sources—dry fields, quarries, factories, towns, parking lots, etc.— are good places from which to linger downwind. Clouds along the ridge are almost sure indicators of lift. If ridge lift is reliable you can wait on the cloud's downwind track for it to arrive.

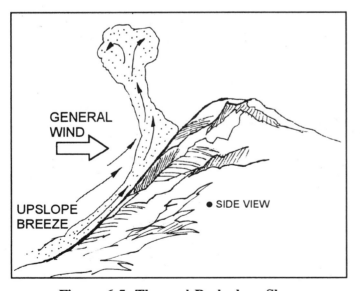

Figure 6-5: Thermal Pushed up Slope

I played this waiting game once in the 1992 East Coast Championships on the west side of the Sequatchie Valley and found a good thermal when the cloud arrived that carried me high to move well ahead of other pilots who had left earlier to scratch along the ridge.

Certain terrain features such as ravines, canyons or bowls may channel thermals up as shown in figure 6-4. A thermal often hugs the ridge, for incoming air is blocked on the ridge side of the thermal. Thus the thermal top may be a bit upwind from the bottom portion as shown in figure 6-5.

In areas with lots of trees we use leaf movement to track thermals. In strong conditions, however, as often as not a vigorous gust on the trees is a sign of a downdraft hitting the

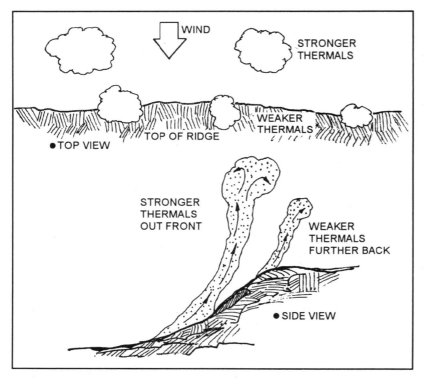

Figure 6-6: Thermal Location

mountain. We have learned over the years not to depend on the tree movement to locate a thermal on stronger days. On light days usually the opposite is true.

The best place to find thermals in comparison to the ridge top is somewhat moot. Stronger thermals tend to exist out front because they rise quicker as figure 6-6 indicates. However, if we explore too far out front we often lose much more altitude and don't necessarily end up higher even if we hit a juicy thermal. I personally favor right along the ridge crest while other pilots favor further out.

✓ Stronger Winds

When the wind picks up, thermals drift further back over the hills as we climb. We must be careful of the venturi directly over the hill and resolve to keep a 2 to 1 glide to the front in moderate winds and a 1 to 1 glide in stronger stuff. Often in these conditions we must use multiple thermals to get high, taking each one back a reasonable distance then heading back out to snag another.

When we do head for the front of the ridge it is important how we do so. We have learned before that thermals are often oval with the long axis aligned with the wind. So it makes sense to head directly upwind to remain in light lift and arrive out front the highest. However, this isn't always the case for sometimes plenty of sink lies upwind of the core we leave. In this case it is better to angle out to the ridge front (see figure 6-7). Generally most of the thermals of the day will be similar so you can set a policy as to which route to take after your first one or two thermals. In any case, if we aren't in danger of being trapped behind a ridge we always angle to the next sign of lift.

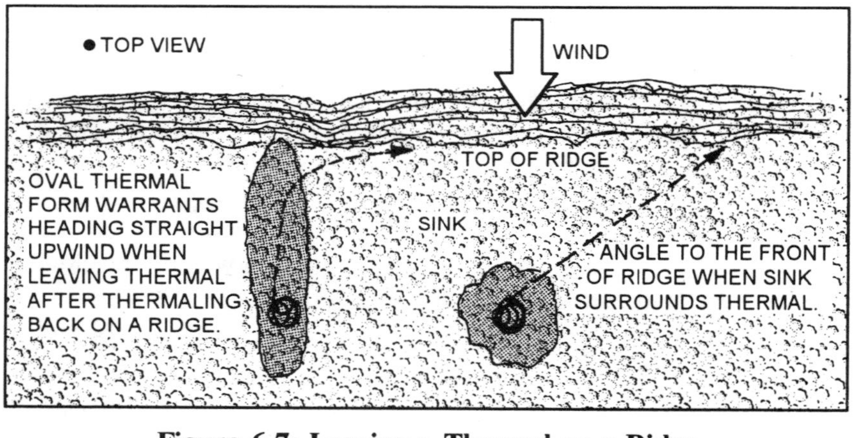

Figure 6-7: Leaving a Thermal on a Ridge

RACING ALONG A RIDGE

The venturi effect was named after the physicist Giovanni Venturi (b. 1822) whose name appropriately enough relates to the wind.

Going cross-country along a ridge has all the implication of landing out and condition judgement that other forms of X-C flights have. We will leave these matters to Chapter 8 and concentrate here on ridge techniques.

✓ Strong Wind Racing

In stronger winds with reliable ridge lift there are two things to consider. First, the lower you remain the lesser winds you encounter so the faster you can fly parallel to the ridge (you don't have to crab as much).

I had this demonstrated to me by Andrew Barber-Starky, Canadian team pilot in the 1978 American Cup Meet. We stayed high and he passed us like we were trailing anchors by hugging the tree tops.

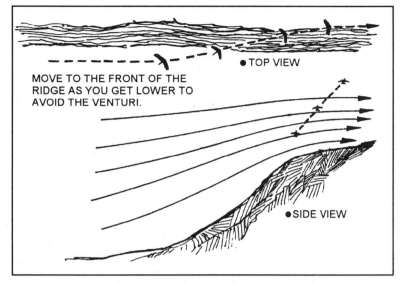

MOVE TO THE FRONT OF THE RIDGE AS YOU GET LOWER TO AVOID THE VENTURI.

● TOP VIEW

●SIDE VIEW

Figure 6-8: Flying in a Venturi

The second point is the lower you do get the more you have to move out front to avoid the venturi. This is shown in figure 6-8. If you descend as you glide, move in front. This is a subtle point, for if you move out too far you are in lesser lift and must slow down to improve your sink rate. There is an ideal position for making time for every ridge shape, wind velocity and glider. At the ultimate races pilots will hug the terrain to maximize their speed along the ridge.

✓ Light Wind Racing

In lighter conditions you have to slow down and indeed may have to use thermals to cross gaps or even get along. *Most pilots new to running a ridge try to stay too high, however.* If ridge lift is reliable, it is only necessary to slow down when crossing gaps. Experiment when other pilots are near and you will see that it is rarely useful to thermal when ridge lift is reliable. As with any type of soaring, slowing in better lift and speeding up in lighter lift or sink will keep you up best and get you along quicker.

Running a ridge is a cross-country skill separate from over-the-back thermal-to-thermal trek.

At the 1981 Masters competition at Grandfather Mountain in North Carolina, Mark Bennett was racing one-on-one against Dave Ledford on a ridge lift day. The task was two laps of a closed course. As Mark tells it, he hit a powerful thermal en route to the first pylon. His thermaling mind set had him circling in 100 FPM up while Dave forged on after two 360s. Dave was just far enough ahead that all Mark could do is chase his tail for the rest of the run. As a result Mark ended up one place and thousands of dollars behind Dave in the final standings. An expensive but well-remembered lesson!

✓ Crossing Streets and Gaps

Thermal streets crossing a ridge can produce so much sink in between the lines of thermal lift that slope lift along the ridge is negated (see figure 6-9). This sink brings down fast moving air that rustles the ground cover as if thermal activity was present. However, nothing but sink will be found. I sat on the ground many times after losing it on a windy ridge in total bewilderment before we figured this one out. I now treat streets like big gaps. I climb under the streets as much as necessary to reach the next one.

Gaps are similar, but usually not so severe. Sometimes gaps, especially those that are backed up by secondary ridges show no diminishing of lift. However, many do, most notably if the wind is crossed. the same applies to the large canyons of high mountains.

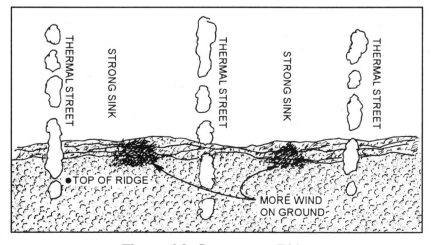

THERMAL STREET
STRONG SINK
THERMAL STREET
STRONG SINK
THERMAL STREET

●TOP OF RIDGE
MORE WIND ON GROUND

Figure 6-9: Streets on a Ridge

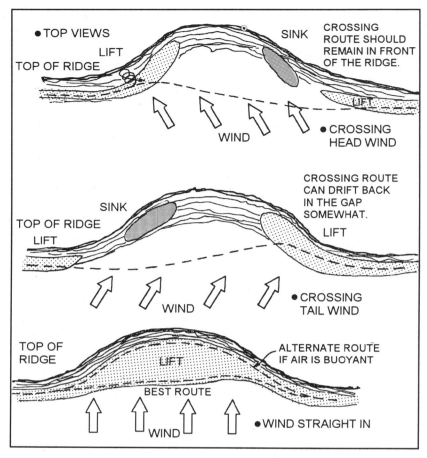

- **TOP VIEWS**

LIFT

TOP OF RIDGE

SINK

CROSSING ROUTE SHOULD REMAIN IN FRONT OF THE RIDGE.

LIFT

WIND

- **CROSSING HEAD WIND**

CROSSING ROUTE CAN DRIFT BACK IN THE GAP SOMEWHAT.

SINK

TOP OF RIDGE

LIFT

LIFT

WIND

- **CROSSING TAIL WIND**

TOP OF RIDGE

LIFT

ALTERNATE ROUTE IF AIR IS BUOYANT

BEST ROUTE

WIND

- **WIND STRAIGHT IN**

Figure 6-10: Crossing Gaps

The sink between streets can bring down fast-moving air that rustles the ground cover appearing to be an area of thermal activity.

If a conveniently placed thermal exists before a gap, use it to climb high enough to attain the other side at a height equal to that you have been traveling. If fate is not so kind as to place a thermal where you want it you can still cross smaller gaps. Slow down before you are at the gap to reach it at maximum altitude. Once there your options depend on the wind conditions as shown in figure 6-10.

If the wind is straight in, you can cross the gap by heading directly for the other side or follow the ridge back as long as you can get back out. I prefer to go straight across although I have seen many pilots take the back route. Neither method seems to be superior since you can usually travel faster on the longer back route. When we have a crossing tail wind gaps are easier to cross. As shown in the figure we do so at an angle to make most use of the tail wind component and catch any lift on the slope that faces the wind on the far side. Be careful of angling in too soon or you may catch sink or turbulence from the upwind part of the gap.

With a crossing head wind we lose the most altitude in crossing. Often we can gain some height by stopping on the face perpendicular to the wind as we see in the figure. Be sure to exploit any thermal channeled up in the bowl. When we head out we make certain our path takes us a little in front of the mountain to avoid the possible rush of wind around the far edge. Sometimes we have to grit our teeth and dive in low to the mountain, on the far side of the gap to seek ridge lift. If landing fields are far out this must be done with care. One bit of solace is that we don't quite have a head wind if we head straight out to land. In any case, use proper speeds-to-fly for distance when crossing a gap as explained in the next chapter.

SCRATCHING CONDITIONS

Light lift on a ridge or hill is all too common, yet not enough pilots hone their scratching techniques. In the words of Pete Lehman, international competitor,..."*you must try to soar on light days. Don't just sit on the hill waiting for conditions to 'get good.' You need to gain experience. If you are afraid of sled rides you won't learn to scratch. The corollary is that the more you master scratching the less sled rides you get.*"

The general overall game plan is to launch in a good cycle, position yourself properly, spend the maximum time in the maximum air and latch on to any thermal scrap that wobbles through.

✓ Launching in Cycles

We have already mentioned the use of launch cycles. We should add how important it is to be ready (hooked up, hang checked and near launch) for the possibility of flying when cycles are few and short. Furthermore, your launch should be a vigorous attempt to put as much energy into the system as possible. If you have to dive too much after nearly stalling you may not be in position to use a bit of light lift.

✓ Positioning

One of the secrets to scratching is knowing the site. Where are the likely lift patches? What bowls or faces are apt to work in the given wind direction? Does the ridge drop off in one direction? Is there a house thermal area?

As soon as you launch turn to get in close. By close we mean as close as your ability allows with a reasonable margin for safety. This will vary with your skill, your glider's handling and the turbulence of the day. Erring on the side of safety is always our intention. Experience teaches us how tight we can be. Remember, some are *not* soarable so don't overdo it and end up with a tree or rock impression on your body. Also very close to trees or terrain you may find turbulence which requires you to go faster and thus sink more.

Some pilots have developed the ability to launch in a turn. This is reasonable in steady conditions but can be dangerous if the air is bumpy. Once you have turned—preferably in the direction of any crossing wind—hug the ridge contours to remain in the best lift. If the ridge drops off in one direction it is often best to head there for you can usually do better above the ridge than below the face, even if it's lower.

If you climb you *must* ease closer to get above the ridge or you will be in weaker lift. This important point is what many early scratchers miss. You want to get above the crest of the hill for the best lift.

Look for bowls or other features likely to have the most upwelling of air (see figure 6-11). Linger in these places as you move along and return to them often. Spines tend to collect thermals as well, so don't neglect their potential.

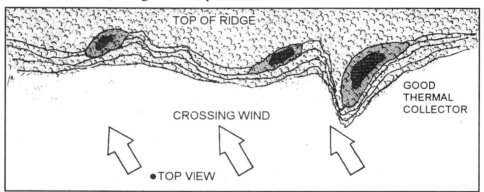

Figure 6-11: Contours Producing Lift in Crossing Wind

✓ Avoiding Sink, Embracing Lift

As you move along, note areas of sink and lift and traverse the former fast and slow down in the latter. You maintain up to best glide speed in more turbulent conditions between areas of lift. When you do hit lift, slow to minimum sink speed but regain control speed before you hit the next patch of sink. If lift is short or turbulent you can turn 180° as you slow so that you remain in it longer and avoid falling out toward the hill. The object is to spend as much time as possible in lift and as little in sink. Look for any other gliders circling and head for them.

✓ Using Thermals

Light thermals in scratching conditions often determine whether launch spectators are seeing the top or the bottom of your sail. You must learn to use every tidbit of lift by turning immediately. Sometimes you only get half a turn in the puff, but that's OK as long as you stay along the ridge. Often we have to perform figure 8s in weak lift below ridge top until we are high enough to 360. It's even frequently necessary to circle in zero sink just to hold altitude until a better ride shows up.

If your ridge is limited in length you have to go back and forth. The ideal is to make each turn in lift. As you 180° note the climb rate and continue the turn all the way around if lift and clearance are ample. Don't neglect to linger in the house thermal area and search back and forth like a shark patrolling a tidewater pool.

Scratching effectively requires observation and flexibility. As soon as you see a hawk or glider circling be there like a lawyer at the scene of an accident. Remember the rule: cooperate and elevate. Lift will move around. Watch what happens, who's going up and where the greatest percentage of climbs take place.

Once you lose it at ridge top level, don't give up. Fight for your right to soar all the way to the landing field. Use your altitude as seed money to help you invest in more altitude by flying over likely lift areas. If you do fail to gain altitude, achieve a gain in experience by analyzing what you did right or wrong. Sometimes a right turn instead of a left makes all the difference. Learning to judge conditions and our sites in this way and making it pay off are some of the real rewards of flying.

Scratching in thermals requires subtle skills and awareness not possible to develop in stronger conditions.

CONVERGENCE LIFT

When air flows meet head on they often well up and produce usable lift. The exact mechanism of the many forms of convergence is explained in our weather book *Understanding the Sky*. Here we note best how to best exploit convergence.

Many times a converging situation doesn't produce enough lift to allow soaring but it does promote thermals. We need to recognize the areas of possible convergence if we want to better understand thermal production. An obvious example of this is the well-known thermal factory at the north end of the Owens Valley—Montgomery pass. Here the valley narrows

"Not two masses can occupy the same place at the same time."
— Ancient Sumerian proverb.

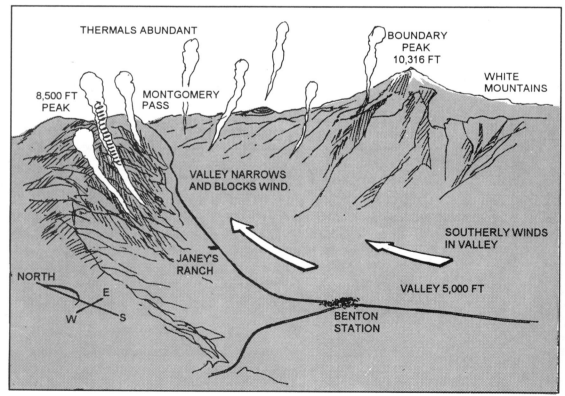

Figure 6-12: Convergence in the Owens Valley

and thermals are abundant in a southwest wind as shown in figure 6-12.

Pure convergence often occurs when the wind from the ocean meets a tortured coastline. Mt. St. Pierre along the Gaspé peninsula in Québec is a notable example. Here the wind enters a narrowing valley and is squeezed upward as shown in figure 6-13. The lift extends far out in the valley sometimes, well beyond the reaches of slope lift.

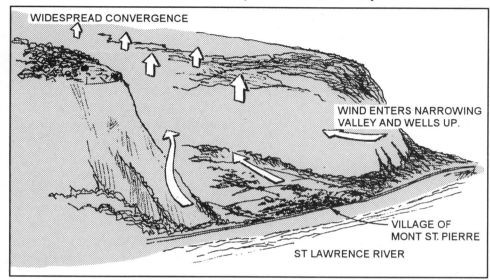

Figure 6-13: Convergence Near Mt St Pierre, Québec

The best way to fly in pure convergence is to slow as much as possible and let nature do the rest. Often climb rates will be 50 FPM or less, but patience rewards you with thousands of feet. If you try to thermal in light bumps you usually end up losing ground. It's better to think of the experience as sight seeing, sit back, listen to some tunes and watch the sunset from several grand up.

Signs of convergence are layers of cloud in a small area or groups of close cumulus. Beyond this the only visual clues are terrain shapes and the possibilities they present. We should be conscious of the probability that some form of convergence is often present and use its unqualified gift of lift whenever it is detected.

WAVE LIFT

Waves are common enough in our flying realm that they should be well understood. Hang gliders pilots have been finding waves more and more usable as glider performance has improved.

In the spring of 1992 a ground-breaking flight took place when Nelson Lewis encountered wave lift over Massanuten Mountain in Virginia. He climbed to over 12,000 feet then proceeded to head downwind to find the second, and subsequent waves after that until he traveled 73 miles in pure wave lift!

Such a flight demonstrates the potential of waves.

Waves forming over the Isère Valley in the French Alps.

To use wave lift we should treat the waves like a combination of ridges and streets. We soar back and forth along their lifting forward edge as if the wave was a ridge. Once we have gained the desired height we head downwind and cross to the next wave in a perpendicular direction as if we were crossing to a cloud street (we cover the techniques of street crossing in Chapter 8). At the next wave we again revert to our ridge soaring act (see figure 6-14).

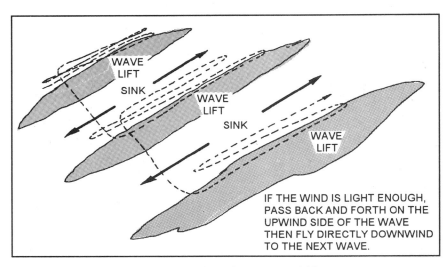

IF THE WIND IS LIGHT ENOUGH, PASS BACK AND FORTH ON THE UPWIND SIDE OF THE WAVE THEN FLY DIRECTLY DOWNWIND TO THE NEXT WAVE.

Figure 6-14: Using Wave Lift

Such ideal repetitive waves are common, but just as frequently the downwind repetitions are weakened by terrain features. As conditions change so do these effects. Thus we must be opportunistic to use waves when they are offered. Waves are best identified by lenticular clouds. However, they can exist without clouds so we will do best if we recognize the lift by its widespread, generally smooth nature. Succeeding waves will be similarly oriented across the wind and commonly three to six miles behind the preceding one. As a rule of thumb, waves are spaced (in miles) about 1/5 the wind velocity (in mph) forming them.

Waves are not without dangers. The first is that abundant lift carries us up to higher winds that we cannot penetrate. The second is that we can't get down while daylight lasts (waves often set in toward dusk). The cure for both of these problems is to recognize the condition early and move upwind until the lift drops off before you get too high.

Waves are frequent phenomena but seldom attainable.

One other danger is the possibility of a severe rotor under the wave crests. Such a rotor may be violent in high terrain such as the Sierra in California. When this mountain chain sets up a wave, magnificent awe-inspiring rotor clouds occur in the Owens Valley. Needless to say pilots are smart to observe this from the ground for such waves have broken sailplanes.

To avoid such rotor in a cross-country situation fly downwind from wave to wave until the waves diminish, fly off to the end of a wave or land heading upwind from the lift in a wave. Figure 6-15 illustrates these flight paths.

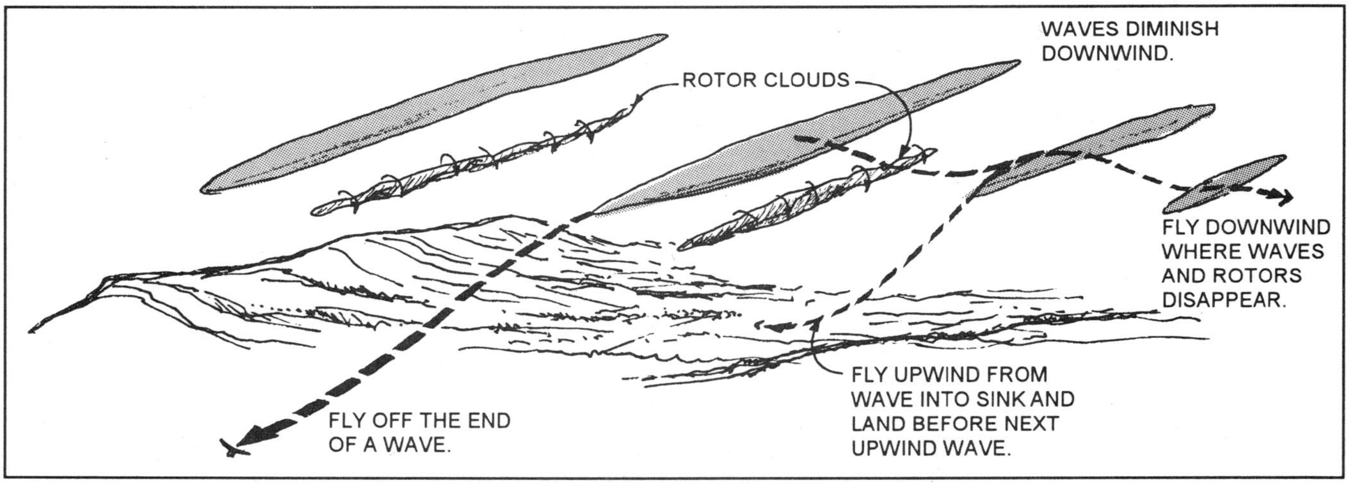

ROTOR CLOUDS

WAVES DIMINISH DOWNWIND.

FLY DOWNWIND WHERE WAVES AND ROTORS DISAPPEAR.

FLY OFF THE END OF A WAVE.

FLY UPWIND FROM WAVE INTO SINK AND LAND BEFORE NEXT UPWIND WAVE.

Figure 6-15: Avoiding Wave Rotors

III - FLYING IN TRAFFIC

Yield unto others in the same way you would have them yield unto you.

Quite often we have company in the air. Usually it's only a couple of friends whose habits or quirks we readily understand. But at fly-ins, meets and popular sites we may meet up with total strangers of questionable skill, humanity or sanity. Here we deal with the other pilot in the air in the same way we hope we are dealt with—the golden rule!

TRAFFIC ON THE RIDGE

Of course we leave the suburbs, the expressways and boulevards to get away from the rat race. Imagine our chagrin when we step into the sky and find it cluttered with a Saturday crowd Sunday driving. All is not lost, however, for here is your perfect chance to compare your performance against that of others.

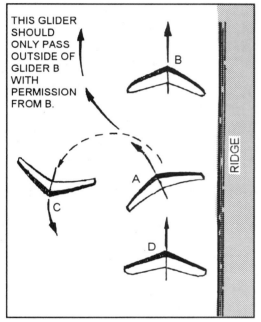

THIS GLIDER SHOULD ONLY PASS OUTSIDE OF GLIDER B WITH PERMISSION FROM B.

Figure 6-16: Traffic on a Ridge

The first matter to assure is that you know the "rules of the ridge". We are careful to pass on the right of an approaching glider, give a low man the right of way and pass on the ridge side of a glider. However, the last rule is impossible to follow if both gliders are low and tight on a ridge. With radio communication a faster glider (A in figure 6-16) may pass a slower glider (B) on the outside, but should *never* remain in the outside position shown for very long because glider B has no options. Indeed in a dump, glider B cannot turn away from the ridge. The safest matter is for pilot A to perform a 180 and go the other way as glider C is doing, being careful to avoid a trailing glider D. If pilot A is heading to a destination in the direction shown, S turns may be necessary to avoid turning back or ramming a slow glider.

✓ Staying on Top

The ideal place to be in traffic is on top. The top dog not only has less to watch for but she or he can readily view the rest of the pack and immediately go to where the best climb is. The key to getting on top and staying there is positioning. You must leave thermals at the right time (just as they die behind the hill), fly efficiently directly toward the next source of lift (a turning glider or cloud for example) and remain in areas that seem to be working best for the day. If you're trying to max out altitude, the techniques for scratching outlined above should be applied even though you may be well above the hill.

When you have to turn, do so in lift. Turning in sink puts you in that sink longer than necessary. If you are still in traffic be sure to clear your turns carefully. It is possible that inferior glider performance will prevent you from rising above the crowd. However, you can still welcome the chance to do the best you can to achieve maximum relative altitude.

✓ Body Talk

Signaling your intentions in a populated sky is necessary for safety. We favor hand signals which are as simple as an arm pointing to one side or straight ahead indicating intended heading. More subtle but obvious clues are when a pilot turns his or her head to look in a given direction. This usually indicates a turn to that direction. When you fly in traffic always be sure to turn your head in this manner to provide such a signal. It is best to turn the head several times to make the signal more obvious.

Body language indicating turns:
- *Arm signals*
- *Turning heads*
- *Side controls*

The final and most unmistakable signal of a turn is a side control. If you are following another glider you can tell instantly when they are going to turn: they move to the side. You

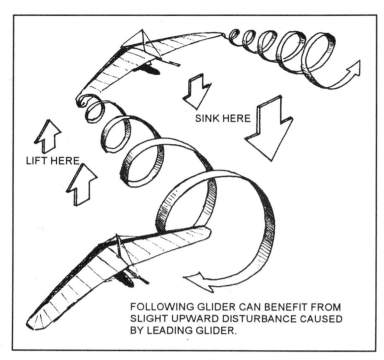

LIFT HERE

SINK HERE

FOLLOWING GLIDER CAN BENEFIT FROM SLIGHT UPWARD DISTURBANCE CAUSED BY LEADING GLIDER.

Figure 6-17: Flying Behind a Glider

can best broadcast your intentions by swinging your body to the side a couple times before you hold the control. In all cases, if you can make eye contact with another pilot you can be assured your signals are being watched. He who fixates on his vario is the one who is likely to miss your signal and hit your glider. This is not an overdramatic warning for in the summer of 1992, for example, six pilots were involved in mid-airs in the USA alone. Two of them did not walk away.

Dusk is the time when gliders are hardest to see. White gliders are most visible at this time so consider yourself invisible if you sport flashy colors that look so brilliant in the strong sunlight. The important thing is to develop the ability to know where all gliders are at all times by knowing pilot tendencies and relative rates of changing positions. This three-dimensional overview is very important in competition as well.

✓ *Following Gliders*

It is often necessary or expedient to follow close behind another glider on a ridge or a confined lift area. We all know about the turbulence behind another glider, especially if it's going slowly and producing the strongest vortices. The best place to fly is just to one side of the preceding glider to remain in the updraft like a goose in V formation as shown in figure 6-17. However, on a ridge where a turn to that side is likely, this is dangerous. Remember, you are in the preceding pilot's blind spot at this point. With a wind on a ridge the vortices are blown toward the ridge so you can remain in their lifting portions and still be in the same track as the preceding pilot.

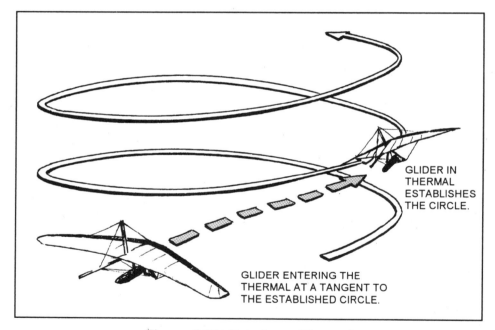

GLIDER IN THERMAL ESTABLISHES THE CIRCLE.

GLIDER ENTERING THE THERMAL AT A TANGENT TO THE ESTABLISHED CIRCLE.

Figure 6-18: Entering a Thermal

GAGGLE FLYING

When a fleet of gliders are swarming in a thermal, chopping it up like boats in a bay, you have to use all your well-learned politesse, thermal skills and awareness. Many advancing pilots are reluctant to mix it up in a thermal-clogging gaggle, but this too is a skill that can be acquired and has its rewards.

To begin we must learn to enter a gaggle properly. As figure 6-18 shows we do this at a *tangent* to any circle already established (in the same direction of course) whether we are entering a little above or below other gliders. To best hit the tangent point, watch the circling glider and aim for the outside of his or her circle as shown. We should take into account thermal tilt if we are at different heights.

We should also begin with the same size circle. Do this by noting the other pilot's bank angle and try to duplicate it. Ideally we would like to enter a traffic circle directly across the circle from another pilot. Sometimes timing doesn't work out and we are next to him or her as shown at A in figure 6-19. The technique here is to fly a concentric circle outside the other pilot's trajectory then move in when the other pilot pulls ahead which will happen since the inner path is shorter (point B).

Sometimes three or more gliders end up at the same level. Usually they slow each other down, as indeed two gliders do in narrow thermals, for no one can tighten up in the core. It often happens that not everyone agrees on the best path to take as well. In this case try to stay with the tighter circling glider for invariably inexperienced pilots flatten out too much in thermal traffic.

The turning radius of other pilots is deceptive. As mentioned in Chapter I, others appear to always be circling wider than you. Perhaps this is why inexperienced pilots circle too widely. If another glider remains opposite your position then both of you are circling with the same rate and radius. If you see other gliders turning inside you it is a good sign you are turning too flatly (unless they are much lighter than you). Tighten it up if the inside is clear.

GLIDER IN THERMAL LEADING

ENTERING GLIDER

A

ENTERING GLIDER

ESTABLISHED CIRCLE

B

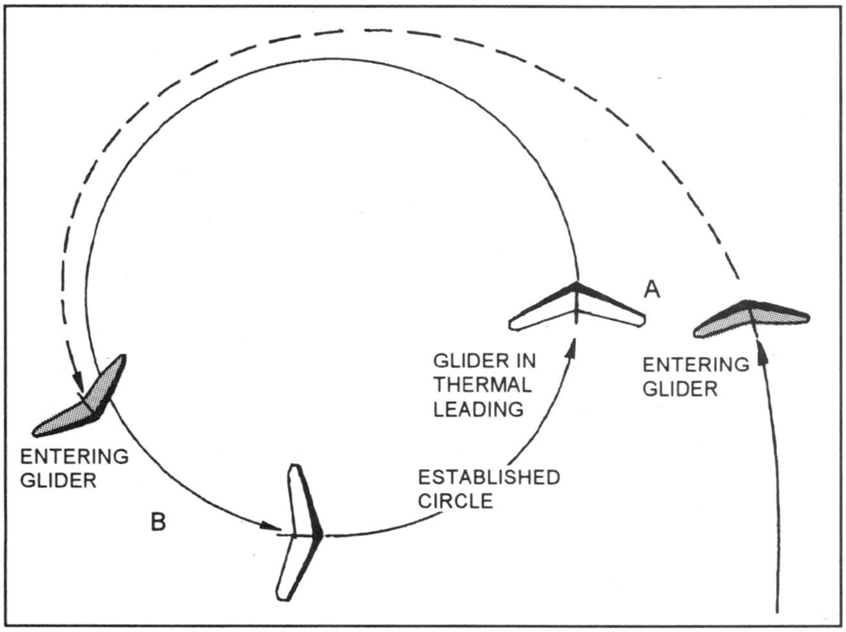

Figure 6-19: Avoiding a Thermal Conflict

When you're thermaling with another glider they will often disappear from your view, especially if they are banked too steeply. They may be gone for several revolutions and not really be above you. In this case be careful to hold the same bank and circle path for you may be invisible to your neighbor as well. As long as you both maintain steady gyrations, you will not collide.

Thermal Gaggle Rules and Techniques
1. Enter a gaggle exactly on a tangent with the same size circle.
2. Space yourself out across a thermal by circling wide until you can join the tighter path.
3. Bank the same as others but recognize that this is probably too wide. If you can catch a core safely do so with a tight turn inside the others.
4. When gliders disappear from view maintain a steady bank and airspeed. Keep a constant lookout for other gliders at all times.

IV - ADVANCED PILOT MISCELLANY

*I*n this part we address a number of additional issues that attribute to a pilot's consummate skill and thus the designation of "advanced pilot."

FLYING IN DUST DEVILS

Dust devil = whirl-wind = water spout = willy-willy

We have learned a bit about dust devils in previous chapters. Here we see how to use them. They arise when a thermal accelerates upward in superadiabatic conditions which means very unstable air (see *Understanding the Sky*). The stronger the solar heating and the lighter the dust, the higher a dust devil column will extend.

✓ Dust Devil Variations

It is no secret that diving into a dust devil will often reward you with bountiful lift, but also occasional wish-I-was-anywhere-but-here turbulence. Part of this matter depends on how low you hook into a dust devil. Mark Newland, Australian World Team pilot and winner of the 1986 and 1990 US Nationals says *"never enter a dust devil below 200 feet above the ground."* Take this with a grain of dust, for tighter, higher, stronger devils should not be entered much below 1,000 feet. Down low the thermal is just forming while up higher matters are more consolidated and organized, meaning less turbulence.

Not all dust is ground equally: The superfine blend of the northwestern United States forms dust devils at the merest hint of a swirl. On some days near Chelan, Washington, for example, almost every thermal forms a dust devil and as many as twenty can be seen at one time, some with tops of several thousand feet. In the American Southwest the sandy, gritty soil requires a hearty thermal to create a dust devil. Nevertheless I have seen dust devils a quarter mile wide in Colorado. Dust devils in the greener areas are rare because there is less dust. But even leaf devils do not occur often for the air rarely gets super heated.

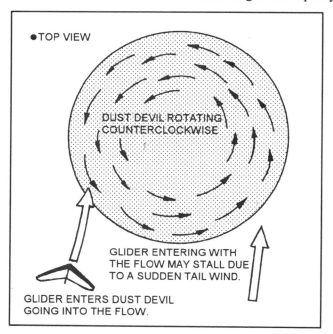

Figure 6-20: Entering a Dust Devil

✓ Using a Dust Devil

When flying into a dust devil it is extremely important to *circle opposite to the dust devil circulation*. This is because a downwind entry can stall you radically (see figure 6-20). Also, going against the flow slows your circling speed so you don't have to bank as much to maintain a given radius and thus can climb better. The majority of dust devils in the northern hemisphere rotate counterclockwise (when viewed from above) so a right turning circle is appropriate. In any case, observe the rotation direction before you enter the devil.

If you are above the dust you can best locate the thermal by recognizing that the dust devil bottom travels at an oblique angle to the wind. This is to the right with a counterclockwise turning column and left with a clockwise rotation. Thus the thermal will be located downwind and to the left of the former and to the right of the latter type of rotation as shown in figure 6-21. In any case we should go into search mode if we don't find a thermal based on a dust devil.

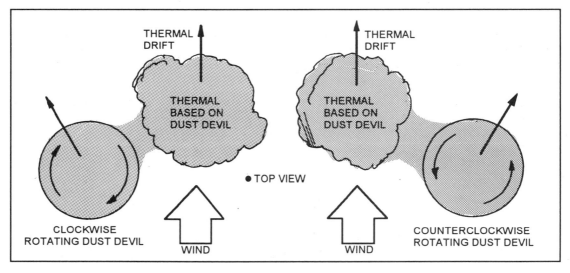

Turbulence in a dust devil will usually be more devilish the lower you go.

Figure 6-21: Locating Dust Devil-Based Thermals

"When getting low in the Owens Valley, I headed out from a ridge to intercept a dust devil. A few hundred yards shy of the center, I hit choppy 200 to 400 up, which encouraged me to think I would get a lot more lift in a few moments directly over the top. I hit only sink as I looked down the funnel of dust, cursing at having missed the thermal downwind of that damn devil."

— Mark Bennett

Often you can find other less rowdy cores on the outside of large dust devils. This is frequently the case with multiple smaller dust devils all dancing around a Mephistophelian core. Sometimes you may dive in a dust devil and find you've missed the elevator. Observing the duration of dust devils on a given day just as you do with clouds will help eliminate such bad luck.

Learn to use dust devils by flying over the smaller ones with good ground clearance. Gradually you'll see which ones portend good lift and minimal turbulence for your usual flying area. If you enter the dust column just be sure to wear your goggles, keep your mouth closed and listen for the grinding away of your wings.

When you are on the ground or at launch in dust devil conditions you should pack up your cover, pads and helmet to keep from loosing them to a passing demon. Also, you must hold your glider as best you can when they come swirling through. If you try holding the nose cables the wing often lifts above you and goes bashing back and forth from wing to wing. The method recommended by Tony Barton, an ardent dust devil wrestler from Arizona, is to keep the tail into the wind and hold the rear of the keel down from underneath as shown in figure 6-22. If the glider picks you up let go and save your bones rather than your tubes.

Figure 6-22: Holding a Glider Assailed by a Dust Devil

There are many astonishing stories of the power of dust devils. We'll relate one that happened in 1991 at Dinosaur, Colorado. Chris Arai was trying to hold his glider down in a dust devil in the setup area when he was picked up several feet in the air. He bailed out before he was slammed. His glider then became plastered up against the rear of a truck and started to push it over the cliff even though the engine was engaged!

FLYING IN CLOUDS

Flying in clouds is like driving drunk at night with your lights off in the desert. You may have no severe consequences or may drive off a cliff.

This subject is easy: don't do it! You rarely benefit from going up into the clouds. I experimented with the experience multiple times in Brazil and would often come out 180° off course even with a compass. We discussed the limitations of a compass in Chapter 4 and how to get out of cloud suck in Chapter 2. The problem is recognizing cloud suck soon enough.

In the Owens Valley in 1992 I was thermaling up with a group of pilots over the Excelsior Mountains. We found some nice lift below a widespread cloud cover. I pulled out of the thermal about 500 feet below the 17,000 foot cloud base. To my chagrin I continued to climb as I stuffed the bar. The edge of the cloud was a long way off and I found myself six hundred feet into the clouds and gyrating wildly before I slowed down. I was so far out of whack I lost a thousand feet and at least six months of longevity before I got back on track.

Clouds rarely provide enough altitude to make up for the loss of visual reference and direct flight. Remember, in the USA the legal limit is 500 feet below the clouds in most places. Also, once you loose orientation you will most likely not regain it until you exit from the cloud in whatever position you may be in. Losing orientation in a cloud is very common and a compass doesn't help once you start turning for compasses have a lag that makes them slower than your glider's gyrations. If you are out of control, slow up gradually (so you don't pull too many Gs if you are in a dive or slip), hold the bar at minimum sink position and let the glider's natural stability take over.

USING A VARIABLE GEOMETRY SYSTEM

A VG system gives you a variety of performance and handling options for different applications.

All modern high performance gliders come equipped with a VG system to tighten the wings for various conditions and purposes. With a looser VG, we have better handling; with a tighter VG, we have better performance up to a point. Using a VG system most efficiently isn't too difficult and is worth learning for it is a waste of performance to leave the line full loose in all situations. Besides, playing with the string gives us something to do instead of boring holes in boring thermals.

✓ Pulling the Cord

Some gliders come with such a long pull on the VG that the cord dangles behind to tickle the pilot thermaling behind you. Long or short it is a good idea to mark your cord at least on the quarter and half points. This will give you instant reference when you're busy with other things like confused traffic. You can thus make a change by grabbing a hank of cord and letting it out or pulling it then checking where you are with the marks.

HGMA certification requires all flight maneuvers—takeoff, roll reversals, landing, stall recovery, etc—be performed in the full-tight configuration. Incidently, most modern gliders with full-tight VG handle no worse than many racing gliders of the previous decade.

Different gliders require different amounts and different forces of VG pull. If yours pulls hard, make sure all the pulleys are straight and the wheels aren't worn (the line can cut nylon pulleys). To pull the line easiest, orient your forearm parallel to the basetube and move your hand directly to the opposite control bar corner. Also be aware that a VG is most difficult to pull when Gs are increased in a turn, a pull-up or in lift.

A word of caution: avoid letting the entire cord go suddenly so that the crossbar smacks up against its restraint. This *stresses* the system. One pilot did this on final and the glider folded. He had a fast acting chute and ended up wowing rather than mortifying the landing field crowd.

✓ The VG in Launch and Landing

We have already advocated several times the benefits of using up to 1/2 VG application for taking off. This tightens the side cables, provides slightly sooner lift off and slightly better performance with relatively little loss of handling. Experiment with your glider in mellow air to find the best setting.

Setting up in a crowd of gliders can be an advanced skill in itself.

Pro Tip: On takeoff, loop your VG line over the rear cable on that side to avoid tripping over it on launch.

On landing we recommend the full loose setting for handling reasons. However, years of experience in glide ratios contests where the entire flight—from ground to ground—is flown with full VG lets us report that the flare portion of landing is most often *easier* with the VG full on. This is because the glider has better speed retention and doesn't slow as suddenly near a stall. However, the wings are prone to "stick" and you can't correct as easily as with a loose VG. The main point is if you forget to loosen your VG, don't panic, just land normally with a straight final and you'll find the flare is fine. You might wish to experiment with this on smooth days.

✓ *The VG in the Air*

When bashing around in the varying air we use different settings of VG according to the amount of turning necessary. We recommend 1/4 to 1/2 VG when scratching (1/4 down low) for the best combination of performance and handling. With clearance and straight ahead lift for instance when cruising a ridge, we use 1/2 to full VG. When gliding between thermals, especially in sink or when racing we use full VG. Using full VG applies in maximizing glide in any condition.

Different gliders allow a different amount of VG travel. Some are so loose with the VG full off that this setting is only appropriate for landing.

When approaching a thermal it is smart to drop the VG off to that used in the thermal *before* you get to the lift in order to avoid locking out in the turbulence surrounding the thermal and to best maneuver into the core. Once you are centered adjust the VG to provide the best climb rate. This amount should be more with flat, weak thermals and less with strong tight cores. When exiting a turbulent thermal wait until you have passed the main turbulence to put the VG full on except in weaker thermals.

VG User's Guide
1. Launch with the VG 1/4 to 1/2 on in all but the most turbulent conditions.
2. Land with VG full off but be able to do it full on.
3. Scratch with the VG from 1/4 to 1/2 on.
4. Glide with the VG full on except when searching for thermals in which case 1/2 on is best.
5. Enter thermals at the expected setting for best climb or less. Adjust once you have centered.
6. Use more VG the flatter the thermal turn. At steeper banks less VG lets you slow down more and helps prevent a lockout.

COPPING A GLIDE

So who wants a glide? We want to soar! But sometimes we end up plunking down hard scrabble money to enter a meet that turns into nothing but doodah days. In such cases all we can do is point our toes, stretch our necks and eke out our best glide. Here's how it's done:

A pilot reaching out with a Moyes XS in the Morningside glide ratio contest.

✔ Launching for Distance

The launch process for distance is simple to describe. You must put as much energy into the system as possible by doing a full-tilt boogie (that's a maximum run for the scholarly reader). This means starting back as far as possible, setting an unvarying nose angle, starting the glider moving gradually then accelerating rapidly. Precision launch technique is the secret to starting a glide with maximum height.

If conditions are not switchy at launch, a full tight VG is necessary for efficiency. Also an immediate moderate turn to the glide direction is required to minimize altitude loss.

✔ The Glide

Set your best glide speed as quickly as possible after launch. This speed varies with various wind conditions as explained in the next chapter. It should be understood here that generally we speed up in head wind and sink, and slow down in tail wind and lift to best stretch our glide over the ground. If the complexion of the air changes while on glide we should be sure to change our airspeed accordingly unless the changes are so quick we end up chasing the airspeed.

Body position is important. Up to half the drag of our body comes from our arms. When on a glide, keep yours tucked to your sides as best as you can even grasp the bar in the center and tuck your head (see figure 6-23). Be sure your harness is pointed longitudinally directly into the airstream. Too many pilots fly feet down because their hang straps are too long (see Chapter 4). There is no use flying in a streamlined harness if it isn't aimed correctly.

In low altitude, short glide situations, maintain this narrow profile and ideal speed for as long as possible —right next to the ground in some cases. The flare should be expertly timed to occur at the last moment with one continuous standup pushout motion. Your job is to perfect all these pilot skills then let your well-trained glider do the rest.

LOW DRAG HARNESS MAIN

KEEP YOUR HEAD DOWN AS MUCH AS POSSIBLE (WATCH OUT FOR TRAFFIC), KEEP YOUR ELBOWS TUCKED AND HANDS TOGETHER AS MUCH AS POSSIBLE (WATCH OUT FOR TURBULENCE), WEAR A TIGHT SLEEVED GARMENT AND YOU'LL BE A LEAN, MEAN GLIDIN' MACHINE.

VG FULL TIGHT

● FRONT VIEW

● SIDE VIEW

Figure 6-23: Best Gliding Position

Gliders waiting in line to be retrieved in a glide contest.

PIONEERING A NEW SITE

One definition of a pioneer is a guy with an arrow in his back. Don't risk your safety in the drive to be the first. Carefully check the various elements of the flight—launch, conditions, landing distance, landing field—to make sure each one is well within the safety limits of a sane person.

The launch should be steep enough with ample clearance from trees or brush below. You can judge this by relating to other familiar launches. However, be aware that wind into launch greatly affects how much forward clearance you need. Remember, the object is to *fly* the site not decorate it with your colors.

New site caution: if a place doesn't look primo it will probably never serve as a good flying area.

Conditions are easy to check as is the glide distance. Do the former by getting your standard weather report to make sure the up you feel is not a rotor. Do the latter by consulting topographic maps or taking a sighting as explained in *Hang Gliding Flying Skills*. Don't hedge on landing distance. Only in the calmest weather should we rely on landing fields beyond a 6 to 1 glide.

The landing field should be of ample size. You know by now what that is. If your site is truly going to be worth anything the landing field must be safe for a variety of pilots. Otherwise you might as well go leap off buildings, land in little parks and claim you have pioneered a new site!

EMERGENCY PROCEDURES

The biggest emergency we can think of in the air is coming unhooked from our glider. If this happens at launch you should drop to the ground as soon as the condition is recognized if on a slope launch. Hopefully your feet haven't left the ground. With a cliff you are going along for the ride.

Practicing emergency procedures is the best way to be prepared if a real emergency arises.

Up in the air, it is preferable to get into the control bar unless you have water to drop into. If a water drop is your destiny, pull on one side of the bar (assuming you are hanging from the basetube) to steer the glider to head parallel to the shore. At least one pilot let go over water but sailed across to the shore due to the rules of trajectory.

If you have ever tried hanging by your hands with harness and parachute, you'll be

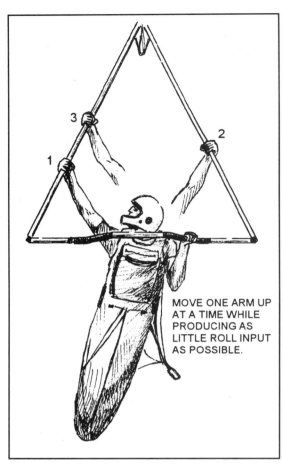

MOVE ONE ARM UP AT A TIME WHILE PRODUCING AS LITTLE ROLL INPUT AS POSSIBLE.

Figure 6-24: Emergency Procedure

surprised at how short you can last—even with a dose of adrenaline. If you can't climb up into the control bar to stand on the base tube immediately, throw your parachute by letting go with one hand and deploying it. If you can hook an arm over the base tube and grab your shoulder strap do so, but don't wait, for you will be diving rapidly and letting go with one hand will put you into a slip that will build up Gs. Hold on as long as you can. The most important thing in such an emergency is to never give up trying to deploy your parachute.

The best way to climb into the bar is to move one hand toward the center of the base tube and quickly reach up to a downtube with the other as shown in figure 6-24. Just as quickly reach up to the other side. The idea is to move your hands up the downtubes a little at a time while producing the least amount of roll input until you can kneel then stand on the base tube. This procedure assumes you can do several chin-ups with 20 or more pounds of gear loaded on or up to 15 chins with just body weight. You can try this procedure by hanging in full gear from a control bar suspended at the apex.

A glider is eminently controllable while standing in the control bar and flare is easy. You might try this control with your feet on the base tube some day you are a grand above in smooth air (keep your feet spread to relieve loading on the basetube). Learning to perform such emergency procedures *before* you need them is highly recommended. It may give you some peace of mind.

With today's pod harnesses you can perform no other maneuver than that outlined above if you are zipped up. If your legs are free it is possible to pull one foot up and in front of the base tube then swing up to straddle the bar. This is very difficult with a chest parachute however, and you would be wise to try it on a horizontal bar no higher than you care to fall.

V - LANDING COMPLICATIONS

*R*egular landings in regular fields are difficult enough for many pilots that we know one club that holds a contest for the most perfect landings in a season. But advanced pilots on advanced flights sometimes complicate matters even more by dropping in on less than perfect fields. We shall see how they are handled.

TURBULENT, SWITCHY CONDITIONS

Often, through no choice of our own of course, we are called upon to set down in a place where turbulence or rapidly changing wind occurs. The best plan here is to come in with a heading splitting the difference between the extremes of wind, aim at the streamers if possible and make a last second correction to favor the current wind as shown in figure 6-25. In all cases we should be prepared to land a little crosswind.

If the wind is swapping 180° in a long and narrow field the best bet is to linger in the middle of the field and make a direction decision at the last minute. Landing at one end of the field often provides the least amount of wind if the field is surrounded by trees or buildings and the wind has turned tail.

In turbulence secure extra airspeed on final and make quick positive corrections. Sometimes strong gusts will pop you up so be ready with a pull in and a prayer. It's also possible to turn a little in their direction if they are crossing.

Some areas with strong local conditions show strange contrary winds in the landing field. Notably at Mt. St. Pierre different wind socks will be steadily pointing at one another. The trick here and in similar situations is to pick one wind sock and land near it into the wind it is indicating. That's why you practiced all those spot landings!

In all difficult landing situations obey the first commandment: **Maintain thy airspeed.**

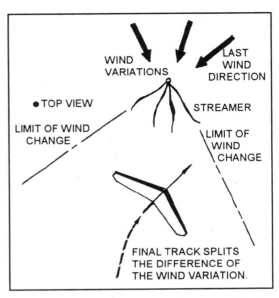

Figure 6-25: Landing in Varying Wind

CROSSWIND LANDINGS

Many pilots are overly concerned with crossing winds so that they perform any manner of gymnastics to turn into the wind in a narrow field. The fact is, crosswinds are not such a problem as long as they are not overly gusty.

First let us understand a glider's reaction to crosswinds. As figure 6-26 shows, our glider enters less wind as it descends due to the wind gradient. This is indicated by the right-hand wind profile. If we are headed directly perpendicular to the wind from our right, our glider is actually drifting to the left so as it descends the impulse of wind it *feels* is from the *left* as shown in the left hand profile of the figure. The results is a tendency for the glider to yaw

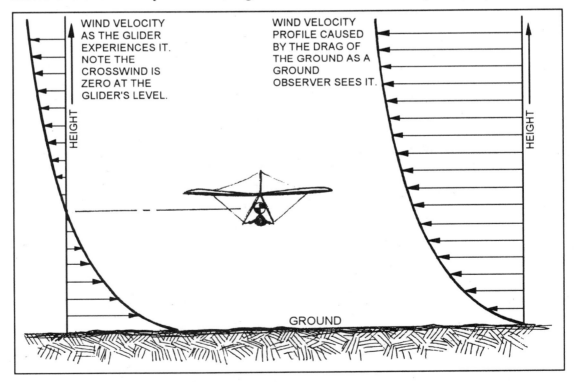

Figure 6-26: Landing in a Crosswind

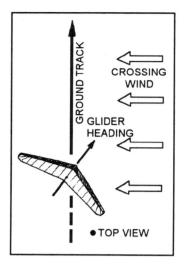

Figure 6-27: A Crabbing Crosswind Approach

left and stall the upwind (right) wing. However, these effects are subtle and diminished by the fact that you are probably somewhat crabbed into the wind to maintain your ground track. This is shown in a top view presented in figure 6-27.

Now when you come in to land in a crosswind, keep your speed up to combat any turn or stall tendency, slow down in ground effect and flare normally with full awareness of any roll tendency. Make a roll control if necessary while you flare. For the most part you'll find that there is no more roll problems than on many into-the-wind landings. In all cases it is important to *feel* the glider's reactions and actively control the beast.

Pro Tip: The faster you fly on final the more time you will spend in ground effect which negates the gradient problem in a crossing wind.

LANDING IN HIGH VEGETATION

No we don't mean trees. We are referring to high weeds, crops or sagebrush. The basic technique is simple: treat the top of the vegetation as if it was the ground and flare accordingly. The secret is to produce a full flare so that you parachute down and your nose doesn't drop. If you are doing this when you flare too early in your regular landings you will prang hurtfully for the vegetation will not slow your descent as it will when you parachute in high crops or brush.

Pro Tip: Maintain prone position so you can get the base tube closer to the plant tops which puts you lower when you flare. Then rotate upright quickly and flare in one motion keeping the nose well up. I have landed in chest high weeds successfully with this method. CAUTION: Do not let your base tube catch the plant tops or you'll be pulled nose down, head first with severe consequences.

LANDING IN SMALL FIELDS

Small fields can be dangerous, make no mistake about it. However, sometimes that's all you've got. We can say without a doubt that it is better to land in a tree than risk catching a wing and spilling into a field as some have done to regret.

The best small field technique is shown in figure 6-28. Here we see a pilot boxing or circling the field to stay within reach, extending a leg if needed just before turning to descend at one corner to go diagonal across the field. Hopefully the heading is into the wind which it will be if you judged your descent and contrived to end up downwind before your last turn into the field.

We prefer to use a slipping (diving) turn into the field to get us down as quickly as possible and provide speed for turbulence. Once you are close to the ground you can use this speed to pay off in a climb and make a very easy turn if necessary. Of course we must be careful of acquiring too much speed so that we float right across our little field and into the arms of a beckoning tree. Producing a series of miniature stalls will help you land shorter, but is very dangerous in turbulence. Resolve to find a bigger field next time and practice these techniques over your normal *big* field.

CROSS SLOPE AND DOWNHILL LANDINGS

We dealt with these difficult forms of landing in *Hang Gliding flying Skills*. For completeness we'll mention here that a cross slope landing in a hang glider is tricky because one wing is

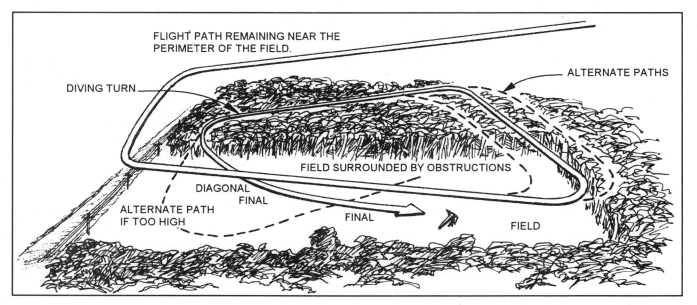

Figure 6-28: Small Field Technique

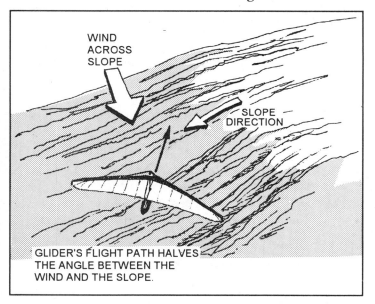

Figure 6-29: Cross Slope Landing

closer to the terrain so lifts more and turns you down the slope. The only way to land successfully in this case is to aim partially if not all the way uphill to split the difference with the slope and the wind (see figure 6-29).

For downhill landings we must realize that the slope falls away as we progress. If the slope is gentle we can eventually slow down close enough to the terrain to produce a vigorous flare that leaves us parachuting down from only a couple feet. This technique requires good timing and a vigorous flare. An ample head wind will let you pull this feat off with aplomb—if you are good at flaring in normal conditions.

At some point a slope will be too steep for you to land down it for your glide will not get you close enough to the ground. If caught with your gear down in this manner it is often possible to perform a flat, low level turn to go somewhat parallel to the slope. However, the side slope landings have their own problems as indicated above. Since you turned toward the slope you probably won't get turned away from it again but the upslope wing will stall first and most likely you'll drop that tip and nose in. The cure is prevention: land upslope.

UPHILL, DOWNWIND LANDINGS

Surprise! Two wrongs do make a right. You can get away with downwind landings and live to enjoy it as long as they are uphill. It is standard practice of many of Europe's grassy slopes for pilots to land like a "fly on a wall." This is popular in England where many hills are walk-ups and pilots simply land as close to the crest as they can when they lose the lift.

The reason such a feat works is shown in figure 6-30. Here we see a wind moving up a slope. As the glider approaches carrying good speed it climbs when the pilot rounds out and

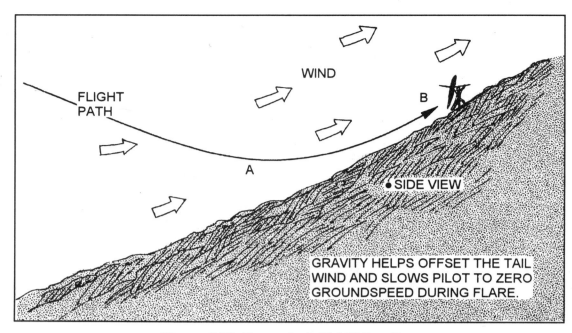

Figure 6-30: Downwind, Uphill Landing

slows down with the aid of gravity. No amount of tail wind (within reason, now) will keep the glider moving up the slope due to gravity operating in the opposite direction. The stronger the tail wind and the faster the approach the higher you go up the hill. It's as simple as that.

Landing uphill downwind is a matter of timing. Don't wait too long to flare or you will become a geologic feature. If you flare too early you will travel up more as long as you don't stall too far away from the hill. The technique is to carry plenty of speed diving toward the hill, pay off into a climb at A then flare smoothly and fully at B. You won't have to run nor will you be able to.

To learn how to perform such landings, start with gentle slopes then steeper slopes *into* the wind. When you first begin this your hypothalamus sends out signals to hit the brakes, for diving at a hill is not your usual practice. However, you need this speed to climb next to the hill. Once you've mastered this and have a feeling for what it's like to dive at a steep face, begin the downwind part using a medium slope in light winds. Then try it in stronger stuff. Remember, you cannot safely handle a strong tail wind on a shallow slope because gravity doesn't help slow your speed as much with respect to the ground. The chart on the side bar provides a guideline to the limits of this practice.

Uphill Downwind Landing Limits	
Slope Angle	Permissible Wind
Shallow	2 - 3 mph
20°	6 mph
30°	8 mph
40°	10 mph
50°	13 mph
60°	15 mph

Landing uphill with a tail wind is not just a spectacular trick. It is a very useful safety device, for in hilly terrain we know that we can always land uphill regardless of the wind direction when a conspiracy of bad air, bad luck and bad judgement catches us by surprise. In the words of Butch Peachy, former US World Team member, *"when in doubt, land uphill."*

Pro Tip: Keep your VG on 1/2 to full tight when landing uphill for the extra speed retention lets you climb parallel to the slope and makes flare less critical.

SUMMARY

*B*ecoming a true advanced pilot isn't easy. We must learn to negotiate tricky launches, washed out lift, jammed up thermals and non-regulation landings. But we persevere and acquire these additional skills little by little. Time passes, life goes on and voilà we have arrived. Oh, but we can smugly strut our stuff at the local hill, awe green fledglings with our hangar talk (there I was, I thought I was going to…) and give sagacious advice at the hill. But wait! Could there be more? Fortunately for the jaded pilot there is. We have a whole world yet to explore even after we've acquired the designation "advanced". The only thing we need to take the next step is to bring our advanced skills along with our advanced judgement and advance by turning the page.

Touch and go in smooth conditions.

Ground handling can be as easy as it seems in this picture.

How to Use Chapter 7

We don't wish to detract from the fun of flying by making you wade through a slough of mucky theory. But speed-to-fly concepts are so important for cross-country and competition flying that the reader should have a basic understanding of speed-to-fly in order to get the most out of later chapters. To help you do this painlessly, we have placed an asterix (*) next to the parts that are essential for an easy working knowledge of speeds-to-fly. With this knowledge and the numbers we provide you can easily use speeds-to-fly to enhance the performance of your very next flight! Later you may be more motivated to learn additional details of the theory to fly further, faster. The information will be waiting for you.

Nelson Howe flies Dead Horse Point in Utah.

CHAPTER 7

Using Speeds-to-Fly

In Chapter 2 we looked briefly at using our glider speeds to achieve the performance variables we choose. Now we go a step further and learn how to best apply this performance in a changeable air mass. The concept we are describing is called "speeds-to-fly".

Speeds-to-fly information can be presented with a lot of onerous mathematics or with graphs for a pictorial understanding. It is our purpose to assist you in using speeds-to-fly as effortlessly as possible so we use the picture method. Mathematicians will find speeds-to-fly formulas to their heart's content in the Appendix.

Make no mistake: speeds-to-fly is one of the most important subjects you can master if you wish to excel at hang gliding. Not only must cross-country and competition pilots understand speeds-to-fly implicitly, but recreational flyers too can benefit from the enhanced performance that speeds-to-fly afford. It is only by constantly flying the proper speed for the conditions at hand that you will achieve maximum efficiency. Only efficient flight will put you on par with the eagles or at least your fellow pilots.

* I - SPEED-TO-FLY BASICS

There is one specific airspeed for any condition of lifting, sinking or moving air in order to achieve the greatest distance over the ground and one specific airspeed to cover a distance the fastest. This statement forms the basics of speed-to-fly concepts and can best be illustrated by an example.

WHAT IS SPEED-TO-FLY

Imagine you and your sleek glider wending your way in still air at best glide speed—say 28 mph. You're achieving a 12 to 1 glide ratio as shown at the left of figure 7-1. In the middle drawing you are still flying at 28 mph but you encounter a 14 mph head wind. Your glide ratio over the ground has deteriorated to 6 yo 1. Finally, the third drawing shows you flying into a 28 mph head wind. If you still maintain your still air best glide speed of 28 mph you will be making no headway, your glide path will be a slow vertical descent, your glide ratio zero. While your sink rate isn't so bad, you get no more glide performance than a brick.

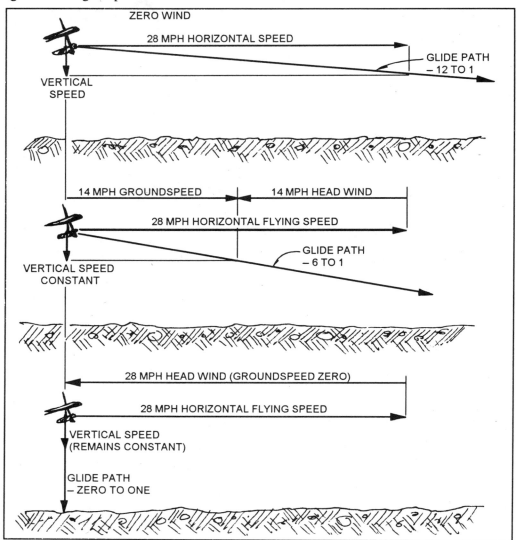

Figure 7-1: Wind Effects on Glide Over the Ground

Now in the latter case we can imagine speeding up a bit. We shouldn't be surprised to find out that although we're sinking faster, we actually are going forward and thus have improved our glide ratio over the ground. If we speed up too much we'll dive too fast and not improve the glide ratio as much. In fact there is one speed that lets us get the furthest in this 28 mph head wind. That's the speed-to-fly.

How we find and utilize this speed-to-fly and those for every other condition is what we will learn in this chapter. We should note that we could have used a tail wind, sink, lift or their combination in our example as well to illustrate the uniqueness of the optimum speed.

A BIT OF HISTORY _____

Speed-to-fly theory was developed immediately after World War II when sailplane flying experienced an exuberant boom. In fact, it was Dr. Paul MacCready—the genius who brought us the Gossamer Condor and Gossamer Albatross (man-powered aircraft) as well as surveillance drones and air deflectors on semis—who laid the ground work for speed-to-fly. Using his newfangled theory he even became World Champion in 1954.

Although we introduced speed-to-fly concepts to the hang glider world with a series of articles in Hang Gliding magazine in 1979 and a previous book in 1978, it wasn't until the latter part of the 1980s that hang glider pilots began using speeds-to-fly on a widespread basis. This is partially because glider performance improved to the point where speeds-to-fly *can* make a noticeable difference in cross-country flying and partially because competition formats have evolved to reward this type of flying. One other factor is the availability of sophisticated flight instruments that include the elements necessary for speeds-to-fly (accurate airspeed indicator and variometer).

Speeds-to-fly revolutionized sailplane competition in the early 1950s. It is impacting hang gliding in the early 1990s.

SPEED-TO-FLY USES

Before we proceed we should make it perfectly clear what speeds-to-fly will be used for. There are two different applications depending on our needs. They are:

Speeds-to-fly give us the exact airspeed to achieve for:
I. Maximum distance from a given altitude
II. Maximum average speed to a given point.

✓ Case I – Flying for Maximum Distance

Reaching as far a distance as possible from a given altitude is a common goal. We need this, for example, when trying to get to a distant landing field or when maximizing our final glide on a cross-country flight. In addition, penetrating high winds or arriving at a patch of lift as high as possible uses this speeds-to-fly application.

✓ Case II – Flying for Maximum Overall Speed

A completely different requirement is flying at the proper speed to provide the fastest possible average speed between two points. This is the situation when racing cross-country. The whole scenario takes into account the necessity to circle in thermals to gain altitude and the fact that flying too fast results in a time penalty due to extra climbing required.

Different decisions are necessary in each of these two cases as we shall see.

*II - THE PERFORMANCE MAP

The first matter we need to attend to is draw a picture of our glider's performance (with us on board, of course). We can do this with a simple graph showing our sink rate at every flying speed. Such a graph is called *a performance map* or *polar*.

POLAR DETAILS

A typical hang glider polar appears in figure 7-2. Since this graph is so important to our understanding of speeds-to-fly, let's take some time to investigate it. To begin we should realize that the values on this graph were taken from measurements of a modern (as of this writing) high performance glider flown in the mid weight range with a streamlined harness and the VG (variable geometry) full tight.

As we shall see later in this chapter, finding data points to produce this performance map is difficult and typically they end up being scattered somewhat so a smooth curve must be fit amongst them. The curve we have presented in the figure is optimistic in terms of maximum glide ratio since we expect gliders to improve steadily in this factor. The maximum glide

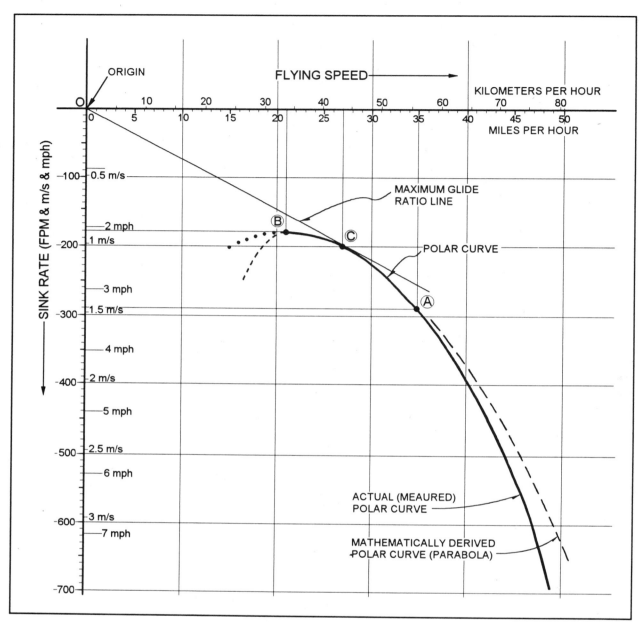

Figure 7-2: A Standard Hang Glider Polar

ratio indicated here is a generous 11.9 to 1.*

✓ The Scales

Looking at the figure we see the horizontal axis is marked in miles per hour (and km/h). This represents our horizontal speed. The further we go to the right on this axis, the faster we are flying. Note: Often the horizontal axis is taken to indicate the glider's horizontal airspeed, but since we read flying speed with our airspeed indicators it greatly simplifies matters to use our flying speed on the horizontal axis. The error this introduces is insignificant as we show in part VIII of this chapter.

- **To convert feet per minute to miles per hour, divide by 88.**
- **To convert meters per second to feet per minute, multiply by 200 (approximately).**

---

* In truth weight-shift gliders at the time of this writing are lucky to get over 11 to 1 glide. However the design potential exists to improve at least 10% in the near future. Also fixed wings achieve a 15 to 1 or better glide. Using the polars we present for a current flex wing is within the error range of our instruments.

The vertical axis gives our sink rate. The further down the scale we go the greater the sink rate. We have marked this in feet per minute (FPM) as well as miles per hour and meters per second. We will use FPM in our discussion.

To see how this performance map defines our glider's performance, let's take any flying speed—say 35 mph—and move down to reach point A on the curve. Reading the vertical scale indicates that our sink rate is about 290 FPM at 35 mph. In fact, in still air we can get *no other* sink rate at the 35 mph flying speed as long as our body position (and thus drag) remains the same. In sinking or lifting air we will get a different net sink rate, of course, but our sink rate with respect to the air will still be 290 FPM.

We find similar unique sink rates for every flying speed within our possible speed range. And thus we have a unique performance map for our glider.

✓ *Below Stall*

At the left most part of the curve we see some broken lines. The dotted line is our theoretical performance if we could slow below stall and maintain proper airflow. The dashed line shows our actual performance as we enter a stall. Note that sink rate increases rapidly as the stall progresses due to extra drag. Also we see that stall occurs right below the minimum sink point since our wings are so twisted or washed out (see Chapter 12).

The dashed line at the right end of the curve is the theoretical polar curve found with the mathematical method which is explained in the Appendix. We speak of this later in part IX-PLOTTING YOUR POLAR.

✓ *Minimum Sink Rate*

We know that our minimum sink rate occurs about as slow an airspeed as we can fly. This point isn't too hard to find on our graph. Looking at the figure we can identify the minimum sink as occurring at point B, where the curve is the highest (lowest sink rate possible) and furthest left. The values indicated are 180 FPM sink rate at 21 mph.

From this we can state that our minimum sink rate (for this glider and pilot) will always occur when we fly at 21 mph. This holds true no matter what the air is doing. Note: at higher altitudes (lower air densities) this speed actually is higher, but this doesn't concern us just yet.

In a glider, a given airspeed relates to a given angle of attack as long as we haven't made sudden control changes. Thus, minimum sink will always occur at *one given bar position*—that which provides the minimum sink angle of attack. Incidently, this bar position doesn't change for different altitudes although the airspeed does.

✓ *Best Glide*

Our maximum glide ratio in still air can be readily found from the performance map. This is most easily understood if we realize that any point on the curve indicates a unique glide ratio. For example, point A with 35 mph indicated on the horizontal scale and a 290 FPM sink rate (3.3 mph) gives a glide ratio of 35/3.3 = 10.6. This is shown in figure 7-3.

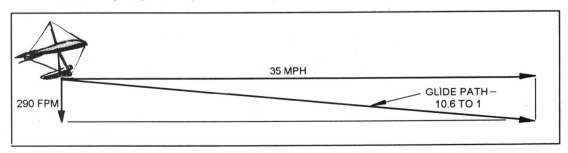

Figure 7-3: Maximum Glide Ratio Values

Similarly, at point B we have 21 mph horizontal speed for 180 FPM (2.045 mph) vertical speed giving a glide ratio of 10.3.

Now which point will give us our maximum glide ratio? We know that this will occur when the ratio of horizontal speed to vertical speed (sink rate) is the highest. Take a straight edge and place one end on the origin of the axes (point O) and the other end on any point on the curve. The angle the straight edge makes with the horizontal axis is a representation of the glide ratio. Note that drawing the line from the origin to the curve does not depict the actual glide angle because the vertical scale is expanded. If we reduced it to be identical to the horizontal scale, a line from the origin to a point on the curve would display the actual glide angle at that speed (however, our curve would not be as dramatic and easy to use).

If you start with point B and move progressively along the curve you'll find the straight edge flattens out for a while then gets continuously steeper. Its flattest value is the maximum glide ratio and occurs where the straight edge is tangent to the curve (touches it without cutting it). This is point C in figure 7-2.

Looking at the graph we see that point C, the maximum glide ratio occurs at a horizontal speed of 27 mph and a vertical speed of 200 FPM (2.275 mph) for a glide ratio of 11.9 to 1. Any other point on the curve will give a lesser value of glide ratio.

Best glide over the ground is a totally different concept than best glide through the air. only in still air are they the same.

*III - CASE I - FLYING FOR DISTANCE

*N*ow we turn our attention to how we use our performance map to figure out speeds-to-fly for achieving the best distance. The idea that must be clear is that various conditions of air movement change the required speeds.

BUCKING A HEAD WIND

We have already seen that a head wind prompts us to fly faster than our still air best glide speed to get our best glide in relation to the ground (see figure 7-1). To find exactly what this new flying speed will be, we must realize that a head wind reduces our horizontal speed over the ground.

Look at figure 7-4. Here we see our original polar as presented in figure 7-2 with the curve shifted to the left 15 miles per hour to reflect the effect of a 15 mph head wind. We have essentially reduced the value of our horizontal speeds by 15 mph. Now we can see that a line drawn from the origin (O) to run tangent to the curve (at point A) is further down the curve than our best glide in still air point (B).

It is a lot of extra work to move the curve and scales on our graph, so instead we just move our origin and thus can use our original performance map for any wind condition. This is shown in figure 7-5. Here we moved the origin (O) to the *right* (for a head wind) 15 mph to get the new origin (O'). Now we draw our lines to the curve and figure the results.

Line O'A is the tangent line that gives us the best glide over the ground in a 15 mph head wind. It is the speed-to-fly in this head wind and occurs at 34 mph with 277 FPM sink. This gives a glide ratio over the ground—the maximum we can possibly achieve under the conditions—as a little better than 6 to 1 (horizontal velocity over the ground: 34 mph – 15 mph = 19 mph divided by vertical velocity: 277 FPM or 3.15 mph).

If we would fly at our still air best glide speed of 27 mph (line O'B) we would get a glide over the ground of about 5.3 to 1 (27 mph – 15 mph = 12 mph divided by 200 FPM or 2.27 mph). It appears that there isn't a great deal of difference between the two glide ratios until we imagine that we have to reach a landing field surrounded by trees, power lines and unfriendly landowners

Speed-to-fly:
- *Fly faster than best glide in a head wind.*
- *Fly slower than best glide in a tail wind.*
- *Fly faster than best glide in sink.*
- *Fly slower than best glide in lift.*

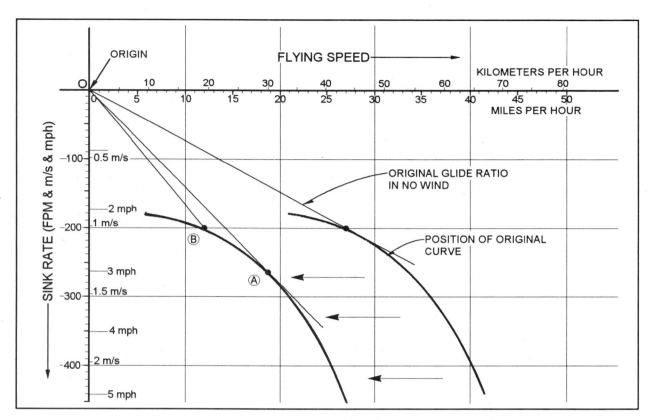

Figure 7-4: Moving a Polar for Head Wind Effects

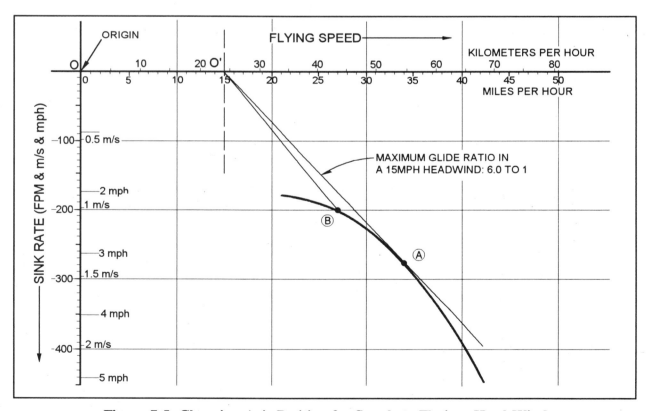

Figure 7-5: Changing Axis Position for Speeds-to-Fly in a Head Wind

with pet alligators that is 5.5 to 1 away in a 15 mph head wind.

A more significant illustration is to imagine two gliders heading into a 15 mph wind looking for a thermal. The slower glider loses 996 feet for every mile it travels at a 5.3 to 1 glide. The more efficient, faster glider loses 880 feet per mile. Thus there is a difference of well over 100 feet in every mile of flight and furthermore our better gliding pilot gets to any available thermal almost 30 seconds sooner for every mile traveled.

We can do a similar analysis for every head wind we care to. Try a few more examples yourself to become familiar with the concept. See what happens if you fly your still air best glide speed (27 mph) in a 27 mph head wind.

From the above discussion we can form our first speed-to-fly ruler as given in the side bar.

Understanding this principle and getting a feel for what speed to fly at in various degrees of head wind is a great step forward in flying with finesse.

Flying in a head wind is like dragging a small parachute in terms of covering ground.

> **In a Head Wind**
> Fly faster than best glide speed to achieve best glide over the ground. The greater the head wind, the faster we must fly.

RIDING A TAIL WIND

A tail wind gives us a boost from the rear and can actually improve our glide ratio over the ground since our horizontal speed is greater. To get the correct speeds to fly in various tail winds, we again turn to our polar.

Figure 7-6 shows our standard curve with a no-wind tangent (line OA), a 10 mph tail wind tangent (line O'B) and a 20 mph tail wind tangent (line O"C). Instead of moving our curve, we moved our origin this time to the *left* to simulate a tail wind adding to our flying speed. The new origin points are O' for a 10 mph tail wind and O" for a 20 mph tail wind.

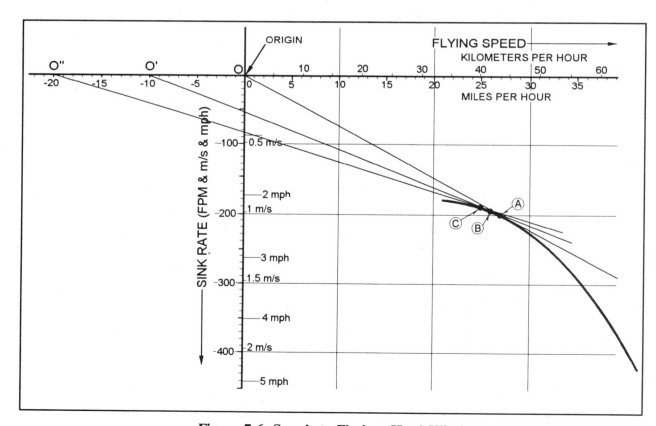

Figure 7-6: Speeds-to-Fly in a Head Wind

This graph construction points out that we should fly slower than our still air best glide speed to max out our distance over the ground. The efficient speed for the 10 mph tail wind is about 26 mph and for the 20 mph tail wind is about 25 mph giving a glide ratio of over 20 to 1 (25+20 = 45 divided by 193 FPM or 2.19 mph). Work out your glide in a 10 mph tail wind for practice.

Use a straight edge to see what happens as the tail wind increases. You'll find something interesting: no matter how strong the wind, you never quite get to minimum sink speed as the best speed to fly. In fact, in most reasonable winds the graph indicates that we should be flying just below best glide speed in order to go the furthest in a tail wind.

Our second rule for speeds to fly is stated in the side bar.

Flying in a tail wind is like having a little motor on board or being buoyed by helium balloons.

Since so much cross-country activity takes place in the down-wind direction, this principle is very important to would-be wanderers of the sky.

> **In a Tail Wind**
> Fly slower than still air best glide speed. The amount is only a few miles per hour at most and is never minimum sink speed (unless lift is present).

In 1978 competitions were quite different than those today. In the Nationals that year one of the tasks required pilots to fly around a pylon course as many laps as possible. Since not much lift was available over the course, this was considered to be essentially a glide ratio contest. However, a wind parallel to the course actually made it a speed-to-fly contest. Those few pilots who understood speeds-to-fly concepts won their heats and even excelled over gliders with superior performance. One unfortunate pilot on the best gliding ship at the time—the Phoenix Mariah—heard rumors of speeds-to-fly but got it backwards. He slowed down on the head wind leg and speeded up on the downwind leg—and landed way short!

GLIDING IN LIFT

The third type of condition we can (gladly) find is lift. If this lift is greater or equal to our minimum sink rate we slow down to our min. sink speed and thus enjoy an infinite (level) glide ratio or a climb. The only time we wouldn't slow to min. sink speed is if the lift was strong enough that we could race in it and remain level, and we would only do that in competition with assurance that we could reach the next patch of lift with good height.

If lift is light—less than our minimum sink rate of 180 FPM—we slow an amount given by our performance map as in figure 7-7. Here we see a 100 FPM lift tangent (O'B) and a 180 FPM lift tangent (O"C) along with the still air tangent OA. Again, rather than move the curve up in lift (representing a reduced sink rate) we move our origin down.

With 100 FPM lift we see that we should fly about 24 mph for best glide over the ground, *not* at minimum sink. (Of course, if we were merely floating around trying to delay our landing, minimum sink speed would do this best.) With 180

> **In Lift**
> Slow down to go further, but don't slow to min. sink speed until the lift equals your minimum sink rate.

FPM of lift we are at our min. sink speed. If the lift is greater (dashed line) we still fly our min. sink speed.

Our third speed-to-fly rule is in the side bar.

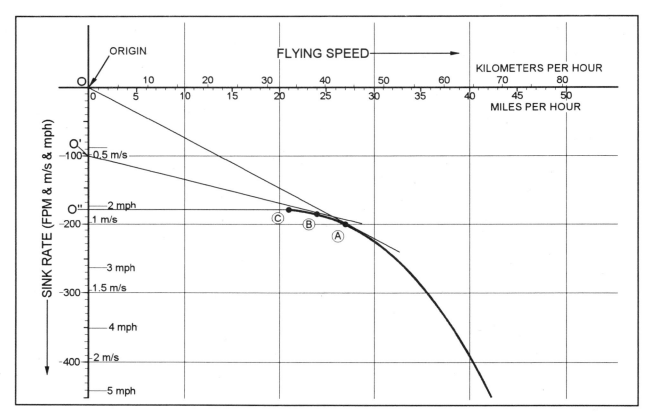

Figure 7-7: Speeds-to-Fly in Lift

IN SINKING AIR

Sinking air is of special importance because we often encounter it between thermals. Whenever we leave a mountain to reach a landing field or cross to another soaring spot we encounter our old nemesis, sink. Getting through this sink as efficiently as possible—that means high—often determines whether or not we can reach our goal.

Sinking air can be treated just like the rest of the air movement we have investigated. As figure 7-8 shows we move our origin *up* when we model sink to simulate moving the curve down.

We show the cases of 200 FPM sink (line O'B) and 500 FPM sink (line O"C). For 200 FPM of sinking air, this construction shows that we should be flying about 34 mph to get our best glide over the ground. Our total sink rate as shown on our vario will be 277 FPM that our glider gives us plus the 200 FPM from the sinking air for a net 477 FPM.

With 500 FPM sink we must go even faster—about 39 mph as indicated by our graph—to go the furthest distance. The result is a total indicated sink of 870 FPM (370 FPM + 500 FPM). We see plenty of this type of conditions on strong thermal days.

Our fourth rule for speed to fly is in the side bar.

To some it may not seem natural to speed up in sinking air since speeding up makes us sink even more. However, when we realize that speeding up gets us

> **In Sinking Air**
> Speed up to achieve best glide over the ground. Generally faster speeds are warranted in sinking air than in head wind.

out of the sink sooner, the logic is clear. Even if sink doesn't quit we go further. A simple illustration should make this apparent. Imagine flying at still air best glide speed in 500 FPM sink. With a glider performing as in our previous polars you would be traveling horizontally

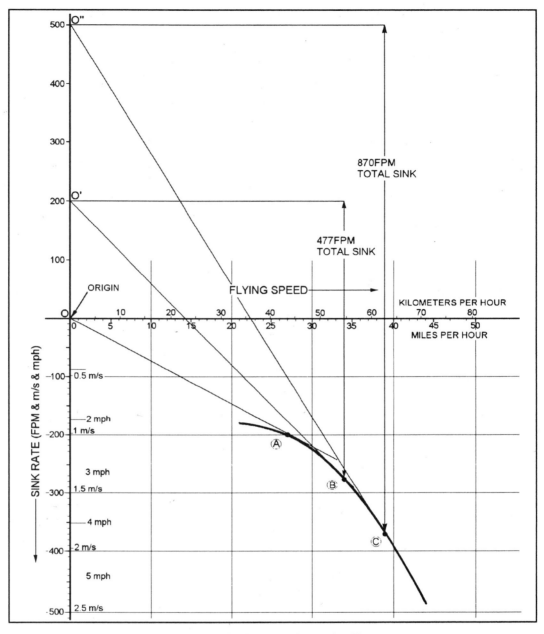

Figure 7-8: Speeds-to-Fly in Sink

27 mph and sinking 700 FPM (500 FPM + 200 FPM) as shown in figure 7-9.

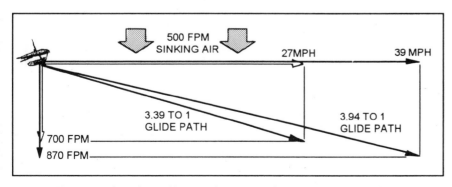

Figure 7-9: The Effects of Proper Speeds-to-Fly in Sink

Now imagine flying at 39 mph with a sink rate of 870 FPM as worked out above. Your glide path with respect to the ground is seen to be better in the latter case. Even though you are plummeting faster, you are covering ground much faster as well.

We rarely encounter head winds, tail winds, lift or sink alone. Next we take a look at condition combinations.

- 165 -

CONDITION COMBINATIONS

We rarely have the luxury of meeting a simple tail wind, head wind, lift or sink. Usually these flows come in combinations. We can handle that too with our handy polar graph. For example, in a 10 mph head wind in 100 FPM sink we move our origin to the right 10 mph and up 100 FPM and draw our tangent line (O′A) as in figure 7-10. The speed-to-fly is then found to be about 34 mph. Notice that this is faster than either the head wind or sink alone would have you fly.

A tail wind with sink would result in a tangent line similar to (O″B). Vary the strength of the airflow components and try the other combinations such as lift and head wind, lift and tail wind to see how this works.

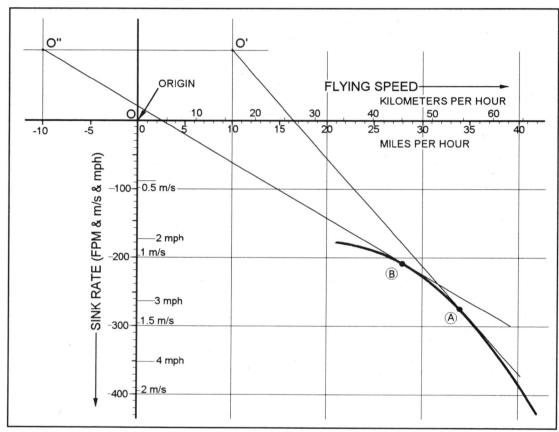

Figure 7-10: Speeds-to-Fly in Wind and Sink

✓ *Crosswinds*

Frequently, we are operating in crossing winds whether we are detouring to a friendly cloud or crabbing across a gap. What is our best speed-to-fly in this cases? Actually, the question is rather complex for the stronger the wind and the slower we fly the more we must crab and the less headway we are making towards our goal. Conversely, if we fly faster we have to crab less but our sink is greater. In addition to varying strength, the wind can also be a quartering head wind or tail wind.

Crosswinds slow our progress like head winds unless they are directed from the rear.

Although such real situations can be worked out mathematically, the equations are very tedious so it is easiest to present the ideas graphically. Here are a few basic rules that you can use as guidelines.

Achieving Best Glide in Crossing Winds

1. With a quartering head wind (less than 90° cross), fly faster than best glide airspeed so that your crab angle remains less than 45°. Your airspeed should normally be less than your speed-to-fly in a direct head wind of the same amount. This added speed decreases as the angle of the crossing wind increases. The left side of figure 7-11 gives the speeds-to-fly for various quartering head wind velocities and angles. Figure 7-12 gives an overview of the speeds relationships in quartering winds.

2. In a quartering tail wind fly faster than your speed-to-fly airspeed in a direct tail wind of the same amount so your crab angle doesn't degrade your glide path. This is shown in the right side of figure 7-11 with an overview in figure 7-12.

3. In a direct crosswind (90°) the optimum crab angle does exceed 45° in non-sinking air. Figure 7-13 indicates optimum crab angles for various crossing winds. Note that head winds require less crab angle (but higher airspeeds) than tail winds for a given crossing wind.

4. In sink or lift combined with crossing winds, speed up even more in the former and slow more in the latter. In lift that provides zero sink, slowing to fly level is optimum for going the furthest distance no matter what the crab angle. (Later when we address speed optimization we find that this isn't the case.)

Speed-to-fly concepts take the guesswork out of venturing into varying air.

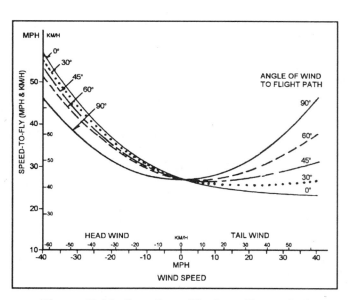

Figure 7-11: Speeds-to-Fly in a Crosswind of Varying Angles

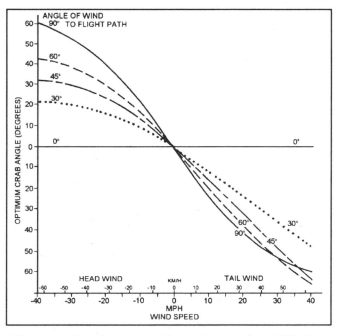

Figure 7-12: Optimum Crab Angles for Differing Crosswind Angles

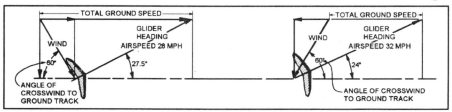

Figure 7-13: Example of a 60° Crossing Head and Tail Wind

We should utilize the best speed -to-fly for distance techniques whenever we want to go as far as possible or get somewhere as high as possible from a given altitude. Examples of these uses are: final glide on a cross-country flight, crossing an expanse of unlandable terrain, looking for lift in weak or spotty conditions, crossing gaps and reaching for a landing field. Sometimes not flying best speeds-to-fly in these situations results in a landing while others are winging depressingly high above us.

We rarely have an exact value for the wind speed at our altitude, but we do know the vertical movement of the air from our variometer's songs and gestures. At best we can only estimate head wind, tail wind and crosswind components. However, we can learn to apply the ideas explained above so we come fairly close to optimum speeds.

Try to judge glide paths watching the horizon and other gliding gliders to tell when you're sliding along the best possible path. Practice speeds-to-fly continuously and you will learn to generate the proper speed almost automatically. Obviously an airspeed indicator can help you achieve these proper speeds. Your reward will be longer-lasting altitude.

➤ **Pro Tip**: When thermals are weak it is more difficult to feel them the faster you fly. It may be necessary to actually fly slower than the optimum speed-to-fly in this case.

The MacCready speed ring tells you which speed to fly in every sinking condition.

An evening sky and a building cloud beckons.

*IV - THE SPEED RING

*I*n the previous section we mentioned that we can know our sink or climb rate from our vario's output. If we have a polar for our glider we can then combine this information to find out what speed to fly for any condition of vertical air movement. Of course, we are mainly interested in progressing through sinking air since we generally stop to climb in lift and the air between thermals is usually sinking various amounts.

A speed ring is a tool that is as effective as a new glider in enhancing your performance.

What we are going to do is construct a scale that goes on our vario which will tell us the proper flying speed according to what our vario indicates. This scale is called a MacCready speed ring after its inventor and the fact that most sailplane instruments used circular dials so the added scale is in the form of a ring. To make the process painless we will use a simple graphical method to construct our ring (the mathematical method is in the Appendix).

THE SPEED RING CONSTRUCTION

To see how to make a speed ring, look at figure 7-14. Here we see our original polar from figure 7-2 with some added points. Now let's imagine we are flying in 400 FPM sinking air. We can find the proper speed to fly by moving our axis up to the 400 FPM level and drawing the line O'A tangent to the curve as shown. This tells us we should be flying at almost 38 mph in this much sink.

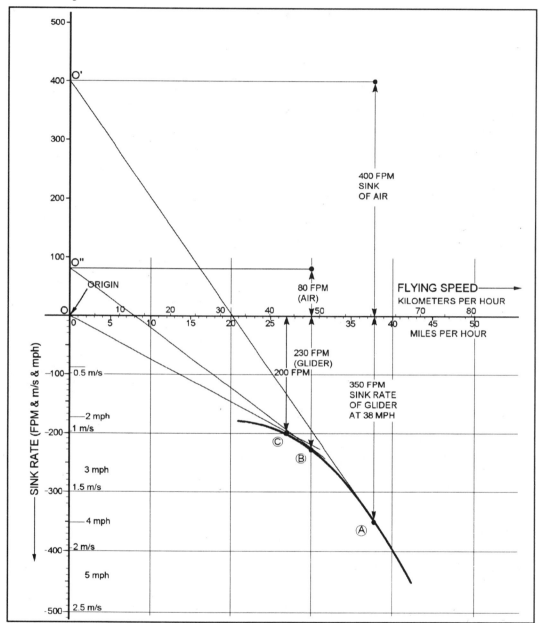

Figure 7-14: Finding Speed-to-Fly Points

Next notice that our total sink rate at that speed in that air will be 750 FPM which is 400 FPM contributed by the air and 350 FPM due to the glider. This gives us a point of reference. We can say anytime our vario is reading 750 FPM down then we should be flying at close to 38 mph. (Note: this does not take into consideration horizontal wind movement, but we already know how to deal with that).

Let's try another reference point. This time we'll work backwards by starting at point B which is the 30 mph point on the curve. Drawing a tangent at B yields the line O″B. If we construct the horizontal axis at O″ we see we have a total sink rate of 310 FPM which is 230 FPM glider sink rate and 80 FPM from the air. We then would use this flying speed whenever the air was sinking 80 FPM. Thus when our vario reads 310 FPM down we should be flying at 30 mph.

One more point to consider in our example is when the air is neither lifting or sinking. In this case we start at our original origin O and draw the tangent to the curve to find line OC. This is our still air best glide line and we see that our total sink rate is 200 FPM at 27 mph.

We can repeat the above process with as many points as we choose. Figure 7-15 shows how a performance map looks with an adequate number of points drawn in. The additional solid line is known as the speed-to-fly curve and it connects the new axis and speed-to-fly points.

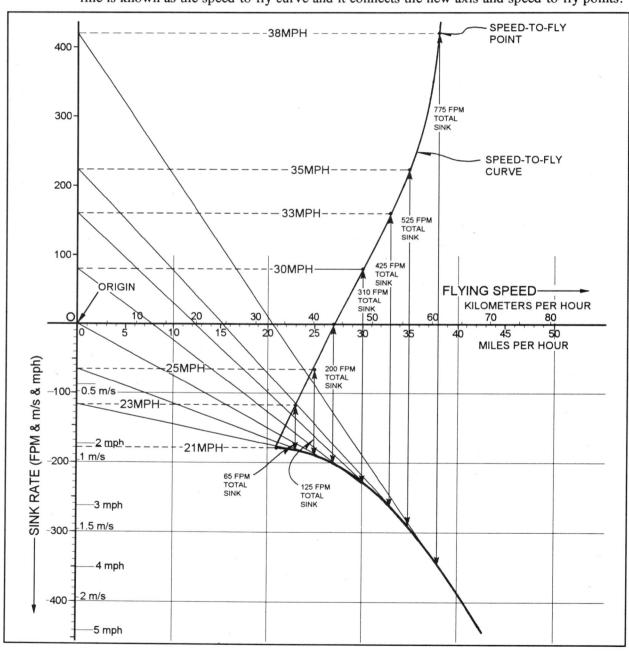

Figure 7-15: A Complete Speed-to-Fly Graph

The data from each of the points we have constructed can be put into a convenient table:

Speed-to-fly Data Points	
Speed-to-fly (mph)	Variometer reading (total sink of air and glider rounded to nearest 5 FPM)
21	0 FPM
23	65
25	125
27	200
30	310
33	425
35	515
38	775
40	970
43	1280
45	1555

*Data for high performance hang glider with VG full tight at 2,000 ft with 1.6 lbs/ft² wing loading.

With the numbers in the table we can now create a speed ring. This is shown in figure 7-16. We simply put a thick mark and labelled the proper speed next to the corresponding sink rate. For example, 30 mph appears next to 310 FPM according to the table.

In the figure we show both a circular and straight vario dial face. The principle is the same. However, we'll see that circular dials are easier to use when we are flying for maximum average speed. (Also an analog, not digital vario display is required). That's your speed "ring", now let's see how to use it.

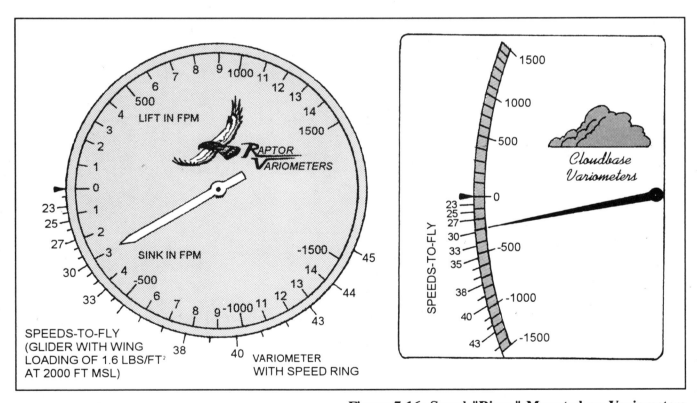

Figure 7-16: Speed "Rings" Mounted on Variometers

USING A SPEED RING – CASE I

Take a flight with your favorite glider at your favorite site. As you glide along out of lift, watch your vario needle. It will indicate some value of sink, 300 FPM for example. At 300 FPM sink, your speed ring says you should be flying almost 30 mph as shown in figure 7-17. If you were flying 25 mph you should thus speed up to achieve the best glide over the ground.

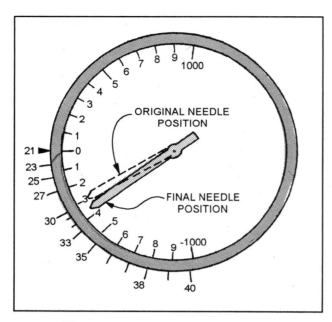

Figure 7-17: Using a Speed Ring

This speeding up makes your vario register a bit more sink which means you have to fly a little bit faster than it originally indicated to match the speed-to-fly and sink numbers. With a little adjustment you'll find the vario needle agrees with your airspeed indicator at 31.5 mph(the best speed to fly for the present conditions) with about 355 FPM sink showing.

If you overshoot and go too fast, your airspeed indicator will read more than the vario needle says you should be doing. For example, if you fly at 35 mph the vario will read 400 FPM sink—you're going too fast and should slow down since the 400 FPM sink mark corresponds to 32.5 mph, not 35 mph (see the figure).

In real life, sink sometimes varies constantly and we must avoid chasing the needle all over the place. Also rapid adjustments will fool the vario into thinking there's lift or sink out there when it's really just pilot-induced swells and dips. The best technique for using a speed ring is to make your adjustments smoothly after you establish an average value for several seconds. Update every time a major change occurs. The whole idea is to spend as much time as possible flying the most efficient speed.

*V - POSITIONS-TO-FLY

Throughout our preceding discussion we have assumed you are using an airspeed indicator in order to fly the proper speed-to-fly. Realistically, many pilots do not have an accurate airspeed installation so they can only guess at the proper airspeed. However, we can eliminate the airspeed indicator altogether if we know which bar position relates to which value of glider sink rate. We call this method positions-to-fly.

HORIZONTAL WINDS

If you wish to use positions-to-fly in horizontal winds you must beg, borrow or steal an airspeed indicator and relate various bar positions to a specific airspeed. Then you can relabel your polar with these bar positions as shown in figure 7-18. Now any amount of tail or head wind relates to a specific bar position for maximum efficiency. However, just as with the situation when using an airspeed indicator, unless you memorize these positions or use a chart you only have a vague idea what position to use. The main point of this exercise is to give you a general idea how fast you should be flying in different conditions.

IN VERTICAL AIR

When the air is moving up or down we can be more precise just as in the case with a speed ring. Here we will use a *position ring*. To set up a position ring, it is easiest to simply make a speed ring chart and substitute bar positions for the related flying speeds.

For example, if we find that we fly 30 mph with the bar at our chest, we should label *chest* next to the 310 FPM sink tick in the figure 7-16. Continuing in this manner, we can create a chart for positions-to-fly much like that for speeds-to-fly.

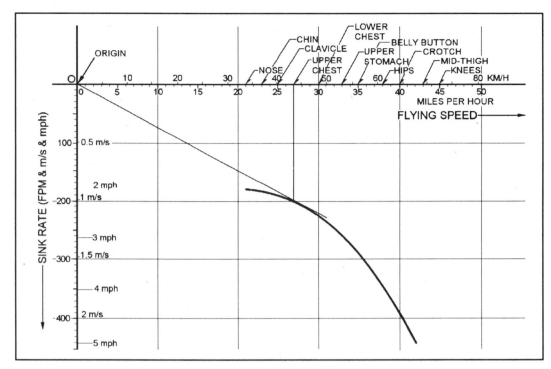

Positions-to-fly give hang glider pilots a much more natural method of maximizing performance than speeds-to-fly.

Figure 7-18: A Position-to-Fly Graph

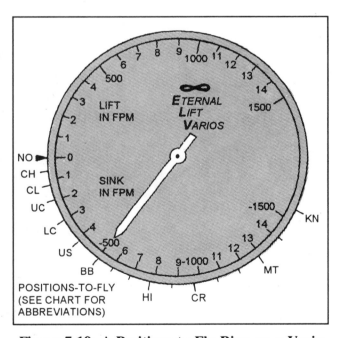

Positions-to-fly Chart

Bar position (1)	Variometer reading (total sink of air and glider) in FPM
Nose (NO) (2)	0
Chin (CH)	65
Clavicle (CL)	125
Upper chest (UC)	200
Lower chest (LC)	310
Upper stomach (US)	425
Belly button (BB)	515
Hips (HI)	750
Crotch (CR)	960
Mid thigh (MT)	1255
Knees (KN)	1610

(1) This is hand position , not belly bar position.

(2) These positions relate to a true reading airspeed indicator, but the error is usually not drastic

Figure 7-19: A Positions-to-Fly Ring on a Vario

Now we can create a complete position ring as shown in figure 7-19. We use this ring exactly as we use the speed ring. For example, if the vario dial points to belly button on the ring and the bar is only at your chest, we must pull in. Once the vario dial is in agreement with where our bar is, we are assuredly flying at our most efficient position (speed) for the conditions at hand.

The beauty of using positions-to-fly is that it eliminates a weak link in the system: airspeed. After all, most of us are accustomed to thinking in terms of bar position for controlling airspeed, and this is as it should be since we can't be staring at an airspeed indicator in traffic, near a hill or during landing. Once you've determined which airspeed relates to which bar position you can continue flying by "feel". This technique is also valid for maximizing average speed as we shall see.

Take the time to transfer bar positions in the chart to your vario now (use a piece of masking tape to write on) and you can use the system tomorrow. Your true numbers may be a bit different than those given, but the error won't be critical.

VI - ALTERING OUR POLAR

$\mathcal{Y}$ou may note that we indicated the altitude and wing loading for which our performance maps were drawn. This is because air density and weight will change the curve shape and position. If we fly different size gliders with ballast or at great altitudes we will want to know these changes so we can minimize our errors and maximize our performance.

WEIGHT CHANGES

✓ Polar Adjustment

Wing loadings for our gliders is expressed as pounds per square foot of wing area. You can find yours by adding the weight of you and your equipment and dividing by your glider's area. For example, a 160 lb pilot + 20 lb harness + 70 lb glider = 250 lbs. Divide this by 155 square feet and we get a wing loading of 1.61.

Now imagine we add 40 lbs of ballast, or the pilot weighs 200 lbs. The wing loading is then 1.87 lbs/sq. ft.

To deal with this we must use an equation (sorry):

$$\frac{\text{New Distance (ND)}}{\text{Old Distance (OD)}} = \sqrt{\frac{\text{New Wing Loading (NWL)}}{\text{Old Wing Loading (OWL)}}}$$

What this means is every point on the new polar curve can be found from the old one by measuring from the origin to the old point, inserting it into the formula and solving for the new distance. An example should make this clear.

If our original wing loading was 1.61 and our new wing loading is 1.87, our equation becomes:

$$\text{ND} = \text{OD} \sqrt{\frac{1.87}{1.61}} = \text{OD} \times 1.08$$

Now look at figure 7-20. Taking a point —say best glide (A)—we measure its distance from the origin. If it was 10 units, for example, the formula would give us the new distance (ND) and (ND) = 10×1.08 = 10.8. This is point A' on the figure. We mark this distance off along the best glide tangent and have the point for best glide of the new polar. We repeat this procedure for as many points as we need to fill in a smooth curve.

Each new point is placed along the line from the origin to the old point (OA, OB, OC as shown). This is because we are increasing the horizontal and vertical value of each position proportionally so the glide path at each angle of attack is the same.

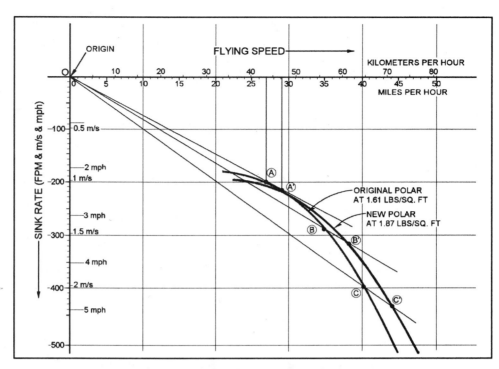

Figure 7-20: Changing a Polar for Different Wing Loadings

✔ *Wing Loading Effects*

The first thing to note on a shifted polar is that all speeds increase for the higher wing loading. Minimum sink speed goes up almost 2 mph as does best glide speed. Minimum sink has increased about 10 FPM but maximum glide in still air *does not change*. We can make further observations by looking at figure 7-21 where we have included a lighter wing loading as well (1.48 lbs/sq. ft representing a 140 lbs pilot).

Using ballast changes wing loading which warrants a change in speed ring scales, but not in position ring scales.

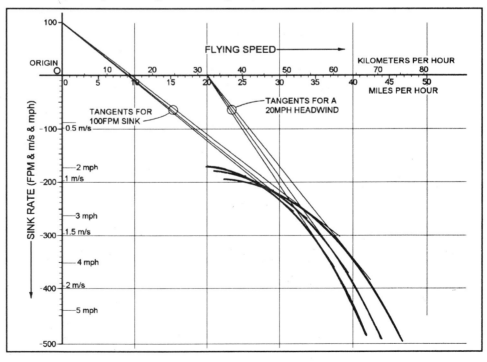

Figure 7-21: Wing Loading Effects on a Polar

It is important to notice that as we add weight the polar flattens out. This means a higher wing loading has a bit more efficiency over a wider speed range. Of course the lesser wing loading affords a better sink rate and slower min. sink speed. This may be significant when turning in small thermals as we saw in Chapter 3.

Now look what happens when we encounter a head wind or sink. It should be clear from the tangent lines that the heavier wing loading achieves a better glide over the ground in these adverse conditions. Conversely, the lighter loaded pilot has an advantage in lift and tail wind.

From these investigations we can form general rules:

Effects of Wing Loading on Performance on a Given Glider
1. Increasing wing loading increases all flying speeds (stall, min. sink, best glide, V_{NE}, etc.) approximately 1/2 mph per 10 lbs of added weight (.7 km/h per 4 kg).
2. Adding weight increases the minimum sink rate (about 4 FPM per 10 lbs).
3. Maximum glide ratio in still air *does not* change when we change wing loading—it just occurs at faster or slower speed.
4. In a head wind or sink, increasing weight *does* change our best glide over the ground—it improves.
5. In a tail wind or lift, decreasing weight *does* change our best glide over the ground—it improves.

Note: In this list we did not include the effects wing loading has on handling and distortion of the glider which may affect performance. We deal with these in Chapter 3 and 12 respectively. Also, please refer to Chapter 9 for a discussion on the advantages of using ballast.

✓ Wing Loading on the Speed Ring

Since we get very different speeds from our polar at different wing loadings, especially at the faster speeds we employ in sink, we should use a different speed ring when loaded differently. Typically we put an unballasted scale and a ballasted scale on the ring. In figure 7-22 we have included three wing loadings on our speed ring to satisfy all tastes and body types (1.48, 1.61, and 1.87 lbs/sq.ft). These rings were taken directly from the polars in figure 7-21 using the method described earlier. If you are flying any other wing loading you can make your own speed ring or estimate your speeds between those shown. Note that using positions-to-fly does not require a change in ring scales as wing loading changes because angle of attack doesn't change with wing loading as does airspeed.

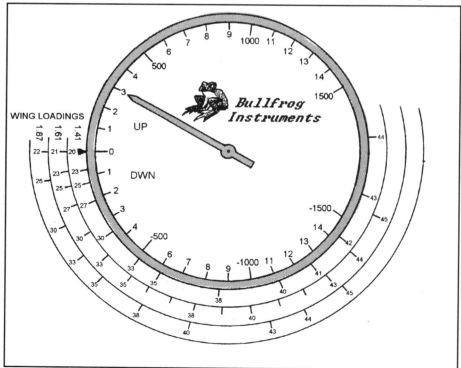

Figure 7-22: Speed-to-Fly Rings for Different Wing Loadings

We have mentioned before that altitude changes simulate wing loading changes. We can handle altitude in the same way as weight by drawing new polars according to the density changes at different altitudes. However, we don't know these changes exactly since differing lapse rate and pressure systems serve to alter the air density. The most effective way to handle this dilemma is simply use the standard rule of thumb (as discussed in Chapter 2) that speeds increase by 2% per thousand feet of increased height.

Thus, we can use the polars for increased wing loadings in figure 7-21 to simulate the polar for increased altitude. The 1.87 wing loading increased all speeds by 8% which is the same as adding 4,000 feet putting us at 6,000 feet (remember the original polars are valid for 2,000 feet). The lighter wing loading polar simulates the polar at sea level (2,000 feet lower).

Altitude changes are exactly like wing loading changes in all respects except handling.

By moving your polar curve a given percentage according to your altitude, you can figure out your speeds for 10,000 feet, 18,000 feet or whatever. However, if you use a pressure or pitot* type airspeed indicator or our positions-to-fly system, *you don't need to* change your speed ring values. The reason is, your airspeed indicator is also affected by the change in density of the air and even though you are going faster at higher altitudes (lower densities), the airspeed indicator reads the same value for any given angle of attack.

Thus, if you are maintaining the bar position for still air best glide at 27 mph at sea level, at 18,000 feet your pitot airspeed indicator will still continue to indicate 27 mph (even though you are actually moving at 36.7 mph true airspeed) and you will still be achieving best glide. This holds true for all points on the polar. Since angle of attack is really what defines the performance of our wings, positions-to-fly values are equally valid at altitudes.

We don't entirely ignore altitude effects of course, for just like wing loading it affects our performance:

Effects of Altitude on Performance

On a given glider:
1. Increased altitude increases all flying speeds.
2. Sink rate increases at altitude.
3. Glide ratio *does not change* at altitude—it occurs at a faster speed.
4. In a head wind or sink, increased altitude improves our glide ratio over the ground.
5. In a tail wind or lift, increased altitude degrades our glide ratio over the ground.

VII - CASE II-FLYING FOR SPEED

We have previously assumed that we wanted to go as far as we could or get somewhere as high as possible. Consequently, all our speed-to-fly or position-to-fly study was directed at achieving our best glide over the ground. However, cross-country or competition pilots are a hungry lot—they want to do more, better. They want to go further, faster. Indeed, going faster often means further for our biggest obstacle on long cross-country flights is limited sunshine duration.

* A pitot is a straight tube pointing into the airstream. The popular Hall airspeed indicators are essentially pitot tubes

Here we turn our attention to maximizing our average speed from point to point. We'll see that speeds-to-fly concepts have a lot to say in this case.

FINDING THE BEST SPEED

The easiest way to illustrate how to fly faster is to use an example. On the left of figure 7-23 we have a gang of five pilots all jockeying for position at 5,000 feet. Miraculously, they all start gliding at the same time towards the next thermal three miles away. On the way our venturesome pilots encounter 150 FPM sinking air and find a 400 FPM climb rate in the next thermal.

Obeying their inner feelings, they all set out at different speeds:

Pilot A - isn't sure what's out there so he flies at minimum sink speed (21 mph) to maximize his time to find lift.

Pilot B - decides this is foolish and flies best glide speed (27 mph) to cover more ground and encounter lift more readily.

Pilot C - is sharp. She just finished reading the first part of this chapter this morning and knows she should fly her best speed-to-fly through the sink to reach the thermal sooner and higher. From her speed ring she knows this is 32.5 mph.

Pilot D - receives some inspiration from heaven and flies at 39.5 mph, ignoring the fact he is getting a poorer glide than his slower comrades in flight.

Pilot E - forgot to drain his bladder at launch and now is in such a hurry to reach goal that he throws caution to the wind and zooms off at 45 mph.

Now see if you can guess which pilot regains the altitude he or she left with (5,000 ft) the soonest.

✓ *The Envelope Please...*

It should be clear that pilot A is flying too slowly as is pilot B. Pilot A reaches the thermal after losing 2829 feet on a glide that takes 8.67 minutes. He then climbs at 400 FPM to reach the 5,000 ft level in a total time of 15.64 minutes. Pilot B glides for 6.67 minutes losing 2332 feet with a 5.53 minute climb for a total of 12.50 minutes. He topped out more than 3 minutes faster than pilot A, but there room for improvement.

From the chart we see that pilot C was wiser than the previous two, for her glide path was the best and she got to the thermal highest. Her total time back to 5,000 ft was only 11.21 minutes.

Pilot D appears to have the least total time with 10.60 minutes even though he flew faster than the indicated speed-to-fly speed. How did he know to fly 39.5 mph? It wasn't inspiration from heaven at all—he went on to read the rest of this chapter and knew how to find the best *average* speed-to-fly given the expected climb rate. Before we pass this trick on to you let's finish the study of our pilots.

Pilot E chose to fly too fast and spent too much time climbing even though he got to the thermal in only 4 minutes. His total time was 10.90 minutes, only 18 seconds (.3 min.) off the pace.

✓ *Further Observations*

If we look at the figure and related chart we see some interesting matters. First we note that pilot D actually achieved a poorer glide over the ground than pilots B and C but got to the thermal much sooner so that he could climb past their positions by the time they got there. In fact, he was 247 ft above pilot C and 762 ft above pilot B when he regained 5,000 ft! Anyone who has flown with other pilots from thermal to thermal will recognize this scenario: if we dally we often end up looking at our former wingmen drawing cute zeros above our head.

It is apparent from this little flight review that big gains can accrue to the pilot that flies with smarts. Apparently, even though we get a poorer glide, we can sometimes get higher sooner. Let's see why and how.

Using speed-to-fly ideas for maximizing speed is one of the secrets of top competitors.

- 178 -

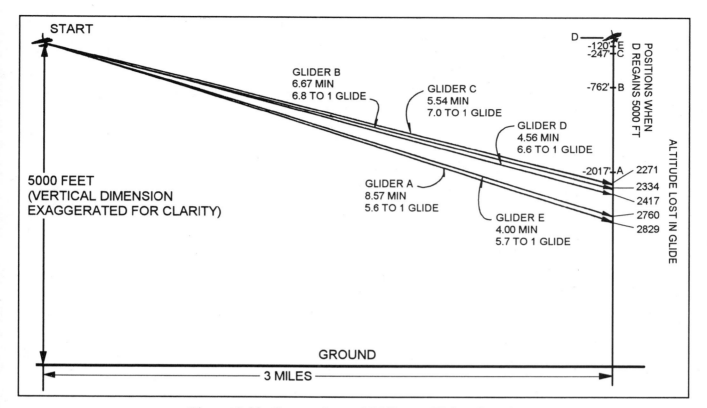

Figure 7-23: Comparison of Different Flying Speeds

PILOT	FLYING SPEED (MPH)	TOTAL SINK RATE (FPM)	GLIDING TIME (MIN)	ALTITUDE LOST (FT)	CLIMBING TIME (MIN) @ 400 FPM	TOTAL TIME (MIN)	AVERAGE SPEED (MPH)
A	21	330	8.57	2829	7.07	15.64	11.50
B	27	350	6.67	2334	5.84	12.50	14.40
C	32.5	410	5.54	2271	5.68	11.22	16.05
D	39.5	530	4.56	2417	6.04	10.60	16.98
E	45	690	4.00	2760	6.90	10.90	16.48

MAXIMIZING AVERAGE SPEED

We wish to make it clear that the reason we can achieve a faster time over a given course is due to the climbs required. By getting to the climbing area sooner we make up for the extra altitude we loose—up to a certain point. As the lift gets weaker, this becomes less and less the case.

The only speed we care to maximize is our average speed. Sometimes we must fly slower to do this, but often, especially in desert conditions, we should fly faster between thermals.

✓ In Still Air Between Thermals

Imagine we must glide in still air to a thermal with a 400 FPM expected climb rate. To find the best speed-to-fly for the fastest time, we again resort to the graphical method.

Figure 7-24 shows our trusty polar from which we have been squeezing so much juice. We take our expected climb rate and mark it off on the vertical axis *above* the origin (O). Then we lay down the tangent to our curve from this point (A) to get line AB. The speed at point is 37.5 mph and is our speed-to-fly for the best time in the glide and climb combination. The distance of the line OC represents the average speed at 20.1 mph. Remember, the average speed is the distance divided by the total time and total time includes the gliding time *and* climbing time.

You may have noticed that normally when we're dealing with lift we move our origin down the vertical axis to simulate moving the curve up. Here, however, we went up the axis because we are saying in essence that our expected climb rate lets us fly as if we were in 400 FPM sink without paying the sink penalty. Hence we move up the axis and get a faster speed. You may wish to try different speeds and make a total time calculation as we did in figure 7-23 (remember, we're assuming zero sink between thermals). You'll find that the 37.5 mph we found graphically will give you the shortest time or best average speed from one point to another at the same height.

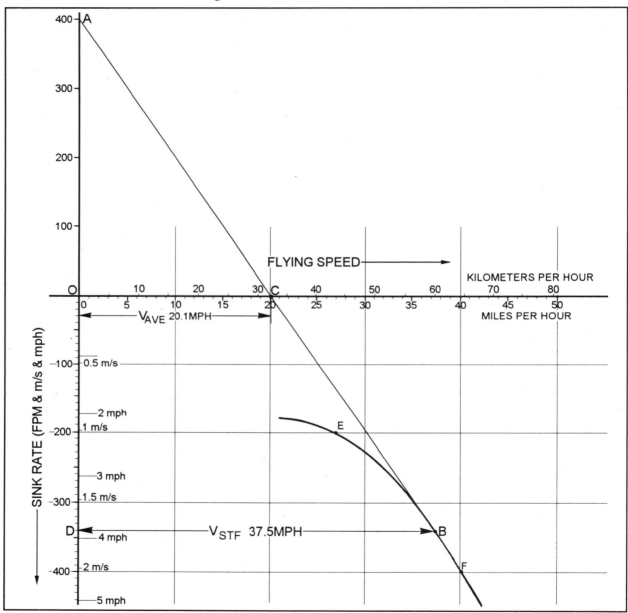

Figure 7-24: Finding the Best Average Velocity

As a further clarification, we should point out that this graphical method works because when we're given a fixed climb rate we maximize our gliding speed between thermals (line DB) and average speed (line OC) by flying at the speed given by the tangent (AB). If we go from point A to any other point on the curve, such as E or F, we see that we end up with shorter speed lines. Also, note that average speed (OC) is always proportional to flying speed (DB) and the greater our expected climb rate, the closer average speed will be to flying speed. The reason these relationships work is explained by the marvels of mathematical analysis in the Appendix, but you don't need to understand the details to appreciate the beauties of nature.

✓ With Inter Thermal Sink

We previously considered the case with still air between thermals. However, we know we usually encounter pesky sink when thermal hopping. Figure 7-25 shows how we handle this graphically. We simply move the origin O up an amount equivalent to the sink, then move it up an additional amount equal to the expected lift.

The example in our figure shows 150 FPM sink between thermals giving an origin O′ and a 400 FPM expected climb giving a starting point A for the tangent line AB. The flying speed (between thermals) is then the distance DB and the overall average speed is O′C. Note the average speed is found along the new axis starting at O′, not O. The flying speed in this case is 39.5 mph and the average speed is 16.98 mph. Note how the average speed decreased compared to figure 7-24 because we had to spend extra time climbing due to the extra sink while gliding. Also we see how these flying speeds found graphically agree with those calculated in figure 7-23.

In a moment we'll see how to use these speeds in the real air.

✓ In Horizontally Moving Air

We are most frequently racing from thermal to thermal in some sort of wind. How do we figure this into our charts or calculations? The fact is, we don't, based on one important assumption: thermals drift with the wind, so in a head wind or tail wind the thermal spacing and frequency at which we encounter them is the same as in no wind conditions. This is analogous to a boat in a river running into equally spaced drifting ice chunks. Our assumption is not entirely true, for the tilting of thermals in wind and their inertia affect their relative position. However, the model is good enough for our work here.

Crossing winds present a special problem, for to maintain a given

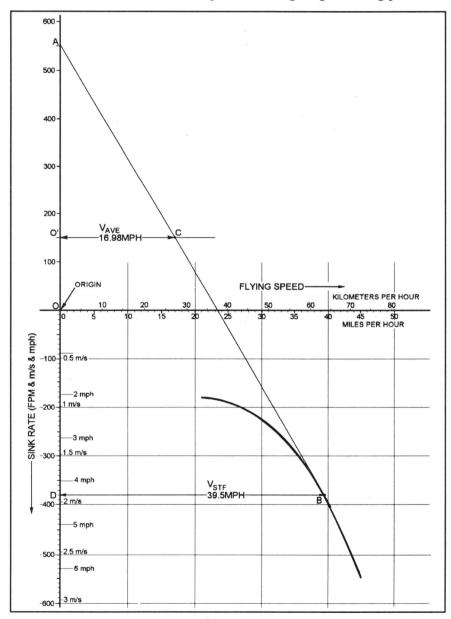

Figure 7-25: Finding the Best Average Velocity With Sink

heading we must crab which slows our progress and effectively reduces our glide path. As mentioned previously crosswinds can be considered as additional sink and our flying speed goes up accordingly.

*USING A SPEED RING–CASE II

✓ The Movable Ring

It is most inconvenient to carry our performance map aloft to make best average speed-to-fly decisions Fortunately, just as with case I (speed-to-fly for best distance), we can get all the information we need from our speed ring. To do this we need a *movable* speed ring. Some varios come equipped with such a ring. If yours doesn't or you have a non circular scale on your vario, make a movable speed ring or scale by using a clear plastic disc or taping a holder and guide for the movable scale as shown in figure 7-26.

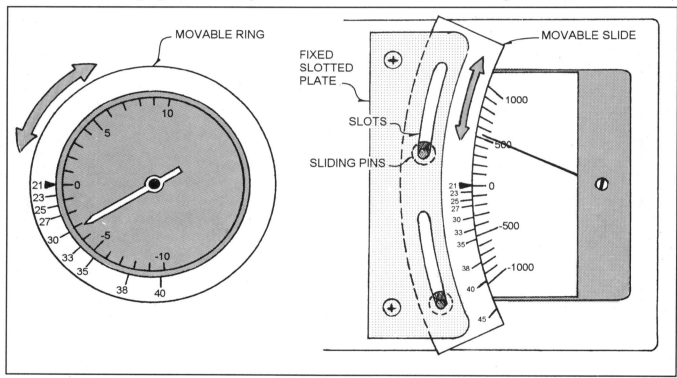

Figure 7-26: Mounting Speed or Position Rings

The numbers you put on your movable ring or scale are the same we found before (see figure 7-16) in the exact same relative position. To use the ring for the best average speed-to-fly, *we move the ring or scale so that our minimum sink speed which we fly in zero sink indicated is set opposite our expected climb.* An example should make this clear.

Using a speed ring is easy—just set it and it will kindly suggest the optimum flying speed.

In figure 7-27 we see a speed ring rotated clockwise so that the zero sink speed (21 mph) is set adjacent to our next expected climb rate, 400 FPM. What does this tell us about speed to fly? It says we should match our flying speeds with what our vario needle is indicating. For 400 FPM expected climb in still air if we speed up until our vario is pointing to our flying speed we'll find it points to 335 FPM down (our glider's sinking speed) at 37.5 mph as shown in the figure.

✓ The Movable Ring in Sink

If we are in sinking air while gliding, our vario will indicate more down so we speed up to again match the needle to our flying speed as in our previous case (see figure 7-17) with the dial set at zero. The movable MacCready speed ring automatically combines expected lift

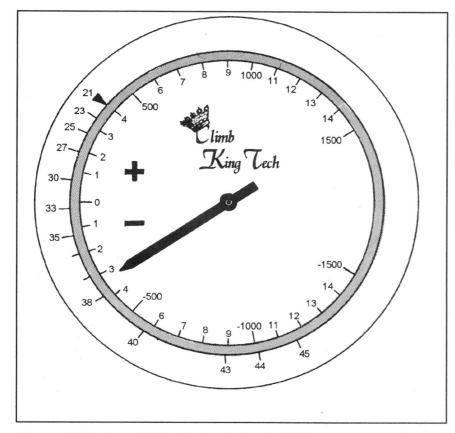

Figure 7-27: Speed Ring Example for a 400 FPM Expected Climb

and encountered sink just as we did in our graph, and therein lies its beauty.

In real flying we typically have to change our flying speed frequently as we encounter varying amounts of sink. However, again, we should be careful not to make our pitch adjustment too abruptly or we'll end up chasing the needle all over the dial.

The reason this movable scale method works is because moving the zero point up the lift scale on the vario is the same as moving the origin up the axis on the graph. Once we construct a speed ring it is so easy to use that we wonder why we waited so long for the privilege.

✓ Positions to Fly for Fastest Average Speed

We should note that a movable positions-to-fly ring works equally well as a speed ring for maximizing speed along a course. Simply make your position-to-fly ring movable and use it as described above for the speed-to-fly ring. With the minimum position set next to the expected climb rate in the next thermal, lining up the needle with bar position will have you flying the proper bar position and thus speed for the best average speed along the course. We can't emphasize enough how simple it is to use positions-to-fly since we all know our strategic body position and can avoid having to look at an airspeed readout.

Setting the speed ring to zero expected climb is a special case of the overall speed-to-fly method. It is this setting that gives us our speeds for best glide over the ground. All other settings assume we'll find additional lift and thus give us a faster speed between thermals and the best average time.

The advantages of using a position or speed ring are important to all competition pilots as well as those who wish to excel at cross-country. We summarize the method here:

> **Using a Position or Speed Ring for Fastest Average Speed**
> 1. Set the position or speed ring for the next expected average climb rate by rotating the dial until the min. sink airspeed lines up with the expected climb rate value on the vario scale. (We discuss this in detail below.)
> 2. Fly towards the next area of lift at the speed or bar position indicated by your vario needle. Make airspeed adjustments where necessary.
> 3. Readjust your ring as you continuously update your evaluation of expected climb rates.

*PRACTICING BEST AVERAGE SPEED TECHNIQUES

✓ Setting the Position or Speed Ring

One of the challenges of using positions or speeds-to-fly for going fast is deciding where to set our ring. The best guideline is:

A pilot heads out X-C from Chabre, site of the 1994 European Championships.

▶ *Set the position or speed ring for the average climb rate in our last thermal.*

This policy assumes that thermals in a given time period are similar and generally they are. More importantly, when we get good at using speeds-to-fly and locating thermals we learn to reject the weaker thermals and only climb in the ones that are up to our high standards. The good thermals we choose to core are what determine our speed ring setting.

In chapter 5 we discussed thermaling in detail, but here let us remark that thermals often vary in strength on their way skyward. They are typically weak down low as they get organized and gain momentum, then they turn on and plume upward in their mid-range and finally dwindle as they approach cloud base (except in cloud such conditions). It is advantageous to climb only in the strongest range of a thermal, so we establish the following well-known rule:

▶ *Leave a thermal when its climb rate dwindles to the expected initial climb in the next   thermal.*

This rule prevents you from wasting time in the slow tops of thermals.

Of course, we can only make educated guesses as to our average or initial climb in a forthcoming thermal, but many days exhibit surprisingly consistent conditions. Part of this judgement is based on how far thermals are spread, for the farther apart they are, the more altitude we will lose trying to reach them. Lower down thermals tend to be lighter so we would naturally climb higher in a given thermal when lift patches are spread far apart.

A summary of position or speed-to-fly rules follows:

Ring Setting Rules

1. Set the ring to the average rate of climb experienced in the day's thermals or the present thermal if conditions are changing.
2. Leave a thermal when its climb slows to the expected *initial* climb of the next thermal.
3. Do not waste time in thermals whose average climb is weaker than the ring setting unless absolutely necessary (this rule assumes lift is abundant and your settings are realistic).
4. Gain altitude in fewer large climbs rather than many smaller bites of height for time losses occur in centering and the slower climbs at thermal bottoms.

✓ *Changing Gears*

Often when we venture afield while airborne we encounter changing conditions of air and terrain. We need to shift gears to reflect the tougher going or the better lift. If we enter a blue hole, flatlands, no-man's-land or soggy ground we need to downshift, slow down, get conservative. We then back our speed ring down—often to the zero expected lift setting—so that we reach as far as possible into the weak area and sniff for lift. As time and distance shows us what to expect in this area we then can reset the ring with some confidence.

In the 1986 US Nationals at Chelan, Washington, a big blue hole squatted over course line along the Columbia river. Pilots flocked into this dismal area and many hit the deck, at first disappointed over the lack of lift, then dismayed over the lack of roads. Those pilots who shifted gears and worked every bit of anemic lift eventually limped into goal with elation and relief.

The Owens Valley and Dinosaur, Colorado are two other favorite flying areas where a gear change is recommended. North of Boundary Peak off the White Mountains in the Owens, the mountains become less spectacular and the thermals change from gut-wrenching to merely uplifting. The real problem is they are often widely spaced. In Dinosaur, west of Cross Mountain a 20 mile flat stretch exists that can sometimes offer thermals with climb rates less than half of those in the higher ground. Cross-country pilots usually fly gingerly across the area until reaching the warm updrafts of Juniper Mountain.

When we enter a better area, our first good thermal lets us crank up our dial and go with glee from boomer to boomer. The whole process is one of assessing conditions, and updating our ring setting with each thermal condition change.

A very important point to realize is that a hang glider with its less than impressive high speed glide may loose abundant altitude—thousands of feet—when gliding fast between thermals. It is important not to blindly follow the proper speed-to-fly for fastest run if thermals are spaced too widely to reach them at these speeds. If you do you'll be quoting the famous line: "I was winning until I hit the ground!"

Judging the spacing of lift is part of your assessment of conditions as you fly along. Start with a conservative ring setting at first and up it as the lift proves more reliable.

The declarations of the ring are not gospel. Don't forget to consult your store of experience and observations to know when to alter your speed.

✓ A Flight Example

Figure 7-28 is an illustration of the preceding ideas. The pilot leaves the thermal at A as it diminishes below 500 FPM, the previous average climbs. The glide to the next thermal is right on the numbers and the climb to B is cut short because the next cloud looks magnificent and promises a better climb. In fact, the speed ring is set higher and a faster glide results. The pilot is rewarded with a rapid, tall climb to cloud base at C.

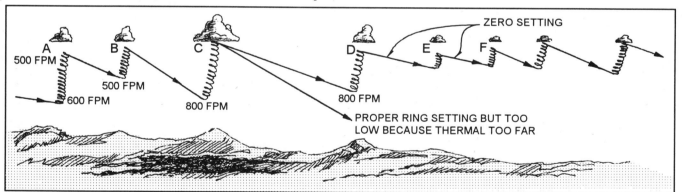

Figure 7-28: A Flight Using a Speed Ring

Next, a promising cloud over a distant hill would warrant a speed ring setting at the average climb below similar clouds (A and B), but it is so far away that our wise pilot sets the ring for zero expected climb, thus getting below the cloud high enough to climb to D. Good thinking, for another pilot alongside flew the textbook speed and ended up scaring squirrels in the trees low over the next hill.

Our brave but cautious pilot keeps the ring setting at zero as she ventures into the lowlands. After two climbs at E and F she realizes the thermals are weaker but consistent so she sets the ring for the average climb at 300 FPM. Eventually her combination of speeds-to-fly for best time and best distance finds her at goal in wonderful short order.

VIII - SPEED-TO-FLY ERRORS

*O*ut in the wilds of nature what appears to be an exact science on paper is often chaotic. There are errors involved with our speed-to-fly method that we need to address.

PILOT ERRORS

The most erroneous factor known to man is man himself. I'm sure most women would agree. Our miscalculations and mistakes cause us undue grief, especially in flying where the slightest error can leave us lonely on the ground picking cinders from our soul.

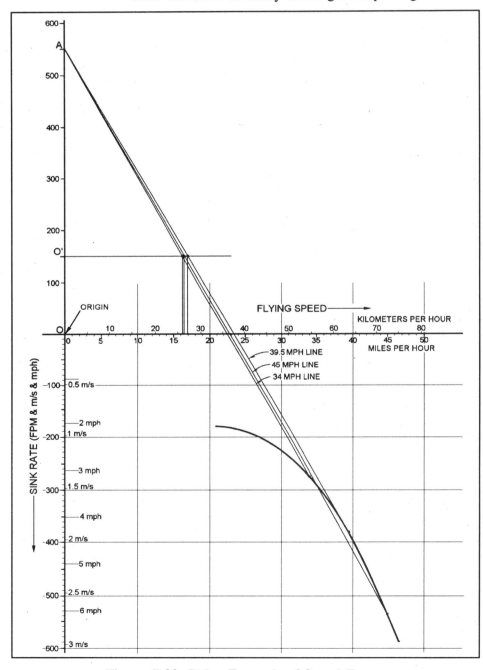

The biggest area of error in speed-to-fly flying is in setting the speed ring. Let us look at an example using figure 7-29 and the data from figure 7-23 shown before. In this earlier figure we found that a pilot flying at 39.5 mph is awarded with the fastest average speed of 16.98 mph. Using the same calculation method as in this previous example or the graphical method in figure 7-29, we can see what happens to a pilot flying 5.5 mph faster and slower. At 34 mph gliding speed the pilot requires a total time of 11.08 minutes for an average speed along the 3 mile course of 16.25 mph. At 45 mph the total time is 10.90 minutes for an average speed of 16.48 mph. This is an error (too slow) of 4.3% and 2.9% respectively. In general, an error of 20% in ring setting (or a 4.0% error in flying speed) only results in a 1% error in average speed.

Going too fast was less of a mistake than going too slow and both errors are fairly minimal. For example, a 50 mile course at an average speed of 16.25 mph would take 7.94 minutes longer than at the best average speed of 16.98 mph and 16.48 mph average speed would require 5.36 minutes.

Figure 7-29: Polar Example of Speed Errors

Here are our general ring setting rules:

While ring errors may result in small losses of efficiency, the pilot who is "right on" is the one who gets to sip lemonade in the shade at goal in first place.

PHYSICAL ERRORS

Sources of errors due to physical factors such as instrument falsehoods and changing air structure enter into our speed-to-fly scenario constantly. We deal with them by adjusting our position or speed ring setting so that the results are consistent. For example, if an airspeed indicator is reading incorrectly it can greatly change our overall average speed. Seeing a deficiency on our part we choose to up our ring settings proportionally from that point on.

Here is a list of potential errors

1. The air below our glider is slowed and does not display true airspeed.
2. Our altimeters are designed to read standard atmosphere conditions which only exist in weather textbooks. Pressure transducer varios do not change accuracy at altitude but when used with a pressure-type airspeed indicator will have us flying too fast as we operate higher. Using positions-to-fly with a pressure transducer vario will eliminate these errors.
3. We assume our horizontal speed is our actual flying speed (see figure 7-30). The error in this case is less than 1/4 mph at high speeds where it is greatest and can be ignored.

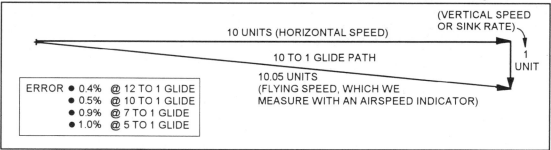

Figure 7-30: Flying Speed and Horizontal Speed Comparison

4. The polars we use only approximate reality and may change as sail stretch occurs in different temperatures.
5. We assume a constant climb in the next thermal as we set our ring.
6. Thermals don't necessarily drift with the wind due to their inertia.

We treat all of these errors essentially the same way: we set up our system as accurately as possible (see the following section) then make minor adjustments to the numbers in the course of our flying if we see error trends. Note that many errors cancel themselves out since an instrument error in drawing a polar and setting up a speed ring will be deleted if that same instrument is used to indicate what speed to fly.

IX - PLOTTING YOUR POLAR

The most painless way to get a reasonable polar is to use the ones offered in this book. You may adjust them for your wing loading, or check a point or two to shift the curve one way or another to match our data. If possible you should draw your own polar to fit your glider, wing loading and instruments.

Another way to get a polar is to use the mathematical method as given in the Appendix. However, be warned that the mathematical method is only intended to be valid for speeds above best glide and that hang gliders do not conform to the theoretical curve at higher speeds due to their sweep and twist. The dashed lines in figure 7-2 indicate the theoretical polar and its departure from reality.

GATHERING DATA

By looking at a polar curve we see that we need to match as many different values of horizontal speed with their respective sink rates as is practical. We do this by taking flights in as calm conditions as we can get (you'll find yourself looking forward to sled rides for a while) and collecting data. We need an airspeed indicator, a stopwatch, reliable vario and an accurate altimeter (digital preferred). You can do this yourself but it helps to have a radio and a friend to talk to so he or she can write down information and leave your brain uncluttered.

Here are the methods:

Making your own personal polar and thus position or speed ring is useful, but requires multiple flights in still air.

Polar Data Gathering Method

Speeds-to-fly

1. Take a flight in calm air and stabilize at one speed.
2. Using the stopwatch, time how long it takes to lose 100 feet at this steady speed.
3. Call down the airspeed and time (in seconds) to your trusty assistant.
4. Calculate the sink rate by dividing the time into 6000 (60 seconds × 100 feet). Example: If it took you 26 seconds to drop 100 feet, your sink rate is 6000/26 = 231 FPM.
5. Above 35 mph, use your variometer to read sink rate since it becomes more reliable at these speeds. (Note: at faster speeds you may have to extend your instruments in order to see them).

Positions-to-fly

1. At the same time you call down your airspeed and sink rate data, you can indicate your bar position.
2. On flights in variable air or when soaring you can relate speeds to bar positions and still collect data since they are not affected by lift. If you already have a speed polar or care to use the one in this chapter, you can notate your sink rate at various bar positions, place these positions on the horizontal scale then proceed with making the position ring.

DRAWING THE CURVE

Once you have this information you can make a polar graph like the many given previously. Put your airspeed on the horizontal axis and sink rate on the vertical axis. Note that you will find it difficult to get consistent data points; you may find them very scattered. It is extremely rare to find perfectly still air and instruments are sometimes cantankerous. Also, it is surprisingly difficult to get more than a couple data points on a flight with 1000 feet of

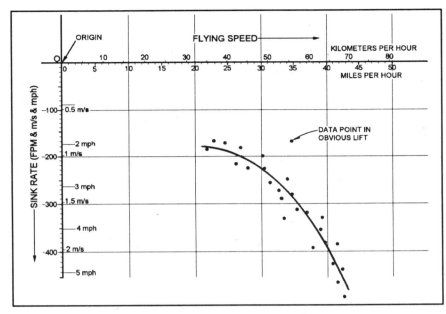

Figure 7-31: Example of Polar Data

vertical drop. But perseverance pays, and the more tests you do the closer you will approach the truth.

Try to get your minimum sink rate data point—it should be with an airspeed in the low 20s and a sink rate below 200 FPM. This will help you start your curve and then you can draw the rest using the ones in this book as a guide and your data points. Figure 7-31 shows a curve drawn in this manner with typical data point scatter. Note that points way out of line are treated like wayward kids and ignored. When drawing such a graph, use scales similar to those we have presented to avoid making the curve too flat and difficult to use.

The final thing to do is the construction for your position or speed ring as shown in figure 7-14 and 7-15. Transfer the numbers or bar positions from the chart you create to your vario ring and go have fun in the sky exercising your new-found performance potential.

X - FINAL GLIDE

*E*very cross-country flight ends in a final glide. If we are on a quest for maximum distance we will get as high as possible in the last available lift and go on a glide using speeds-to-fly for best glide ratio over the ground. On the other hand, if we are competing and trying to reach a goal as fast as possible the final glide is a bit more complicated for we must not only decide what speed to fly, but also when and how high to go on final glide.

FINAL GLIDE FOR MINIMUM TIME

The final glide is as important in a competition situation as in a cross-country flight for distance. The latter uses a strategy to eke out miles or kilometers while the former uses a strategy designed to shave seconds from the total time of passage.

When we are flying toward a goal we progress until we reach a point and altitude at which we know we can make goal on a glide. If we are climbing or encounter lift from that point onward we must make a decision whether it is better to glide to goal or to keep climbing and fly later but faster to goal.

The rules for final glide in a race are similar to the rules for flying fast toward expected lift.

Final Climb for Final Glide
Once within reach of goal, continue climbing in a thermal until you reach an altitude where you can fly at optimum speed for that climb rate and reach goal.

In one case we climb first, then glide; in the other case we glide first, then climb. We can thus give the law in the side bar.

The optimum speed is found on the speed ring when the ring is set to the climb rate. You set the ring to your average climb while you're in the thermal and your vario dial will then point to the most efficient speed to fly once you are on glide. The only problem is, knowing how high to climb depends on how far you are away from goal and what the air is doing.

To solve this problem we approach it from the back door: We assume various glide ratios to goal then calculate what the desired climb altitude is at different climb rates. This "best climb altitude" depends on our position which we get from our altimeter and properly marked maps (we discuss map preparation in Chapter 9).

At least one pilot flies with a calculator and figures this all out in the air. For the rest of us mere mortals the calculations appear in the chart below. This chart can be reproduced and placed inside your map holder and is quite easy to use with a little practice.

Finding Additional Climb Height for Best Average Speed to Goal (h in thousands of feet) (1)			
Average climb rate in present thermal (set your ring to this)	Assumed glides		
	8 to 1	10 to 1	12 to 1
100 FPM (2)	25 h	40 h	25 h
200 FPM	30 h	80 h	115 h
300 FPM	70 h	110 h	155 h
400 FPM	105 h	165 h	225 h
500 FPM	135 h	215 h	295 h
600 FPM	165 h	270 h	355 h
700 FPM	190 h	315 h	405 h
800 FPM	230 h	360 h	450 h
900 FPM	260 h	395 h	515 h
1000 FPM	290 h	435 h	570 h
1100 FPM	315 h	480 h	615 h
1200 FPM	370 h	510 h	660 h

(1) In the chart h is the height of our chosen glide ratio at our given position in thousands of feet.

(2) For metric users, a similar chart can be made by equating each 200 FPM with 1 m/s and using h in thousands of meters with the same numbers in the chart. The additional climb will then be given in meters.

To use this chart, decide what glide ratio you expect to get to goal based on the conditions you have been experiencing (head wind, tail wind, sink) and reports from teammates or ground crew. Then go down the appropriate glide column to the climb rate you are in. Read the number given which you use to multiply times the height (h) which is the height that allows you to glide to goal at your expected glide ratio over the ground.

For example, suppose that you have determined that you can achieve a 10 to 1 glide to goal. If you are in 500 FPM lift, the chart gives us 215 h so you multiply the height of the glide path at your position (in thousands of feet) by 215 to get the proper additional climb height above 10 to 1 glide path (see figure 7-32). At position A, this height (h) is 2000 feet, so we multiply 215 by 2 and get 430 feet, the additional height to climb.

At other positions we climb different amounts. For example, closer to goal we climb less as shown at B in the figure. Further away we climb more. From the chart you'll note that the poorer your expected glide path is, the less you climb in a given strength thermal for optimum speed. You may think otherwise, since severe conditions seem to warrant getting higher. However, the chart reflects the fact that the poorer your glide path is, the closer you must be to goal at any given height, so the proper additional climb is less.

In the example, our vario will tell us to fly at 39.4 mph (this is where the needle and speed will match up when the ring is set for 500 FPM climb) to reach goal once we have left our thermal at the proper altitude. This reading automatically takes into account any sink that is reason for our original expected 10 to 1 glide (which is below our maximum glide in still

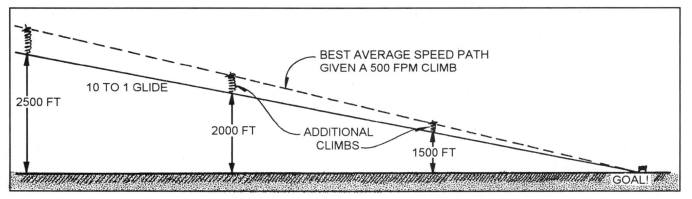

Figure 7-32: Using a Final Glide Calculation

air). If a head wind is causing our devalued glide the vario will say to fly at 39 mph and we'll have to add a tad according to our best judgement. Note that as little as 5 mph head wind will change our maximum glide from 11.88 (in still air) used in our polars to 10 to 1.

There are many other considerations when judging final glide, such as altitude insurance, use of maps, checkpoints and varying conditions. We will cover this material—along with competition matters in Chapter 9. For now familiarize yourself with the use of the final glide chart so you can finish with finesse.

SUMMARY

*T*he theory developing speeds-to-fly can be as involved as an individual pilot cares to make it. Most of the time we can't solve complex problems in the air, but we can use speeds-to-fly concepts to improve our tactics and thus our overall performance.

The highlights of this chapter are:
1. There are two cases of speeds-to-fly: maximum distance in varying conditions and maximum average speed over a course.
2. For maximum distance, fly faster in sink and head wind, slower in lift and tail wind.
3. For maximum average speed use a movable speed ring or position ring on your vario.
4. Most pilots fly too slowly when lift is abundant.
5. Positions-to-fly are easier to use than speeds-to-fly.
6. Final glide calculations are involved but can shave many minutes from your total time over a course.

Finally we repeat our statement that speeds-to-fly are perhaps the most important concept to understand in order to improve performance, especially in cross-country flying and most assuredly in competition races. While we don't all yearn to compete, we all are eager to receive maximum rewards for our efforts.

CHAPTER 8

Cross-Country Flying

Flying X-C is X-citing. Once you cut the home ties and head for parts unknown, a whole new world is presented to you. It's not so much that you are calling on new skills, but you are given new viewpoints, new possibilities and new problems to solve with the old skills.

Cross-country flying is perhaps the most rewarding thing you can do to garner a sense of accomplishment and adventure. Think about it: You use only your abilities, judgement and the wings on your shoulders to ride the natural air currents for miles, letting yourself wander where your heart leads. You are achieving something above and beyond what 99.996% of the population doesn't even dream is possible.

I - BEGINNING YOUR ODYSSEY

We must be fully fledged before we can leap. For that reason we outline the gradual procedure for learning X-C safely. We also address solving such problems as retrieve and landing fields then turn our attention to going further. The know-how is delivered here, all you have to do is supply the excitement.

WHY FLY CROSS-COUNTRY?

" Why did you climb Mount Everest?" "Because it was there."

We have touched on the rewards of cross-country (X-C) flying in our introduction. We can assert that once you have learned to fly X-C you will see new possibilities for flying you never dreamed existed. You will learn much more about the air and conditions because the source for experience will be spread across the sky rather than stuck in a fish bowl above takeoff. Finally, you will come to realize that hang gliding will never lose its appeal because each cross-country flight is a totally unique experience—an adventure equal to no other.

Why not fly X-C? There are several objections that can be argued for staying put with the other minnows. These include the hassle of retrieve, the danger of landing out and desire for guaranteed airtime. In this part we'll answer all of these arguments so there's no excuse not to travel by personal airline.

LEAVING HOME THE FIRST TIME

A bit of anxiety about leaving the home port the first time is natural. However, you can reduce such nervousness considerably by being escorted by an experienced X-C pilot preferably with radio contact. Most such individuals will enjoy coaxing and coaching a neophyte. The other thing you should do is make your first X-C a short one directly to a field only a few miles away that you have previously scouted. Make it a big field and plant a wind sock in it for security.

A view of the endless Eastern US ridges from 6,000 ft on an X-C flight.

The above trick can be repeated with multiple fields along your intended course. Make sure they are close enough to one another so that you don't get caught in the middle. Perhaps the best route for a beginner is along a ridge or mountain chain with plenty of good fields out in front. Of course, if you live in desert areas your landing options are greatly expanded.

If you don't want to risk cutting your day short by leaving your hill, wait an hour or two then go cross-country. This will give you time to assess the day which is good to do anyway as long as you aren't expecting to set a record. It may take a number of X-C flights before you are able to separate the good days from the also-rans, but remember, even the experts can't call 'em all right. The point is to *try*.

Flying cross-country is the ultimate freedom...it changes our perspective of the world.

Pro Tip: If a trusty experienced pilot is leading you, follow his or her suggestions carefully. *We were guiding one new X-C pilot who didn't listen to our advice not to cross a gap at the end of a 20 mile flight. He crossed anyway, sank out and had to land in a postage stamp field and broke his glider when he ran out of room.*

LANDING CONSIDERATIONS

Before you attempt cross-country flying your landing skills should be top-notch. This especially means being able to set up a landing consistently (review this in Chapter 2 and see Chapter 6 for more challenging landings). It also means eventually becoming comfortable with slopping terrain, tighter fields and reading wind conditions from the air. We'll deal with these matters later. For now, a learning X-C pilot should choose large, easy fields.

"The first thing a prospective cross-country pilot must do is become very capable at landing. This is the first thing to practice. Total confidence in landing gives you the freedom necessary to concentrate on finding lift."
— Tony Barton, US World Team member and 1991 US National Champion

The number one requirement for beginning cross-country flying is good landing skills.

One very important point that addresses a major problem in many pilots' mind is that when flying X-C you usually have many landing field options and can often choose an *easier* field than your normal landing field. When you aren't pushing the limits you'll find your X-C landings are usually less challenging than those made in the DLZ (designated landing zone) of many sites.

In any case the policy you should adhere to throughout your X-C career is to fly from one reachable safe field to the next. As you gain more experience you can better judge what is reachable and safe from a distance and what is not. Thus your fields, like stepping stones, will be further apart. Crossing territory without adequate landing fields is foolhardy and tilts the risk-to-reward balance in favor of dire consequences.

The best practice for cross-country landings is to fly as many new sites as possible. The only difference between this and going X-C to a field you have previously scouted is that you can usually see the landing field from launch.

RETRIEVE—SOLVING THE MAIN PROBLEM

Amazing: Territory you covered so rapidly in flight takes so long to traverse in a car.

Perhaps the biggest problem we face is getting *back* along the ground once we've gone *to* in the air. There are several solutions. The first is obviously to hoodwink an unsuspecting friend, loved one or beginner pilot into the great adventure of chasing you. Glorious tales of your escapades may even make them eager to do this. However, sooner or later the bonds of friendship are strained, love meets up with reality and the beginning pilot takes to soaring. You can forestall with occurrence by offering meals, tenderness or instruction (to the appropriate party), but eventually other possibilities need to be explored.

✓ *The Retrieve Pool*

The best solution is to form a cooperative with other pilots to hire a driver. This is mostly what takes place at competitions. Retired folks or high school students have been very useful drivers at reasonable prices.

If the above isn't feasible, get a group of two to five cross-country pilots to rotate driving days. Here's how it works: On your day to drive you fly as long as you want but must land

Crossing Seven Mountains in Pennsylvania—seven miles of unlandable territory.

within easy reach of the retrieve vehicle so you can go get the other pilots expediently. The next cross-country day another pilot is responsible for retrieve and you are free to fly as far as you wish. If a pilot is absent a given day, the rotation proceeds as normal. If it was that pilot's turn to drive the rotation goes to the next pilot and the absent pilot retrieves on the day of his or her return. One other rule you may wish to try is that a pilot is only on duty to drive two days in succession even if no one goes X-C.

We have been using this system for some time and will testify to its effectiveness. This frees you up to try cross-country flights even on so-so days which is great practice.

The more viable and reliable your retrieve system, the more you will fly cross-country.

Other ways to manage retrieval is to call a spouse or friend waiting at home (by prior arrangement of course!). This works but often means a long wait. Buy a newspaper or fly with a paperback in this case. Be sure to supply a phone number where you can be reached, for nothing is worse than having the two of you lost for many hours with no way to contact. The best solution in any case is to get to the nearest settlement on the map and meet your party there. Roads that appeared simple from the air can be very convoluted on the ground and you may have trouble giving directions over the phone.

✓ Riding your Thumb

Hitch hiking is a reasonable alternative, especially if you are in any country other than the United States where the high rate of violent crime intimidates drivers out of stopping for a pilot with helmet hair and a suspicious way of glancing at the sky for signs of other pilots. The best way to flag a ride is to use a foldable sign that says: pilot needs a ride. These are available from dealers or High Energy Sports.

Sometimes you can even get a ride from witnesses who saw you land. Usually the subject of "where'd you come from" and "how're you going to get back" is one of the first things in the standard spectator question manual. Your subtle hints often elicit offers to take you back to your origin. Your counter-offer for gas money is a naturally polite gesture. If your glider is to be carried in the back of a pick-up it's best to leave the tail gate down and pad the back of the cab with your coat or harness.

It is often necessary to leave your glider while you get a ride back to your car or hitch hike. If it will be a fast turnaround you can leave it fully set up provided you can plant it against some tall brush or a building and the wind is light. This is the best way to prevent it from being stolen. The next best thing is to leave the control bar up. If you break it down all the way, we strongly suggest you hide it carefully in brush or weeds. Cover it if you can. Leave your harness in an entirely different place so you only lose one major item if theft occurs. Some pilots use camouflaged X-C bags for this reason. Don't underestimate the chances of getting your gear stolen, for it's happened on occasion almost everywhere.

PREPARING FOR X-C

The best way to be prepared for cross-country flying is to always fly with the necessary ingredients. In terms of equipment we list them here:

X-C Gear
In populated areas:

1. Radios	6. X-C glider bag
2. Maps	7. Hook knife
3. Books	8. Food and water
4. Money	(optional)
5. Phone numbers	9. Warm clothes

In deserts or hostile country:

1. All of the above	5. Signal mirror
2. Space blanket	6. Food and water
3. Survival gear	7. Plastic trash bag
4. First aid kit	

The trash bag is a trick I learned from Nick Kennedy and used to put your harness and instruments in if you get caught in rain. Curiously, this happens most often in desert conditions because of the frequency of unpredictable thunderstorms. The hook knife is for flights over wooded areas or water. The space blanket, survival gear and signal mirror are in case you *really* get lost and have a few days to figure out why X-C flying is so much fun. Dress warmly! Hours in the air at X-C altitudes will cool your core.

✓ Radios

We discussed radios in Chapter 4. Here we repeat that an auxiliary telescoping antenna is advisable for better reception on the ground especially if your antenna is rigged in your harness. You can fly with this auxiliary antenna and put it on after landing. Many times you have to walk to a phone or road and should always keep your radio with you.

Some pilots fly with extra batteries. Most radios will hold enough charge for hours of flight and retrieve if you use them sensibly. That means being sure they are fully charged before your flight and not yakking about your personal life as you fly. We suggest you review the information about getting full performance from your batteries in Chapter 4.

Your retrieve vehicle should have a radio for effective pick-up. Such base units are usually much more powerful than hand-held units. You can often hear your driver but he or she can't hear you. For this reason it is useful to work out a code for "yes" or "no" that you can use to key your mike and cause a CHHHHT noise on the retrieve receiver. Two breaks for yes and four for no are advised to avoid confusion. Use this to respond to questions from your driver such as: "Are you south of that big mountain where all other gliders are soaring so easily?"

✓ Maps

If you are flying a known area, along a highway or mountain chain, chances are you can get by with carrying a map in your harness. In this case a road map is best for you can easily identify towns and routes for your driver. If you need a map to figure out where to go in the air, it should be mounted to your base tube with a map holder (see Chapter 4). For this consideration a sectional (aviation) map or a large scale (1:250,000) topographic map is best. The sectional is preferred if you expect to fly more than 60 miles or air traffic restrictions impinge on your course route. The topographic map is better for shorter flights because of the greater detail. Make sure your driver has the same map so you can communicate. Sometimes it helps to divide the map into a grid so you can identify where you are such as "M7" (row M, column 7). We will deal with navigation and air traffic rules in a later section.

The first thing you should do when contemplating crossing country on the wing is to study maps of your flying area. The allows you to plan the most likely safe and effective flying routes as well as retrieve routes. Maps showing the topography are best for this purpose. The more you engross yourself in maps, the more you'll feel at home in the air over new territory. You can solve many of the decision dilemmas that crop up in a cross-country flight simply by familiarizing yourself with the route ahead of time. Don't leave out the fun of developing new routes in your old familiar territory by using detailed maps.

✓ Phone Numbers

Your driver's phone number or a third party number if your driver is following you is the minimum necessary. An ideal solution is to get a answering system or service that lets you retrieve messages by remote control. That way you can communicate with your driver after a fashion even when you are both away from the phone. A backup number is wise in any case.

II - CROSS-COUNTRY STRATEGIES

Once you have done your home work and preparation, it's time to form an overall plan and start adding distance. Such a plan is an extended flight plan and will depend on several factors as we shall see.

DIRECTION TO FLY

Wandering off into the blue has its charms, but a planned route will usually result in longer flights.

If your are flying from a ridge or mountain chain, one obvious direction to go is along the mountain to make use of the abundant thermals collected by the high ground. However, if this is a 90° crosswind tack your average speed and therefore your total distance will be somewhat limited. An average speed of 15 mph is typical for ridge running when you consider thermals to work and gaps to cross. Nevertheless, following a mountain chain is a good way to get started in X-C flying and is great fun. Even better is linking a series of short mountains or long ridges for some impressive distances. The multiple ridges of the eastern

United States are prime examples of an ideal setup for this type of flying.

✓ Going with the Wind

Naturally we can go faster and often further when we have the wind at our tail. Even on a ridge it is much better to go away from the wind if it is crossing from one side. On a thermal day we prefer to go downwind which is the direction of thermal drift and generally over the back of the mountain.

In significant wind we must be concerned with turbulence on the lee side of a mountain. For this we have presented several rules in *Hang Gliding Flying Skills* which we summarize here:

Nothing is more discouraging on a cross-country jaunt than hitting a wall of wind.

> **Over the Back Rules**
> 1. Remain on a 1 to 1 glide (45° angle) to the front of the mountain as you thermal back unless you are high enough and intend to go over the back.
> 2. Do not go over the back of any mountain with less altitude than the height of the mountain except in light wind or a very crossed wind (see figure 8-1).
> 3. Land behind a large object (mountain or building) a distance at least equal to the height of the object (in feet) times the wind velocity (in miles per hour).

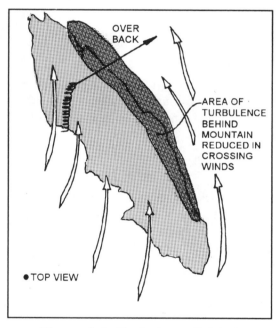

Figure 8-1: Turbulence Behind a Mountain

In post cold front X-C conditions the wind remains fairly constant in direction for 100 miles or more. The most it changes is about 30° clockwise in the course of a day's flight. However in the desert local effects can create very different winds in a short distance.

For example, on a flight from Slide Mountain near Reno, Nevada I landed in a 25-30 mph south wind. My wife, Claire, landed 10 miles north of me in a light north wind.

Winds along the coast or near the mountains can greet you with a head wind after you've been making such good progress with a tail wind.

In the 1992 Owens Valley meet two tasks running way to the south of Big Pine became extremely difficult as the northerly wind turned to a strong south at the far end of the valley.

It pays to learn the typical wind patterns in your area of operation and go with the flow accordingly.

✓ The Terrain and Sky

Realistically we can't always fly directly downwind. For example, one of my favorite cross-country sites has a 15 mile sea of trees directly over the back which must be skirted. Beside terrain problems, it is often wise to follow a given highway for a reasonable retrieve. Avoiding dinosaur country is forever a safe and sane policy in casual cross-country endeavors.

Often lift sources may demand a deviation. It makes sense to zig to well-placed mountains and zag towards promising clouds, especially if they are in streets aligned with the wind.

✓ Deviations

We must learn to be circumspect deviates. That means we have to know when to go straight and when to alter our course for highly probable lift. When flying for distance time is of the essence somewhat because we are racing the sun. However, generally it's reasonable to make larger deviations in this mode of flight because we don't have to stick to a particular track to make a turn point or goal. We'll see in the next chapter that deviations demand more consideration when racing.

Experience and practice will tell you when it's reasonable to make jogs in your path. When you are high these deviations should be mainly to clouds. When lower you should head for ground sources such as mountains and thermal generators. With time you'll learn to prove some ancient Greek geometrician wrong: the shortest distance isn't necessarily a straight line.

✓ Avoiding Air Traffic

Air traffic and restricted airspace are real good reasons for avoiding a certain X-C path or altering our course. The areas hang gliders must avoid in most countries are: Type A, B, C and D (formerly Positive Control Areas, TCAs, ARSAs, Control Zones, Airport Traffic Areas) as well as Restricted areas and Prohibited Areas. These chunks of territory are explained in *Hang Gliding Flying Skills*, and a sectional map available at airports or hang gliding shops tell you where these areas are.

It is not always possible to determine your exact course due to drift in thermals or unforeseen obstacles. Consequently, if you are put in a position where you must skirt one of these areas of high traffic, high danger, keep a keen lookout for other aircraft. Try to plan ahead and angle across the wind to avoid the undesirable area rather than waiting until you're upon it and having to detour directly crosswind. In any case, try to stay high before you make your route alteration for your crosswind travel may reward you with sink if the lift is organized into streets.

Air traffic can be a problem with all flights, but specifically on X-C flights where you may enter areas where aircraft pilots have never considered a hang glider could venture. A spokeswoman for the US Air force advises hang glider pilots to put aluminum foil in their leading edges to "paint" on the radar of jet jockeys barreling along with their head in their instruments. See ESCAPING AIRCRAFT in Chapter 2.

FLYING OUT-AND-BACK AND TRIANGLES _____

A specific type of cross-country flight known as out-and-back has its own rewards, records and problems. Usually this must be accomplished in lighter winds for you have to go one way then come back. The exception is if you use ridge lift to help you along. Sometimes it's possible to find an aiding wind at one level then change to another level on the return trip. Out-and-back flights are more difficult than one-way trips, but they have one added benefit: if you're successful, you can land near your car.

Triangle courses are very popular in Europe and have their own record categories. In order to define an official FAI triangle, the shortest leg must be at least 28% of the total distance. Triangles are also easier in lighter winds.

An out-and-back flight is about 15% faster in a 90° crosswind than if one leg is directly upwind and one downwind (the downwind leg doesn't make up for the upwind leg because it lasts so much shorter in duration). No wind produces the fastest average time for both out-and-back and triangle courses.

SPEEDS-TO-FLY / POSITIONS-TO-FLY _____

The previous chapter dealt with speeds-to-fly and positions-to-fly extensively. If you didn't absorb all of it, don't worry, the understanding will come gradually. The point is to remember that there is a specific speed to fly for every given condition of lift, sink or wind. In the case of cross-country flying for maximum distance we use the method that gets us our

For each glider and pilot there is an optimum airspeed in every air condition to fly furthest. This airspeed changes often, adding challenge and reward to X-C flying.

best glide over the ground. This means our speed ring or position ring is generally set to zero and we speed up in sink and head wind, slow down in lift and tail wind an amount given by our polar graph. We can alter this somewhat on good X-C days for we want to go as fast as we can (being reasonably conservative, for as long as we remain aloft in a tail wind we are making distance) so we don't get foiled by sundown. This means setting the ring higher for higher speed.

The main point to remember is all of cross-country flying is concerned with speeds-to-fly. The pilot who understands it best will have the best chance of finding that next thermal.

CROSS-COUNTRY NAVIGATION

Navigating in a hang glider is generally incredibly easy because we go so slowly that we basically have time to read the landmarks just as we do when we drive a car and compare roads and towns to the map. However, sometimes when you are high and concentrating on thermals, mountain ranges and rivers can look very different from what you expected, and it's possible to get lost.

In the 1990 Nationals at Dinosaur, Colorado a goal was called at Meeker along the White river. Some pilots thermaled high and drifted south of the river. When they finished their multiple laps around the lift they found the river and resumed their trek. Unfortunately they followed the wrong river and ended up 40 miles south of the intended goal.

✓ Compass Variation

The main tools for hang gliding navigation are a *heading* compass (one where the swinging part is a dial) and a map. To use a compass we need to understand *compass variation* or *magnetic variation*. The north and south magnetic poles are not located exactly at the north and south geometric poles so the compass needle doesn't always point to true north. This can be a great deal of difference—as much as 20° east in the American Northwest and 20° west in the Northeast for instance (see figure 8-2). With a west variation, the compass needle points to the west of true north; with an east variation the compass errs to the east. We must compensate for this when we figure our headings.

To navigate on a hang glider, follow these simple steps:
1. Draw the desired course on your map.
2. Figure out the heading in degrees using a protractor as shown in figure 8-3.
3. Now apply the magnetic variation. This can be found on a sectional chart. If the variation is to the *east*, subtract it from the heading. If the variation is to the *west*, add it to the heading. Remember the memory aid: east is least and west is best.

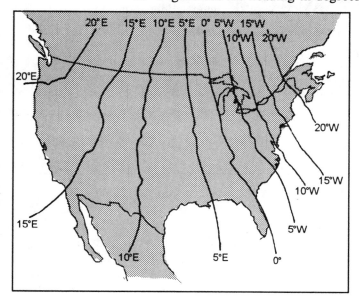

Figure 8-2: Isogonic Lines in the USA

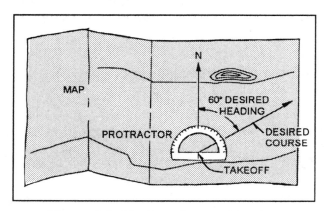

Figure 8-3: Finding Course Heading

4. The compass heading you end up with is the direction you should fly to reach your goal.

✓ *Alternate Method I*

This is my favorite method for it doesn't require you to know the variation. It is so simple you can be brain-dead and use it.

1. Stand at launch and orient your map to the hill (if you're looking west, for instance, the west side of the map should be facing away from the hill). The easiest way to do this is to find a distant land mark or a road and align that feature and its representation on the map.

2. Now set your compass on the course line on the map and your heading will be what the swinging dial is pointing at as shown in figure 8-4. If you have multiple course lines you can read their headings in a similar manner as long as you don't move the map.

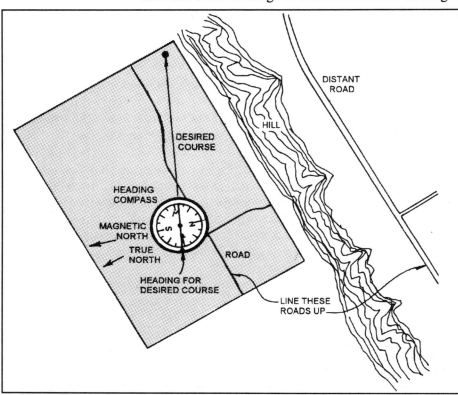

Figure 8-4: Finding Compass Heading

✓ *Alternate Method II*

This method can be used if you know the variation but can't orient the map to the local terrain.

1. Set the map on a flat surface with the compass upon it and turn the map until its north axis is angled to the magnetic north (indicated by the compass) the amount of the magnetic variation.

2. Now set the compass on your desired course line and read the heading.

✓ *Navigating in Wind*

With standard airplane or sailplane navigation the wind factor is added into the course considerations. However, with a hang glider our slow progress and general attention to the terrain lets us ignore this factor as long as our flight direction takes us toward distant land marks. While our glider heading may be different from our path or course line, we can easily read this course line on the compass. Most immediate orienting is done with our map and local land marks. The compass is only used for occasional course line checks or crossing unmarked terrain.

GETTING LOST

"I've never been lost in the woods. However, I have been confused for a couple days at a time.." —Daniel Boone, woodsman

If you do find yourself lost, the most important point is to remain calm and gain some altitude. From the highest vantage point possible you have some time and the perspective to figure out where you are. Look back toward launch (sometimes visible from 50 miles away) or the route you recently traveled to see if you inserted a dogleg in your path. It usually doesn't help to look close by for land marks, since mistaken identity is probably what got you lost in the first place. Use the wind direction or sun position to help orient yourself, but remember that these factors change.

Take your time to consider where you could be by using your map and lining up prominent features. Help prevent getting lost by checking your path and position as you circle in thermals—you can see launch as you come around—all along the way. If you are absolutely and irreparably lost it is usually better to land at a convenient spot (a house perhaps) than to continue on in a competition, for the way distance is measured actually leaves you farther from goal if you are considerably off course. In an open distance X-C flight it is reasonable to continue flying even when lost, especially if you are still following the wind and you're not heading into no-man's-land, god's country or both.

GETTING FOUND

If you land in the boondocks with no idea of which way to go to reach civilization, you are in a survival situation. You can probably stay warm enough overnight wrapped in your harness, parachute or sail. Your big concern is water. It should be conserved until you are sure a rescue is imminent.

...and down in the dirt directions can be very confusing compared to aloft with a bird's eye view.

In almost all cases it is better to stay with your glider, leaving it open on the ground. In rough country this will be the only way you'll be spotted from the air. A fire for the light at night and the smoke during the day can alert a rescue team, but in open country such a small plume may be difficult to spot. A signal mirror is a very effective device for attracting attention. Fly with these light-weight items when you're reaching for lost horizons.

Radios are essential for flying in hostile country. However, they are only as good as their battery pack. It takes the most juice to transmit, so keep your broadcasting short and turn the radio off when you can. A wise plan is to arrange with drivers and flying buddies to only use the radio on the half hour (or hour) in the event of a rescue situation.

There are many good books detailing survival skills which may be essential information in some cross-country situations. We do not have space here to do justice to this material, but we can only repeat the Boy Scout motto: be prepared. The best way to avoid spending the night with the varmints even if you are lost in the air is to fly toward a road or buildings when a landing is coming up on the agenda.

ALTIMETER SETTINGS

When flying cross-country we can unequivocally say that altimeters should be set to *sea level* (MSL). This is so everyone is conversing in the same tongue and you can completely comply with air traffic rules. You can easily set your altimeter to MSL if you have a topographic map, for altitudes of the contour lines are MSL. Sectional maps also give MSL heights, but they are less detailed. Usually local pilots know the MSL height of a site.

A reliable altimeter integrated with your variometer is an important cross-country aid.

Sometimes it is desirable to have your altimeter set for zero at takeoff, even when flying X-C. One reason for this is if the mountain tops are all at essentially the same height so you know how much altitude you have to play with if you are ridge-running or gliding to a mountain. Newer varios with multiple altimeter functions are ideal for this use.

We should note that our altimeter setting will change as pressure systems move across our area. As a high approaches the altimeter will read low (more dense air). Likewise, if we fly toward a high our altimeter will read low by as much as a couple hundred feet.

TIMING YOUR DEPARTURE

The time to leave on a cross-country flight depends on your goals. If we are not in competition we leave so the majority of our flight takes place in peak conditions. We can generally consider this to be from 1:00 to 4:00PM, local sun time (depending on where you are located in your time zone, this may be as much as 1/2 hour off indicated time—earlier on the east side, later in the west). If you expect your flight to take longer than this three-hour stretch, space it out so the flight extends the same amount before and after this window.

Other considerations include wind and terrain effects. If you expect a wind change early that will help you, you may wish to leave early. If it is expected later you'll want to start later. If you are flying an out-and-back course you may wish to leave earlier or later so the upwind leg is in lighter winds. Similarly, if an area is difficult to cross because of poor lift generation (lots of water or vegetation perhaps) you may want to time matters so you are over that area in the peak conditions).

✓ Getting off Early

Of course, if you are trying for your personal distance record you'll want to start your flight as soon as conditions permit. Generally earlier conditions exhibit thermals with lower maximum climb rate and heights. These characteristics increase during the day and towards evening thermals get weaker, larger and remain high with less severe sink in between, on the average (see figure 8-5).

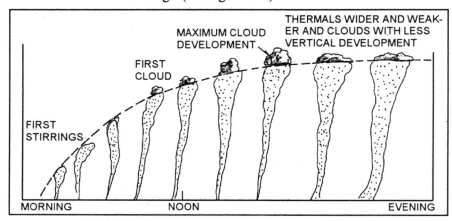

Figure 8-5: Daily Progression of Thermals

How early to leave can be a hard decision to make without other pilots in the air helping marking thermals. Generally, if you are alone and have a fairly easy time finding thermals above launch it is reasonable to think about going X-C as soon as you can combine thermals to get one half of the way to cloud base. This doesn't mean you leave then for the ideal time to go is when you catch a thermal strong enough to carry you to base as you ride it over the back of your mountain.

Another consideration is cloud formations. A good time to leave the mountain or hill is when good clouds are building on course. If these are streets, so much the better. If you are between streets on a mountain it is usually best to head for the nearest street before going X-C downwind. If this isn't possible you may have to wait until the streets move over your area (sometimes they don't).

The early bird gets the thermal worm.

On one cross-country flight I launched at noon and was cruising high on an exceptional day. Thirty miles downwind I was on the ground having run off the end of a street. On my way back a friend who hadn't launched until 4:00PM sailed over my head at 8,000 feet and landed after 7:00PM with a 57 mile flight. His radio transmissions inspired my self-reproach and depression. Getting off early doesn't always garner you the most mileage!

Despite this story we advocate getting to the site early if you are serious about cross-country flying so you have options. I have unfortunately missed some high mileage because our slot-in-the-trees launch was blown out by the time I was set up.

Sometimes there's only one train a day that leaves the station for distant parts.

If you are planning a ridge run, you should leave as soon as the ridge lift is filled in—usually by 11:00 to 12:00AM. If large gaps need to be crossed you may have to wait until thermals are healthy, but you can wait on the ridge rather than on the ground.

We believe it's better to be in the air waiting for conditions to improve in general rather than waiting on the ground, for on some days lift gets good early then deteriorates and you may miss the good conditions. A common occurrence is for a big release of thermals to happen as soon as the ground inversion is broken in late morning. Then a somewhat calm period sets in as the sun replenishes the warm air. Finally a regular production of thermals takes place and you are on your way. Look for this type of cycle to occur when a strong ground inversion caused by a cold night is present.

Here we summarize the X-C departure time guidelines:

When to Leave Cross-Country

1. Center your flight in the day's best thermal production period (usually from 1:00 to 4:00).
2. Alter this time for terrain or wind considerations.
3. If open distance is your goal consider starting as soon as you can easily achieve 1/2 cloud base height.
4. Leave over the back when you get a strong thermal that caries you to cloud base.
5. Leave when good attainable cloud formations appear downwind.
6 On a ridge run leave as soon as ridge lift is consistent and sustains you several hundred feet over.

Searching for thermals should be part of an organized system based on knowledge, experience and a "read" of the area.

III - FINDING AND USING LIFT

In Chapter 5 concerning thermals we discussed at length sources and signs of these elevators to cloud base. Here we look at strategies for putting together a whole series of thermals and lift patches—hopefully an infinite series. We'll also see when to leave a thermal and how to cross nonproductive areas.

THERMAL SEARCH PLAN

We saw in Chapter 5 how we can divide the sky into thirds in elevation and use different signs at different heights. In cross-country flying the trick is to start thinking further and further ahead.

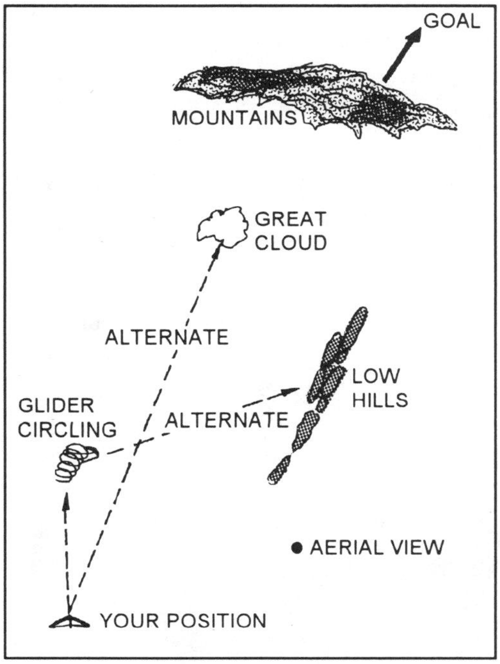

Figure 8-6: Alternate X-C Plans

"One should always think ahead—don't wait until cloud base to make a decision where to go for that is too late. It is essential to have reserve plans A and B."

Judy Leden — 1991 Women's World Champion

This statement points out our strategy. We observe the best looking signs ahead—ground sources, hills, clouds or circling gliders—and see which ones we can get to without too much deviation long before it is time to leave. This is in-air flight planning that gets constantly updated and revised.

At the same time we form our primary plan we create backup plans or escape routes. For example, assume you see a circling glider ahead. Your primary plan is to use the thermal your fellow pilot has generously marked, then fly to the cloud beginning to form beyond, which should put you in a good position to reach the mountains ten miles further as shown in figure 8-6. Your backup plan may be to deviate right to some low hills if your friend's thermal doesn't pan out. An alternate plan is to glide all the way to the forming cloud and arriving lower but earlier. Which alternate you use will depend on the altitude you have when you reach the place of the first expected thermal, and the state of the building cloud ahead.

When looking along our course, we need to try to see potential sources as far as our vision reaches. With thermals this includes distant mountains, factories, towns and quarries as being the most visible.

Cross-country is a game of connect-the-dots. But you must first find the dots.

✓ Ground Sources

Cone-shaped mountains are very good for thermaling since they release thermals in a small area as in figure 8-7. Juniper Mountain near Maybell, Colorado and Black Mountain near Bishop, California are two cone-shaped mountains on popular X-C routes. Longer mountain chains or ridges placed perpendicularly to the wind are effective for ridge soaring, but their length may have to be worked to find a thermal. A cone is a more sure-fire thermal source with limited altitude.

Figure 8-7: Thermal Production From Mountains

The general survey of the terrain in front of us should include a search for ground sources and clouds within our glide path, higher terrain five miles or so beyond our glide path and distant potential cloud routes or mountain routes ten miles beyond our glide. When we reach our next lift source we update and extend this serial planning.

"I first look for clouds, but since we don't have many in my home state of Arizona I have learned to read the terrain effectively. I pick likely lift sources just on the edge of my glide, particularly peaks or the edges of depressions on large flats. I'm always watching for anything in the air—dust, leaves, butterflies, swifts, particles, seed tufts. I am constantly looking ahead not down."
— Tony Barton, US World Team Member

✓ Clouds and Wind

As we have mentioned, long streets are most common in post cold front conditions, but desert areas often display short lines of clouds that can be used as streets for a spell. An example of a flight in such conditions is shown in figure 8-8. Here we look down from space as a pilot on a general northwest course dodges from cloud to cloud to find the best lift.

When we are going across the wind as often happens when we are running along a mountain chain, detouring a *verboten* area or flying a triangle, we have to predict what cloud will reach us on our course or rather what clouds we can reach as they drift across our course. This judgement is easy to do if you know the simple trick in the side bar.

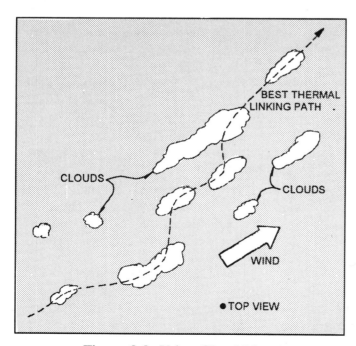

Figure 8-8: Using Cloud Lines

In a wind crossing your course, whichever cloud is pointing at as you crab along will intercept your path.

To see why this works look at figure 8-9. Here we see a glider following a course line AI. Because there is a crosswind the glider must head a little into the wind or crab to remain on course as shown. The amount of crab is so the arrow AF, the upwind component of the flying velocity AE, is exactly equal to the wind velocity. Then AD is the velocity made good along the course. Now assuming the clouds are drifting with the wind, we will meet cloud C at point B because triangles ADE and ABC are similar (proportional). We complete the distance from A to B in the same time the cloud drifts from C to B. Notice that our glider is pointing exactly at cloud B.

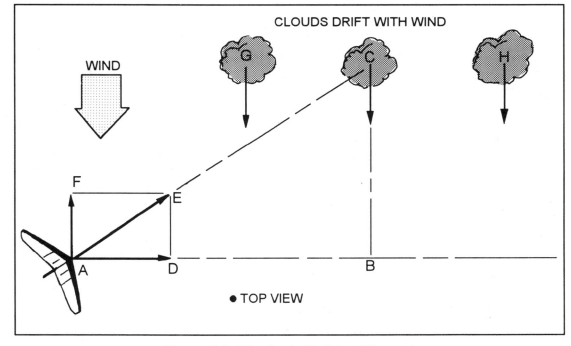

A cloud sailing on the wind is your transport to parts unknown.

Any cloud remaining on the same viewing angle as you progress will meet you in the air.

Figure 8-9: Meeting a Drifting Thermal

If we wish to intercept a cloud at G, we would have to slow down or better yet, point our glider at it and we'll reach it somewhere to the left of course line. The only way we can reach cloud H is by speeding up. We must increase our speed until our glider is pointing at the cloud. If this is too fast for the altitude we have, we will have to set our sights on another more likely catch.

By using this technique you'll connect with more clouds and avoid those fruitless long glides when the ride leaves just as you get in position.

LIFT PROBABILITIES

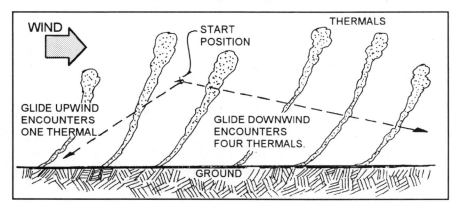

Figure 8-10: Encountering Thermals Upwind and Downwind

In wind thermal columns tilt as shown in figure 8-10. Even shorter thermals may show some tilt. As a result of this tilt we have a much higher probability of finding thermals in the downwind direction than upwind (with crosswind being in between) as shown. The stronger the wind, the more this is the case. In no wind of course, all directions are equal.

As a rule of thumb thermals are

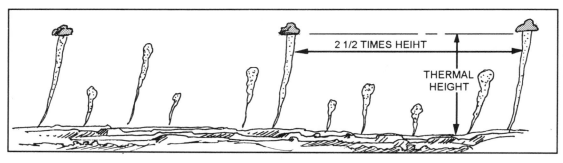

Figure 8-11: Thermal Spacing

spaced about 2 1/2 times their height. The stronger ones go higher as shown in figure 8-11. Lower down there's more thermals. That's the good news. The bad news is that the majority of them are weaker so the higher we remain the more likely we are to only encounter stronger thermals. If thermals are spaced 2 1/2 times their height and if we get an 8 to 1 glide (remember all that sink), then we should meet the next thermal about 1/3 of the way down from the top as shown in figure 8-12.

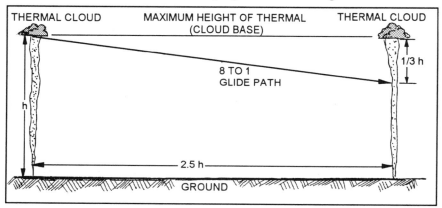

Figure 8-12: Loss Between Thermals

✓ Probability Curves

The higher thermals go, the more chances we have of at least finding something even if we have to settle for the weaker stuff down low. In desert conditions we generally can expect at least two thermals in a glide from cloud base, while in greener conditions we often only get one. Both the extra distance we are afforded due to higher cloud base and the higher frequency of thermals account for this. We can put this concept in chart form as shown in figure 8-13. If we assume we have a 50% chance of finding a thermal in our glide distance, we can see that by doubling this distance with twice the height (or twice the performance) the probability jumps up to around 75%. Note that the only way we can assure 100% probability of finding a thermal is to have an infinite glide path (a motor!).

The curves for poorer and better days are shown as dashed lines. It should be clear that on better days we may go faster because we don't need to conserve our potential gliding distance. Also we don't blindly fly along course but head to our best guesses for finding lift. The better your skills at this, the better this probability curve becomes.

✓ Escaping Sink

As we have seen in Chapter 5, lift is often organized in clumps, patterns and lines (streets). So is sink. A trick suggested by Tony Barton when massive long-time sink oppresses you is to turn 90° to maximize your chances of finding lift.

I recall gliding to goal with Al Whitesell in the 1991 US Nationals north of the Owens Valley. We were headed for the Tonopah rest stop after topping up about 15 miles away. Al was 1/8 mile south of me and encountered heart rendering sink. I was in still or buoyant air most of the way and made goal on a fast glide. Al continued on and found nothing but sink for miles, finally having to stop and search for a thermal before he could finish the course. Just a mere 1/8 mile to the side on a parallel course made all the difference.

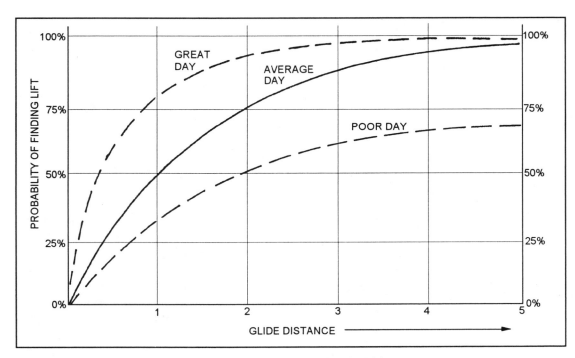

Figure 8-13: Thermal Probability

READING GAGGLES

We use gaggles as thermal markers like a frog uses lily pads—we hop from one to the other (hopefully). It is very important to be able to read what a gaggle (or single glider) tells us before we deviate our course to reach it or race to join it.

Gaggles are usually sure signs of lift. But remember, the term means a grounded flock of geese!

The more vertically a gaggle is strung out, the more reliable the thermal is. It is a column if gliders are working the same thermal at various altitudes. Be wary of gliding to a gaggle if the lowest pilot is at your height, for you might not find the lift when you get there. Be doubly wary if the gaggle is in a group with no lower gliders. the thermal is probably a limited bubble in this case.

The steeper gliders are banked, generally the stronger the core. This is the best sign for telling thermal strength. It is very difficult to tell climb rates as you approach a gaggle because your sink is variable. Look at several gliders if possible to see how they are doing at different levels. If pilots seem to be working different cores, look for the one banking the steepest and seemingly climbing the best as you approach. Latch on to that pilot's core.

When circling pilots are scattered near each other, or they frequently change bank angle, direction or position you should expect broken or elusive cores. If the thermals of the day have been broken according to your immediate past experience, it's best to go to the marked thermal. If solid thermals have been the norm, don't invest too much altitude in getting to the broken thermal.

Concerning deciding to go to a confused, moving gaggle: if it ain't fixed, don't break it.

If several gaggles are visible like swarms of albino gnats, it is sometimes profitable to go to the distant one if it is lower and showing good climb rates. Part of the decision is based on how much of a hurry you are in. Our strategies will change when we consider racing cross-country in the next chapter. Often it helps knowing the pilots in the gaggle to tell if they are likely to be circling too flat for conditions. Also, in most free X-C flying only one or two pilots are available to key on so our options are considerably reduced. We take what we can get. A good cross-country pilot must always be an opportunist!

We have discussed streeting actions before and explain their cause in *Understanding the Sky*. Here we see how to maximize their use for going far. In the next chapter we exploit them for going fast.

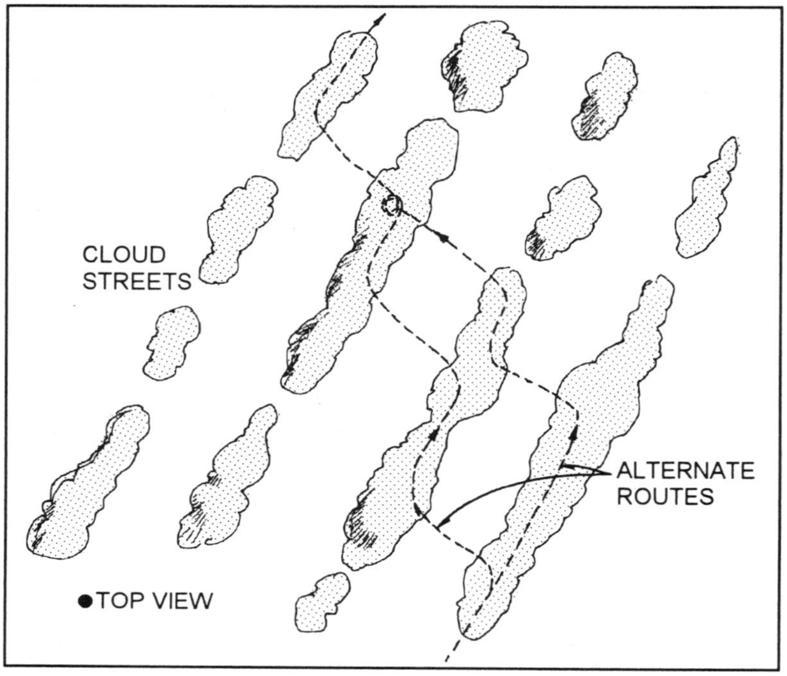

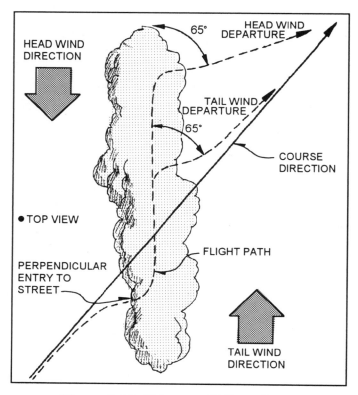

Figure 8-14: Crossing Cloud Streets

The main thing we need to remember is that while lift under cloud streets is typically the stuff of dreams, *between* the streets is what nightmares are made of: sink which is often stronger than the average between thermals. Streets are normally separated by 2 1/2 times the top of the convection. This is typically a distance of 2 to 5 miles. Crossing such an avenue of sink requires some thought.

✓ *Crossing Streets*

If we are traveling with the wind and thus the street and we must make a detour to the side, we should cross the sink directly perpendicular to the street as shown in figure 8-14. If several streets must be crossed we should do so one at a time and regain height by traveling under each street if possible as shown. If we must stop and circle to climb we naturally do it under the best cloud available. It is more important to cross *to* a healthy cloud than leave *from* one, but ideally we wait to cross where two good clouds reside next to one another. It can be shown mathematically that the most efficient crossing of a street is at an angle, but the loss of altitude in this crossing —usually thousands of feet—will put you on the ground or at least below the most vigorous lift. We cross perpendicularly to minimize the altitude lost.

On a few occasions our course will be oblique to the cloud street. This will most often happen in competitions and the street may be a cloud line, not true streets, but the ideas are the same. Figure 8-15 shows our course line at an angle to the street. Does it make sense to use the street? If so, for how far? The answers depend on the strength of the lift in the street and the wind direction. Mathematical analysis can show that we should use the street until a precise departure angle is reached. We can't do such analysis in the air, so we settle for the general rules in the side bar below.

These rules are illustrated in the figure. Notice that we actually approach and leave the street almost perpendicularly to it in order to beat through the strongest gutter of sink that usually borders the street. Once through this sink we set our proper course.

Figure 8-15: Using an Oblique Street

Using Streets at an Angle to our Path
1. Depart from the street with a course heading between 45° and 65°.
2. The stronger the head wind and the stronger the street, the greater the departure angle.
3. In a tail wind or lighter lift we depart at a lesser angle.

▶ **Pro Tip**: Use these same ideas when encountering a single cloud on a crosswind leg if the cloud shows elongation with the wind and a dark base along its length (see figure 8-16).

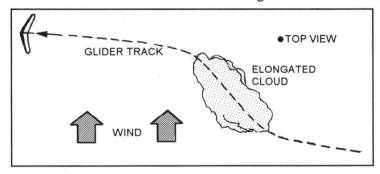

Figure 8-16: Using an Elongated Cloud

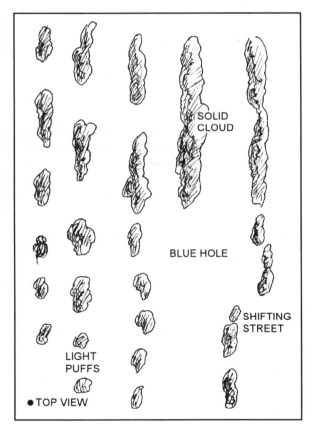

Figure 8-17: Cloud Street Variation

✔ *Solid, Broken and Blue Streets*

Cloud streets come in 57 varieties, 21 flavors and 4 races. Some are solid, some are intermittent and some are in between. Frequently streets end and a blue hole exists beyond. Streets are often not perfectly straight and tend to bend clockwise downwind in the northern hemisphere—counterclockwise in the southern. At times the streets are more like short paths that are spaced somewhat willy-nilly. All of these variations are shown in figure 8-17.

When thermals in a streets are fairly spread out or weak, we use them like individual thermals, generally climbing as high as is practical in each one before heading to the next. Practical means not wasting time in piddling lift if you're less than a thousand feet below cloud base. When clouds and lift are in a solid line, we can fly straight using only the best patches of lift under the thickest cloud to circle if necessary. In such a situation we use dolphin flight techniques which we discuss later.

When streets end we should cross to another street at a good cloud. If this crossing is impossible and we must venture into the blue we *always* top out our altitude to be as high as possible for crossing the expected anemic conditions in the big blue hole.

If streets peter out in general we should expect that the air mass is simply drying out and streeting action *is still present* (unfortunately, sometimes the air mass truly has changed and blue sky ahead means you will soon be on the ground feeling blue). Streets without clouds are known as blue streets and are flown exactly the same way as visible streets. But in this case you have to use your imagination, intuition and any psychic powers you may possess to find the streets, then stay with them by flying directly downwind.

With blue streets you never know whether you flew off the end of a street and should turn 90° to find another or if you are simply between thermals in the same street. Generally it's best to continue straight parallel to the wind in the blue streets unless you are in long-lasting sink in which case you blundered into a sink street and must extricate yourself with a change of course. When flying in any "blue" condition we must use all our thermal detection know-how, including scoping ground sources, airborne debris, smells and haze domes.

CROSSING BLUE HOLES

Blue holes are generally areas of poor or no lift on an otherwise day of good clouds as depicted in figure 8-18. This is different from a blue day that is blue because the air mass is too dry or warm to form clouds (or an inversion stops the thermals).

One of the best ways to cross blue holes is to go around them. If good clouds border your impertinent blue hole and they are not too far off course, by all means use them to avoid a struggle and possible grief.

Flying a blue street is like walking a steel girder on a ten story construction site blindfolded. Great care must be taken to track straight ahead to avoid falling off the edge.

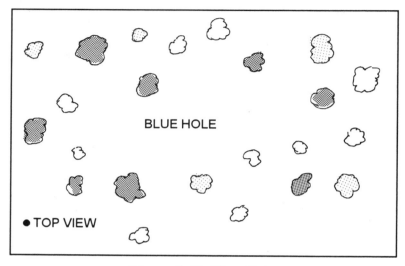

BLUE HOLE

● TOP VIEW

Figure 8-18: Blue Hole

A large gaggle was traveling to a turn point across the Doce river near Govenador Valadores in the 1990 Brazilian Pre-World Meet. A large blue hole existed on course. I vacillated between heading into the hole straight on course or veering to the clouds about a mile east. My vacillation turned into herd instinct and I followed the crowd into the blue unknown. I watched one brave pilot head east alone. It was Judy Leden, unmistakable with her Citroën sponsored billboard glider. I couldn't watch her long; soon we were struggling to grab every scrap of stingy lift. Some of us went down and some of us limped across the blue hole and eventually made goal. I found out that Judy had an easy go of it around the blue area and beat us by half an hour. It was a memorable lesson.

Crossing a blue hole is like going out on a blind date—you never know what to expect and you can only get through it with luck, a good attitude and patience.

If you absolutely must cross a blue hole, as is often the case, you will do so only with tenacity, patience and perhaps a little luck. Venture into a blue hole as high as you possibly can and shift gears into survival mode. Work every surge and shred of lift unless you see other gliders or birds showing you better stuff within reach. Besides other gliders, your main focus should be on ground sources and triggers. Thermals do often exist in blue holes, but they tend to be weaker, lower and shorter-lived than their hearty neighbors under the clouds.

OVERDEVELOPMENT

We caution all pilots to avoid flying near thunderstorms. However, when storms find you unexpectedly you should know their dangers and how to escape them. Reread the material in Chapter 2 and *Understanding the Sky* and fly safely.

Note that invariably we end up on the downwind side of thunderstorms because they approach us from upwind. There is often lift on this downwind side, especially under any bench that forms. We should use this lift to quickly skirt the storm and get as far away as possible as in figure 8-19.

When a bench forms, some fallout and gust front action is taking place. It is of utmost importance to gain your height and leave the storm far behind, preferably in the crosswind

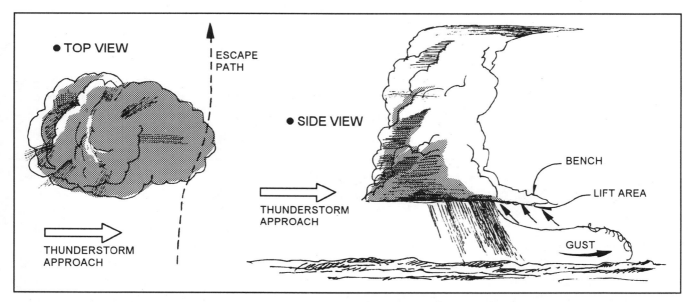

Figure 8-19: Escaping an Approaching Thunderstorm

direction. Also under the bench is the ideal place to be sucked up into the clouds. Know well what you are doing if you fly with thunderstorms in the vicinity.

Heavy virga or rain means heavy sink. Light virga or rain often has light lift.

Sometimes general overdevelopment thickens the clouds to produce rain or virga. It is reasonably safe to fly in these conditions as long as we're aware that cloud suck can exist and the cloud buildup is not too great a vertical extent (we must discern this long before we reach the clouds). Heavy virga or rain usually announce lots of sink and should be detoured if at all possible. Light virga and rain are often accompanied with light lift and may be crossed. Hail or sleet is often the makeup of the virga. As a rule of thumb, anytime 1/4 inch or larger hail is encountered the overdevelopment is dangerous with vigorous updrafts, turbulence and lightning. Of course, a storm may be dangerous long before that.

Hail of 1/4 inch or more in diameter is a sign of dangerous overdevelopment.

During a competition flight north of the Owens Valley, I was faced with two patches of virga under a street leading to a turn point and back to goal. I traversed virga three times and one patch extended over the turn point so I could hardly get a clear photo. At times this thick patch obscured the ground and changed from rain to sleet to hail. The reason for this change was that I climbed continuously higher in cloud suck as I flew straight, bar to my waist! Virga doesn't always mean sink!

HITTING THE FLATLANDS

When we leave the mountains for flat lands we should expect some changes. These changes include: a more regular spacing of thermals, often weaker thermals as the lift is distributed more evenly and possibly lower cloud base as thermals starting lower down reach the dew point at lower altitude. Another reason for lower thermals over the flats is that mountains tend to raise inversion layers in their locality (see *Understanding the Sky* to see why this happens).

When the terrain changes dramatically on an X-C journey, be ready to shift gears.

As when crossing blue holes, venturing into the flatlands often demands caution and lower expectations. Indeed, the area immediately surrounding a massive mountain chain can often be a blue hole. Mind you, all flat areas are not Slough's of Despondency for they often work quite well, especially if they are desert. The flats east of Chelan, Washington, east of Sandia Peak in New Mexico and many other places work fine, but they are still probably not as reliable as the mountainous terrain in the same areas. North of Boundary Peak in the Owens area and east of Cross Mountain in the Dinosaur area are examples of flat areas that rarely result in as good thermal hunting as on the higher mountains.

IV - GOING FURTHER

he ways we go further are twofold: First we must go faster where appropriate to beat the sun. Secondly, in seeming contradiction, we must learn when to be patient and slow down. We'll see how to apply these strategies.

TEAMWORK

A cooperating pilot can do more than double your search area and thermal finding prospects.

Flying faster means flying more efficiently. One of the best ways to do this is to take along a buddy. You can cover twice as much sky searching for thermals and can help each other follow better glide lines. The ideal thing is to have your friend be as good or better than you at cross-country skills, because then you learn faster. You should be connected by radio, but even without a radio hand signals or just general observation lets you work together.

I once had a cross-country partner who always seemed to be right with me when I topped out a thermal and automatically became my wingman with nothing being said. We'd invariably land within hailing distance of one another either because we worked do effectively together or seduced each other into bad conditions—I haven't figured out which.

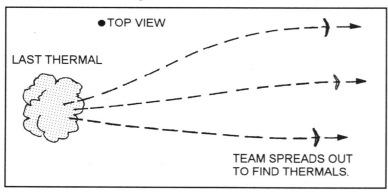

Figure 8-20: Team Flying for Thermal Searches

To work with another pilot or two you should call each other over to good sources of lift once you have found a sure thing. When you top out and leave (sometimes it's worthwhile for the top pilot to linger in the lift until the lower one catches up) all pilots should spread out in order to cover more sky as illustrated in figure 8-20. How far you spread out depends on how high you are, how strong the lift is and how long it lasts. The higher, the stronger and the longer the lift duration, the more you should be separated for you can afford to glide further to reach your flying partner if he or she finds lift. This separation should be from several wing spans to as much as 1/2 mile in extreme conditions.

With radios you can discuss the best routes and next possible cloud or thermal generator to head for. This is a great learning experience for you can find out how other pilots think and assess the same information you have at the same time. Nothing is finer than setting a record or having a milestone flight with a friend!

ALTITUDES TO FLY

When flying X-C with a buddy, separate more on glide:
- *the higher you are*
- *the stronger the thermals*
- *the longer thermals last.*

We should know that our speeds vary with altitude, with true airspeeds increasing the higher we go. It should be apparent that when we are bucking a head wind we should remain as high as possible to achieve the best glides over the ground unless the wind is significantly stronger at higher altitude. Generally in Western conditions the winds are actually lighter aloft. Similarly in any crossing winds remaining as high as possible is more efficient in most cases. On the other hand, in a tail wind the lower altitudes are best. In the last condition we need to take into consideration the realities of lift distribution both in the horizontal and vertical dimension and only remain low if we are guaranteed lift.

The vertical velocity of thermals usually varies from the ground to cloud base. It makes good sense to find the band where the climb rates are highest and try to stay within this band.

In addition, where inversions are common, sometimes a band between inversions or above an inversion to cloud base exhibits the best lift. It is to our great advantage and delight if we can remain in these bands as shown in figure 8-21.

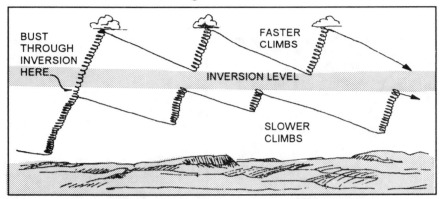

Figure 8-21: Flying in Lift Bands

DOLPHIN FLIGHT TECHNIQUES

Flying like a dolphin swims involves slowing down in lift and speeding up in sink. Ideally the flight is straight ahead and no circling is required. In a hang glider this ideal is rarely achieved and usually only occurs under premium streets, cloud lines over a long mountain or with ridge lift helping out.

Dolphin flying gets much press, but true dolphin conditions for hang gliders are a rare affair.

Dolphin flight methods can be used whenever you are flying straight and will get you to a particular point higher than any other form of flying. You slow down when you detect lift and speed up when sink strikes. This is simply classical speed-to-fly technique. With a speed ring set to the climb rate of the next expected worthwhile thermal this will result in a gradually descending path until the good thermal is met at which time you should circle back up.

"In the 1984 Owens Valley Cross-Country Championships, I got to cloud base just north of the Mazourka Laguna, flew across a pass to the Silver Canyon turn point, and back south to Black Mountain without *circling once! Later during that same meet, I flew from Coldwater Canyon to the Boundary Peak turn point to goal at White Mountain ranch, a 45 mile flight with only 180° of direction change. I thought I had an engine attached!"*

Mark Bennett, Multiple US team member

✔ *Forced Dolphin Flight*

It is possible at times to set our speed ring at zero and fly a straight level path by slowing down in the good lift. However, this is "forced" dolphin flight and is slower than setting the speed ring for the best expected climb, flying the appropriate speeds and circling when lift reaches our expectations. In a hang glider our performance is such that we often have to combine circling climb with straight climb in all but the very best of conditions. The most efficient speeds are those given by the speed ring or position ring even if we could avoid turning by slowing down.

Figure 8-22 shows a hypothetical flight with a street of lift and areas of sink. The initial climb under a good thermal induces us to set our speed

500 FPM

500 FPM

Figure 8-22: Dolphin Flying

- 213 -

ring for 500 FPM, the expected lift under the best cloud we can reach downwind. As we pass through other areas of lift we slow down but do not circle unless they meet our minimum criterion: 500 FPM. We could have climbed higher initially, but would have arrived at the end of the street later. Here are the general rules for dolphin flight:

An out landing in outrageous Utah after an outstanding X-C flight

Dolphin Flying
1. Slow up in lift and speed up in sink according to the ring setting.
2. Set your ring for the best expected climb in a street or line of lift.
3. Do not force dolphin flight by slowing too much to remain level—the ring tells you how fast to fly.
4. Circle to climb if you are low, about to run out of cloud street, the local lift is exceptional or you can't sustain level flight at the indicated speed-to-fly.

When you are gliding through general sink, be careful of pushing out in little shots of lift that are too small to make a difference. You'll often do worse than if you maintained a steady speed since you slow yourself too much to cross the sink next to the lift blob. This is frequently the case in turbulent conditions or when you encounter the trashy tail of a missed thermal.

If you find yourself speeding to escape cloud suck under a street or isolated cloud you are actually loosing time for the most efficient way to fly is to slow in lift, not dive. The error here is not going on glide sooner. Learn from your experience and try to avoid a repeat. With practice you'll be bounding through the sky like a jolly dolphin in that other great fluidic expanse.

LEAVING LIFT

One of the elements of good social grace is knowing when to leave a social affair. it is a equally desirable trait to know when to leave a thermal. We learned in Chapter 7 that in racing situations (trying to go far, fast) we leave when the lift = our speed ring setting = the expected average climb in the next thermal. When we are flying for maximum distance we alter this somewhat.

When lift gets weaker or towards the end of the day our goal is to remain high. To do this we should take thermals as high as they are willing to carry us. If clouds are flattened or an inversion exists it is usually not worth our time to ride all the way to cloud base unless we latch on to a unique boomer.

With taller developing clouds it makes sense to climb higher—often to near cloud base for the strongest lift may be just under the cloud. Generally the higher the cloud buildup, the stronger the lift and the closer to cloud base the good lift extends. Figure 8-23 illustrates these matters.

Figure 8-23: Cloud Development Indicating Lift Quality

When we fly over the back of a mountain we

often encounter nothing but sink over the valley, at least for a distance of five miles or so. In this case and when we are crossing "enemy territory" we are tempted to stay with our thermal in jumbled lift or zero sink after we've topped out to drift with it. This is a reasonable tactic only if nothing promising—a cloud, a ridge, a hill, a smokestack—is ahead. If we do adopt this policy we should only use it in dire need and realize that it is a s-l-o-w way to accumulate mileage on the meter.

One of the hardest skills to develop is knowing when to leave lift and head off into the unknown.

Pro Tip: When you leave a thermal look back once you have some distance to see what a cloud looks like that produced the lift you left. On that same day any cloud with a similar appearance should reward you with similar lift.

THE FINAL GLIDE

We discussed most final glide concerns in Chapter 7. Here we need to make it clear that when we are trying to fly as far as possible our final glide can be an important addendum to a great story. In this case we should use speed-to-fly techniques for flying the greatest distance over the ground. This means setting our ring to zero expected climb (after all if there is more climb we are not on final glide!) and slowing in lift or tail wind, speeding in sink or head wind the appropriate indicated amount.

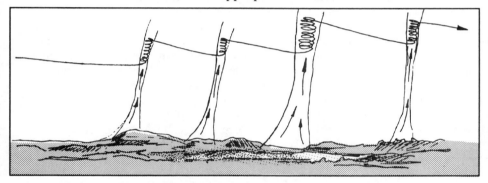

Figure 8-24: Using Light Lift in Final Glide

Towards the end of the day our tactics change somewhat. While thermals tend to be high, they are weaker, spaced further and climbs are slower. Also sink is generally more gentle so we try to remain as high as we can and float directly downwind using anything we find as indicated in figure 8-24. If we detour it should be to apparent areas of ridge lift (magic air perhaps), convergence or late evening release of heat such as towns, quarries and deep valleys. All our scratching ability is brought into play and even a drifting zero sink circle is worthwhile to help us delay the inevitable.

To max our distance after leaving our last thermal we must fly the proper speed-to-fly.

Often the air will be buoyant in early evening and we can glide much further than initially expected. Plan for a series of downwind landing areas. At the end of a long flight you will be tired, so remind yourself to hang tough to squeeze out that last bit of mileage and concentrate when the call of gravity says it's time to land.

"At the end of the day, landing safely is more important than one extra mile. Choose a safe area for touchdown."
Johnny Carr — Multiple British Team Member

V - LANDING OUT

*B*y their nature cross-country flights have us landing in unfamiliar areas. Such ad hoc landing zones need not be terrifying territory if we learn to read them properly. We review such skills here.

LANDING HAZARDS

The ideal landing site is a long, smooth, flat grassy strip next to a restaurant bar located, why not, on the grounds of a nudist colony in July. I almost had such an experience when I landed in the midst of the world's largest kegger in 1977 near Missoula, Montana, but that's another story. We rarely see the ideal, so let's get prepared for the reality. Here we discuss how to handle potential hazards.

✓ *Field Hazards*

Hidden fences, sprinklers, ruts, ditches and rocks can hurt our landing gear or wings. Most often there is some sign of these dangers such as unmown patch or strip or change in ground cover color. Ditches are invariably darker green than their neighboring fields and often contain high weeds. Fences and rocks cannot be moved or harvested over, so are deeper in weeds. Some potential hazards are illustrated in figure 8-25.

As you fly over an unknown landing field, circle around to detect any anomalies or differences in ground cover. If long lines appear in your field expect hazards that you wouldn't want to tangle with and land parallel to them—even if you have to land crosswind.

In Brazil one pilot was strained through a barbed wire fence that had been in the abandoned field so long the weeds had covered it. The greatest hazards here, however, were the huge cement-like termite mounds and the dark green inviting fields which were swamps that would soak you to your waist!

Here is a potential cross-country landing after a flight downwind from the mountains in the background. The field at Ⓑ looks promising but beware of the two brush areas that are probably growing in rock piles. Also note the gust lines in the grass. Corn at Ⓒ , and wheat at Ⓓ are forbiden while the plowed field at Ⓔ and new mown hay at Ⓕ are less desirable landing spots. The field at Ⓖ is promising because you can get close to the road. However, it must slope downward towards the stream Ⓗ and the power line limits it. The field at Ⓘ also slopes toward the river Ⓙ while the field Ⓚ appears to slope uphill into the wind. Both of these fields are made more challenging by the power lines Ⓛ. The field at Ⓜ has cattle and possible turbulence downwind of the trees, if you can even reach it. Fields further back on your track at Ⓝ look fine, but are a long walk from any road. Landing closer to the mountain than N may result in dangerous turbulence given the indicated wind. Notice the smoke showing the wind at the nearest farm and the hawk at Ⓞ which is within easy reach if you backtrack and may be marking a thermal you missed--your ticket out of the illustration.

Ⓐ = WIND

Figure 8-25: X-C Landing Hazards

✔ Crops

We have seen in Chapter VI how to land in high crops and weeds. We should learn to recognize the typical crops in our area. Corn is the worst and appears a rough dark green in obvious rows from the air or pale brown and green when ripe. Wheat is dark green and uniform in the spring with a golden yellow color when ripe. Oats are pale green when growing and pale yellow when ripe. These are the high and expensive crops—recognize and avoid.

Alfalfa is fine to land in, but watch for hay bales that are often in a line after cutting. A bare dirt field can be fairly lumpy just after it's plowed—watch your ankles. Dry dirt fields can harbor heated air that lifts off just as you come in, greatly increasing your work load on landing. Better to choose a grassy field. Finally, corn fields that have been cut leave very hard stalks about 8 inches high that can trip or impale you. Step high if you land in corn country.

✔ Trees and Brush

The lone bushes you spot from the air are *always* higher than they look. Do not expect to go over a bush and drop down on the other side, for you may end up in it or worse yet in a heap just beyond it. If you have no clear space, find another field.

Trees are frequent obstructions in fields, and a proper setup will take into consideration the need to give them a wide berth. If high trees surround your field figure that it is reduced in size by about six times the trees' height unless you can maneuver within the field boundaries (see figure 8-26). We repeat the admonition that it is better to land in a tree than to catch a wing and topple head first to the ground.

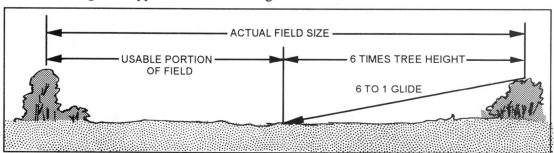

Figure 8-26: Obstructions Limiting Usable Field Size

✔ Power Lines

Too many pilots have had power lines tangles.

An expert pilot in Ohio was electrocuted when the glider he was trying to hold down was blown up to contact a wire. I saw a photo sequence of a pilot in Washington who survived the pyrotechnics of a power line landing, only to drop two stories into a raging brush fire ignited by his sparks. Finally we witnessed a pilot intent on making goal at dusk fly into a huge high tension line carrying enough voltage to power Las Vegas. His light bulb imitation flashed the whole valley. He cut himself free with a hook knife, landed in a molten pile of glider pieces and staggered away looking like Wily Coyote after a particularly bad day.

We must keep a constant vigilance for spiderweb-like power lines in order to keep from ending up in like a moth in a bug zapper.

The problem with power lines is that they are difficult to see. Frequently the smaller ones have poles nestled in the trees with wires stretched across otherwise good fields. Because of this basic invisibility we adopt a general outlook:

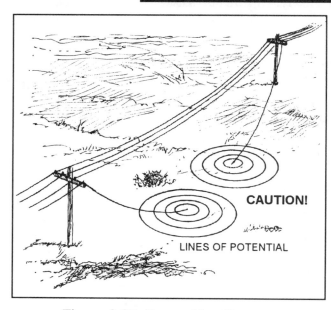

Figure 8-27: Power Line Dangers

If you or a fellow pilot land in power lines here are a few things to know:

▶ You will *not* get electrocuted as long as you do not complete a circuit.

▶ *Do not* touch more than one wire if you can avoid it. You can hang on one wire and not get electrocuted.

▶ *Do not* struggle or touch a pole or the ground if you are stable and in no danger of falling.

▶ *Do not* get near a glider caught in a line. A pilot was killed when a glider hung up in a power line shifted in the wind and touched his head.

▶ *Do not* get near power lines broken and dangling on the ground. A dangerous electric current can exist near live wires as shown in figure 8-27. The power company advises leaving the area with *small* steps in such a case so as not to bridge too much potential.

▶ *Do* notify the power company or police immediately to turn off the power so the pilot can be rescued.

LANDING COMPLICATIONS

Expect sloping ground within a distance of five times the height of a hill or mountain.

Once we scope out all the potential hazards in our chosen field we should look for further complications such as slopes, turbulence and cattle. Finally, we have to deal with the land owner.

✔ Sloping Ground

We have seen in Chapter 6 how to deal with sloped landings. Here we see how we can tell that the terrain is sloped from the air. We can say unequivocally that anything that looks sloped from aloft is *very* sloped in reality. If you can't detect a slope and you are in generally hilly country, expect slanted ground anyway. Here are some signs from the air:

If you don't have a cape and a suit of lights along with a matador union card, the best way to survive the angry attention of a bull is to play dead.

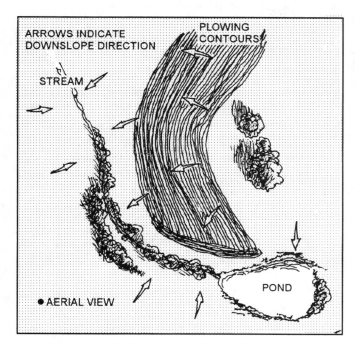

Figure 8-28: Detecting Slopes From Aloft

✓ Turbulence

We should expect turbulence downwind from all objects that can disrupt the flow, including: trees, buildings, hills and machinery. Land as far away as possible from these rotor generators.

✓ Cattle and Other Creatures

A very delicate matter is landing in a field with horses. These type A animals along with sheep spook very readily. Sheep aren't much of a problem when they rush away, but horses can injure themselves in fences and any other thing you can imagine. Crippling a $100,000 stud was probably not your intended purpose when you took off. If at all possible, do not land in a field with horses. If you must, do it as far away from them as possible.

Cows are another matter. They have two things on their mind generally: eating and getting milked. They are curious when their routine is disrupted, however, and will amble over to lick, taste, trample, fold, spindle and mutilate your glider. If you can't toss your glider over the fence, at least break down quickly while you shoo bossy back.

In areas where bulls are allowed to roam free, they can present a real danger (see figure 8-29), especially if you look like the type to threaten their harem. Generally any bulls you encounter will be beef cattle. Herefords (brown with white faces) tend to be more docile than Angus (totally black) and I, for one, will walk an extra mile before I'll land in a field fenced in with an Angus bull. Since I can't tell the difference between a cow and a bull unless I look under them, I always overfly them by a good margin.

Figure 8-29: Animal Hazards

Land next to a party in progress and you'll be guaranteed a hearty reception.

✓ Landowners

Landowners are like most people in that they come in varieties. Some are gentle, kind, friendly and eager to introduce you to their 200 lb daughter. They let you use their phone, give you a ride to town and invite you to "drop in" any time. Others are exactly the opposite, threaten to call the cops, confiscate your glider and generally spread their misery.

You never know which type you'll encounter, but fortunately the former is most common. In fact, in all my out landings I have only met up with one irate landowner. When you approach a landowner smile, be polite and explain that you "ran out of air" (something a landowner can

John Heiney in a Florida sky promising much distance.

understand) and hope it was OK to land in this open field. Don't wait for the landowner to come to you or you'll seem less friendly. If he objects, apologize and say you'll remove your glider from the property immediately. Then do so.

If the landowner objects strenuously and prevents you from getting your glider, do not argue for landowners think they have the moral high ground. In fact, in the USA at least, you have a right to land wherever you consider safest in an emergency such as running out of options. You are *not* trespassing until you've been warned once. Since you cannot read *no trespassing* signs from the air you are not guilty. If you are booted off a property without your gear contact the police to get it back. If a landowner threatens you with violence he is committing a crime which you should let the police handle. The landowner acting in such a way is in much more trouble than you, but you are not in a position to administer this trouble. Incidently, once you've been told not to land in a particular place then you are more likely to be charged with trespassing.

Make no mistake about it, you are an ambassador for our sport and your reasonable behavior and smiles will be remembered.

LANDING CONVENIENTLY

While we are still in the air and feeling an impending landing in our bones it is time to scope out the lay of the land to facilitate our retrieval. We should look for the roads that lead to the nearest towns or prominent landmarks. We should try to land by a major road if possible. Landing near a house with a telephone line is always a smart move. Finally, check out rivers and streams to be sure to land on the side that has the most traveled road or within reach of a bridge.

> *One pilot landed across a river in New Mexico. His only route to civilization was to swim the river. He removed his clothes to float them across but underestimated the current strength. He lost the log they were on and ended up across the river naked as Adam. Not knowing what to do he finally decided to walk to a house and describe his fate. As luck would have it an innocent housewife came to the door, screamed and called the police. He had a lot of explaining to do but certainly ended up with a memorable cross-country flight.*

DETECTING WIND DIRECTION

In strong winds we have little problem detecting the wind direction. In moderate to light winds we must be more observant. The standard wind indicators such as smoke, flags, clothes on a line and drifting dust are familiar to most pilots. Dust from farm machinery or trucks can be deceptive for it occurs in a line that may appear to be the wind direction but is really very different from the true wind because the dust source is moving shown in figure 8-30. To keep from being fooled, try watching an individual puff or observe the tractor dust as the tractor changes direction.

Wind lines on water are one of our favorite wind indicators. Because water lies below the bank there will be a calm area next to the bank the wind is coming *from*, then streaks beyond this as shown in figure 8-31. The longer the streaks and the more they dance around, the stronger and more gusty the wind.

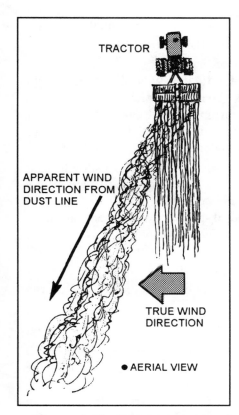

Figure 8-30: Wind Direction From Vehicle Dust

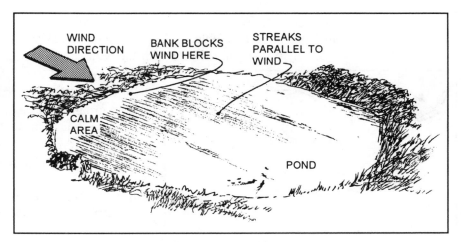

Figure 8-31: Wind Direction From Still Water

In stronger winds the waving of grass indicates the wind direction. Trees work also because they are most active on their upwind side. This is a good indicator in light winds as well if you carefully observe which side rustles. Palm trees are confusing because they tend to wave their fronds no matter what the wind direction. Look at the tips of the fronds for wind indicating stringers.

In moderate winds you can detect the wind from your drift. The method is shown in figure 8-32. Here we see the top view of a pilot flying over a ground track for reference. A crab angle is necessary to remain along the track. Therefore the wind comes from somewhere in the shaded directions shown. Next the pilot turns 90° towards the shaded area and notes the drift or crab angle. Since the glider must be pointed to the left the wind is from the narrow angle illustrated which is close enough for comfort.

If foreground objects are crossing background objects, you are drifting sideways and should adjust your direction accordingly. To see how this works, look out the window and move your head forward and back. Objects near and far do not move to the side relative to

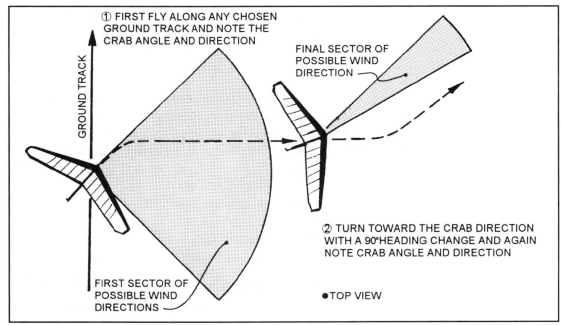

Figure 8-32: Wind Direction From Crab Angle

each other. Now move your head to the side and you'll see that closer objects move sideways in front of farther objects. You can look ahead across your field or use sagebrush in this manner to line yourself up with the wind.

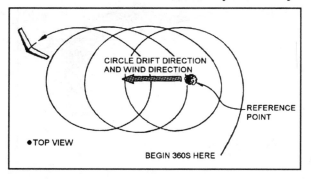

Figure 8-33: Wind Direction From 360 Drift

My preferred method for finding wind direction in very light winds is the 360 trick. To use this, pick a spot below you on the ground and begin turning smooth 360s. After two or more turns your drift will tell you the wind direction as shown in figure 8-33. This method works in stronger winds too.

It should be noted that local factors such as valley flow or outflow from canyons can make the ground wind direction very different from that a few hundred feet up. Therefore we should be ready to use both methods if space allows and certainly make adjustments if the wind is moderately strong or we are landing in unrunnable ground cover. In case the wind is too light to tell the direction we should always opt to land uphill.

Pro Tip: If all else fails, have your driver toss up dust, hold a streamer or you can drop a precious smoke bomb!

FINDING YOUR DISTANCE

After almost any cross-country pilots our log book, if not our fellow pilots, wants to know how far we went. In our experience, a good road map will provide the point to point distance within 1/4 mile if care is taken in pinpointing launch and landing. University libraries often have much more detailed maps, but these may have to be strung out along several tables for measurement accuracy and so are less convenient. If you use a car odometer to measure your landing distance from an obvious way point, and your basic Exxon map will suffice for all but competition and distance records.

In competition the meet organization supplies a map of suitable scale. For official records we use a mathematical method that is discussed in Chapter 11 (SETTING RECORDS) and the Appendix.

SUMMARY

Flying, to most people, is a wonderful feat. Flying a hang glider is even more astounding. Flying cross-country in hang glider is something beyond belief. But before we can extend ourselves so unbelievably in all conditions, into every possibility, we need to start slowly and build solid skills. The most important of these skills are reading signs of lift and landing. We remind all inexperienced voyagers that it is better to land shorter than to alight in a scary place that deflates your confidence.

On the other hand, once you get adept at choosing fields and finding lift you can press on from point to point, even in tough conditions. The two skills enhance each other, for in the words of Butch Peachy, US World Team Member: *"It is easier to find a thermal than a landing field."* Butch isn't trying to point out the scarcity of good fields, but illustrating the mind set of a good X-C pilot. Mark Bennett, Butch's teammate has this to say: *"Less experienced pilots spend too much time fixating on landing areas. They fall victim to landing field suck. They need to look at how to go up rather than down. If you think about landing too much you will never get up and go far."* Mark isn't preaching a devil-may-care attitude but a self-confidence that characterizes winners.

CHAPTER

Competition Flying

Once you have worked hard on your advancing skills, it's a great challenge to see how they measure up to your expectations. Competition affords you the chance to do just that in a somewhat controlled situation. It also gives you a direction for honing your skills, polishing your techniques, applying your knowledge, exercising your judgement and displaying your humility.

Yes, the early stages of competition can be quite humiliating as you learn that your local hero act doesn't play in the big time. However, you'll meet some of the most helpful pilots at competitions and your store of lore will expand at a rate equal to your skill.

To ease your passage into this somewhat elite world of racers, masochists and stoics, we give you guidelines for starting competition with minimum stress. We also provide insights for training and winning from some of the world's best pilots. Your final step into the hierarchy from which true champions are selected should be a fun and exciting adventure.

I - PREPARING FOR COMPETITION

There are two main differences in personal cross-country flying and competition. In competitions we are generally flying with many more pilots than we are used to and we are usually trying to race. Because of these factors we are in an ideal learning situation for we can observe multiple decisions of our own making and that of others and get a quick return as to the outcome. We can't help but become better.

"One week of competition flying is worth months of free flying in terms of experience."
— Jim Lee, US World Team Member and World Record Holder

BEGINNING COMPETITION

"I have to say that competition is the best thing that happened to my flying. It eliminated the boredom of turning circles at my home site, the lethargy of general free flying. It introduced me to the best people I know, and got me flying some of the best sites in the world. It' challenging, it's fun. Most of all, It improved my flying skills. Competition is the best teacher I've found."
— Nelson Howe

The best way to enter competition is to start on the local level. Here you can test your mettle with less stress, less cost, less time and less fear of failure. Once you have learned some of the dos and don'ts, the whys and whynots, you should graduate to larger and longer meets.

Here's a long-term schedule to work on:

▶ 1. *First get off the hill.* This may seem obvious or even ridiculous, but many pilots get intimidated by the larger crowds in front or launch or launch conditions themselves and fail to get into the air in a timely fashion if at all. At any large meet there are always some pilots who are left on launch. If you aren't ready for all the traffic, get off *first* not last. If you wait to the end to launch you will never see the better pilots in the air and will learn slower. Your first principle should be to launch early.

▶ 2. *Next work on making goal.* Don't necessarily expect to do this on your first competition or your second. Or your third. Some pilots compete on a casual basis several years before they are making goal consistently. Be patient and learn. Your first goal will be just cause for celebration.

▶ 3. *Finally, get faster.* Once you make goals consistently you must then learn to complete them in shorter time. This is how meet winners do it, but such abilities take years to develop. At this level you may or may not win a meet, but to be in the top of the standings time after time is something only a few can achieve.

To start competing all you need to develop is consistency and concentration. As your experience and judgement grow you can see the improvement in your results. This is the reward for your efforts. Later when you've acquired experience you can start dreaming of becoming a superhead.

TRAINING FOR COMPETITION

The first thing to do to prepare yourself for competition is to gain as much weather and theoretical flying knowledge as you can. This comes through study and talking to other pilots. The next thing is to practice specific skills and put this knowledge to use. Here's how to proceed:

▶ Practice your takeoffs in all types of conditions. *"A pilot with bad takeoff skills will miss conditions in challenging situations,"* warns Butch Peachy.

▶ Practice flying in traffic. Learn to get comfortable flying close to and cooperating in thermals with other pilots. Reread the material on this matter in Chapter 6 and put it to use. In general the pilots at competitions are very competent and can be trusted to work in close as long as you fly consistently and follow the rules.

▶ Practice getting low and thermaling up quickly. If you are getting outclimbed, figure out why and correct the problem. Remember, it takes several different days to see if this is the case, for some thermals are close to the ideal smoke ring model where the center rises fast but slows at the top so that high gliders get a slower climb (see figure 9-1)

▶ Practice in weak conditions. Contests are often won or lost on the weak days.

▶ Practice racing cross-country. Merely flying from point to point is not the way to practice for competitions that are races to goals. You have to try to go fast.

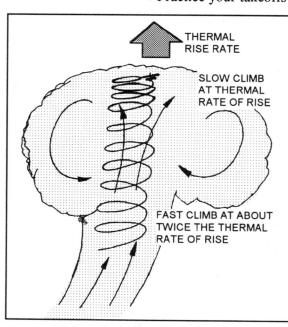

THERMAL RISE RATE

SLOW CLIMB AT THERMAL RATE OF RISE

FAST CLIMB AT ABOUT TWICE THE THERMAL RATE OF RISE

Figure 9-1: Slower Climb at Top of Thermal

"A pilot must race in everyday cross-country flying or he (she) is not training for competition or flying as far as possible. We must strive to fly as efficiently as we can at all times, especially in turns."
— John Pendry, 1985 World Champion and multiple European Champion

Of course, gaining knowledge and practicing are not totally separate items, for we go back and forth enhancing one with the other. We must accumulate information from experience. After every flight think back on your mistakes, not to mortify yourself, but with an interest in avoiding them the next time (we have previously mentioned Tony Barton's mistake book with which he reminds himself of rights and wrongs). There are thousands of things to think about and thousands of things that can go wrong, but little by little we learn the right responses automatically and move on to the next level of achievement.

COMPETITION EQUIPMENT

When we enter competition it is a good idea to have the best equipment possible so we know

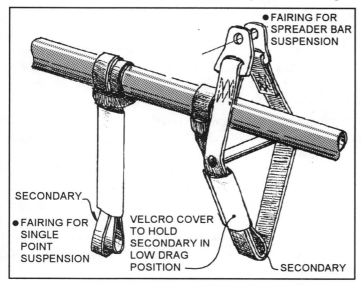

Figure 9-2: Cleaning up Hang Strap Drag

that our successes or shortcomings a result of *our* performance not our glider's. That way we are best able to figure out what to practice. However, if you can't afford the latest and greatest wing, do not despair or shun competition. You can still learn and have fun. We are also reminded that Joe Bostik won the 1988 US Nationals on a Wills Wing *Sport*, designed for intermediates and recreational advance flying.

✔ *Preparing your Glider*

We discussed performance tuning of a glider in Chapter 4. The only thing we can add to that material is the use of faired downtubes and a fairing on the hang straps as shown in figure 9-2. If your downtubes are faired but do not have boundary layer trip strips extruded into them you can readily make some from automotive pin-stripe tape. Use the 1/4 or 3/8 width size and place it on the tube on either side of the leading edge just in front of the high point so it doesn't increase the thickness (see figure 9-3).

Be sure your base tube has some grip material on it. Even with bar mitts your hands can sometimes slide and this makes you grip tighter, which leads to fatigue unless you have forearms like Popeye.

Sometimes you have a choice in glider sizes. Larger gliders generally sink better and smaller gliders are faster. Use these guidelines:

Glider Sizes
- Choose a larger glider in light lift, lighter winds and inconsistent conditions.
- Choose a smaller glider in stronger winds or lift and predictable conditions.

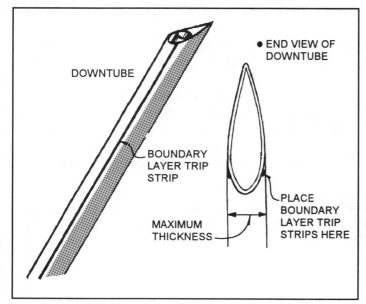

Figure 9-3: Boundary Layer Strip on Faired Downtubes

Note that with a larger glider you can achieve smaller glider characteristics by using ballast for more versatility. Also it bears repeating that we cannot truly tell a glider's performance from one or two contest results or one or two flights. It takes many flights in varied conditions to discern all-around performance differences.

✓ *Cameras*

About the only goody we need to add for competition if we are already engaged in X-C flying is a camera. This is necessary for photographing turn points. Cameras in competition have perhaps produced more anguish than the Spanish Inquisition. They malfunction or are hard to access. Most pilots use two cameras for security. If you are only using one we suggest it be a mechanical one for they are more fool-proof than electronic cameras. Make sure you can work the mechanism with gloves on.

If you shop around you can find cameras for fairly low prices, but we suggest you don't buy the very cheapest ones for the rewind mechanisms do not last. You don't need or want an expensive camera for the dust and abuse they are subject to turns them into a cheap camera and you are not going to win any awards with a picture of a lonely intersection turn point anyway.

If you use two cameras you may wish both to be electronic, for trying to wind and snap a couple of photos on two cameras in turbulence can be like trying to juggle five ferrets on a Ferris wheel. One camera should always be your primary and the other your backup. Typically the film in your backup camera will not be developed unless the primary fails.

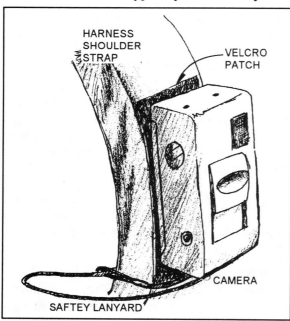

HARNESS SHOULDER STRAP

VELCRO PATCH

CAMERA

SAFTEY LANYARD

Figure 9-4: Convenient Camera Mounting

You must mount your camera system for easy use in flight. Some harnesses come with pouches or Velcro patches for this purpose. Some pilots make special racks for their cameras on their base tube. This is very handy but subjects the cameras to extra dust in dirty desert conditions. My favorite system is a Velcro patch on my harness shoulder straps shown in figure 9-4. Sticky-back Velcro is then applied to the camera back and everything is nice and convenient. Naturally your camera must be safe-tied to your body. Check to make sure the camera lanyard is strong enough to take some jerks when you drop it in the air.

Later we discuss some of the tricks for efficient and accurate camera usage.

Pro Tip: We must always try to avoid the mistake of using new equipment for the first time just as a meet starts. We should be well familiar with our cameras, oxygen system, instrument, harness and glider. We should try them in actual flights so their use is automatic well before we need them for competing. Many times pilots take delivery on new gliders just in time for a competition only to find out that their old glider would have served them better because they couldn't dial into the new one soon enough.

COMPETITION TYPES

Modern competitions involve cross-country tasks in several different formats. There are races to a goal either in a straight line or more commonly around turn points. Usually these latter courses involve some crosswind flying and occasional beating upwind. All our X-C skills are called for in these cases.

Open distance tasks are used in some less structured meets. These are easy to administer but not kind to pilots, for on any reasonable day this results in many hours of retrieve. In

The aim of the game in modern competition is to cover a cross-country course as quickly as possible.

desert conditions this often means getting back in the middle of the night. As the days wear on the best pilots accumulate a sleep deficit which isn't conducive to safety or fun. A folded course open distance task is more reasonable if meet organizers want to test a pilot's ability to stay up. In that case the expense of film developing must be incurred, but this is worth it for the increased pleasure of the meet.

Don't neglect your spot landing skills for some meets have nice prizes for getting closest to the spot at goal. Sometimes these prizes are more rewarding than a good meet placement.

SCORING FORMATS AND RULES

Most cross-country style meets use a scoring system awarding 1000 points for the fastest person to goal on each flight. Slower pilots get a portion of these points depending on how much time behind the winner they are. Pilots not making goal always get fewer points than pilots who make goal and the points of the pilots who fail to finish are proportional to the distance made of course.

With this scoring format, days that result in few pilots to goal or very little distance achieved will be devalued by a formula. This is called the *validity factor* and multiplies the results of a pilot's distance and speed points. The scoring formats of this type were developed by Paul Mollison of Australia among others in the late 80s.

Another method of scoring is the Total Elapsed Time (TET) whereby a pilot's score is kept as the total time it takes to make all goals. If a goal is not completed the pilot gets a time based on the time of the slowest finisher and the pilot's distance achieved. The problem with this system in its simplest form is that it doesn't account for days of low validity and is not kind to pilots not making goal. The TET scoring system works for the top 10 to 20 percent pilots, but is discouraging for lesser skilled pilots. For this reason we do not encourage the use of TET scoring.

Don't let yourself get beat by the rules—learn them, heed them and use them to fly intelligently.

In any case, scoring systems should be printed in a meet's rule package. Take time to understand the scoring system to see where to emphasize your strategy. For example, if speed points are a small percentage of the overall score, it is best to slow down a bit to increase the odds of making goal.

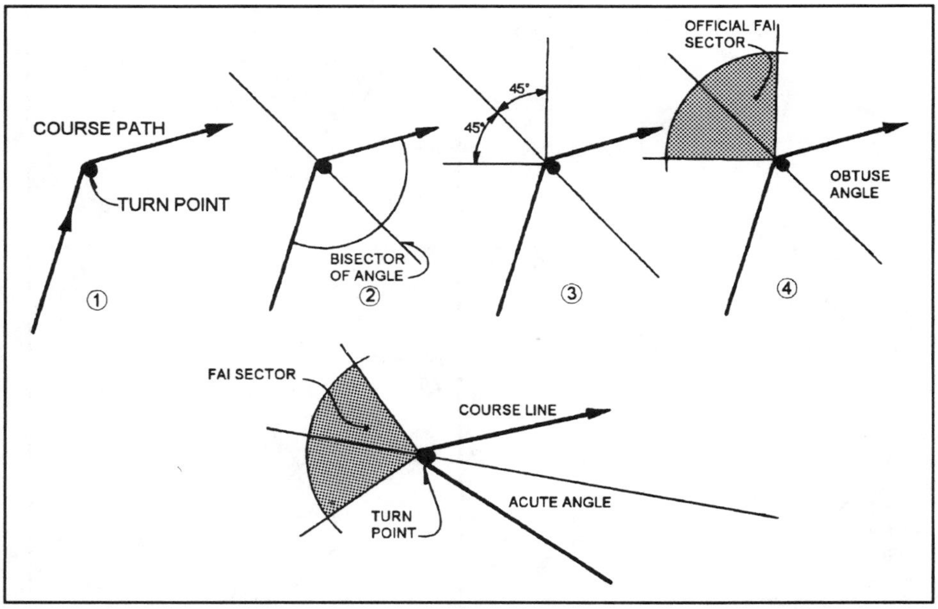

Figure 9-5: The FAI Turn Point Sector

✓ FAI Turn Point

When cameras are used in a contest to photograph turn points and thus allow doglegs and triangles in a course, the photos must be taken from a particular position in order to prove that you have passed the turn point. The official position is within a 1/4 of a circle wedge area called the FAI sector.

The FAI sector is found by bisecting the angle of the course lines to and from the turn point. Then we draw radians (lines) at 45° to this bisector on the opposite side of the bisecting angle. Next we draw an arc with a 1 kilometer radius connecting these two radians and end up with the shaded pie-shaped sectors shown in figure 9-5.

Note that we have drawn an FAI sector for both an acute (narrow) and obtuse (wide) angle. You should become familiar with these sectors and learn how to put them on your map or better yet automatically set them up mentally.

In a later section we'll see how to best photograph FAI sectors.

✓ Pinning a Map

If you do not make a goal, your distance to that goal must be measured. The way this is normally done is you place a pin in a large map of the entire course.

Great penalties can be incurred if you pin yourself in the wrong place. Be sure you are placed where you were.

If you are close to goal you can measure your distance with a car odometer to pinpoint your landing position. If not, use a notable landmark such as a road intersection or river crossing to mark your relative position. Be sure to remember to take an odometer reading to this landmark. If you are far from a road use natural landmarks that are large enough to show up on the pin map back at headquarters. If you have a compass, notate the heading to two or more landmarks and you can triangulate your position (remember to include magnetic variation).

Pro Tip: Always note the name, pilot number and position of other pilots landing near you or short of as you return. This will help establish your position accurately which is very important for the fairness of a competition. Also, don't forget to fill out your landing form and get witness signatures if required.

✓ Measuring Distance Achieved

A course in a cross-country competition flight is a straight line from takeoff to a turn point, from turn point to turn point or from either of these to goal. The closer you land to the course line, the better because of the way distance is measured.

To determine distance made good along a course, the distance you are from goal or your next turn point is used as a radius for an arc which is drawn back to the course line. Thus, the further you are from the course line, the further back you get moved as shown in figure 9-6 for several situations.

It should be clear from the figure that the

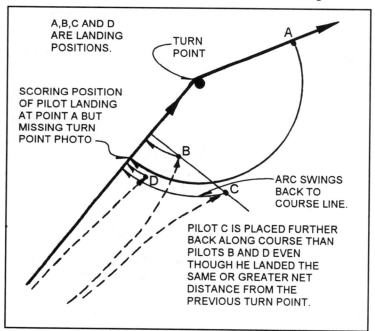

Figure 9-6: Maximizing your Score When off-Course

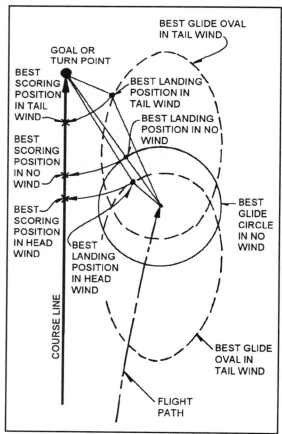

Figure 9-7: Maximizing your score in Winds

closer you are to goal, the greater penalty you incur for being off the course line. If you pass a goal without crossing the goal line or a turn point without taking a photo as pilot A in the figure, you are placed back with the same arc method as shown. It should be understood that if you cannot get a turn point photo, landing as close as possible to the turn point is to your advantage. If you fail to get a turn point photo do not continue on course for you will ultimately achieve less distance. If a photo fails to come out you will be swung on an arc back from the next photographed turn point past your last good turn point.

If you find yourself off course due to drift or terrain problems and you are likely not to reach goal or the turn point, you should glide directly to these points for maximum distance as shown in figure 9-7. Here we see a pilot at A with a possible glide circle determined by the present height. By heading directly to goal the pilot produces the shortest arc to swing back to the course line as shown. In wind the circle of glide becomes an oval and the best heading is altered somewhat as shown. The case for a tail wind and head wind along the course is shown.

It should be clear that all parts of the meet rule book should be well understood to avoid confusion in the air and to best plan your flight. Takeoff systems are especially important to understand and we discuss them in the strategy section.

PRE-MEET PRACTICE

Every site has its own rhythms, quirks and secret sources of lift. The more time you have to learn these factors, the better you will perform.

If you are going to be competing at an unfamiliar site it is important to learn its secrets. These secrets include best times of day for maximum lift, location of house thermals, best routes for various tasks and normal weather cycles. Most areas have places where thermals are to be expected along a course. Learn them. Find out if the safe launch window exists only for part of the time. Many pilots were stuck on the Dinosaur launch, fretting and stewing, in the 1990 US Nationals as the wind would turn tail in the afternoon.

Local pilots are the best source of information about these matters. They tend to be most willing to give up their hard-earned secrets because it is a pleasure to be an aerial guide. The best preparation is to take a flight with a pilot experienced in the area to learn thermal sources, good landing fields and landmarks. Here is a list of what to look for when reconnoitering a site before a meet:

Just as a house thermal often exists near a flying site, so to do semi-reliable thermals exist along a course. Learn their place of residence if not their visiting hours.

Pre-Meet Checks

1. Locate the best launch point allowing the best chance of launching in varied conditions or the least crowd.
2. Determine the earliest reasonable launch times and the normal length of the launch window.
3. Locate the house thermals and best soaring spots near launch in different wind directions.
4. Determine the best routes for the different expected tasks.
5. Locate dependable lift sources out on course.
6. Fly the expected tasks, especially the more difficult ones and locate goals. If conditions do not allow flying to goal, drive the route looking for lift sources and check the approach to goal from the ground, looking for obstructions and the highest altitude on the course line.

All this gathering of information may take several flying days. However, we should be careful not to overstress ourselves before the meet starts either by flying too long or too intensely. A good plan is to fly at about 3/4 throttle for a few days then take the day before the meet off to do laundry, take a hike, relax in the shade and make new friends. Who knows, those new pilot friends might locate thermals for you, or rescue you from a Nowheresville landing area, or even end up marrying you as with my case.

Pro Tip: Use this pre-meet practice to familiarize your drivers with their duties and the retrieval routes.

II - THE HUMAN ELEMENT

*W*e can readily state that the factors that lead to success in competition are equipment, pilot skill and the human element. Just what is this human element and why is it not included in pilot skill? We shall see that it involves many factors we have not previously discussed and has more to do with the mental side of the picture rather than the physical.

ATTITUDE _____

If we were to single out one aspect of the human psyche that determines whether or not a pilot is destined to be a winner it would be attitude. Gren Seibels in his book *A Gaggle of One* (concerning sailplanes) states it best:

> *"Flying skill is invaluable of course, but it will never prevail over a pessimistic attitude. The impregnable optimism of the consistent winners in their most priceless asset. To be sure, all of us—even the mightiest—have assembled a grisly catalog of disasters and humiliations, for such is the essential nature of our sport. We also know that so long as we persist in the game, potential pratfalls lurk just beyond every thermal. It is our reaction to this knowledge, how we cope with it, that largely determines our chances of winning a given contest."*

✓ *Accentuate the Positive*

We all know pilots like Mark Gibson or Kenny Brown whose enthusiasm for flying even on the toughest contest day is unbridled. Contrast this with pilots who carp about the conditions, gripe about the task call and grouse about their past performance. These latter pilots never finish at the top, for only by focusing on *solving* the problems at hand with an aggressive, positive attitude will a pilot excel.

"The impregnable optimism of the consistent winners is their most priceless asset..."

Some pilots let one dismal day affect their performance for the rest of the meet. Others pick themselves up and become more determined. There are many examples of pilots winning meets after starting off poorly.

> *"There are top pilots who lose confidence after a bad day. The mark of a true champion is being able to pick oneself up and excelling after a serving of bad luck."*
> — Judy Leden, 1991 Women's World Champion

Many pilots, especially those new to competition, let themselves be intimidated by the presence of legends of the sport. They don't realize that even the seasoned ace is human and susceptible to human error. The point of the whole competition exercise is to make the fewest errors which you can quickly learn to do if you continually work on observation and awareness.

"Pilots who think they will be beaten are beaten"
— George Moffat, World Champion sailplane pilot

My own attitude adjustment came on a day in the 1989 East Coast Championships in Tennessee when I was at the tail end of a launch line. I was bemoaning the fact that the top pilots had already launched and left while conditions looked like they were deteriorating. One of the three pilots left on launch turned to me and said simply: "your problem is that you have a bad attitude!" He promptly launched, climbed forever and made goal with one thermal to win the day. I launched a bit later and needed only three thermals. It was suddenly apparent that my perceived misfortune was just the opposite and such negative thinking can block the desire or ability to perform well.

Since that time I have developed a positive outlook. Curiously, the modicum of success that I have experienced in modern X-C competition has dated from that change in attitude. We urge all pilots interested in competing to adopt a positive viewpoint from the start.

✔ It Ain't Over 'till it's Over

It is especially important to never give up in the course of a meet. Even if you are floundering at the bottom of the daily placings you can still salvage something by practicing things you wouldn't try if you were a contender. If you compete for any length of time you will witness many occasions where the final standings are radically different from what was in place half-way through. Things can even change dramatically on the last day.

In the 1991 East Coast Championships (USA), Bruce Case was well down in the scoring due to one bad day. The last competition round appeared to be an easy ridge run down to a turn point and back to goal. Pilots piled off launch in bar-stuffing mind set. Little did they suspect that the wind was extremely cross and lift was at a premium: once a pilot got low there was no saving grace. Many top pilots hit the deck while six made goal through a combination of early recognition of the situation and excruciating patience crossing gaps on the upwind return trip. Tim Arai won the day but Bruce was one of the finishers and his performance on this day vaulted him into first place at trophy time.

THE WAR OF NERVES

There seems to be very little "psyching out" of fellow competitors in modern competition except for the flaunting of a new piece of equipment or besting someone soundly in the air. Those are the most efficient psyche outs anyway. Actually, trying to intimidate someone on the ground can often have the opposite effect of that intended if the psyche*e* is of the mental makeup to become more determined in adversity and in fact goes on to beat the psych*er*. If you try to intimidate someone and he or she manages to beat you, it is you who will end up being intimidated as well as looking foolish. Let the daily contest results do all the necessary psyching.

Launch setup at the 1989 World Meet in Fiesh, Switzerland.

✔ First Place Jitters

The most nervous spell in a competitor's experience is not when facing tricky conditions, but when in first place. The pressure of being in the lead is only experienced by a few and handled well by fewer. If by chance you find yourself in front of the pack, the best thing to do is ignore the placings and concentrate on each day as a separate entity, reminding yourself that all you have to do is relax and apply the same skill and judgement that got you where you are. Most of us are not in first place enough times to practice the development of confidence, so we must acquire dead certitude and supreme security in our abilities long before we reach the top.

✔ Dealing with Delays

One other situation where we may have to battle with nerves is when there are long delays due to bad conditions or crowding. The ability to relax in such a situation can affect your later performance in the air. Some pilots always have reading material handy at launch for just such contingencies (we humbly suggest this book). Other suggestions are a short walk, a diverting conversation or a game of hacky sack. If you have to stay with your glider due to gusts, try dozing in your harness or mentally reviewing your love life or some equally diverting exercise if your love life was sacrificed to hang gliding. Remember, the more you can relax on the ground, the more energy you will have to expend in the air.

MENTAL TOUGHNESS

Hang gliding competition is a manic-depressive pastime. We are sometimes overwhelmed with joy as our good decisions carry us to goal with an elite few and other times we wallow in despair as we sit on the ground picking cinders from our soul while flocks of gliders pass over our heads. It is in these most inglorious situations that we have to call on our reserves of mental toughness to get back into the fray and give it all we got.

Mental toughness means:
1. *Tenacity*
2. *Patience*
3. *and good decisions under pressure.*

✓ Tenacity

Steve Blinkensop, Australian World Team member, recommends distance running to develop the mental toughness that declares "never give up." This is a good suggestion, but no matter how it's acquired, an attitude of never quitting is a great asset to a competing pilot. When you are scratching low and seeing pilots looking like specks, or watching pilots hit the deck all around you, that is the time to call on your hidden reserves of tenacity, single minded stubbornness and unwillingness to give in to almost certain fate. The qualities that are so hard to live with are exactly those that make us shine in tough competition situations. We have all seen pilots we have counted out rise like a phoenix from a seemingly hopeless situation.

The launch site at Govenador Valadores, Brazil, during the Pre-World Meet. Tony Barton sets up in the foreground.

✓ Patience

A second part of mental toughness is patience. Impatient pilots will not do well on weak days. Often we must wait until conditions improve and hang on like a bulldog in a weak cycle. The toughest time to exercise patience is when we are floundering alone. Again let's listen to Judy Leden who has given much thought to the mental side of competition: *"When above the pack it's easy to make decisions. The best pilots can exercise patience and make good decisions when the rest of the field is flying away over their heads."*

✓ Decisions

The ability to make good decisions under pressure is the third factor that results in mental toughness. Continually learning from mistakes, and knowledge from attention to detail and observation are the keys to good decision making. A natural pilot is one who automatically makes good decisions based on awareness, precise motor skills and the development of the right responses.

A bad decision can leave you grounded and spouting language as salty as whale tears, but you must use such insults from fate to learn, learn, learn.

Learning to make good decisions and staying with them until they are proven correct or erroneous is an important part of hang gliding competition. Many times in meets you'll see pilots leave a thermal and go on long, long glides expecting to catch a faster elevator further along the course. If they waffle in their decision they end up working weaker lift or diverting their course which costs precious minutes. Tony Barton is a master at such courageous glides away from the pack. His secret: self-confidence and the mental toughness to stay the course.

One other matter contributing to mental toughness is proper diet and sleep during the contest days. Eat a good breakfast just like your mom said for the day-long energy needed to keep on top of the decision demands. Some pilots forswear alcohol during competition for the accumulated dehydration effects that hurt decision-making (see Chapter 13). It should be obvious that lots of sleep helps you concentrate better on those tough choices at cloud base or treetop level. We might also add that oxygen use where appropriate is extremely beneficial to decision-making and ultimately competition results.

CHEATING

It is possible to cheat in some ways in modern X-C competition, most notably by declaring an improper landing point. However, such an act is often found out or suspected and the pilot is forever labeled a "cheat" in the small community of hang gliding. He or she finds fewer friends and less cooperation among other pilots.

"We should fly for ourselves rather than against someone else." Helmut Reichman, World Champion sailplane pilot.

Looking at it another way, cheating is patently ridiculous because most of the rewards of competition are a sense of self-accomplishment and respect from your peers. If you cheat you are cheating yourself for you will not gain an ounce of self-worth if you know you really didn't do what you reported. If your peers suspect you cheated you are lower in their eyes than if you bombed out every day! Save your cheating for Las Vegas if you must.

Setting proper priorities and goals can eliminate the urge to cheat. The proper approach to put things on the right track is to fly *to achieve the best possible performance within our range of abilities rather than against others*. This attitude makes each day an exploration and a discovery of our own resources rather than a tense combat against other pilots. With such a viewpoint you'll find that the pressure of competition is greatly relieved, the pleasure is greatly enhanced and you'll still improve.

GROUND AND CHASE CREW

The people that care about you on the ground and in the air can have a big effect on your performance in several ways. First, their assistance with your equipment and the logistics of getting pre-launch photos and meet information can greatly alleviate your work load, thereby giving you more time to plan your strategy, watch conditions and relax. Secondly they can keep an eye on other pilots in the air and on the ground so you can best judge when to take off.

A good driver can greatly enhance a pilot's performance through encouragement. Likewise a poor driver can be a distraction and detract from performance.

Thirdly they are invaluable for providing information out on course. Every driver should be equipped with drinks, a radio, a good map, a compass and a wind indicator. Periodic reports on the wind direction and speed are useful for helping you plan routes and look for thermal sources. Also the presence of a good driver nearby provides amazing confidence when you venture into hostile territory. Pilots without drivers are often seen sticking within reach of a good road which may or may not be the best choice from a competition point of view.

Finally, a good ground crewperson can go a long way in alleviating the stress and disappointment of a bad day, especially if the two of you share mutual fondness. Despite the chuckles that such a statement elicits, we refer to words of encouragement and support that helps us pick up and go with grace the following day.

➤ **Pro Tip**: A driver is as important as any member of your team—if not more so. Treat your drivers with courtesy, praise and good meals. Let them share in your successes and let them know they are part of the team. Never, never take your frustration at failure out on a driver (you don't pay them enough).

If you do not have a ground crew, try to link up with a pilot friend or any other pilot with a driver who would like to share expenses. Sometimes it works out fine if you can supply a car while the other party supplies the driver. The most valuable thing you can offer is experience and information freely shared with such an ad hoc teammate. In any case, you should expect to share all expenses.

III - WINNING STRATEGY

$\mathcal{S}$trategy refers to our overall plan. That some planning for competition is necessary can been seen in the simple example whereby the pilot that thermals downwind on a crosswind course may never make it back upwind to goal. Here we'll review the strategy necessary to enhance our performance and decision-making.

THE OVERALL PLAN

We should be aware that strategy won't win a contest like tactics (specific skills and actions), but having a broad plan is extremely important in order to avoid taking unnecessary risks. An overall plan should take into account our strengths and weaknesses. For example, if our combination of skill and glider results in great climbing ability but slow speed we have to plan to win on the weak days. Conversely, if we are fast but not such great climbers we plan to win on the stronger days.

The best strategy to win at hang gliding is to become consistent at making goal.

✔ Changing Strategy

We should also be aware that our strategy should change as our placement changes. For example, if we fall way behind we can afford to take more chances in an attempt to catch up. This "go for broke" style has a lower percentage of good results, but when we do hit it lucky our performance is impressive. At the very worst we acquire practice at making more risky decisions (in terms of success, not safety) than we normally would.

If we rise close to the top of the scoring we should be more conservative. However, we will never win by being too conservative. The top pilot knows that pilots just below will probably be going all out to beat him or her, so their chances of making a bad mistake are increased, but if he or she gets too conservative the lead will be lost. Such short term strategies are subsets of the overall strategy which operate in all but the last 1/3 of a meet where the advantages of change in approach are more clear.

Be as flexible in the air as a world class gymnast.

✔ New Pilot Strategy

An overall plan that makes good sense for a pilot new to competition is to fly conservatively to make goal every day. If this is achieved a pilot is almost assured to place in the top five to ten in almost every meet. With such a record this consistent will probably make the World Team of his or her country. However, this is not how meets are won, and such a consistent pilot will have to get faster to be a winner. A few pilots come into the system racing from day one. They endure much humiliation as they fall short repeatedly, but ultimately they become winners when they learn to put it all together. If your self-image can handle a rash of defeat, by all means go this route, but for the rest of us thin-skinned, lily-livered mortals, an overall conservative strategy is best in our early competition experiences.

BECOMING A WINNER

There are three ways to become a winner:
1. Have better equipment.
2. Perform better in some facets of flying.
3. Specialize in avoiding mistakes.

Most pilots have access to the same equipment you do. Vast strides in performance improvement are not currently being made, so we should look elsewhere for the magic that makes a winner.

Some pilots *do* perform better than others in certain conditions. For instance, a pilot may climb exceptionally well in light air. However, over the extent of a contest, conditions usually vary greatly and our one field of expertise may be utilized only rarely, like the skills of a master kazoo player in the New York Philharmonic orchestra.

Thus the best avenue for *being* the best appears to be reducing our errors in what sailplane champion George Moffat in his book *Winning on the Wing* calls "low-loss flying."

✔ *Low-Loss Flying*

In order to improve our performance we do not expect to find a secret elixir that turns us into superhumans, but rather we minimize our losses by shaving a few seconds here and a minute there from our takeoff-to-goal transit time. Here is a list of items where time can be saved:

Avoid these common mistakes whenever possible:
1. *Lingering in weak lift*
2. *Not shifting gears when conditions change*
3. *Not flying straight to the goal or turn point.*

> **Saving Time**
> 1. Becoming efficient at the takeoff and starting gate.
> 2. Finding thermals as quickly as possible.
> 3. Flying fast through the stronger sink approaching a thermal.
> 4. Converting speed for altitude when entering a thermal.
> 5. Centering a core as quickly as possible.
> 6. Bypassing weaker thermals.
> 7. Shunning weaker gaggles and going to steeper turning groups.
> 8. Leaving the thermal when it begins to weaken.
> 9. Crossing the center of a thermal and gathering speed when exiting a thermal.
> 10. Flying best speeds-to-fly between thermals according to a speed ring.
> 11. Avoiding large diversions from course line.
> 12. Deviating only to make the best use of lift streets.
> 13. Taking efficient turn point photos.
> 14. Using accurate final glide calculations.

In later sections we review each of these items which are considered tactics. The overall strategy is to combine all of these factors to achieve low-loss flying.

PRE-LAUNCH PREPARATION

Takeoff strategy begins before takeoff by being prepared. This means getting to launch early and setting up quickly so you don't have to rush at the last minute. Get your equipment in order and ready to go. It helps to have a quick setting up glider or a system that helps you rig as efficiently as possible. One clear way to save time is to have your battens separated left and right then stand a bundle on the tails to display them biggest to smallest as shown in figure 9-8. Now lay the bundle about 1/3 of the way out on your wing and you can quickly pick up and insert the largest to smallest battens all the way along the wing without wasting time laying each one out.

The time saved in the setup process is time you can spend relaxing, grabbing a bite, watching conditions and planning strategy. If you are always rushed you can never focus on the flying.

When a task is announced, take a photograph of the task board immediately (if necessary) so you don't forget to do so. Failure to photograph the start board which identifies the flight is a tragic

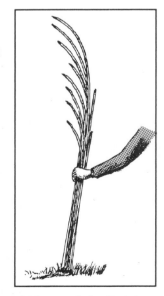

Figure 9-8: Quick Sorting of Battens

mistake which you'll only make once. Also prepare your maps at this time and plan your course with compass headings and landmarks to guide you. Go over probable routes with your driver, check your radios then relax until launch time.

Pro Tip: If launch positions aren't assigned get to launch early enough to set up in a place where you won't get jammed in by other gliders. It is also desirable to be near pilots' meeting areas and in position to watch conditions.

A typical official task board.

WEATHER BRIEFINGS

Daily weather briefings are normally presented at each morning pilot's meeting. These briefings may consist of anything as detailed as a complete soaring report to something as limited as "expected scattered blue sky". As a competitor it is to your advantage to glean as much useful information as possible. We can't present a total guide to weather lore here—that's in *Understanding the Sky*—but we'll outline the important points.

If information on thermal activity is provided, note the expected time of first thermal lift. Also look for the time of maximum heating, maximum height and expected climb rate in thermals. Use this information to decide the optimum time to launch either to perform your flight in the best part of the day with an open launch or to maximize your position with a tarp start.

Typically, wind check pilots will be in the air marking thermals. However, sometimes they sink out or the meet director has not budgeted therm properly. In such a case other signs such as birds or wind changes must be used to identify thermals. If it looks soarable in your best judgement—even if the weatherman reported a later trigger time—it's not unreasonable to launch about ten minutes after the first pilot stays up. If wind check or other pilots are in the air and conditions are doubtful, your chances are enhanced if you launch as soon as you see a glider starting to climb. Most beginning competitors plant themselves on launch and wait until a climbing pilot is well above them before they launch. This often results in a missed thermal.

✓ Winds

Another factor to determine at the weather briefing is the expected winds aloft. Typically wind velocities are provided for surface, 3000 feet, 6000 and 9000 feet levels (12,000 ft in high terrain) and are given in knots along with the compass heading they are coming *from*. Sometimes these winds are predicted for both early and late in the day. You should use such information to determine which legs of your task will be easier (downwind) and which ones more difficult head wind or crosswind). You should allot more time for the difficult legs and may wish to seek a level where the winds are lighter.

✓ Other Weather Items

Other matters to look for are indicated inversions, predicted storms and weather trends. If thermal tops are forecast to be higher than any indicated inversion(s) it may be possible to climb above the inversion and this will be desirable if long distances are required. The lift should be expected to be weaker and possibly more ragged in the inversion. Storms usually develop later in the day so earlier launches are in order when storms are called for. Weather trends such as a pickup in winds, the arrival of a cloud bank or a sea breeze will necessitate a change in tactics and timing to avoid or exploit the new environment.

Finally, at the end of each day you should review the conditions you experienced and compare them to what was prophesied. This allows you to judge your weather person's tendency to undercall or be overly optimistic about the conditions. You can use this judgement on succeeding days to fine-tune your decision making process.

TAKEOFF STRATEGY

There are currently two types of start formats used in competition. The first is timed launch either as an open window (you can launch wherever you wish) or in a specific order in a limited launch site. In this case your time starts when you take off and stops when you cross goal.

The second format is a universal start where pilots launch at will before a specific time when a tarp or some other signal device is displayed for a photograph to be taken. Here everyone's time starts when the tarp appears. Let's look at the pros and cons of each method and the strategy for maximizing performance in each case.

✓ Time Factors

With timed launches (first case) you can choose your launch time if the launch format is

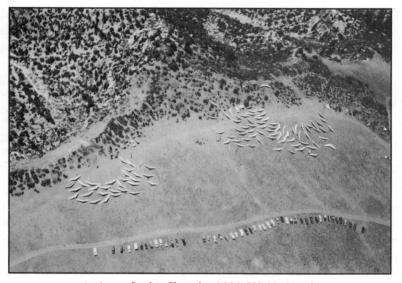

A view of takeoff at the 1990 US Nationals.

open window. This has the philosophical advantage of allowing the pilot to use judgement of the weather to maximize performance. If you are faced with such a launch you should estimate your total flying time based on the expected thermal strength and the distance to goal. For example, if climb rates are expected to be 500 FPM and goal is 60 miles away, we need about three hours in the air (two hours at 30 mph to cover the distance and one hour at 500 FPM climb to gain the 30,000 feet needed for a 10 to 1 glide). If expected climb rates are not available, use your best guesstimate according to the look of the day or use an average of 20 mph in desert conditions and 15 mph in green country.

With this estimate of total time, figure out when to launch so that your flight will take place during peak conditions. Maximum surface heating lags behind the maximum sunshine and occurs around 2:30 local sun time. Remember, there is an hour difference in local sun time from one side of a time zone to the other. Ideally you want the middle of your flight to occur right at the best heating. In our example above, we want to be flying 1 1/2 hours before 2:30 (local sun time) and 1 1/2 hours after 2:30. This means we should launch at 1:00 PM.

It is far easier to compensate for launching too early than too late. Cure a too-late-launching syndrome by practicing getting off the hill as soon as it looks possibly soarable when free-flying.

Of course, there are exceptions to this strategy. If worse weather is due later in the day you should launch earlier. If conditions are weak you should launch later. If your course is a triangle or if any portion of the course is into the wind, plan your flight so the upwind leg occurs during the strongest lift of the day (between 2:00 and 3:00). Finally, if top pilots are launching in a flurry of flights, you should consider going for they may know something you don't or at the very least you may be able to join them in their express gaggle.

Pro Tip: If top pilots in the meet are waiting on launch it is a good idea to heed their wisdom and avoid launching until they appear ready to go.

On an open distance day we resort to a different strategy for we wish to fly as long as possible. A good guide here is to launch about 15 minutes after the first pilot is able to soar, or 20 minutes after the first sign of thermals. If thermals suddenly appear with vigor be aware that the initial surge of thermal activity often dies off to be replaced with more regular production. All of these strategies require practice and observation to modify for best results, but are well worth using.

✓ Ordered or Crowded Launches

When you must launch in a given order, you don't have a clear choice of launch time. The same is true of an open but crowded launch. In such a case it is usually better to get in the air sooner rather than later. Try to launch as soon as about 1/10 the total number of pilots have left the hill. To do this, line up accordingly. Remember waiting on launch is a disease that is hard to cure.

Most ordered launches have a right of refusal which means you go to the back of the launch line. Generally you should take off at your appointed time whenever conditions look good even if you are first. If conditions look questionable and no one is in the air to tell you otherwise it is reasonable to refuse launch. However, in very marginal conditions it takes a long time to launch pilots so you may find yourself in later conditions which are worse. The important guideline is to go when you think you can stay up, but don't get impatient and reward yourself with a sled ride if the air looks dead.

✓ The Universal Start

You should train for competition by flying often and long if possible. The physical development you thus acquire lets you get off early without a thought for the hour you may have to wait for the start time.

More and more competitions are using the start tarp system where everyone launches early and everyone's time starts when the tarp appears. In some meets you must remain in a certain area before the tarp appears while in other cases you can be anywhere and simply have to take a photo of the tarp at the appropriate time.

The main advantage of a tarp start is that meet directors don't have to time each launch. Top pilots like this system because they have an easier time keeping track of their opponents—everyone in front of them is beating them. Also this format is good for spectators for the first pilot across goal is the day's winner.

The drawbacks to the tarp start system is the crowded gaggles that occur and the frustrating time spent trying to stay high before the start tarp appears. Near misses are not uncommon and a few mid-airs have occurred. Furthermore the choice when to head out on course is taken away from the pilot so less judgement comes into play.

There are two tricks to maximizing tarp starts. First, you must get off early. This allows you to get high and go from thermal climb to thermal climb and stay on top of the pack.

That's the theory at least, but often it's difficult to time when to leave the lift you've topped out in to head for an up and coming gaggle. You can practice this at home by simply trying to always stay the highest for a period of say an hour. The problem is, if your timing is off you can find yourself at the bottom of a cloud of gliders.

The other trick is to time yourself from various points to the start tarp photo sector so you know when to head for the tarp. Also note the altitude it requires. If you are late you not only lose the time but you also miss the lead gaggle which is the fastest group on course (note that the lead gaggle tends

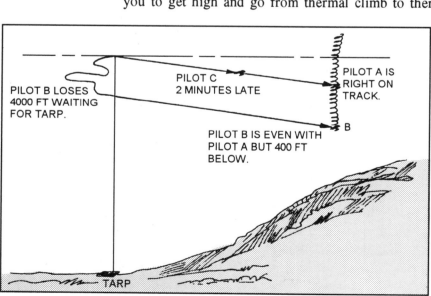

Figure 9-9: Achieving Start Tarps

to be slower with a tarp start since everyone is keying on everyone else, but it's still the best thing going).

Usually it takes longer than you think to reach the start tarp and in any case it's better to be early at the gate than late. The reason for this is that if you are late you lose that amount of time on the leaders. If you are early you lose altitude while waiting but at a slower rate than you can gain it back (if major sink isn't in the holding area). To see this look at figure 9-9. Here we see pilot A who has timed the distance perfectly and gets a photo right when the tarp appears then returns back to the mountain. Pilot B is two minutes early and loses 400 feet sinking at 200 FPM while waiting for the tarp. This pilot arrives back at the mountain at the same time as A only 400 feet lower. Pilot C arrives at the tarp at the same height as the other two but two minutes late. If pilot B finds a thermal of only 200 FPM he or she is even with pilot C when this pilot reaches the mountain. If the thermal is stronger which is usually the case, Pilot B will be well above C. For example, a 500 FPM thermal will put B 600 feet above C. In such a thermal B is only 48 seconds behind A which is the time takes to make up 400 feet at 500 FPM.

Starting tarps are typically 1 to 3 miles upwind of launch. In varying wind you'll need to adjust the amount of time you allow for reaching the tarp. It is almost always better to start for the tarp and be there when it opens no matter how high you are unless you expect to get back to the lift too low to get back up efficiently or you are in a screaming thermal that won't be there when you return.

Sometimes the thermal cycles are such that everyone is low just when it's time to head for the tarp. You should still go for it as long as you can get back high enough to get up, for your sink rate while gliding to the tarp to reach it at maximum altitude isn't much greater than if you stayed at the mountain if the air is not moving vertically. Of course, sink is often stronger away from the mountain, but even so, other pilots who wait will also encounter the sink when they venture out. Again it is better to reach a start tarp early than late.

It's better to be out front and low than way back and high when the tarp opens.

IN THE AIR

Imagine yourself in the air battling feisty thermals, dodging an armada of gliders and scrambling for altitude. What should you be doing? First, if at all possible, find uncluttered lift away from the pack so you can climb freely and concentrate on other things. However, this doesn't mean blindly leave gaggles, for sometimes that's the only place to find up air. But remember, there is a herd instinct at work and sometimes you can go to a cloud or a thermal source and have lift all your own, at least for a while.

During the initial stages of flight whether you are on course or holding for a tarp start, you should try to scope out as much as you can about the conditions and course strategy. Look for:

With a universal start system use your time in the air before the tarp to scope out the conditions and plan your initial route.

The Aerial Checklist
1. Orientation of the sun to imagine the best thermal generators and as an aid in navigation.
2. Cloud drift (watch shadows) to know the upper wind.
3. Thermal types—are they weak, strong, wide, narrow, short or long?
4. Cloud lift—where is the best climb available in relation to the cloud?
5. Inversion layer or effective ceiling to know where the best climb levels are.
6. The best routes toward goal due to the cloud distribution and terrain features.
7. Areas of strong lift.

The sooner you can determine these factors, the sooner you'll be able to fit your overall plan to the specific conditions and task of the day. What follows is one type of strategy to which you can relate these factors.

USING LIFT BANDS

In Chapter 5 we discussed how we can divide the sky vertically to determine where to look for thermal sources. In a similar manner (but not necessarily at the same levels) we can imagine the sky divided into bands or layers that help determine our strategy.

A good way to do this is to divide the sky into three more or less equal bands from cloud base on down as shown in figure 9-10. They are:

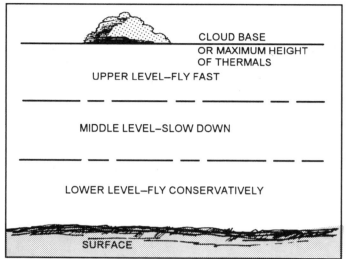

Figure 9-10: Flight Levels

Flight Bands
- *Upper band* —This is where you go fastest using exact speed-to-fly theory and your speed ring.
- *Middle band* —Here you are lower and slow down by decreasing your speed ring by 25 to 50%.
- *Lower band* —This level calls for caution so you set your speed ring to zero to maximize distance over the ground and work almost any lift.

As a day progresses or conditions change you may move your bands up and down to maximize your speed. In good conditions or when getting a later start your upper band should be expanded downward. When setting up such imaginary bands use the following guidelines:

Flight bands are a way to organize your strategy.

☐ Be conservative in blue conditions, over bad terrain or if not flying for time (move bands up).
☐ Use more speed when good thermal indicators abound or when battling a head wind (move bands down).

Flight bands of these nature work best when there is a large distance between the clouds and the ground. They are most useful on the good days and help you increase your speed by budgeting altitude.

FOLLOWING LEADERS

As soon as possible, learn the numbers and the colors of the top ten pilots in the meet. The reason to do this is not to follow them around, but to be able to select the best thermal to go to when many gliders are circling. If you use other gliders for signposts as you should, it is important to know who is giving you the best information.

Following others may be a good way to learn a few things early on, but the secret to competition success is making good decisions—some thing you'll never learn to do if you always follow.

Following a well-known pilot around a course has a built-in recipe for failure: you will be at a loss when he or she leaves you behind. That's not to say that you can't try to keep up with the better pilots, but using them to guide you around the course without venturing out on your own is being a leech.

John Pendry is often plagued with pilots following his every move because of his great skill. In the 1988 World Meet he led a group over the mountains in New South Wales, Australia that became known as Pendry's minnow pack. When he dove for a turn point at the Murmungee launch, he found nothing but sink and alas had to land. His fate was not a lonely one, however, for he managed to deck about twenty minnows, all of whom felt let down by the big fish!

In my own experience I find myself doing better and going faster when I am alone because I often get bogged down in slow gaggles where excess caution seems to be contagious. It is very difficult to be the first to leave a circling group for it is easy to think that all these pilots boring holes know more than you do. Whenever you can, practice leading a group of X-C pilots for it prepares you for the times you are alone or miraculously leading the field. Too often pilots get out in front and get nervous and conservative. That's not the way to win.

A few pilots—notably the legendary Steve Moyes—specialize in launching later and jumping gaggles to achieve very fast times. Such an act requires confidence and the ability to read distant gaggles with accuracy. Not many pilots can do this, but it is not a bad skill to acquire for the times when you get behind. With a tarp start, such an intentional strategy is not possible, of course.

SHIFTING GEARS

In the previous chapter we saw how important it is to shift gears (either up or down) as the terrain or conditions change. In competition where speed to goal is the quest it is even more important to change speeds, yet harder to do. The urge to race is difficult to put aside, especially if things have been going great hitherto.

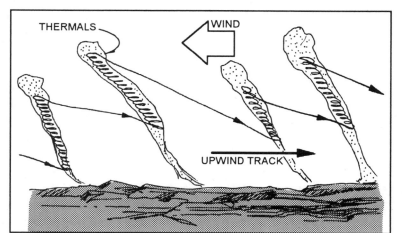

Figure 9-11: Upwind Flying in Thermals

Sometimes it helps to know ahead of time the point where a gear shift is needed such as when leaving the mountains or turning upwind. In this case we are already prepared to exercise the patience of Job and the hope of Bob. Saw-toothing upwind and barely making headway on each climb and glide cycle (see figure 9-11) is a necessary skill for a top pilot as much as racing downwind. If you never practice in "low gear" you'll have too much tendency to stay in high gear.

"It's one thing to go fast, but the hardest thing to do is to know when to slow down."
— Mark Bennett, multiple US World Team Member

IV - WINNING TACTICS

*W*e think of tactics as the specific ploys, tricks and techniques that we use to get us through the sky. In this part we learn about marshalling all of our skills to win little skirmishes against the forces of nature and the wiles of our fellow pilots.

TEAM FLYING

Whenever possible, getting together with one or two pilots in the air is beneficial to all for the trade of information—either verbal or visual—as well as the mutual encouragement works wonders for your performance. *"Two can do it better than one!"* quips Butch Peachy.

Most beneficial to any of us is to be linked up with a pilot slightly better than we are. Least beneficial is to be with one who is always behind, but in the frequent reversals of fate that flying hands us, this is rarely the case. A pilot that is of lesser skill can offer encouragement and observation of conditions.

When two pilots are near each other they should communicate their intentions such as when they are going to leave a thermal and where they are heading next. Even if two pilots are not at the same height they can leave together since the lower pilot generally runs out of lift first. If the wind is crossing once the pilots head on course, the highest pilot should remain on the downwind side of the other since he or she can spend more altitude in reaching a thermal.

The lead pilot along a course should briefly relay information concerning general conditions (weather changes, weak areas, fast flying stretches, etc...), routes that work or prove difficult, specific thermal sources, climb rates and thermal heights. Middle of the group pilots can do the same for teammates further back. Pilots in the rear should mainly keep quiet except to ask for specific information or report a potential problem such as a thunderstorm. The exception to this is when the course is out-and-back in which case the rear pilots can lend aid for a while to the lead pilot returning.

Let's hear what Mark Bennett has to say about team flying:

"The lagging pilot can easily make the mistake of acting like an anchor, dragging the lead guy back with too many questions, or a poor attitude in general. The lead guy is busy trying to maintain his position and distractions from the rear can be of little use. It's a fine balance between willingly helping those friends behind, and having your focussed concentration on winning irreparably broken. In general, minimize radio use."

Once a team pilot is on the ground either at goal or short, he or she can lend a very useful hand reporting ground winds and observations of the sky and other pilots' positions. This is especially helpful if this grounded pilot gets picked up and is traveling right along with you. With a teammate at goal you can be apprised of the winds conditions on final glide (lift, sink and wind) and whether or not pilots are making goal too high or if some are coming up short. This information helps you judge your own final glide (see below).

In the 1992 Pre-World Meet, my teammate Rich Pfeiffer won the day with a blazing speed on a 99 mile flight from Gunter Launch in the Owens Valley to Gabbs, Nevada. when I approached later, lift had diminished considerably and my chances of making goal dimmed. However, I went on glide about 15 miles out and Rich's constant reportage of wind shifts and pilot's circling helped me steer my course for maximum distance. When I came closer he could see my glide maintaining in relation to the landscape which helped keep a positive altitude. A final word on the wind let me know I could land in the flight direction and I crossed goal with at least six feet to spare!

✓ Ground Crew

If you have only one driver and vehicle for the entire team, it is best that he or she supports the lead pilot by remaining with him or her all the way until being informed to go to goal. A driver should be at goal before the first pilot to provide valuable information as indicated above.

If the driver does stay with the lead pilot it is important for pilots in the air to relay the position of downed pilots for later retrieve. This alleviates endless searching for all concerned. If the lead pilot goes down, a quick breakdown can get him or her in the vehicle which is most valuable to the pilots remaining in the air. The mark of a good teammate is the ability to encourage and aid pilots still flying once he or she has fallen short.

A lone driver should be sent out on course in position as soon as the time starts. With timed launches this is when the first team pilot goes. With a universal start, this is when the tarp opens. If more than one driver is available one can stay behind to help pilots launch and the other can be in position to follow the lead. Out on course the trailing vehicle can then stay with stragglers and pick up dropouts while the lead vehicle eventually goes to goal.

✔ Radio Use

"Winners aren't talkers."
—George Moffat

"No matter what you hear on the radio, you must make the ultimate decision."
—Butch Peachy

"Hie, a pox on voxes!"
—Shakespeare *(probably)*

It is an axiom of aviation competition that the more time spent talking on the radio, the less chance you have of winning. It is important to keep transmissions short and concise. Lengthy transmissions usually get lost partway through since the listeners can't break in to clarify points. It is desirable to give route information, lift information and your position information when pertinent. It is not alright to discuss sex, politics, religion or the doubts you have about ever making goal. Keep a positive attitude on the airwaves.

When pilots are trying to concentrate it is very annoying to listen to a pilot giving directions to a ground crewperson. For this reason it is wise to have a second channel available for retrieval once a pilot is downed. Also teammates may occasionally request radio silence when engaged in extricating themselves from a sticky situation. It is important to remain quiet during these periods (except for essential information) and equally important for the environmentally challenged pilot to report when the situation becomes unstuck.

It is illegal to use codes on FM radios in the United States. However, to keep your transmissions short and avoiding letting everyone know how you are doing you can divide your team's maps into a grid system and report your position with a vertical letter and a horizontal number such as: "I'm at C9 at 10 grand." Some teams go further and use colors or specific words that relate to how they are doing. Generally though, this type of skulduggery is more trouble than it's worth, unless you are trying to protect a lead.

The final point we'll make on radios is to put your vox in a box and mail it to Shangai to avoid spreading anguish and enmity among all your fellow pilots. VOX systems on a hang glider invariably turn on inadvertently and every one has to listen to the offending pilot grunting, cursing, panting and singing in an unconscious comment on his personal situation. The blithe culprit is the only one unaffected because he is the only one hearing nothing. Woe to you if other pilots find out you're a hidden radio offender.

RACING WITH GAGGLES

We have spoken of gaggles in previous chapters. Here we reiterate the importance of leaving slow groups, going to good climbs and the best gaggles. It is amazing how often unaware pilots let another nearby pilot climb up to them and past without moving to the better lift. The sooner you determine someone is climbing better and move, the more time you save.

When heading for a thermal glittering with gliders, aim for the steeper banked ones (see figure 9-12). Look for the best pilots' gliders as well, for one reason they are good is that they find the strongest lift. In large confused gaggles, keep a lookout for better climbers outside your thermal for very often so many pilots in a small volume reduces everyone's climb rate. A separate core that you can share with only one or two pilots is ideal.

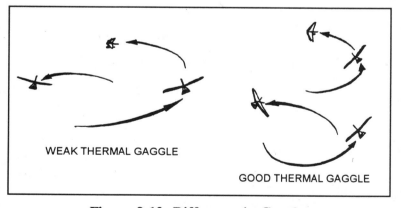

WEAK THERMAL GAGGLE

GOOD THERMAL GAGGLE

Figure 9-12: Difference in Gaggles

"Don't get distracted by gaggles, attracted by cloud base or caught wasting time in slow climbs. The better you know an area the better you can apply these principles. Always concentrate on lift indicators while gliding and learn to watch for the next gaggle while thermaling."
— Chris Arai, US World Team Member

At all times you must be observant to see the signs that other gliders give as to the location and heft of lift. One of the best things you can do is obtain a helmet with good peripheral vision to allow you to see gaggles up ahead while you have your head down in glide mode.

When you start slowly you get with slow gaggles that can slow you even more. In this case it's better to break away and do it alone.

Remember, everyone in your gaggle is your friend and ally until final glide. An informal truce should take place where everyone cooperates to help each other go faster. If, however, some pilots tend to hang back and feed off others it is easy to leave them behind by departing from a thermal when they are out of position to see you anytime there are multiple choices to make.

Finally, be aware that while gaggles are fairly reliable indicators of lift they are not necessarily indicators of wise decision making. I don't know how many times I have landed out with a whole gaggle plopping down in the surrounding fields. We learn to use gaggles as information sources, not as directors of our flight.

✓ The Leading Gaggle

The gaggle that leads the pack is usually made up of most of the meet aces. Despite the fact they are out ahead and have no markers they still pull away from the trailing gaggles. It is of great aid and comfort to be with this lead gaggle, but usually difficult to stay there. As Al Whitesell says of his lead gaggle flying, *"Racing up front with the leaders is an intense experience requiring great concentration. You must watch every pilot every second for if you let your attention stray they are gone, leaving you floundering in their wake. The up side of this experience is that time goes by unnoticed until surprise (!) you're suddenly at goal."*

Being in the lead is no comfort, for a moment's lapse leaves you lagging. But the intensity of the experience is well worth the effort especially when you finish with the winners.

The only way to get with the lead gaggle is to launch when the best pilots launch, stay as high as they do and get the start gate on time. The only way to *stay* with the lead gaggle is to perfect all the techniques we have discussed. This perfection, of course, makes winners. Even if you can't keep up with the leaders, your time spent with them will show you some of the necessary ingredients for producing excellence. Here is how one leader does it:

"When in the air you must observe everything around you as if you had eyes in the back of your head."

— Mark Newland, 1986 and 1990 US Nationals Winner

ENTERING AND EXITING THERMALS

We have previously seen the importance of coring a thermal quickly. Here are a few other matters to consider. The sink around a thermal is usually more intense than elsewhere. Therefore we should try to pass through it as quickly as possible. Figure 9-13 shows a pilot flying the ideal speed between thermals and near thermals. Note how speed is acquired before hitting the near-thermal sink. This speed is paid off in the thermal, gaining some additional altitude and

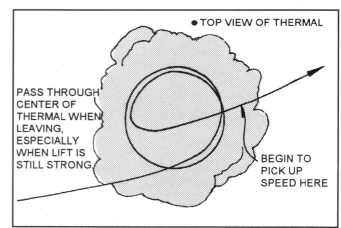

FLY FASTER IN STRONGER SINK

FLY FASTER IN STRONGER SINK AROUND THERMAL

● TOP VIEW OF THERMAL

PASS THROUGH CENTER OF THERMAL WHEN LEAVING, ESPECIALLY WHEN LIFT IS STILL STRONG

BEGIN TO PICK UP SPEED HERE

Figure 9-13: Negotiating Sink Near a Thermal   **Figure 9-14: Technique for Leaving a Thermal**

There is a great tendency when approaching a gaggle to slow up to find what the pilots are climbing in. Their climb coupled with our sink can be deceptive, making the thermal look better than it is. We must emphasize the necessity to observe gaggles well in advance to get a true picture of what they are in and carry speed until you are out of sink to minimize your losses.

When exiting a thermal we should pull on extra speed to get through the strong sink *before* it is encountered as shown. Our exit path should begin on the far side of the thermal with a straight line through the center of the core as shown in figure 9-14. Little details like this can save you 100 feet or more.

Remember, we normally leave thermals when our climb rate falls to that expected in the next thermal (our speed ring setting). Never leave a thermal without a definite destination in mind.

We deviate from our course:
- *For better lift*
- *To avoid dangerous terrain*
- *As soon as possible for minimum losses.*

COURSE DEVIATIONS

We have mentioned that the successful racing pilot is the one who can maintain the straightest course as well as make slight deviations to use cloud streets, mountain chain sources and lift bands.

The sooner we detect the need for deviations, the better, for we can minimize the angle of deviation. This is shown in figure 9-15I where the pilot A headed for the cloud earlier and has a shorter path than pilot B. Once a deviation is made we should follow a new course to goal or the next turn point as shown in figure 9-15II. Here pilot A again has the shortest path.

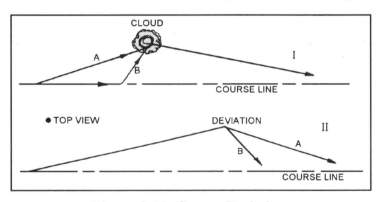

Figure 9-15: Course Deviations

Deviations of less than 10° are inconsequential. Altering our path up to 30° is good practice as long as we find better lift. Changes of 45° or more should only be considered if we are likely to sink out going straight or terrain problems block our route (a sea of water or trees). Finally, going backward on course should only be used in extreme situations where we are almost sure to sink out otherwise and we will definitely find lift by retracing our path. Even so, all pilots need to develop the ability to make the tough decision to go back when necessary.

TURN POINTS

We looked at the official turn point sector above. Here are some tips on achieving turn points efficiently:

Approach a turn point:
Downwind as high as you can.
Upwind as low as is practical.

Getting Turn Points Photos
1. Identify your turn point from the meet photos and from the air long before you reach it. Place it accurately on your map. Have your camera ready *before* you reach the turn point sector.
2. Head a little to the good side of the turn point and take your photos while rounding it as shown in figure 9-16. If you cut the turn point too closely you don't have enough time in the sector to take multiple shots.
3. Place the turn point in one corner of the picture frame so the FAI sector shows in most of the photo area as shown in figure 9-17.
4. Pass the turn point at least by 300 feet to be sure you have no interpretation problems.
5. Avoid drifting downwind off the course line or a turn point if possible.
6. Plan your next thermal past the turn point long before you reach the turn.

Knowing exactly what turn points look like and where they are is extremely important. View any posted photos or those on the rule book to form a visual image of the turn point. Turn the photos so you see the turn point in the same direction with which you will be approaching it. Some pilots carry copies of turn point photos in their map holder for easy identifying. Turn points with their altitude (MSL) should be clearly marked on your map.

My own lesson was learned in 1990 in Brazil. One turn point on this particular day was an island about 20 miles west along the brown Doce river. The turn point photos were not posted at the pilots' meeting but I was sure I could find the island. Out on course I took a couple good turn point photos and flew on over the rugged hills of Minas Gerais state. That night I found out the sad truth. My island was the wrong one, even though it was the only one apparent. The real turn point island was in fact no longer there, for the river was low and only a muddy track separated it from the mainland. Had I seen the photos I would have recognized the shape of this quasi-island and enjoyed my evening and indeed my meet results more.

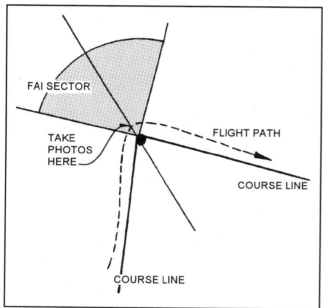

Figure 9-16: Taking Efficient Turn Point Photos

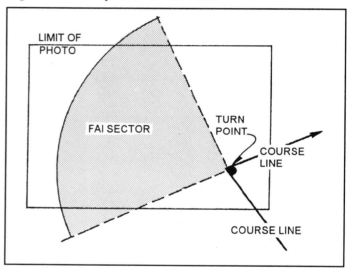

Figure 9-17: Placing Turn Point Photos

Turn point success:

* *Know well what it looks like*

* *Spot it from as far away as possible*

* *Fly directly to it if possible*

* *Do not cut it too closely unless you are low or a vertical structure guides you*

* *Don't get downwind of a turn point if you can help it.*

Placing the turn point at the corner of your picture (figure 9-17) is a trick that can save a lot of grief for there will be no doubt that you get the turn point.

Aerial photography can be confusing as shown by the experience of Tim Arai. The meet director claimed he didn't get a proper turn point photo. Tim was sure he did, but on viewing the photo had to agree with the meet director. Tim was about to become suicidal when his brother, Chris, walked in, turned the slide upside down in the viewer and it became obvious that Tim had a perfect photo!

Passing a turn point by a reasonable amount is very important. If a vertical structure is near the turn point use it as an indicator of where you are. Remember, we mentioned how you are usually well behind where you appear to be. Don't leave any doubt in a meet director's mind about your turn points or you will be continually scrutinized.

"Pilots should be aware to balance the risk against the reward and make turn points by at least a 100 meter margin. Cutting a turn point too closely is a foolish risk for a few seconds saved."
— Paul Mollison, 1988 World Meet Director

Before you achieve a turn point , look along the departing leg for gaggles or clouds. View the sky and terrain from the angle you will be looking to note the different appearance of clouds and shadows. This helps you judge conditions and orientation. Such planning ahead can help prevent the common malady of some pilots that results in a landing near turn points.

Remember, a turn point is not a goal but a simple jog in your flight path.

If your course is a crosswind track to a turn point it is important not to drift too much to the downwind side. Stay upwind as much as you can.

An official turn point photo from the East Coast Championships showing a pilot well past the hairpin turn.

In the 1992 Sandia Classic in New Mexico we flew east 70 miles to a goal at Milagro. A strong north wind was blowing and those pilots who drifted south had a hard time beating back upwind to goal. Some landed tragically short.

Use thermals near a turn point to your advantage. If you are approaching downwind, you should try to stay as high as you can. If you approach a turn point upwind, do so as low as you dare for maximum average speed (see figure 9-18). If pilots are marking a thermal near a turn point it is not a bad idea to get your photos then come back to the thermal especially if the thermal is tall and the turn point is close by or the outbound course is a retrace of the inbound.

I once was in the turbulent top of a thermal with several pilots. Two of us left to achieve a nearby turn point and returned to the thermal lower but in a stronger position allowing us to climb up almost to the stay-at-home pilots who still had to get the turn point.

Pro Tip: It's easy to misjudge the altitude needed to reach an upwind turn point. Also leaving a thermal to reach a turn point then return to the thermal takes longer than you may think. Only a column thermal can be used in this manner.

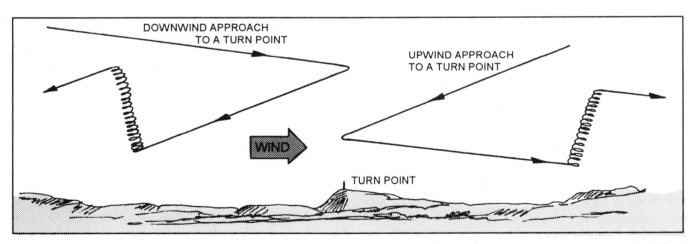

Figure 9-18: Approaching Turn Points in Wind

USING BALLAST

We saw in Chapters 3 and 7 that ballast increases our wing loading which increases all flying speeds. We must balance this with the reminder that increased circling speeds reduces our climb rate. From our understanding that good climb rates can be the most important part of achieving a fast average speed, we should use ballast with caution.

Tight or weak thermals require a lighter wing loading as does a tail wind. Once we know these simple laws (and their converses) we can form some general guidelines in the side bar.

In desert conditions where thermals tend to be narrow but strong ballast can be an aid for it can help in handling which makes up for the loss due to tighter banks. Indeed, in gaggles sometimes a lighter wing loading provides less response and therefore no climbing advantage.

When using ballast, make sure your load is water or small particles. Sand is the material of choice. Typically 20 to 50 pounds of ballast is used, although you better hope for wind on takeoff at the upper limit. Needless to say it is unsportsmanlike conduct to dump ballast on another competitor and you should always dump your load before landing to avoid alighting like an awkward goose.

Using Ballast
I. Use ballast if:
- Flying into a head wind.
- Thermals are large.
- Thermals are strong.
- Strong thermal streets exist.
II. Remove or avoid ballast if:
- Flying in a tail wind.
- Conditions are weak.
- Thermals are small.

DOLPHIN FLYING

True dolphin flying is difficult to achieve in a hang glider partially because good energy retention is needed to gain in lift with a pushout what we lost in sink. However, the experience of some pilots in streets and lift lines indicates that dolphin flying is possible on exceptional days.

The dolphin flight rules for competition racing are the same as those established in Chapter 8 for going far. One additional point is that the success of dolphin flying often depends on the pilot's ability to not just vary speeds straight ahead, but to make small side deviations to the best lift, most readily by reading clouds.

We can relate dolphin flight to the flight bands discussed earlier. If we can stay in the higher band with abundant lift we can perhaps achieve dolphin flight, at least for a portion of our trek. In any case, be cautious of being overzealous in the desire to fly straight with a minimum of turns. Many charging pilots have raced themselves to the ground in some miscarriage of dolphin flight philosophy. True dolphin flight entertains the possibility of circling when you get low.

THE FINAL GLIDE

In Chapter 7 we discussed the theory of final glide. We found that for maximizing speed the final glide decision making is a bit more complicated than for simply gliding the furthest. You should reread this important material to understand how to save minutes in final glide.

In that previous discussion we discovered how to judge the amount of climb we should obtain in thermals of different strength once we are within reach of goal. However, to know the height of different glide ratios over the ground at different positions it is necessary to mark our maps.

✓ Marking Final Glide Maps

The final glide in competition is typically 1/10 to 1/3 of the entire flight. It behooves us to maximize this portion of our flight if we wish to do well.

Figure 9-19 shows a goal with a series of concentric arcs drawn at 5 miles, 10 miles and 15 miles away. If we know the MSL altitude of the goal, we can post the MSL altitude we need at each of these points for any chosen glide ratio to goal. The easiest way to get these numbers is to make a chart. In the following example we assume goal is at 2320 ft MSL as in the figure.

Note that we have added 500 feet of insurance in our calculations. This is highly recommended when you first start competing. After making multiple goals and learning to judge conditions better you can reduce or eliminate your insurance. If you are consistently coming

Altitude Needed for 5 Miles Away (26,400 feet horizontal)				
Glide Ratio	Vertical feet needed	+ 500 feet insurance	Height of goal	MSL altitude needed
8 to 1	3300	3800	2320	6120 or 6.1 thousand
10 to 1	2640	3140	2320	5460 or 5.5 thousand
12 to 1	2200	2700	2320	5020 or 5.0 thousand

Glide altitudes on our map are invaluable aids. These are minimum altitudes and we must learn how to determine how much to climb above them with our final glide chart.

in to goal too high, you should lower your numbers or more specifically increase your expected glide ratio. Screaming along final glide with the bar stuffed is an indicator that you wasted time somewhere in an orgy of climb. Ideally you should come in with about 100 feet to spare which you convert to speed in the last 1/10 mile or so.

From our chart we see the right hand column gives us the altitudes we need above sea level for the different glides. We convert this to thousands of feet (such as 6.1) to reduce clutter and label our maps appropriately as shown in the figure.

We follow the same process for the other distances as shown. The handy chart below provides the vertical distance needed for various horizontal distances and glides. To get the MSL altitudes you need for your map, simply add your insurance allowance and goal altitude to these numbers and label your map.

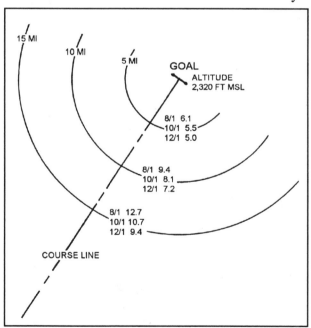

Figure 9-19: Marking Maps for Final Glide

Final Glide Heights				
Glide Ratios	5 miles	10 miles	15 miles	20 miles
8 to 1	3300	6600	9900	13200
10 to 1	2640	5280	7920	10560
12 to 1	2200	4400	6600	8800

For metric final glide heights, divide the arc distance in kilometers (use 10, 20 and 30 km) by the glide ratio to get the height.

Note that we include the heights for a 20 mile glide for in the high desert it is possible to attain these altitudes.

In general we work with the 8 to 1 and 10 to 1 values. We choose the glide ratio based on the day's conditions and our overall experience. Only with a tail wind and relatively little sink do we ever achieve 12 to 1.

To use these numbers it is important to relate the arcs drawn on the map to actual points on the ground. Sometimes they fall directly on something obvious like a road intersection and sometimes they lie over nondescript ground in which case we must estimate our position from a landmark shown on the map.

As we fly along between the arcs we should use checkpoints midway between them to monitor our progress. A little mental math tells us what altitude we need at these midpoints. If we are high we can speed up. If low we should slow down or work lift.

At the end of Chapter 7 we provided a final glide climb chart that tells how high to climb in a given strength thermal before going on final glide. To use our map glide altitudes with the final glide climb chart of Chapter 7, we simply climb above our glide altitudes the amount appropriate to the thermal strength we are experiencing. Of course, nature doesn't conveniently place thermals at the mileage markers, so again we must do some mental math to figure the altitude we need for the glide ratio we have chosen at the position the thermal is encountered. Of course, if we are already above the climb height our climb chart indicates, we should simply slow down a bit in the thermal then bid it goodby on our way to goal.

> **Pro Tip:** Be sure to check your map scale when drawing the distance arcs. One meet head provided a map scale that was too big since he reduced the map size when he photocopied them. Had we not caught this the outcome would have been tragic (a lynching may have occurred).

Once you have drawn and labeled your arcs, cover the map with clear contact paper. This will keep it fresh in rain and dust. Use these glide calculations just once and you will be a convert. They instill great confidence!

MAKING GOAL

If you're going to make it, rejoice but continue concentrating until you have safely landed. The sky often rains gliders as multiple crossers circle down. This is prime time for a midair if the landing area is tight and pilots go into relax mode.

If you possibly can, call in to goal frequency to inform officials of your approach or have your ground crew do so. This will help alleviate any confusion if you are excessively high or cross with several pilots. Once you are on the ground and your glider is safe, walk to the goal keepers to make sure they got your time and number. In most meets this is OK as long as gliders aren't crossing goal. This is a fail-safe factor for you and the meet organization—don't forget it.

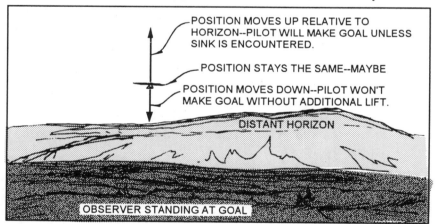

Figure 9-20: Judging Final Glide of an Approaching Glider

Your crew or teammate at goal should inform you of other pilots' crossing altitudes so you can adjust your speed accordingly. Sometimes lift abounds and pilots cross at the moon. Other times sink lurks that drops pilots agonizingly short. You need to know these things and spend or save your altitude accordingly. A good teammate can judge your glide with the horizon and tell if you're high or low so you can speed up or slow down (see figure 9-20). However, woe to he who calls it wrong and lands his teammate short!

We have seen pilots land just short of goal who could have made it either by diving into ground effect and floating across, choosing to land in a high tail wind or landing on their belly. These are not techniques to be practiced everyday, but are sometimes reasonable in the heat of competition. You be the judge. On the other hand, many inexperienced competitors come over goal too slowly, too high. Practice flying with the bar stuffed well away from the terrain in thermal conditions so you can make a safe dive at goal.

Once the flurry and excitement of making goal is over, break down quickly so everyone can return as soon as possible for a good night's sleep. On the way back to base explore the flights of you and your teammates to find out where you made good and bad choices so you can repeat the success and avoid the blunders. Congratulations and celebrations are in order all the way around, but tomorrow's another day for you to prove your mettle.

SUMMARY

*C*ompetition flying is one of the pinnacles of achievement for it calls on all our resources of psychological discipline, planning, knowledge, experience and skill. Once we have built our skills to the advanced level the real development begins, for competition is 95% a mental exercise as Judy Leden states. Perhaps the most important mental aspect to acquire is a positive attitude. This translates to confidence, eagerness to meet a challenge and knack for winning.

We become a winner every time we pick up our glider and attempt a task that extends our abilities. As we repeat this practice we refine our strategy and improve our tactics until we see real progress in the meet results. However, most of us will compete for years and never actually come in first. But the friends we make and the hours of exciting flying we share give us a sense of accomplishment that cannot be found anywhere else. That's a win in our book.

Pilots staging during the 1990 Hobbs, New Mexico tow meet.

CHAPTER

Towing Aloft

Hang gliding started in the late sixties with the towing of primary designs. Soon foot-launching was discovered and towing became a launch method of secondary focus as mountain sites afforded soaring of all types. However, the decade of the eighties witnessed a resurgence of towing worldwide. This was due to improved towing methods, improved ultralight tow vehicles and improved glider performance which allowed great soaring possibilities, even over flat terrain.

Today we have many methods of dragging pilots into the sky. They all have their advocates and applications. We will review each of them in this chapter to give the interested pilot a solid background for learning to tow safely.

The practice of towing should be recognized as adding an ordinate of complexity to the art of flying a hang glider. For this reason learning to tow should take place only under the guidance of an experienced towing instructor. This book cannot possibly cover every detail that can go wrong with all the different systems in varied conditions. Use it as a groundschool guide so that you are fully prepared to learn effectively when it's your turn to be pulled gently aloft.

I - THE BIG PICTURE

The various forms of towing have been developed to suit different needs, not the least of which is the human need to explore new possibilities. The different towing methods have different advantages and disadvantages. Here we'll look at how towing developed and how the different methods have solved the problems of towing as well as provide an overview of safe towing practices.

TOWING HISTORY

Towing has been around at least since the early 1850s when Sir George Cayley hitched his coachman up to a team of horses and successfully pulled him aloft in one of Cayley's designs. Hopefully the coachman was getting hazard pay. Sailplane pilots perfected towing in the 1930s, but early towing of hang gliders developed from another source. Water ski enthusiasts had learned to tow flat kites behind their boats so when the more controllable standard Rogallo glider designs appeared in the 1960s, the transition was readily made. With the invention of the control bar system, the Rogallo had one big advantage over a flat kite: you could release from the line and fly like a bird (well sortta).

Because of the water ski heritage, towing was promulgated by such luminaries as Bill Moyes, Bill Bennett and Michael Robertson who specialized in ski shows. Places like Cypress Gardens in Florida became hotbeds of towing and for many years an annual towing competition took place at this venue. When towing moved to land sites the same practices developed for towing over water were used. These consisted of a fixed length of line attached between the tow vehicle and the glider's control bar.

An Odyssey rigid wing trike tows a Swift.

The problem is, towing over ground is less forgiving than over water. A rash of accidents in the 1970s put many pilots off towing so the activity waned. However, a few brave souls persevered and developed safer and safer systems for towing. Notably, Donnell Hewett in Texas analyzed the problems and came up with center-of-mass towing as well as a series of rules which he calls the Skyting Criteria. Jerry Forburger, from Oklahoma at the time, invented the ATOL system which is a payout winch combined with a platform launch on the tow vehicle. Gerard Thévenot and others in France solved the problems of towing air-to-air with an ultralight as a tug. The perfection of reel-in winches such as those designed by Paul Yarnell in New York or Bob Bailey in Florida completes the picture to give us the great variety of towing we have today.

With towing who needs mountains? They just block the view and get in the way when you're trying to go far!

With the maturation of towing we can now say that hang gliding is accessible to everyone be they hillbillies or flatlanders. Furthermore with the performance of today's gliders, mountains are just a luxury, for Larry Tudor's world distance record (303 miles) and Larry Bunner's United States record east of the Mississippi (176 miles) were both made of tow. Towing has come of age with new tugs and techniques, competitions and fly-ins as well as the opening up of airports for towing operations. This healthy development will only continue unabated if we maintain our standards of safety.

TOWING TYPES

The several types of towing are somewhat distinct with their own items of unique equipment and problems to solve. Here we'll define the different types then treat each one separately later.

1. Static line – This system is the old method of hooking a line to a vehicle and pulling (see figure 10-1). It requires at least twice as much runway as altitude achieved and requires a careful operator since the only thing to regulate tow force is the speed of the vehicle.

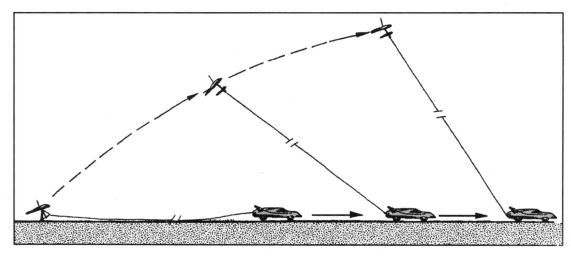

Figure 10-1: Static Line Towing

Towline wear is also a problem with this method since the line is typically dragged along the ground during restaging. With modern methods employing weak links and pressure gauges this form of towing can be safe and provide the fastest turnaround.

II . Payout winch – With this system a winch providing a regulated amount of drag is mounted on the tow vehicle. Typically a platform for carrying the glider up to flying speed is also incorporated and is known as a *platform launch*. The great advantages of this system are its gentleness and ease of control as well as the close contact between the pilot and the operator at launch. The disadvantage is that the runway length required is three to five times the desired altitude because the line is paying out as the tow vehicle advances.

III . Air-to-air – This type of towing uses an ultralight to tow the glider aloft. Its main advantage is the towing height is limited only by fuel, time and legal ceiling. Also, a good tug pilot can tow a glider into a thermal much better than with a ground-based system. The main drawback is the need for more extensive training on the part of the tug pilot (he or she must be an experienced ultralight operator) than with other systems.

IV . Static winch – With this system a motor-driven winch is situated at one end of a field and reels a line that pulls the glider aloft. The advantages of this system is it allows very fast turnarounds. It requires about twice the runway for altitude gained. The disadvantages are that it is bulkier and requires more maintenance than payout winch systems (but not more than an ultralight tug).

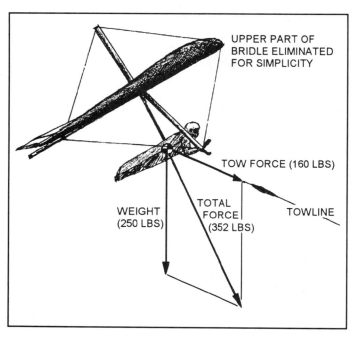

Figure 10-2: Forces on a Towed Glider

TOWING PROBLEMS

The main problem that towing presents over free flight are the increased forces on the glider and pilot and the misplacement of these factors. Other problems include oscillation, stalls, communication from pilot to ground crew and suitable operating areas.

✔ Glider Forces

The extra force on a glider results from the pulling of the towline as can be imagined. In figure 10-2 we see the effect of a tow force added to our normal weight. The two forces combine to give the net force that the glider feels. This force is greater than our normal weight and increases the loading considerably while it is directed forward of the normal gravity force. As a result the glider wants to fly in a nose-up attitude due to added thrust and airframe distortion as it climbs to maintain its trim angle of attack.

The more forward the net force is directed (determined by how far forward and how high the tow force is), the steeper our angle of climb and the higher our attitude. As a result, the trim position of the bar tends to be different than when free flying as shown in figure 10-3. Note that bar position for trim varies with towing speed, position in the tow and towing type. We'll find out more about this later.

Towing adds an order of complication to flying. However, sailplanes fly almost exclusively by towing.

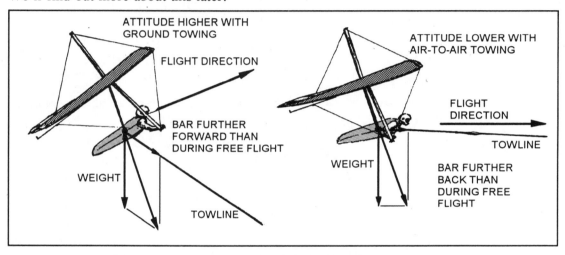

Figure 10-3: Flying Positions With Different Forms of Towing

We limit the forces on our gliders by adjusting towing speeds, using a brake or clutch system on the winch and a weak link in the tow line. These devices are necessary to avoid overstressing gliders, but more importantly to prevent lockouts.

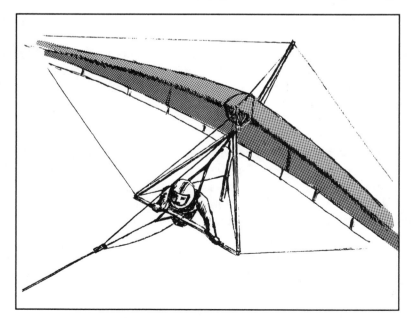

Figure 10-4: Beginning Lockout

✔ Lockouts

Next to a low stall and line break due to a gust, the event most likely to maim on tow is a lockout. A lockout occurs when a glider gets tilted to one side by a gust or overcontrol and continues arcing to the side as speed and forces build up. The outcome of a serious lockout can be pounding the ground with fatal intentions.

Figure 10-4 illustrates a typical incipient lockout. Here the glider is heading to the viewers right and the pilot's correction control is rendered less effective because the tow force is already pulling the pilot to the side where a correction must be made.

Once a lockout proceeds to a certain point a pilot can no longer correct for it and must relieve tow tension to escape either by releasing, having the vehicle freewheel the winch, back up, or doing both of these actions at the same time or experiencing a weak link break. The longer a lockout situation continues before any of these actions happen, the more severe the recovery will be (imagine being in a 45° bank under a high tow force that suddenly is released).

We do not have to analyze the forces acting to create a lockout, we have all seen or experienced lockouts when flying hand-controlled kites. When they oscillate to the side, then arch to the ground with a resounding thwack!, we have witnessed a lockout. Here's a summary of how to prevent and cure lockouts:

A lockout is preventable with:
- *Light tow forces*
- *Stable gliders*
- *Smooth conditions*
- *Straight head winds*
- *Capable control*

Lockout Procedures

1. Remain pointed at the tow vehicle at all times (even in a cross wind).
2. Prevent oscillations by flying slowly and correcting heading changes immediately.
3. At the first sign of a lockout, the pilot should make a quick correction while the tow observer should lighten tow pressure.
4. If the lockout doesn't get corrected immediately, the pilot should release or the tow vehicle should stop (or reverse direction) or freewheel a winch.

An exception to step 4 is when the pilot is below 50 feet above the ground. A wingover created by releasing during a lockout can have its own dire consequences. The phase of towing during the first 100 feet is critical for this and other reasons and should be done with as light of forces as possible.

✓ Oscillations

Oscillations on tow are mostly pilot-induced. Some gliders when flown faster tend to oscillate with inexperienced pilots. The timing and amount of control input are out of phase in this case. Pilots inexperienced under tow tend to fly too fast because they aren't used to the forward bar position necessary with ground towing. To make matters worse, once they get off center in the oscillation their body is pulled to the side by the towline which alters their perception of the control required.

"Make all controls subtle and wait for a reaction while on tow to prevent overcontrol."
–Jerry Forburger, Atol designer and tow guru

The cure for oscillations is to first be informed of the different feel of controls, bar positions and forces while under tow. Make all controls quick and small and wait for the glider to respond before adding more control. An experienced pilot should indicate where the bar will be during climbout. the other important factor is for all tow pilots to be well able to prevent or stop oscillations when flying fast during free flights. It should be clearly understood that some gliders are much more prone to oscillate than others under tow and this can be tested for during free flight by making fast turn reversals.

✓ Stalls

Stalls usually aren't apparent while on the tow line for they quickly become lockouts. However, during a weak link break or unexpected release when a low stall can occur because the attitude is way too high for a non-towing situation. The worse possible situation is when a break occurs right after launch. This can be a non-problem if the pilot instantly recognizes the need to pull in for speed as soon as the break occurs and before the kinetic energy of the glider dissipates.

Severe gusts at low altitude can cause serious stalls. Light tow pressures down low when thermals abound make good sense.

If you wait too long the consequence is a severe stall near the ground, the ogre that haunts all pilots' dreams. If you are very close to the ground, there may not be room to even pull in so you'll have to parachute the glider down the few remaining feet. Again the best way to prevent dangerous stalls is to use lighter tow forces for the first 100 feet.

CENTER-OF-MASS TOWING

The decade of the eighties witnessed the maturation of hang gliding. Safer and better performing craft evolved, a renewed interest in fixed wings was expressed, paragliding appeared, pilots got older and towing became safer. Much of the improvement in towing safety is the result of the work of Donnell Hewett, a quiet, unassuming man but obviously a great thinker.

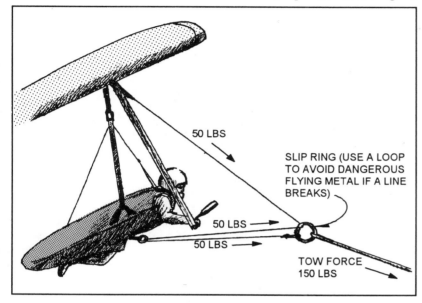

Figure 10-5: Skyting Bridle Force Distribution

Donnell saw the problem with the original systems as being a misplacement of forces. Originally, towlines were attached to a release at the bottom and (sometimes) the top of a special control bar. The glider was towed and the pilot was mostly along for the ride. Lockout problems were common because the towline would pull from the bottom of the control bar rolling the glider deeper into the turn. The solution Donnell devised was center-of-mass towing whereby the towline pulls on the pilot and glider in the same place and sense as does gravity in free flight.

The essence of this solution is known as the *skyting bridle* shown in figure 10-5. There are two lengths going to the pilot's center of mass (near the hips) and one going to the glider's center of mass (the keel or apex of the control bar). These lines are actually all one line and all have the same tension in them (neglecting friction effects) as if they were acting around pulleys. Thus, the pull on the pilot is twice that of the pull on the glider (see the figure) which is exactly what we want since the mass of the pilot is about twice that of the glider.

With this Hewett bridle, towing becomes much less stressful with nearly normal controls, generally lower forces are imposed on the glider and there is no need to add a heavy towing bar to the glider. We highly recommend that all towing operations use a skyting bridle with possible alterations for specific styles.

THE SKYTING CRITERIA

Donnell Hewett went on to define other facets of safe towing. He eventually developed the Skyting Criteria which describes an ideal for which all towing operations should strive . They are listed below.

If you wish to tow in observance of the laws of the universe (physics), follow the Skyting Criteria.

Skyting Criteria

1. Constant direction of tow
2. Constant tow tension
3. Distribution of tow forces proportional to mass
4. Center-of-mass bridle attachment
5. Gradual transition to and from tow
6. Reliable releases
7. Use of infallible weak links
8. Safe learning method
9. Adequate tow vehicle power
10. Capable crew
11. Reliable communication
12. Suitable environment

These criteria when met will not absolutely guarantee a safe towing operation, but they greatly reduce the possibility of an accident. Let's flesh them out.

✓ Simulation of Free Flight

The first four criteria are intended to produce as close a simulation to free flight as possible.

▶1. The tow direction on the glider should be straight ahead to prevent control problems. The longer the tow line the easier this is to assure. With modern payout winches and air-to-air towing, this criteria is difficult to follow, but still should be considered.

▶2. Tension regulation is essential to overcome the effects of wind gradient and gusts. A payout winch brake or clutch device serves the purpose here. With air-to-air towing this criteria is difficult to meet, but some elasticity in the tow rope and tug inertia help.

▶3. We discussed the 2:1 distribution of tow forces to pilot and glider above.

▶4. It may not be possible to attach to the center of mass of a glider so we compromise by using the keel just in front of the control bar apex. Likewise, an air-to-air situation may require attachment at the pilot's shoulders which does not meet the skyting criteria.

Not all operations can strictly confirm to the Skyting Criteria. We must understand where we differ and the potential consequences.

✓ Transitioning

The next four criteria address safe transition to and from tow.

▶5. The force on the towline should be as light as possible when tow is initiated and before release. This is effected by a stretchy towline or light brake pressure on a winch. The release should take place after the tow vehicle has stopped (not possible with air-to-air) and the line has slackened.

▶6. Releases must be sturdy and rapid in their action. They must not require excessive release force and be capable of releasing under very light or heavy towline pulls.

▶7. A weak link is perhaps the most important safety device in the whole operation. It is intended to limit the ultimate forces in a towing situation and obviously must be very reliable.

▶8. Any system of towing should include a method for learning the system gradually. Such a system can include tandem flight, simulation, a low and slow tow, etc. Each step should be mastered before passing on to the next as with any form of learning. As Donnell Hewett suggests:

A. *Never* try two new things at once.
B. *Never* allow yourself to be pushed beyond your comfort zone.
C. *Never* exceed the limits of your equipment or skills.
D. *Never* go more than twice as high, fast or far than you have already mastered.

✓ Practical Towing

The next four criteria address the practical implementation of towing.

▶9. It should be clear that an underpower towing system will not allow a glider to climb adequately and thus it will be in the near-ground danger layer too long. Typically we want a minimum climb of 300 FPM at around 25 mph for safe towing.

▶10. A skilled and able crew is essential to safe towing. This should always consist of a spotter to monitor the tow and driver where practical. An additional crew pilot to help the pilot stage or signal readiness is also desirable. Obviously a spotter cannot be used in an air-to-air situation and is not necessary with a static winch for the operator must be the spotter.

▶11. Radios have proved to be reliable and effective means of communication when towing. A backup system of signals consisting of leg motions should also be used (see later).

▶12. Any area of towing operation should be clear of obstructions to the sides and include an area in front of the towing system for a pilot to bail out in case of a malfunction. Power lines or other objects that can entangle a towline should not be present. Likewise, obstructions that can cause turbulence should not exist close upwind of the operation.

TOWING EQUIPMENT

The different types of towing operations require some specific equipment, but some items are general to all towing. We review them here.

✔ Towlines

Towlines must be sturdy and resistant enough to withstand the force of tow and the abuse of dragging on the ground or binding on a winch. One of the cheapest yet longest-lasting lines available is the popular 3/16 to 3/8 inch polypropelene. It is tough, waterproof and stretches just the right amount. It is the ideal line for air-to-air towing.

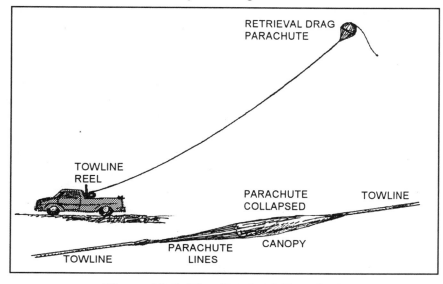

Figure 10-6: Line Retrieval Parachute

The problem with polypro' is it is heavy. Thus a glider with 1000 feet of line out is experiencing a greater tow force than one with 100 feet out. As a result weak links and tow forces are hard (but not impossible as experience shows) to regulate. Thus, a better choice is the newer synthetic lines of either Kevlar or Spectra. They are made from stronger fibers and thus are thinner and lighter. A typical diameter is 3/32 of an inch.

Ideally a towline should have a parachute attached at the pilot end as shown in figure 10-6. Under tow this parachute is deflated since it is pulled by its apex. After release it opens to let the line drop slowly. most winch systems

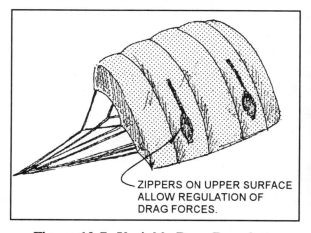

Figure 10-7: Variable Drag Parachute

Drogue chutes for line retrieval.

can thus reel the line in before it hits the ground. This saves entanglements and wear on the line.

It is necessary to use different size parachutes in different wind velocities to get a uniform line dropping rate. This can be a hassle and costly so we suggest you use the trick we learned from Dave Kinchloe: put zippers in the parachute to change its drag production according to the day's conditions (see figure 10-7).

Care for your towline as you would your glider. Keep it out of sunlight when out of use. If it falls in salt water rinse it out with fresh water and unreel it to dry in the shade. Towline is expensive and you can greatly expend its life with some tender loving care.

✓ Bridles and Releases

The connection from the towline to pilot must be carefully considered to ideally meet the Skyting Criteria and allow easy release. A typical system is shown in figure 10-8. Here the towline ends with a loop with a weak link connecting it to the release. The release ends with a ring that accepts the skyting bridle. The skyting bridle itself should run through rings at the pilot's hips (attached to where the main harness risers attach to the harness) and up to the carabiner. This prevents the force of tow from pulling apart a faulty harness. The carabiner itself should be steel.

A reliable release is a life-saving device.

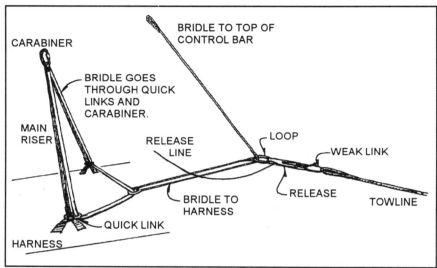

Figure 10-8: The Complete Skyting Bridle

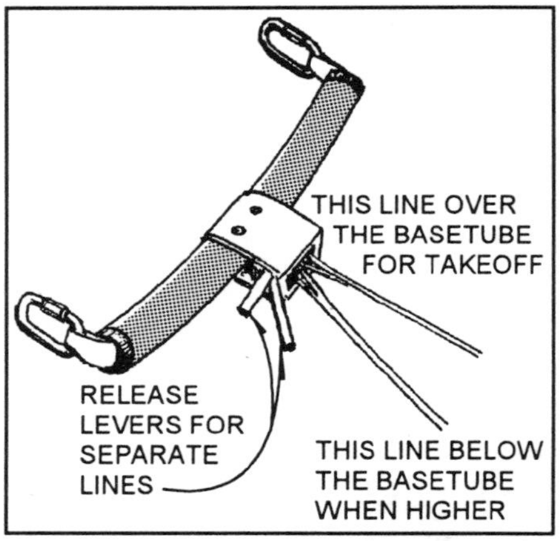

Figure 10-9: Dual Shoulder Release System

There are two different problems with such a release setup. First, the metal ring can rebound and hit the pilot with a sucker punch in the face in the case of a weak link or towline break. Second, the pilot may not be able to reach the release in the event of a malfunction. One way to address these problems is to replace the metal ring on the release with a cloth or rope loop and keep a suitable knife in a handy position for cutting the bridle. Unfortunately, cloth loops rubbing on bridle lines can wear quickly and must be inspected and replaced regularly.

A system developed in Germany consists of a spreader bar that attaches to the harness shoulder straps with a one or two point release in the center as shown in figure 10-9. The beauty of this release is that no metal exists in front of the pilot and it is entirely accessible. However, it does not distribute force to the glider and thus doesn't meet the skyting criteria.

A final hookup system consists of a two point threaded bridle where by the top of the bridle attaches to a release at the glider keel and the bottom to the pilot's shoulder straps as shown in figure 10-10. When the top release lets go the bridle line slips through the cloth loop on the tow line and releases the tow. This system distributes the force equally to the

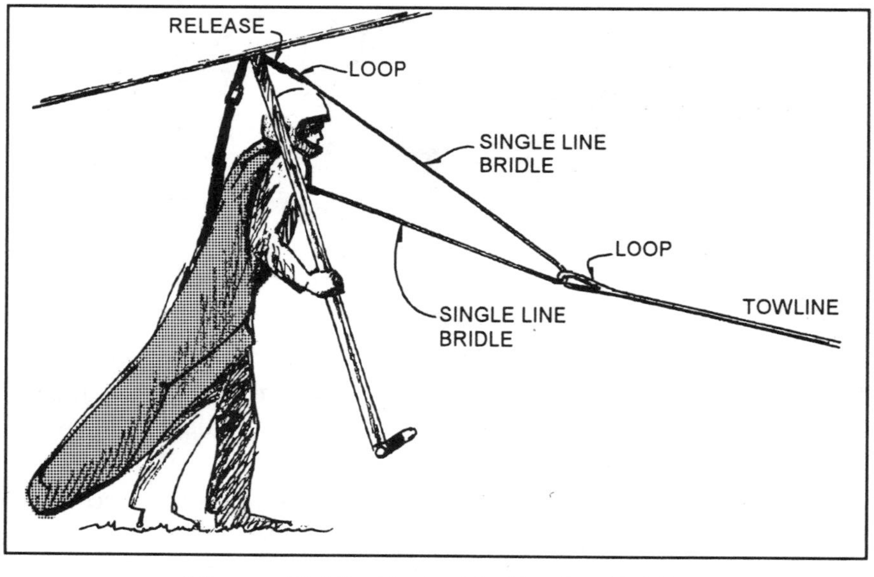

Figure 10-10: Air-to-Air Towing Bridle

A double loop towing release.

pilot and glider and works best for air-to-air towing since the almost horizontal tow force of such towing, the relative drag of the pilot and glider are more important than the mass. A problem can occur if the threading bridle snags on the tow loop or a glider part and the release is not reachable by the pilot. A handy knife is necessary with this system.

✓ *Releases*

There are many types of releases to choose from, so we'll just highlight the common ones and point out potential problems. The most popular release came from parachute technology and consists of a series of line loops that serve to reduce the force on each succeeding one as shown in figure 10-11. This release may use two or three loops. It is very reliable under high force but may require shaking to release under little load. Also it must be inspected frequently for wear of the loops.

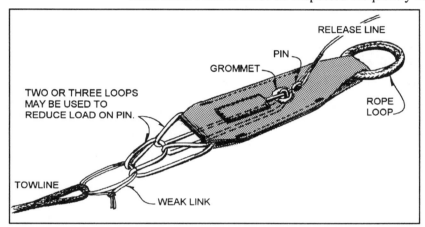

Figure 10-11: Multiple Loop Release

One design fault of such a release is to have one of the loops in shear as shown in figure 10-12. This is a side view of the last loop with the release pin (top drawing). If such a system is loaded heavily, it may (and has) fail to release with light loads due to the shear force on the loop (middle drawing). The situation is remedied by using a longer final loop as shown in the bottom drawing. We should note that the end of the release pin should be covered so that the trigger line cannot loop around it, preventing release.

Another German designed release is shown in figure 10-13. This release is intended to be hooked to shoulder straps and is quite simple. The secret is two stiff rods about 3 inches long sewn inside a tubular webbing. They are folded over and held in position with a tube as shown. When the tube is pulled back either by hand or with a trigger line, the free rod flops forward and release is effected.

The final type of release we'll look at is the sailplane release shown in figure 10-14. Its method of deployment is apparent from the drawing. It is best mounted on a solid object and is especially effective on the tug end of the towline.

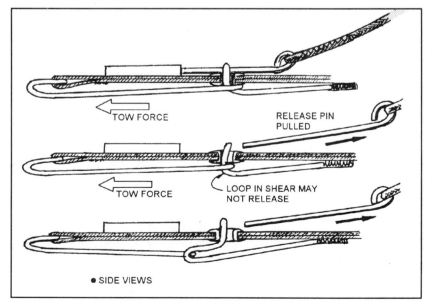

Figure 10-12: Faulty Loop Release Design

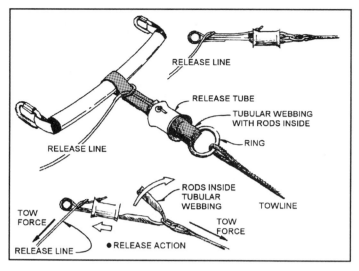

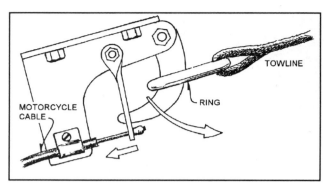

Figure 10-14: Sailplane-Type Release

Figure 10-13: Shoulder Release System

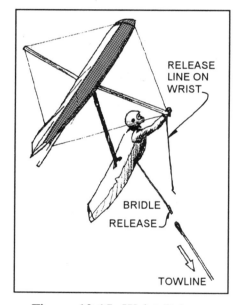

Figure 10-15: Wrist Release Problems

A tow release must work infallibly under all loads and pull directions.

✓ Release Criteria

In order to be safe a release must operate in a wide variety of conditions. To test yours, load it to 300 lbs and try releasing it in all directions up to 45° from the line of load. The trigger line force should be no more than 25 lbs.

Next, load the release to 300 lbs then reduce the load to 5 lbs. The release should work with the trigger line in all directions up to 45° angle from the load with a pull of no more than 5 lbs.

Finally, with about 20 lbs load on the bridle, release and towline system, take the trigger line in both hands and run it up and down the release while maintaining the line taut. Make sure it doesn't catch on the release. If it does there is a design flaw that must be corrected.

The trigger line should always be connected to a shoulder strap or some other appropriate easy to reach place on the body. It should not be connected to the pilot's wrist, for a severe stall while on tow can result in an inadvertent release as shown in figure 10-15. Once you are hooked into your bridle, it should be moved to all extreme positions to make sure it doesn't release on its own. The trigger line should be long enough to prevent this, but not so long that you have to reel it in like a fish.

Keep your release and bridle system free from dirt and corrosion —clean it if necessary. Also, be aware that sunlight deteriorates most synthetic fibers. Test your entire system routinely.

✓ Safety Weak Links

Weak links are small in size but humongous in importance. They are the fail-safe unit of a towing system. A weak link should be incorporated in *all* towing systems at the pilot end of the towline and at the tow vehicle end as well where appropriate (air-to-air and static line).

The most popular weak link is the readily available 205 Dacron leech line (so called because it is regularly sewn in the leech or rear a the sail). This is the line with which most battens are held. In various tests, it has been determined that two loops attached as shown in figure 10-16 will break at over 250 lbs. The breaking strength for more loops is shown.

From the rule in the side bar, if you and your harness weigh 180 lbs and your glider weighs 70 lbs, the total is 250 lbs and the weak link should break between 250 and 300 lbs. The one loop of 205 leech line works well. For heavier pilots or tandem towing, more wraps or different

> The ideal breaking strength of a weak link is from 100% to 120% of the total flying system weight.

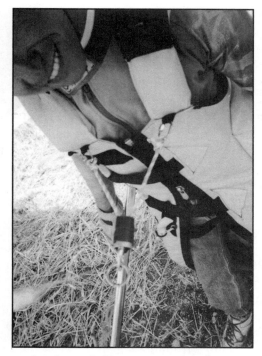

An air-to-air European made release.

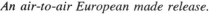

Figure 10-16: Weak Link Combinations

diameter chord is necessary.

If you find yourself breaking weak kinks repeatedly, try using lighter tow forces initially. Remember, the glider and reel have inertia that is lowered once they start moving. Also keep in mind that it is better to break weak links than bones. In general, a little experimentation lets you find a system that provides the safety margin your life depends on, but doesn't break needlessly.

✓ *Radios*

We mentioned radios as being essential for good towing communication. Despite our previous advice, for towing they will ideally have a VOX system so you can talk while both hands are busy flying. It is desirable to give a constant report to your driver or observer on the radio so that they know things are fine and any lack of commands isn't due to a dead radio.

In water operations, radios are tricky to use for they're too expensive to risk a soaking. For advanced pilots this may not be a problem, but for unsure pilots the best case is to mount the radio in the glider with a remote VOX. In any case, back up visual signals are necessary and can be used below 1000 feet.

II - PAYOUT WINCH / PLATFORM LAUNCH

One of the most popular forms of towing is with a payout winch mounted on the back of a truck or boat. The reason for the popularity is that most of us have a car, some of us have boats, so all we need to have our own mountain is a winch. Let's see how to proceed.

THE PAYOUT WINCH SYSTEM

The idea behind a payout winch is to have the towline conveniently wrapped on a reel that gradually feeds it out under a constant regulated pressure. This solves several problems: First,

Bill Moyes mans a payout winch.

the tow pressure can be kept to a minimum or more importantly kept below a maximum so control problems including lockouts are greatly reduced. Secondly, the towline is not dragged along the ground and is usually reeled in while it's descending so it doesn't tangle with ground objects including other boats or cars.

Mounting a payout winch is most readily achieved in the bed of a pickup truck. Some smaller trucks have the winch mounted in the front of the truck with a launch platform in the rear. Where there's an urge there's an angle, and many winches have been mounted on vehicles ranging from a small Volkswagen to vans and station wagons. Almost any automobile is suitable for winching since plenty of power is available.

✓ Platform Launches

A payout winch tow is very easy to adapt to for a new towing pilot.

We speak of platform launches in the same breath as the payout winch since they so readily and frequently go together. A platform launch system consists of a method for carrying the glider right along with the tow vehicle in flying position. The glider is fixed at its nose so it cannot fly away until the vehicle reaches flying airspeed at which point the nose line is released and the glider rises rapidly, pulling out the line from the winch.

Such a launch is easy, forgiving and fun. You pop up just like at a windy cliff launch without all the stress. In fact, platform launching is generally simpler than foot launching.

EQUIPMENT FOR PAYOUT TOWING

Besides the *matériel* described earlier, the main thing we need for payout winch towing is the winch system. There are many designs commercially available. Most are permutations of the original ATOL system. Some are better than others.

To discuss winches we'll break the components down to a reel, braking and pressure control system and rewind system.

✓ Towing Reels

The ideal reel is light, strong, wide and not too small in diameter. The diameter factor has to do with changes of tow forces as line pays out. The wide reel in figure 10-17 has a larger diameter hub than the narrow reel. As a result the narrow reel provides a much more variable tow force since the inertia is greater as the tow starts (more of the weight of the rope is distributed away from the axle) and a greater change in the radius of the pull occurs during full-line payout.

WIDE REEL WITH A LARGE HUB MINIMIZES CHANGES AS LINE PAYS OUT.

NARROW REEL HAS A SMALL HUB WHICH CAUSES A CHANGING TOW FORCE.

Figure 10-17: Reel Designs

✓ Controlling Line Tension

The braking system often consists of a disc brake mounted to the winch. A good automobile braking system is advised here due to all the work it is going to expend. The most important matter of concern here is to keep the disc and pads clean of oil and other fluids that can change brake effectiveness and therefore tow force reliability. Semi-metallic brake pads are recommended because they are impervious to these contaminants. If your discs get rusty the towline should be hooked to a tree and pulled out with normal brake pressure until the rust is worn off or accurate tow pressure will not be possible.

Typically, a braking system is hydraulically activated with a gauge and a control for the driver or observer to use to monitor and set pressure. It is important to know that pressure indicated does not relate linearly to tow forces. The reasons for this include the initial inertia of the reel, the friction of the brake being greater when stationary than when it's moving, the brakes heat up which changes their effectiveness and the reduced radius of pull as the line pulls off. The ultimate determinant of safe tow pressure is the rate of payoff of the winch, the rate of climb of the pilot and the pilot's radio feedback.

Line tension can vary throughout the tow due to:
- *Changing towline weight*
- *Changing diameter of reel*
- *Changing side angle of pull in crossing winds*
- *Changing friction as brakes heat*

✓ Rewinding the Line

Rewind systems consist of a hydraulic or electric motor to reverse the winch and a level winder. If an electric motor is used, batteries should be of the type designed to be drained and recharged such as boat or RV batteries. The motor should be geared to run at high speeds to avoid burnout (a slow running electric motor uses more current and generates more heat).

Rewind motors should be strong enough to wind the line in fast and tight, thereby preventing line from burying itself in the spool once tow pressures are exerted on it. All winches need some sort of level winding system to prevent uneven spooling. This can simply be a wooden block with a hole in it that the operator passes back and forth or a sophisticated double helix worm gear as used on the ATOL system. If the hand systems are used, beware of snags or knots in the towline that can grab the line guide and pull you into the winch.

Besides routine maintenance on all your towing equipment, the best way to keep it in good working order is to cover it when not in use. This prevents UV damage and rain complications. Some operators like to store their line loosely by pulling it off the reel and into a barrel. This action greatly reduces the stress on the line.

✓ Platform System

A typical platform system is shown in figure 10-18. Here we see control bar supports that are placed right below the downtubes. Stops in front and behind the base tube prevent the bar from walking as the vehicle travels. Safety hooks are also placed on the base tube for moving faster over uneven terrain.

Also shown in the figure is the nose release line. This holds the glider at the proper attitude until launch speed is achieved at which point it is released. A sailplane type release is used here with a trigger line routed to the pilot or operator. Usually an additional safety webbing is hooked to the nose to override the release and prevent inadver-

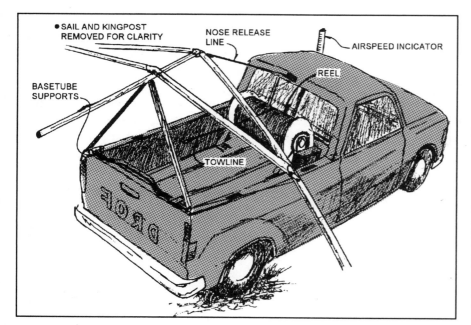

Figure 10-18: Typical Platform Launch System

tent release until the operation is ready to initiate launch procedures.

Finally, we have depicted an airspeed indicator visible to the pilot and driver. This allows both parties to monitor airspeed which is the determinant of launch release time.

PAYOUT WINCH PROCEDURES

There are many details to consider for smooth, safe and successful winching. We'll highlight the important ones, but ultimately every pilot new to this type of flying should have instruction on the specific rig he or she is using.

✔ Pilot's Procedures

A pilot is greatly responsible for his or her own safety during tow and should be in complete command of the towing operation (except in a student situation). Here is a review of the steps:

► 1. Load the glider. Do this by lifting on the control bar while an assistant on the keel rotates the nose to the proper position.

► 2. Preflight the glider, harness and bridle. Do you have a steel carabiner? Leg loops in?

► 3. Attach the nose release and adjust its length. The way to determine the adjustment is to hook in and hang in normal prone position with your hands off the bar. The nose should be raised or lowered until your body position in relation to the base tube is exactly where it is at best glide in free flight. This is usually at your shoulders.

► 4. Hook in and hang check if you haven't just done so.

► 5. Attach the tow line to the bridle. The tow line on a single point attachment should go *below* the base tube. Putting it above will prevent you from climbing as shown in figure 10-19. The tow line only touches the basetube in the first 10 feet or so of climb.

Follow a pre-scribed checklist every time for safe tows.

► 6. Pretension the towline. This is often done by the driver or observer and is extremely important for a slack line will have you jerking the winch and probably breaking the safety weak link. The tow line should pull you forward slightly as you hang in your harness.

► 7. Perform a radio check. *"Testing, one two"..."Check!"*

► 8. Do your final pre-launch check. These steps are:
   a. Check the airspeed indicator for function.
   b. Check the bridle release for proper attachment.
   c. Check the release trigger line for proper placement.
   d. Remove the basetube safety hooks.
   e. Confirm the nose safety is removed and the nose release is in ready position.
   f. Give the driver your desired tow pressure setting.

► 9. Initiate launch procedures. These procedures consist of specific commands and actions on the part of the pilot. The list of possible commands should be short and sweet. We suggest those indicated in the side bar.

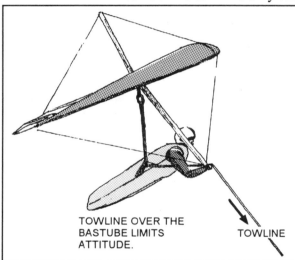

TOWLINE OVER THE BASTUBE LIMITS ATTITUDE.

TOWLINE

Figure 10-19: Towline Over the Basetube Prevents Climb

Upon the command *"cruise"*, the driver accelerates to about 20 mph airspeed. If matters are stable the pilot then commands *"accelerate"* in which case the driver steadily accelerates (note many operations omit this command and simply use *cruise* for going from stopped to launch speed). When the airspeed reaches between 25 and 30 mph, the pilot should yell *"clear"* and actuate the nose release.

What happens next is a sudden and beautiful grasp of altitude. The built-in

Towing Commands	
Go to cruise	Increase pressure
Accelerate	Decrease pressure
Clear	Release
Abort	Stop

speed and the increase of angle of attack will raise you 30 to 50 feet rapidly. Your job at this point is to keep the glider pointed in line with the vehicle using small, rapid controls and *maintain the proper airspeed.*

As Jerry Forburger says, almost everyone new to towing pulls in too much because of our habit of taking on airspeed when things get strange. However, as explained earlier, the proper nose position will be at a higher attitude due to the added thrust of tow. Thus the bar position for best glide will be further out once we get under way. About at the chin should be good for the initial climb out. If you go too fast you increase the chance of oscillating. If you go too slow you increase the chance of a stall or lockout. Keep your eyes looking toward the horizon for orientation with occasional glances at the truck to look for hand signals.

Once you have climbed above 100 feet you are in a safer situation and can let the bar move to trim or minimum sink position. Adjust the speed a little to check for the best possible climb rate. The maximum safe climb rate is about 300 FPM. If you are below this and flying slowly you command more pressure: *"increase pressure."* If you are climbing too fast, command *"Decrease pressure."*

At any time during the launch procedure a problem which you cannot correct should be handled with a command to *"abort."* At this command the driver should stop immediately. One exception to this is when you are "crooked, tight and low" as Jerry Forburger aptly titles the situation where you're knocked off course soon after launch. A release in this situation can be dangerous if you go into a wingover a wingspan up. The best thing is to dump winch pressure on command of *"release pressure"* or for the driver to slow down gradually. The real secret to preventing such problems is to use light tow forces—from 100 to 150 lbs.

As you climb higher the tow vehicle typically slows down, for you usually enter into higher winds and pull off line faster. Your angle to the truck steepens until the truck stops due to reaching the end of the line or the runway. Then, as you overfly the truck you should pull the bridle release trigger and prepare for free flight. Figure 10-20 shows the sequence.

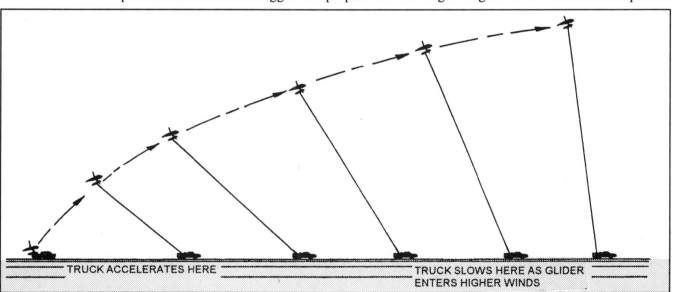

TRUCK ACCELERATES HERE   TRUCK SLOWS HERE AS GLIDER ENTERS HIGHER WINDS

Figure 10-20: Platform Tow Progression

The tow bridle system should be properly stowed to prevent entanglement in your legs and in your parachute. You wouldn't want to reach for your parachute and throw your tow bridle for the bridle won't slow your descent much. Some pilots like to stuff the bridle between their legs then zip up their pod, but watch for snagged zippers.

If you are nearly above the truck when you release you will not notice much change in the glider's attitude because by then the tow force is pulling almost straight down just as gravity does. One note of caution: If you fly too far forward the towline will go behind you and be out of sight. It is better to release before this so you can observe the operation in case of a malfunction.

Now go have fun, but be sure to land back at the staging area for another flight—unless it's a cross-country day, hooray!

✓ Emergency Procedures

About the biggest emergency you can imagine is if the towline fails to release. In that case you simply take out your knife and cut the bridle, right? You say you forgot or dropped the knife? You can still survive. First call down to the ground crew and inform them of your problem so they don't start reeling in the line. Meanwhile fly circles around the truck, small enough to maintain slack in the line. Watch the line to control where it goes. As you get lower the line gets lighter and you'll feel less force.

Once you get half way down, move your circles to the rear of the truck so you aren't looping the truck. When at normal landing setup altitude, do a typical downwind close to the runway with a 180° turn to final as shown in figure 10-21. You will be coming down faster, as if you had a drogue chute on, but otherwise the landing should be normal. The crew on the ground can help by whipping the line to the center of the field as you descend to make sure it doesn't snag on brush or devil sticks.

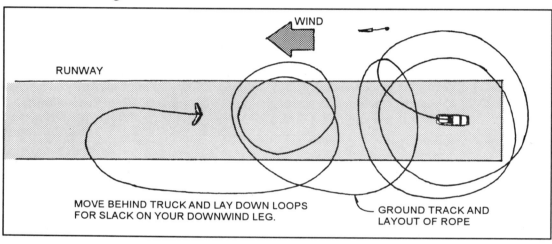

Figure 10-21: Emergency Procedure in Case of Release Failure

✓ Driver's Procedures

A good tow driver makes all the difference in the safety of a tow situation.

The driver's responsibilities are to maintain the pilot's safety and provide a smooth, even tow. The steps mirror those of the pilot. If an assistant or observer is not available, the driver should assist with steps 1 through 7 then move to the launch position while checking for air traffic or ground traffic. Remember to drive slowly with no sudden starts and stops or the glider may tip over. The final pre-launch check should proceed next during which the driver may visually assist the pilot or verbally talk him or her through a list. Such lists should be printed and posted in easy view. This check includes a final check on the airspeed indicator.

Finally, set the winch pressure upon the pilot's command and verify it by repeating the value once you have it set. Then stand by for launch commands.

Proper winch pressures should vary with pilot weight, pilot skill, glider type and the gust factor present. Lighter or less able pilots take less pressure.

When the pilot commands *"go to cruise"*, smoothly accelerate to 20 mph indicated airspeed, shifting gears carefully if necessary. When the pilot commands *"accelerate"*, speed up until ten seconds after the pilot has launched. The launch should take place at about 25 to 30 mph airspeed but you must continue to accelerate to produce a good climb. After this ten seconds, slow the vehicle to produce a constant, steady payout of the winch. If the reel spins rapidly, slow down. If it slows or stops, speed up. *Once the pilot has launched, you should monitor winch payout speed not airspeed or groundspeed.* A front mounted winch facilitates watching the winch.

At the same time you are monitoring winch payout speed you should watch the pressure gauge to keep a constant towline pressure and make adjustments accordingly. If the pilot commands *"abort"*, decelerate slowly to a stop. Otherwise, once you run out of line or runway, stop, pull to the side and get ready for reel-in procedures. The pilot should release once he or she is above the truck. If not, provide a reminder with a release command.

FLYING IN CROSSWINDS

Crosswind launches are very easy with most tow systems.

When the wind is crossing the runway somewhat, towing is not difficult but requires some awareness of the differences. First, the gilder may tend to yaw in the direction of the crossing wind, but roll away from it immediately after launch. The important thing is to *keep the nose of the glider pointed at the tow vehicle at all times.* Do not attempt to crab into the wind for this can cause oscillations. The proper procedure is to let the glider drift downwind while maintaining its aim at the vehicle as shown in figure 10-22.

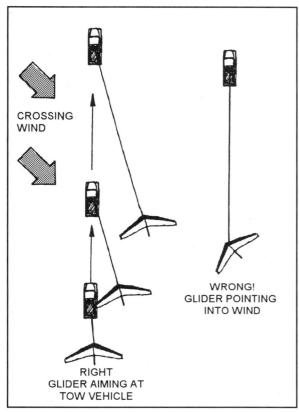

We should note that tow forces may be increased by the crosswind angle since the line isn't pulling off the reel perpendicular to the axle. Lessen the winch pressure accordingly. A reasonable limit for crosswind angle is 30° at 10 mph (less wind may accept up to 45° crosswind). The forward motion of the glider reduces the effective crosswind component so you can get by with more cross in lighter winds. Remember though, crosswinds gusts lead to oscillations and lockouts.

A payout winch system applied to boat towing. Note the floats.

CROSSING WIND

WRONG! GLIDER POINTING INTO WIND

RIGHT GLIDER AIMING AT TOW VEHICLE

Figure 10-22: Proper Crosswind Technique

WATER TOWING

Water towing is great fun for it combines the kure of sun, sand and bikinis with the thrill of flight.

A popular way to tow is on a platform with a winch mounted on a boat. The procedures are about the same as for land towing with the addition of a few special considerations. First, we must understand that boats are tippy so crosswinds can be a problem. Any time the glider is turned across to the wind it can tilt the boat and drop a wing into the water. A solution to this problem is to move a passenger to the upwind side as the boat turns. For this instability reason, boat launches should take place into the wind which isn't a problem on most waterways.

A second problem is the change of angle of attack of the glider as the boat planes. It is < important to set the glider's attitude for the proper angle of attack when the boat is in planing mode. If a wave is encountered, this can suddenly lift the glider. The driver should check for traffic or wake *before* beginning the launch run. It is difficult to see during the initial nose up position of the boat. If a wing gets lifted under way, the driver should turn toward the high wing to equalize the lift on both sides.

Liftoff on water. Note the flotation devices.

The third problem is communication. If you don't want to waterlog your radio you must use leg signals. Standard signals are to move the legs forward and back as if running when you desire more speed (or pressure). Open the legs to command slow down (or reduce pressure) and wave to legs open and close to indicate an immediate stop (see figure 10-23).

The final matter is the use of floats and water safety devices. All water operations should include floats on the rear of the glider's keel and corners of the control bar. The pilot should have a flotation device as well and should at least know how to dog paddle. What about parachutes? Designers claim that parachutes will work when soaked so by all means wear one. The new air rockets are the wise choice, but chemical rockets are also waterproof. Be sure to open and dry your chute after such a bath. If you're landing on floats in the water you *will* get wet.

The tow vehicle must have a minimum amount of buoyancy and power to push all that water and pull all that glider. We recommend at least a 150 horsepower motor on a 20 foot boat for tandem. An inboard engine is most easily set up with a platform.

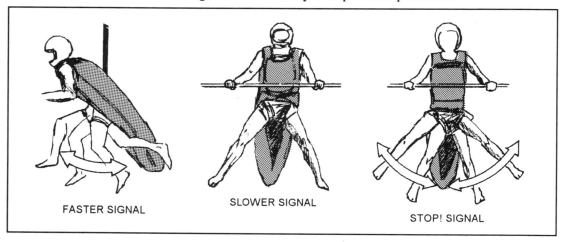

FASTER SIGNAL   SLOWER SIGNAL   STOP! SIGNAL

Figure 10-23: Towing Leg Signals

III - AIR-TO-AIR TOWING

*A*erotowing as it is sometimes called can be great fun and with recent developments in slow trikes or flapped ultralight tugs is about as easy as any form of towing. Here's how it's done.

The Moyes/Bailey tug tows a glider aloft in a beautiful Australian sky.

Bob Bailey, designer of the Moyes tug.

AEROTOWING OVERVIEW

The first regular aerotowing of hang gliders was developed in Europe and performed behind "trike" design ultralights. Trikes are essentially hang gliders with a pendulum seat, motor mount and landing gear.

The whole secret to aerotowing comfortably is to use a tug that can tow as slowly as a hang glider flies near best glide—about 30 mph. Today both trike designs and 3-axis controlled (conventional wing and tail format) ultralights are made specifically for towing hang gliders and work very well.

Multibladed props, lots of power and slow wing designs have resulted in safe and effective ultralight tugs.

Unlike other forms of towing, the glider can affect the tow vehicle. An interplay of speeds and positions can take place that present control problems. For that reason, aerotowing takes a bit longer for a pilot to perfect. For example, it usually requires about ten aerotows before a pilot is ready to handle towing in thermals.

Bill Moyes, one of the pioneers of hang gliding is the only person on record who has towed behind an airplane—a dubious distinction. He was dragged through the turbulent air and released several thousand feet up. A film documents his success and lack of helmet or parachute. And this was on a standard Rogallo!

AEROTOWING EQUIPMENT

One of the obvious items unique to aerotowing is the tug itself. Describing the ideal towing ultralight is beyond the scope of this book, so the reader is directed to operations currently using tugs to find the best system. Most pilots will be candid about the pluses and minuses of their aircraft.

The towline is much shorter for aerotowing than other forms. Europeans use short lines—from 200 to 230 feet while American pilots use from 250 to 300 feet of towline. Shorter lines allow better view of the tug pilot's hand signals and shorter operating spaces, while longer lines are a bit more forgiving on tow. A weak link and release system must be incorporated at both ends of the towline. The weak link at the pilot's end should break at 75 to 80% of the combined pilot and glider weight (about 185 to 200 lbs for a 250 lb flying ensemble). The lighter weak link is used because the towline is not pulling down on the glider or suspending much weight.

A parachute should be incorporated in the towline, but it should be about 45 feet from the pilot so as not to obstruct the view of the tug. The parachute should be about two feet in diameter or less and not deploy until the pilot is off the line.

Three views of air-to-air towing takeoffs. Note the dolly in the top left photo.

As mentioned earlier a reasonable bridle for aerotowing consists of a threaded skyting bridle that releases at the control bar top, slips through a loop in the towline then attaches to the pilot's shoulder straps. Another system attaches to the shoulder straps exclusively. This latter system results in the pilot being pulled through the bar so that trim position is about at your sternum (if you don't know where your sternum is, ask your significant other to show you).

Your harness should ideally have adjustable leg loops or they should be snug. Otherwise the harness will be pulled forward and you may not be able to get your feet in your boot or stirrup. An alternative when using a dolly launch (see below) is to put one or both feet in the boot before the tow starts.

A dolly takes the worry out of switchy winds or poor running ability.

One final item of equipment that is not essential but is advised is a dolly to rest the glider on and get pulled into the air. As soon as the glider lifts about three feet the pilot releases his hold on the dolly and flies away. The pilot holds the dolly with loops through a finger on each hand. The reason for carrying the dolly a little ways into the air is to avoid rolling into a ball in case of a sudden drop. This technique allows a pilot to get in flying position from the start and eases the problem of hard running and control during the period of hand transitioning. Big wheels on the dolly are a necessity if any rough ground is present.

In a recent aerotow situation without a dolly I was prepared to launch in light and variable wind. Just as the signal was given to launch the wind turned tail. There was nothing I could do but give it my best sprint. I didn't gain enough airspeed and I hereby give thanks to the inventor of the wheel and the weak link.

AEROTOWING PROCEDURES

Again, we can't teach everything there is to know about aerotowing. The material here should be used to form the background for a sound instruction program. The important matter is to understand the problems and solutions for aerotowing before attempting the feat.

✓ Launch Procedures

Here is a step-by-step method for safe launching:
- ► 1. Preflight the glider, harness and bridle then move to the launch point.
- ► 2. Hook in and do a hang check. Don't forget this important procedure for it's embarrassing to leave your glider in your wake of dust and dirt clods as you plow a furrow

down the runway and your friends howl with delight.

▶3. Hook into the towline. The assistant should pull on the line while you test the release. If you are a beginner you should have several trials at releasing without looking at the trigger line. CAUTION: It is crucial that steps 2 and 3 not be reversed to avoid forgetting to hook in to the glider after being hooked to the towline. Make it a point to verify you're hooked in *before* each time you get attached to the towline.

▶4. Perform a radio check. If you are learning or radios are not used, the assistant should signal your readiness. Check for air traffic.

▶5. Signal the tug pilot to take out slack. The line should be pulled tight and you should resist.

▶6. Check the wind one last time.

▶7. When the tug pilot signals readiness, stand up with your control bar on your shoulders while holding it with the beer can grip and give the launch signal (GO GO GO) or have the assistant signal by dropping a flag.

▶8. As soon as you feel the line tug on you, resist until you are pulled into a run. This run will be about the same as on a slope because the towline helps you accelerate. Do not overrun the line, let it initiate the motion. After a few steps you will be airborne and should drop to the basetube immediately to effect better control. If you are dolly launching, hold the bar position until you are airborne at the proscribed height.

Once you are in the air you should use pitch control to remain about 8 to 10 feet off the ground while the tug accelerates to its takeoff speed. If you climb too high the tug will not be able to rotate its nose upward to climb. You will have to hold the bar in at this point.

Now, while watching the tug, ease the bar out to climb with it as soon as its wheels lift off the ground. Again if you rise too high you will make the tug dive. Too low and it will climb away from you. The tug will be forced to do the opposite of what you do if you get too far out of whack. The idea is to follow the tug exactly in a dance on air. The best way to do this is *to always aim at the tug's keel or center tube and keep the nose of the tug exactly on the horizon* (see figure 10-24).

Once you are safely above the ground you should concentrate on maintaining good position behind the trike. A list of signals for both pilots from launch to release is given on the side bar.

It is extremely important to hook in to the glider first and to the line secondly. You will not get injured if the tug takes off without you and the glider but consequences may be severe if you get dragged by the ultralight without your glider.

The position of the glider in relation to the tug is very critical in all phases of aero-towing but especially during takeoff, thermals and turns.

Aerotowing Verbal Commands
1. Take out slack
2. Pilot ready
3. Tug ready
4. Go go go
5. Speed up
6. Slow down
7. Release towline

Hand Signals (Given by Tug Pilot)
1. Point left = left turn
2. Point right = right turn
3. Point down = get lower
4. Point up = move higher
5. Crooked arm pumping up and down = release!

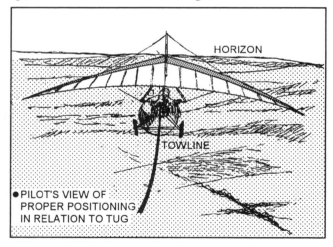

Figure 10-24: Proper Positioning Behind a Tug

If you get well below, to the side or above the trike you should make instant but small corrections. The trike and glider have interplay that results in feedback that can get out of hand. For example, if you push out you climb but also increase the drag on the tug so it drops. Then if you pull in to get down to tug level your dive results in less drag on the tug so it climbs. To stop this chain reaction, wait for things to settle then make small control corrections. The closer you are to aligned with the tug, the smaller corrections you should make.

The secret to perfect towing with air-to-air is to keep the tension in the towline constant. You can sense this tension in the force at your shoulders or under your armpits and watch the slight curve in the towline.

✓ Towing in Turns

Aerotowing is the easiest way to troll for thermals, so unlike other forms of towing turns are common-place as you hunt the sky. The problem with turns is that if you track to the outside of the turn you are accelerated like a water-skier and the line gets taut. This action can slow the tug and make it turn tighter thereby worsening the situation. The best way to handle a turn is to track slightly inside the tug's turning path, all the while trying to keep the towline tension constant.

A pilot's view showing positioning slightly too high (tug is below horizon)

✓ Releasing from Tow

The release from aerotow is quite simply effected by pulling the trigger line. You may speed up a little to relieve the towline forces, but do not allow slack to occur in the towline for it can catch on glider parts and the release may not work. A signal should be given to the tug pilot when you are ready to release (only reliable with radios) or you should release upon his signal. The standard procedure for turns after release is a left turn for the tug pilot and a right turn for the glider pilot to avoid mishaps.

✓ Emergencies

As with all towing, when matters get out of hand clear of the terrain you should release. If weak links fail to operate or you are entering a lockout get off the line before you cause severe consequences to yourself and the tug pilot. If the weak link breaks at the tug, the towline will quickly fly behind you and you should either release it at your end or pull it in so you can drop it on the airstrip. Always check for the towline after you release.

✓ Tug Pilot Guidelines

The tug pilot must be highly qualified as an ultralight pilot as well as undergo training to learn to tow. We cannot cover all these matters here but will point out some towing concerns.

The tug pilot should learn and use the towing commands and hand signals. A mirror should be located on the tug so the pilot can monitor the glider at all times. The tug pilot must learn to use this mirror and inform the glider pilot of necessary corrective action.

Each tug pilot has unique characteristics that glider pilots come to know and talk about. Good tug pilots generally fly slower, maintain a smooth and steady flight with gentle turns. The important thing is to keep one throttle setting and pitch control when cruising for thermals so the glider pilot can determine when the air is lifting the tug.

As indicated, the glider and tug are intimately connected in controls and both pilots need to cooperate for an enjoyable flight. After a tow confer with the glider pilot on matters such as the takeoff power setting, rotation speed, climb angle, relative position during tow, rate of turn and post-release maneuvers. Such feedback will help you become the most sought after tug pilot.

For your safety as a tug pilot we suggest you test your release frequently and drop the towline during a flyby of the runway to prevent snagging.

FLYING IN THERMALS

Aerotowing is the best way to troll for thermals. A good tug pilot will drag you through the sky and drop you off directly in the middle of a fat, succulent core.

Thermals or any varied vertical air movement present more challenges because it initiates relative position changes of tug and tuggee. Also, it is difficult to distinguish between a pilot-induced and thermal-induced vertical motion. One sure sign that the tug has entered a thermal is that the line stays tight even though the tug is climbing relative to the glider.

In thermals the glider pilot must expend more effort to maintain level with the tug for the length of the tow means there is about a 5 second delay between when the tug hits lift and when the glider hits it. Indeed, the tug may be in lift and the glider in sink or vice versa. Being on tow is a great way to visualize the size and extent of thermals, but you must keep level with the tug or you'll soon have to release and miss them.

CROSSWIND TOWING

Maintaining a proper position with the tug on a crosswind leg is extremely important. Just as with ground towing, you must point *exactly* at the tow vehicle as shown in figure 10-25. If you stray to one side either due to a gust or a crosswind, make your corrections carefully as shown in figure 10-26. The secret is to point the glider nose directly at the center of the tug and the correction will occur smoothly.

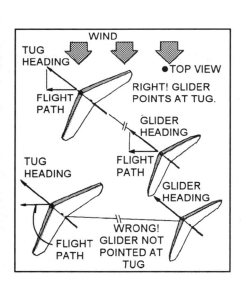

Figure 10-25: Air-to-Air Towing in a Crosswind

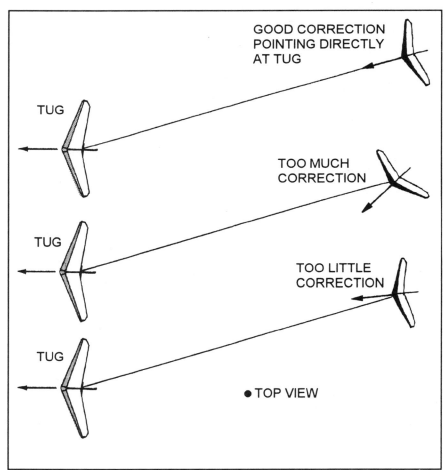

Figure 10-26: Correcting a Misalignment in Air-to-Air Towing

IV - STATIC WINCH/STATIC LINE TOWING

he final two forms of towing are really not the same but have some of the same elements. They both consist of foot launching (although a dolly could be employed) and start with the pilot a long ways away from the tow operator. Let's look at each one.

STATIC LINE TOWING

With this system of towing a line is fixed between the pilot and tow vehicle. The total length of line laid out determines how high the pilot gets and how much runway is needed. This is perhaps the method of towing requiring the most care and expertise on the part of the operator, because it is more difficult to regulate tow pressure, but it is certainly the cheapest (no winch required). With new towing methods, i.e. center-of-mass towing and all the Skyting Criteria, static line towing incorporating a pressure gauge in the line, weak links and radios for communication can be reasonably safe.

A good static line system can fling gliders into the air with less delay than any other method.

One big problem is the difficulty of regulating tow pressures in gusts. This is what caused lockouts in the past. The use of proper weak links reduces this problem.

Static towing can provide the fastest turnaround, for the tow vehicle simply drives to the stage point as soon as release occurs. With a modification matters can be even faster. Some operators use a fixed pulley at the upwind end of the field so the tow vehicle drives *toward* the glider as shown in figure 10-27. The added benefit here is the driver can watch the tow. With two tow vehicles both ends of the towline can be used one after another and gliders can be sent aloft as quickly as they can be hooked up. With this form of towing be sure to inspect your towline often for wear.

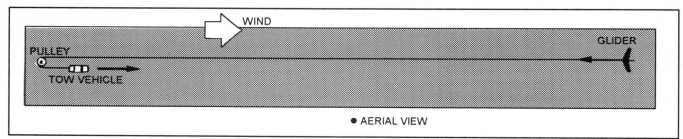

Figure 10-27: Aerial View of a Pulley Tow System

✓ Launch Signals

With both static line and static winch towing, some sort of signalling system is necessary to communicate with the tow operator. An assistant with a flag is commonly employed. Holding the flag up means the pilot is ready. The tow operator then signals equal readiness. At the command of the pilot the flag is dropped and the tow commences. An alternative to this is picking the glider up to signal readiness, then shaking it when the pilot wishes tow to commence. Finally, a VOX operated radio solves all communication problems. A backup for in-air adjustments are the leg signals described in water towing earlier.

✓ Pop Starts

With boat towing the drag of the water prevents the boat from accelerating until it planes out. Thus "pop starts" were invented. In this case the boat backs up and gets a running start. The natural stretch of the rope prevents too much of a jerk on the pilot. Pop starts are not too difficult as this author can attest, but it is advisable to have some part of the bridle hooked to the glider or the pilot will be dragged ahead of the wing at the start. The angle of attack of the glider should be set fairly high, for as soon as the tow starts its natural attitude will be nose high, as with any type of towing. Also, the pilot should resist the tow somewhat so a quick pop off the ground occurs. If a water start is the method, the drag of the floats in the water will provide all the initial resistance necessary. Pop starts will break many weak links unless the driver is very skilled.

STATIC WINCH TOWING

Static winches were popular for a while then fell out of favor for they were in bloom before safer towing methods developed. Now however, a good static winch system with some means of regulating the tow force can be every bit as safe as payout winch or air-to-air towing. In our experience, a payout winch tow is gentle, non-stressful and easy.

Norm Lesnow controls a static winch during a tow in Michigan.

✓ Equipment

Very little is required besides the winch system which is sold as an entire unit on its own trailer. The winch must incorporate a reel, a pressure-regulating system and an engine to pull the line in. Not many of these systems are being built today, so good systems in good shape are valuable.

Other items of use are signal flags, radios and a machete to cut the line for a sudden release. This last item seems crude, but it is very effective and necessary because the winch reeling in with all its inertia cannot be reversed quickly enough. One final item to make things efficient is a small motorcycle or scooter to pull the line back to the start point. With this addition, static winch towing has a very fast turnaround time.

✓ Flying Procedures

The takeoff with a static winch is the same as for the foot-launched aerotow or static line. The pilot pre-flights, does a hang check, hooks to the line, checks the release then moves into launch position. The pilot should back up to pull the towline tight and hold back pressure with a leg forward as in figure 10-28. This position gives a good solid liftoff with less surge.

The glider should be angled nose high as shown. This is approximately 15° higher than you would have it when running on the flat. You should expect to take two or three steps on launch, then you will be airborne.

Once in the air, keep pointing at the winch as with any type of towing. Quick, small corrections are necessary. As you climb higher and approach the winch, you will feel

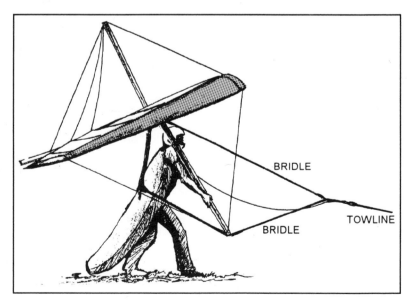

Figure 10-28: Foot-Launched Towing Launch Position

more downward pressure on the bridle. At about 60 to 70° up from the winch, the operator will stop the reel and let it freewheel. The whole process is shown in figure 10-29. If you fail to release you will pull out line from the reel and should fly around the winch and land

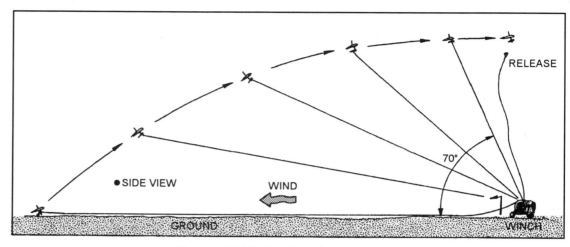

Figure 10-29: Static Winch Towing

just as with a payout winch. Of course this should never happen for you should have a reliable release and a safety knife on hand.

STEP TOWING

The problems associated with space and drag of the line on the ground usually limit how high we can tow. With a static winch we can actually tow up in stages. This method developed

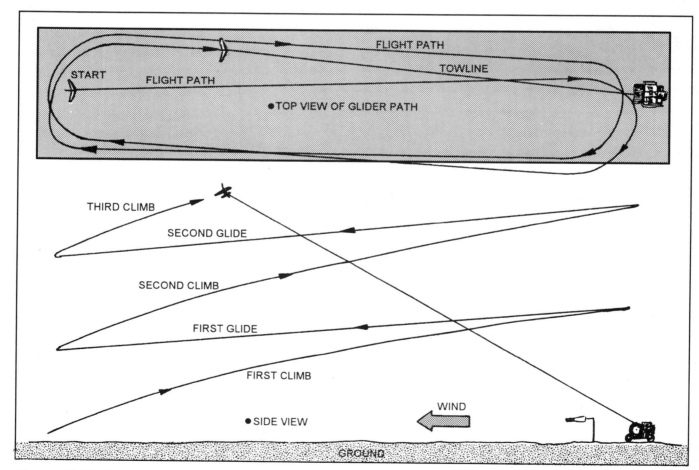

Figure 10-30: Step Towing Flight Path

thermaling height without to have to start with too much line stretched out. Figure 10-30 shows a typical step tow flight.

Step towing is not for beginners and requires a carefully coordinated act between the operator and pilot. The main problems consist of a possibility of a backlash or snag on the reel stopping the pilot or the glider hooking the towline as it turns. The first problem is prevented by using a system to produce tight winding on the reel. CAUTION: By the time the glider is ready to turn around for the first time, no part of the bridle should be attached above the base tube (to either pilot or glider) so the control bar is not pulled backwards when the towline is behind the pilot.

The second problem is prevented by the pilot being very careful to watch the lower wing during the turn at the downwind end of the field. As figure 10-31 shows, the turn at the winch end of the field is not a problem because the high wing swings over the line and the line is directed forward and down. However at the opposite end of the field the low wing swings over the towline and the line itself is directed rearward (out of sight when the turn is initiated) and not as much downward.

Step towing can be fun and is an added benefit to static winch towing. The use of radios and safe attitudes on the part of all concerned will continue to render it attractive to flatland flyers.

The High Perspective winch near Toronto uses 6,000 feet of Spectra line to step tow pilots to over 3,500 feet!

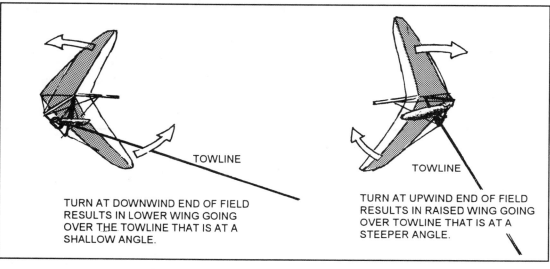

TOWLINE

TURN AT DOWNWIND END OF FIELD RESULTS IN LOWER WING GOING OVER THE TOWLINE THAT IS AT A SHALLOW ANGLE.

TOWLINE

TURN AT UPWIND END OF FIELD RESULTS IN RAISED WING GOING OVER TOWLINE THAT IS AT A STEEPER ANGLE.

Figure 10-31: Turns During Step Towing

SUMMARY

Towing is a whole realm to explore with its own disciplines and advantages. It can actually be less time-consuming and more conducive to cross-country flying than foot-launching in some places. However, to be safe towing must take place under a strict set of guidelines because we are adding more "Murpheys" to the system.

The Skyting Criteria are designed to be an ideal for which all towing systems should strive. Naturally the constraints of some methods will not allow this, but it is important for us to recognize where we depart from these standards and exercise extra caution.

There are currently four main types of towing we can choose from. Like a kid in a candy store it's hard to decide which one we want to try. Our best suggestion: try them all! Your mom isn't looking over your shoulder with a switch, so go indulge yourself with unlimited airtime.

CHAPTER 11

Further Adventures

Once you reach the level where your advanced skills are in full flower, you may look for other challenges. Certainly we acknowledge that competition is not appealing or affordable for every pilot. What else is there? Try tandem, aerobatics, fixed wings, record attempts, aerial ballets or hang gliding safaris to mention a few.

In this chapter we'll explore these diversions with one eye on the safety valve and one eye on the fun button. The real challenge is to maximize safety *and* fun.

I - TANDEM FLIGHT

*H*ave you ever imagined sharing the exact feelings and experience you find in the sky? Think of the fun of showing a friend where to find lift and how to work thermals. Could anything be more rewarding than taking a passenger on a little cross-country jaunt to parts unknown?

These and other fantasies are possible with tandem flying. However certain legal and physical rules must be learned and obeyed in order for your daydream to avoid becoming a nightmare for you and your friend. In *Hang Gliding Flying Skills* we discussed tandem flying from the viewpoint of the passenger. You should review this material. Here we discuss the considerations from the viewpoint of the tandem pilot in command.

PILOT QUALIFICATIONS

Before you consider flying tandem, you should consider your qualifications. To begin you need to have exemplary takeoff and landing skills. You should always have a fast aggressive takeoff style with perfect control of glider attitude. If you have doubts about this, ask other advanced pilots—they'll tell you. Your landings should be perfect 9 times out of 10. The 10th time should not be a nose in. A perfect landing is a *no-step* landing.

Tandem flying implies a great level of pilot responsibility.

As a further qualification you should be properly trained. In the United States this means you have attended a tandem clinic presented by a certified tandem instructor. All tandem operations in the USA take place under an exemption granted by the Federal Aviation Administration (FAA). Consequently all tandem flights are closely regulated. There are three categories of tandem pilot in the USA:

1. *Class 1 Tandem* — This pilot may fly tandem with any other Class I rated pilot.
2. *Class 2 Tandem* — This pilot must pass more stringent requirements and may take any passenger from student rated pilots and above.
3. *Tandem Instructor* — This pilot holds a Class 2 rating plus an instructor's rating and logged lessons. He or she may take any individual as a passenger under an instruction format.

One other qualification a tandem pilot should have is reasonable size and strength to handle the larger size of tandem gliders. Control bars are necessarily wider for two people and gliders are generally heavier than their single place counterparts.

EQUIPMENT CONSIDERATIONS

There are two problems with tandem flying. First the extra weight increases flying speeds even with larger gliders. Secondly, the passenger can trip or cause control inputs that overpower the pilot. We'll deal with the first problem here.

Teddy Hasenfus and his flying companion Leeanne go tandem in the Sequatchie Valley in Tennessee.

✓ The Glider

It should be obvious that you need a larger glider to fly safely with a passenger—even a light one.

I remember a pilot a decade ago who insisted on flying his 165 Comet with his girlfriend on board. After several whacked landings and replaced downtubes (and who knows how many private arguments) they gave up the practice. Landing with such a load was like landing downwind with a tangle of four legs to coordinate.

There are a number of good tandem gliders on the market. Most of them are single surface designs. Large double surface gliders do exist, but they tend to be more tricky to land, are heavier and are best flown by two experienced pilots. Some tandem gliders are tail heavy, some don't perform very well and some are difficult to handle. We suggest you try the glider you intend to buy.

When two pilots fly tandem they must agree before hand who is pilot in command. Two Ohio pilots were gyrating wildly until they both realized that they each thought the other was in control.

A glider used for tandem should have a wing area with a minimum of 200 square feet. Even at this size you will be going faster than normal. For example, a single surface tandem glider would have to be around 300 sq. ft and a double surface tandem glider around 250 sq. ft to obtain the typical wing loadings of single place gliders. If a glider was originally designed for tandem it probably lands and handles adequately. If it wasn't, it should be checked out by an experienced tandem pilot.

As we know increasing wing loading increases our flying speeds. The chart below shows how much this increase is when adding a passenger compared to your original speed flying solo on a given glider. For example, let's assume you and your harness weigh a total of 180 lbs, the glider 65 lbs and you stall or land at 20 mph. Now assume your passenger weighs 135 lbs with harness. Divide your total weight plus glider weight into the passenger weight to get the increase in weight ratio (IWR). In our example it is .55. Now looking at the chart we find our speed increases by 1.24 (halfway between the .5 and .6 values) giving us a stall speed of 24.8 mph at sea level. The chart also gives the speed increases at different altitudes.

Tandem Speed Chart										
IRW = Increase in Weight Ratio = Weight Passenger ÷ (Weight Pilot + Weight Glider)										
Alt (ft)	0	.1	.2	.3	.4	.5	.6	.7	.8	.9
0	1.00	1.05	1.10	1.14	1.18	1.22	1.26	1.30	1.34	1.38
1,000	1.01	1.06	1.11	1.16	1.20	1.24	1.28	1.32	1.36	1.40
2,000	1.03	1.08	1.13	1.17	1.22	1.26	1.30	1.34	1.38	1.42
3,000	1.05	1.10	1.15	1.19	1.24	1.28	1.32	1.36	1.40	1.44
4,000	1.06	1.11	1.16	1.21	1.26	1.30	1.34	1.38	1.42	1.46
5,000	1.08	1.13	1.18	1.23	1.27	1.32	1.36	1.40	1.45	1.48
6,000	1.09	1.15	1.20	1.25	1.29	1.34	1.38	1.43	1.47	1.51
7,000	1.11	1.16	1.22	1.27	1.31	1.36	1.40	1.45	1.49	1.53
8,000	1.13	1.18	1.24	1.29	1.33	1.38	1.43	1.47	1.51	1.55
9,000	1.15	1.20	1.25	1.31	1.36	1.40	1.45	1.50	1.54	1.58
10,000	1.16	1.22	1.27	1.33	1.38	1.43	1.47	1.52	1.56	1.60
11,000	1.18	1.24	1.29	1.35	1.40	1.45	1.50	1.54	1.59	1.63
12,000	1.20	1.26	1.32	1.37	1.42	1.47	1.52	1.57	1.61	1.66

✓ Glider Trim and Hang Straps

When we load up a glider we distort it somewhat. In a tandem glider the general lighter construction and major difference in load with and without a passenger changes the trim noticeably. With a heavier load the wings bow up and the glider becomes nose-light. The hang point on the glider must be moved forward when you carry a passenger and back when you fly solo. The amount of movement depends on the glider, but 1 to 3 inches is typical.

Hang straps should include a separate primary for the passenger and pilot and a common secondary. The reason both individuals are hooked into the same secondary is in case of a keel breaking near the hang straps both will be attached to the parachute.

✓ Harnesses

We have seen all manner of harnesses used for tandem flying. Any one will work in an ideal situation. However, here are some considerations: Knee hanger harnesses tend to hold the legs up on landing and should be adjusted to allow the knees to sag. They also hold the passenger up relatively high when vertical because the leg straps must be tight. Pod harnesses are bulky, get in the way at takeoff and should not be zipped up by the passenger unless he or she has plenty of tandem experience (a busy pilot may forget to unzip the passenger). Stirrup harnesses and cocoons may trip the passenger unless the stirrup or boot is held up with a catch or Velcro. The system we prefer is a pod for the pilot and a knee hanger for the passenger.

✓ Parachutes

The minimum parachute size that should be used is a 22 gore triconical or a 20 gore PDA (see the discussion in Chapter 4). Such small chutes for two people will probably result in some injury except in the best of conditions. We recommend a 24 gore PDA.

The problem of a passenger hugging a downtube or swinging the opposite direction to your control is serious and must be addressed. The only way to solve this problem is to have the passenger hold on to the pilot's harness for the duration of the flight. One hand should be across the pilot's back and gripping the far shoulder strap and the other holding the near shoulder strap as shown in figure 11-1.

Ideally the passenger and pilot should be one—in the secular sense.

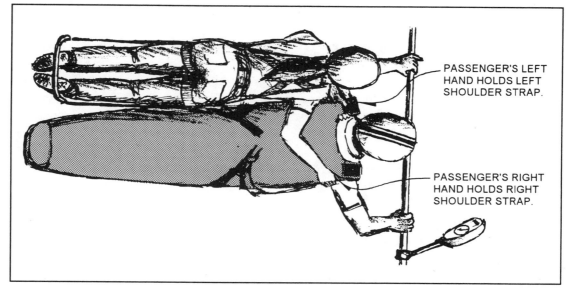

PASSENGER'S LEFT HAND HOLDS LEFT SHOULDER STRAP.

PASSENGER'S RIGHT HAND HOLDS RIGHT SHOULDER STRAP.

Figure 11-1: Tandem Passenger Arm Position

The hand reaching across the back must be routed through the pilot's shoulder lines carefully or it will be pulled off when the pilot lies down. Some pilots have handles sewn to the back of their harness for the convenience and security of passengers.

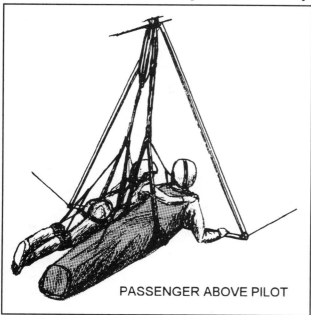

PASSENGER ABOVE PILOT

Figure 11-2: Tandem Flying Positions

Ideally the passenger should hang a few inches higher than the pilot so that he or she can place the arms properly and remain prone as shown in figure 11-2. More importantly, however, is to have the passenger's feet leave the ground first. This will occur if the pilot's harness straps are a little loose while those of the passenger are tight when the glider is held in launch position. Tight harness straps on the passenger at the beginning helps prevent the common occurrence of the passenger suddenly feeling a tug on the harness and lying down.

The passenger should be on the side opposite your parachute bridle so he or she doesn't get hung during a deployment. This means the passenger will be on the left for right-handed throwers as shown. This brings up a problem, however. Most right-handers prefer to turn left, but it is much better for the mental security of an inexperienced passenger to turn so they are on the high side. The remedy is to be competent turning and setting up landings to your bridle side.

TAKING OFF TANDEM _____

It is desirable to have the passenger run all the way into the air. Only about half of them do. The other half sags and becomes baggage when the harness tugs them after a couple steps. The best way to motivate a passenger to run is to have them push you off the slope. The passenger starts the run with this push action and you finish it, of course. Two or three dry runs on the flat with full gear are also necessary to coordinate running procedure. Don't skip this important part.

Tandem gliders being the behemoths they are, do not always respond as fast to control inputs as single human gliders. For that reason you can tolerate less cross and gusty conditions when flying tandem than when solo. Besides, you have another soul along that depends on you to make conservative condition decisions. Ideal tandem conditions are with a straight in wind blowing 5 to 15 mph (20 mph can be tolerated at coastal sites).

Be sure you do a careful hang check of both you and the passenger. Numerous mistakes have been made.

At the 1977 US Nationals near Heavener, Oklahoma, a moderately experienced pilot was wooing a local lady by inviting her for a tandem ride. They prepared to launch into a nice sky and had a good takeoff. Up to the point, that is, when the pilot discovered he wasn't hooked in and tumbled down the hill. Our helpless local lady found herself chief pilot-in-command of an aircraft she had never even seen before her lucky day. As it turned out she was indeed lucky, for the glider flew away and performed a slow arc to crash back at the hill in soft bush. Our heroine left distinctly unimpressed with the bungling pilot who slunk away with his tail between his legs.

TANDEM IN FLIGHT

Flying tandem in an open sky is about the same as solo except you have more weight to sling around. Control forces are usually higher and response is slower. For this reason you can't scratch as close.

Most passengers are anxious about the whole deal. This anxiety combined with the new prone position and new sensations can lead to airsickness and that four-letter word we most dread: barf. You don't do yourself, your passenger or the sport any favor by creating sick passengers. We suggest you use gentle turns away from the passenger for the first few flights. The shear beauty and excitement of hang gliding alone will be enough for the great majority of new passengers.

LANDING TANDEM

The biggest complication in tandem flying is landing. Because even a slight biff can have consequences when passenger slams into you or vice-versa, we recommend using large wheels on the base tube.

Set up your landings conservatively with a long straight final. The passenger should be stood up before the pilot so the pilot can rotate easily when necessary. Practice the procedure and command when doing your harness adjustments before launching. Your flare should be well-timed and strong for your sluggish glider has to lift quite a load to a standing position.

The flare-timing is most critical because although the glider is moving fast across the ground the flare window will be relatively brief. Chances are you'll have to run a few steps, so it is smart to remind your passenger to watch the ground out in front and get ready to run. Then when the flare comes command "run" again. Half the passengers collapse when they touch down and they should be reminded to land on their feet.

Your attitude as tandem pilot has a great effect on the outcome of the flight. If you exude confidence, competence and composure it will go a long way to allay the fear of the passenger. A more relaxed passenger can better follow your instructions and is less likely to panic. Remember, this is all supposed to be fun, not death-defying.

II - AEROBATIC FLYING

*W*e do not condone aerobatics and wish to discourage pilots from performing them. By aerobatics we mean maneuvers outside the tested limits of our gliders. The fact that aerobatics are outside these limits should say something about the wisdom of getting radical.

Getting radical requires a conservative approach.

Unfortunately we frequently see aerobatics performed on hang gliders. They look easy and are fun, but they are difficult to learn safely because you must learn them solo. Many pilots try to learn aerobatics on their own and make dangerous mistakes. We have watched several pilots stall their gliders in aerobatics attempts. It is for this reason that we present this short course on aerobatics although we urge you not to do them.

The only possible good that aerobatics serve is to familiarize a pilot with severe attitudes and banks and teach the right action for recovery during turbulence induced upsets. On the other hand, it is our contention that high G maneuvers stretch our sails and is not beneficial to a competition glider.

WANGS, SPINS AND LOOPS

The aerobatic maneuvers we are going to discuss are known as wangs, spins and loops. Wangs are another name for rollovers or climbovers which are descriptive terms for the maneuver many pilots call a wingover. A true wingover can only be produced by an aircraft with a rudder to create a yaw control at the top of a climb as shown in figure 11-3. If a hang glider attempts this stunt a dangerous maneuver known as hammerhead stall occurs as shown in figure 11-4. Don't try these maneuvers if you plan a healthy future, for a stall at such severe attitudes has worse consequences than most maladies we can imagine. To emphasize the fact we are not performing wingovers, we term our maneuvers *wangs*.

Spins are described in Chapter 3. They consist of stalling a wing in a turn and turning rapidly around this wing. Loops are straight dives and climbs over the top. We wish to point out here that many pilots on viewing a 180° wang mistakenly think they witnessed a loop. This is a dangerous assumption because pilots trying to emulate the experts performing these maneuvers may be induced to experiment with loops. A loop is more dangerous than a 180° wang because it consists of no roll input whatsoever and has more severe consequences if a stall occurs.

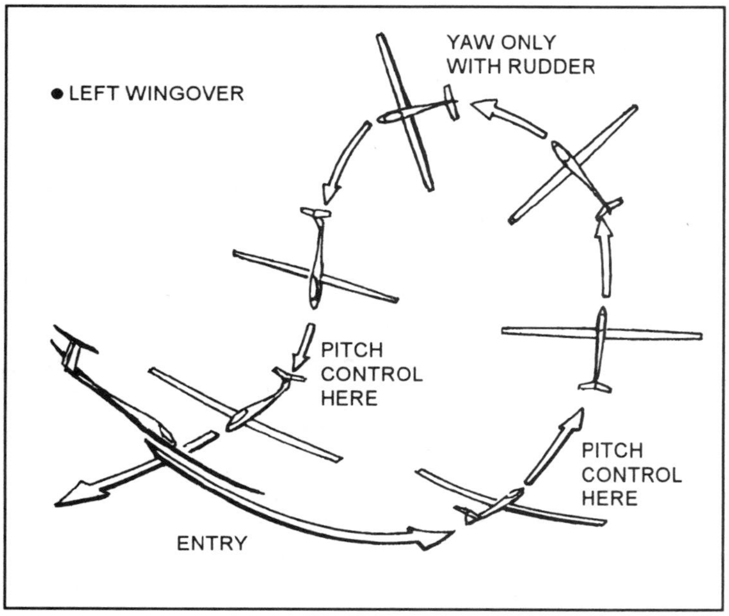

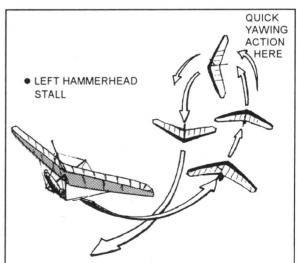

Figure 11-3: Sailplane Performing a True Wingover

Figure 11-4: Hang Glider Hammerhead Stall

PREPARING FOR AEROBATICS

To prepare for aerobatics, first make sure your equipment is sound. This means a thorough inspection and perhaps replacement of the lower side cables if they are more than a season old. We also recommend you use two parachutes, one of which has a rocket deploy system.

Your glider should be a double surface design for good speed retention. All of these maneuvers are to be performed with the VG system *full-on* for speed retention as well.

John Heiney enjoys a steep wingover near Salt Lake City.

You should do all your early maneuvers in smooth air. Evening wonder winds are suggested. Long before you begin considering any serious maneuver you must become very familiar with your glider in steep turns, slipping turns, spirals, dives and stalls. Stalls do *not* mean whip stalls. This latter maneuver is perhaps the most dangerous thing you can do on a hang glider short of trying to fly through an open boxcar on a moving train (yes, it's been done). The turns have been discussed in Chapter 3.

To dive you pull in on the base tube. If you hold this position your glider's stability will make it pull up eventually. If you let the bar out during this climbout you will stall and probably tuck (a whip stall after all). Thus you must start with very shallow dives. End them by slowing up gradually. Next try dives with a little more pull-in. Eventually your glider will pull up itself at which point you must *pull in more* to prevent a severe stall. Once the glider slows its climb and starts to dive again, you ease the bar out to resume normal flying speed. One or more oscillations may occur before you can stabilize your speed.

CAUTION: You can only dive so steeply before your glider climbs out so strongly due to its "artificial stability" (see Chapter 12) that you cannot stop it from stalling at very nose-high attitude, no matter how much you pull in. Only a roll control (that produces a wang) will prevent such a dangerous stall (sometimes). Dives should be practiced with great care using the gradual approach.

➤ **Pro Tip**: There are limits we all must set according to our own experience, practice, time, equipment and natural abilities (like spatial judgement, eye-hand coordination, equilibrium maintenance, strength, etc...).

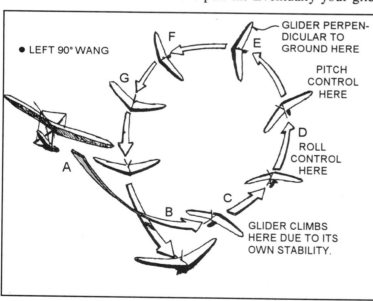

Figure 11-5: A Hang Glider Wang

LEARNING TO WANG

Essentially, a wang is a climbing turn involving roll and pitch as shown in figure 11-5. The added G loading due to centrifugal force during the pullout from a dive allows you to produce slightly faster roll control although the *roll control forces are much greater*. Your body's trajectory during the climbout is ballistic in nature, while your glider continuously pulls away from you. The secret to a properly performed wang is to produce the right amount of roll before the speed slows at the top of the climb. There is more roll required (a steeper wang) for a greater entry speed.

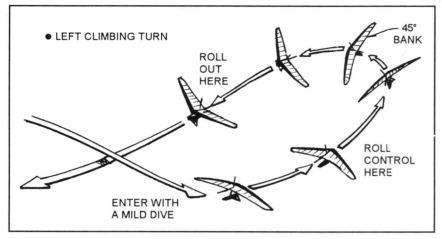

Figure 11-6: Climbing Turn

To learn wangs, start with gentle climbing turns. Pull on a little speed, ease the bar out and roll into a turn. You must practice hundreds of these until you fully anticipate your glider's reaction. Do these one at a time. Linking them builds up too much speed and changes your orientation. Work up to a 45° bank angle climbing turn as shown in figure 11-6. Do this in both directions.

CAUTION: Although this maneuver sounds simple, we are in no way suggested that it be tried by beginner or novice pilots. In fact, if you listen to common sense, there is no reason to practice the above maneuvers. Even at this stage of the game you can make a deadly mistake. Be sure to maintain a minimum of 1,500 feet ground clearance throughout all this practice.

The next step is to create linked climbing turns in a figure eight pattern known as lazy eights (see figure 11-7). The reason you perform a figure eight (which requires reversing turns) is to maintain your heading. If your turn the same way every time you produce a multi-lobed figure.

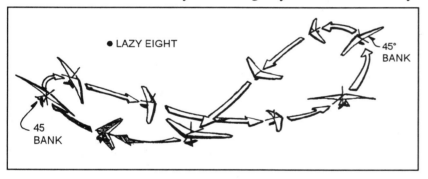

Figure 11-7: Lazy Eights

After hundreds of lazy eights you are ready for a change of pattern and a little more speed. When producing steeper wangs, it is better to do them continuously in the same direction to preserve roll momentum. This can help prevent a stall that can occur if not enough roll is produced. If you get behind on roll control, your glider's natural yaw stability will not rotate the nose downward before you loose too much speed.

Now you may be ready to try steeper wangs. To do this you must gain more speed by pulling on the bar in level flight mode. Increase the amount and sharpness of the pull-in until you gain the desired speed. Here are the essential controls (refer to figure 11-5):

Serious aerobatics should not be performed below certain parachute deployment altitude—do you know what that is?

1) Pull in at A to initiate the dive. The glider will begin to pull out on its own at B while you hold your bar position. Do not push out here!
2) When you are past the level point and beginning to climb, ease the bar out while at the same time producing a roll input (point C). You will feel a strong G force from point B to D.
3) The roll input is given almost totally at C while pitch control is fed gradually from C to D ending up about at your nose. These controls are held while the glider does its stuff, climbing and rolling to E. At E a little more pitch out may be eased into the bar if airspeed is still way above stall. By F you should begin to roll out of the bank (move to the high side) and bring the bar back to neutral pitch, about chest position. The pitch control should be completed by G while the roll control continues until the wings are level.

Rob Kells describing arcs at the Telluride aerobatic championships

The dangers and mistakes many pilots encounter are applying too little or too late roll input or pushing out too soon or too much. Remember, every glider has a characteristic *roll and pitch* response that requires a specific amount of roll and pitch control to produce a proper and safe wang. If you effect too much roll control or too little pitch control, you will simply enter a slip and then a spiral.

Once you do steeper wangs one at a time, the next step is to link them (going the same way). This will require you to maintain your orientation and will provide you with much greater entry speed (maybe too much!) as you exit each wang with a dive. Again, proceed with caution and link only two at a time, then three, etc...

SPINNING A HANG GLIDER

To understand spins, please see the description in Chapter 3. To produce a spin we must produce a stall in one wing and hold it. This is best done by entering a 20° banked turn and gradually pushing full out while high siding to keep the inside wing from dropping.

Flex-wing hang gliders are typically difficult to spin which makes them a great wing for scratching in close and low.

Spins are difficult to do in most gliders and may load the sail up inordinately, thereby stretching the tip area. Also some wild gyrations and surprising attitudes can occur in a malfunctioning spin. Finally, the human spatial orientation system (see Chapter 13) is limited in its ability to visually track longer than about 16 seconds in yaw and five seconds in pitch and roll changes. As a result, inexperienced pilots often get disoriented or suffer vertigo after a few spin turns. In an airplane spins are taught with an instructor so the student can build up a reference in the central nervous system, the "computer" that handles our sense of balance inputs.

For all the above reasons we discourage you, dear reader, from attempting spins.

LOOPS

We could likewise explain the dynamics of a loop and warn you of their dangers, but let us refer to John Heiney, aerobatic demonstration pilot and World Champion. John says:

Over the top is a routine experience for John Heiney.

"My first advice is: do not do aerobatics, at least not the radical maneuvers. All certified hang gliders are strong enough for properly performed aerobatics, but many will not build and retain the energy necessary to loop safely. Even those that will loop can be broken by pulling up too abruptly, especially if you are a heavy pilot.

"What makes inverted maneuvers in a hang glider unwise is that you hang from the wing by a flexible support. If you mismanage your energy, and get too slow upside down, you fall into the wing. This can result in a broken glider, or a tumble followed by a broken glider.

"A tumble is the very quick and violent 'reward' for stalling a tailless wing at the wrong attitude. The glider breaks due to a heavy object (your body) impacting airframe components. Sometimes body components break too.

"In stark contrast to this dose of common sense reality is the seemingly effortless performance by an advanced aerobatic pilot of smooth loops, rollovers and spins. Unfortunately beginning hang glider pilots will witness such a display and decide to emulate this advanced flyer without understanding the years of practice and dedication that allow him or her to do aerobatics safely.

"There is yet another factor involved in being a safe aerobatics pilot. Aside from strong desire, there is an intangible 'something' in your mental makeup that makes you capable of functioning at unusual attitudes. If you do not have it, you will never feel comfortable with aerobatics. Just as flying is not for everyone, aerobatics are not for all flyers. It is OK not to loop."

Petr Nestorov of Russia performed the first loop not long after the Wright Brothers' first flight of a powered aircraft in 1903!

AIR SHOWS AND AERIAL BALLETS

Air shows are an ideal opportunity for us to display our stuff to the public. However, full aerobatics with smokes should be left to the experts and paid professionals. The positive PR of scores of successful air shows is negated by one accident in front of the public. If this accident involves the public, the effect is worse. Most spectators uninitiated with hang gliding are just as awed by the performing of a few turns and a perfect landing as they are by aerobatics which they can't follow or understand anyway.

Air shows are much safer and please more crowds than any degree of extemporaneous aerobatics.

A very successful air show was that which ran in 1992 at Disney World in Florida. Under the direction of Malcolm Jones, an expert hang glider pilot since the early era of our sport, a well-choreographed *aerial ballet* wowed the international tourists daily. Aerial ballet involves coordinating the maneuvers of two or more pilots to create a pleasing dance in the sky. The possibilities are unlimited and we recommend this type of display over aerobatics for its crowd-pleasing appeal, safety and challenge.

III - FLYING FIXED WINGS (CLASS II)

Fixed wing flying is much less strenuous than the weight shifting type —except during takeoff and landing.

The international bodies governing hang gliding (see below under Setting Records) define Class I gliders as those controllable by weight-shift only. Class II gliders use movable surfaces—directly controlled by the pilot— to affect roll and possibly pitch changes. The differences allow various configurations that can provide performance gains and certainly enhances handling. Let us explore this different realm of hang gliding.

THE FIXED WING STORY

We call Class II gliders fixed wings because their wing structure tends to be solid which allows for better control of washout, higher aspect ratios and more defined airfoils (these matters are discussed in Chapter 12). The freedom from the need to be flexible for weight-shift control allows this. As a further benefit, fixed wings usually have the pilot reclining in comfort in a streamlined pod right underneath the wing, thereby reducing drag.

Fixed wings were very popular in the early days of our sport for they vastly outperformed the contemporary flex-wings. The extra weight and complexity of fixed wings seemed to be worth the extra setup time. In 1979 Eric Raymond won the US Nationals on a Fledgling, a Class II glider. In 1980 Tom Haddon won the US Nationals on a Comet, a Class I hang

glider, and ushered in the era of the flex-wing as the best all-around performer. But the process again reversed itself at the 1989 US Nationals when Brian Porter won on the *Odyssey*, predecessor to the *Swift*.

Now a new era is dawning with the introduction of the Swift, the most sleek, high performing hang glider yet devised. Other designs currently in the works are sure to be equally as impressive. These gliders are composites which means they are constructed from combination of fiberglass, Kevlar or carbon fibers.

The impressive Swift shows its sleek lines.

FLYING A FIXED WING

There are some considerable differences between the flying techniques of the two classes of hang gliders. This is a result of the different control systems and configuration. Let's see how this works out.

✓ Taking off

Fixed wings tend to be heavier because of the rigging and structural demands of movable controls. Also, longer wings can be used which results in more structural weight. Creating a composite fixed wing below 100 pounds would be quite a trick, but this must be compared to a 70 pound flex-wing plus a 20 pound harness and parachute. If ballast is used, the comparison is even closer.

Because of this weight, fixed wings tend to be harder to tote around and hold up at takeoff. On the other hand the aerodynamic controls make them easier to hold steady in turbulence. The real problem on takeoff with some designs is often a longer run required, even with flaps. This longer run is due to the higher stall speed resulting in part from the smaller wing areas used, but mostly from the lack of undercambering on the fixed wing airfoil which makes it

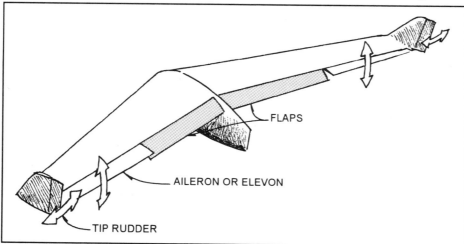

FLAPS

AILERON OR ELEVON

TIP RUDDER

Figure 11-8: Fixed Wing Control Systems

faster. The technique for takeoff is to stabilize the wing, launch in a good cycle and keep running with long strides until you are in the air. Your run may be up to twice as long as that with a flex-wing, so judge your sites accordingly.

✓ In the Air

Flying a fixed wing may involve weight-shift control for pitch and a "joystick" control for roll or a stick for both (see figure 11-8). If weight-shift is used for pitch, it is generally quite sensitive and in some cases may be performed by moving a leg forward and back. A full stick-controlled craft demands that you coordinate the turns just as with a flex-wing. To do this you initiate roll then apply pitch (nose-up) in conjunction with the amount of bank so that airspeed is held constant throughout the turn.

Flaps may be used to slow the wing down and provide better thermaling capabilities. If so this is an extra matter to master, just like using a VG. Sometimes it is possible to use a sailplane trick and slip inward in a thermaling turn to remain in the stronger core area. This is only efficient with full 3-axis control gliders. In general, fixed wings cannot slow as much as a flex-wing and therefore cannot core a small thermal as well even though their straight ahead sink rate is much better. This is similar to the experience of sailplane pilots.

One problem with some fixed wings is they are prone to spin because of their limited twist or washout (see Chapter 12). As a result a pilot must be careful when scratching close to the terrain. Almost every pilot flying the Mitchell wing as a hang glider experienced a spin. As an ultralight this design is great since slow flight in turbulence is not a normal practice.

Speed is the big bonus of fixed wings. For going cross-country there is nothing better that lands and takes off on human power. The great performance advantage here—1 1/2 to 2 times the glide ratio at all speeds—renders fixed wings' all around performance tops.

The Cirrus Class II by Danny Howell.

A close-up of a prototype Cirrus' layout.

✓ Landing a Fixed Wing

Landing a Class II glider can be tricky in rough terrain because even with flaps and a full flare some running is required except with a wind of 5 mph or more. Anyone used on running their landings on a flex-wing will have no problems in general. However, deep sagebrush or weeds may be difficult on a fast fixed wing.

All in all, fixed wings are a welcome facet of hang gliding for they show us possibilities of performance and provide new aspects of our sport to explore. The last word in hang gliding development hasn't been spoken and we look forward to the appearance of new designs.

IV - BALLOON DROPS

A renewed interest in balloon drops has occurred due to the popularity of air shows and gee, it's a great way to get gobs of altitude in still air. A balloon is a man-made thermal and you can ride it as high as you wish. However, there are some dangers that must be considered.

BALLOON DROP EQUIPMENT

Besides a glider and a balloon, you need a connection between the two. This umbilical cord deserves much attention for it must work flawlessly or you may be seriously injured. An inadvertent release below a couple hundred feet will result in a vertical dive that may splat you on the ground. Consequently, the system must be fool-proof and strong.

A balloon is a man-made thermal. Like a thermal it carries you where the wind blows.

✓ *The Balloon Hook-up*

The first thing to do is to figure out an attachment method for the balloon. It should be secure and not easily released. One attachment system consists of running a loop below the basket from at least two of the basket suspension points (see figure 11-9). A knife in the balloon can be used to release the suspension line in an emergency. A release on the balloon is not recommended for a mistaken release by the balloonist can kill the hang glider pilot.

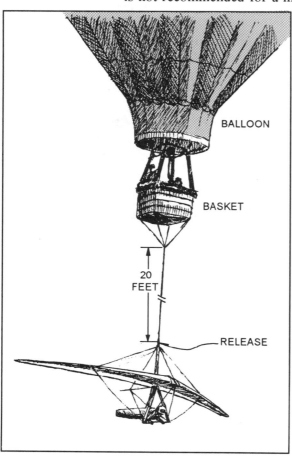

Figure 11-9: Balloon Drop Attachment

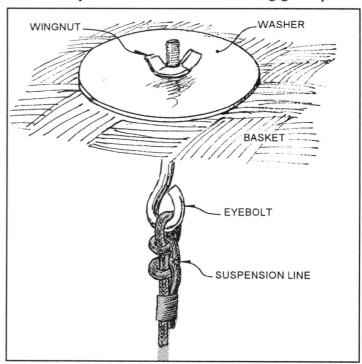

Figure 11-10: Balloon Basket Attachment

An alternate attachment is to hook the connection line to a *strong* eyebolt passed through the center of the basket floor. A strong circular plate with a hole in it should be used to spread the load on the basket as shown in figure 11-10. A wing nut on the eyebolt will allow the balloonist to release the line in an emergency.

A small line looped around the main suspension line will allow the balloonist to pull the suspension into the balloon after the hang glider releases so the line doesn't snag on ground objects. The suspension line itself should be stout and not twisted or the glider will spin when dangling. We recommend at least 1/2 inch braided nylon rope. Use secure knots at either end (a figure eight or 1/2 grapevine knot).

✓ *The Glider Release*

A release must be placed on the glider end of the suspension line so the glider can drop away when at the desired altitude. This release must be strong and fail safe. For the actual release mechanism we recommend a sailplane type release or a 3-ring type release similar to that used in towing (see Chapter 10) but much stronger. The release should be able to support at least 1,000 pounds. Rings used in the release system should be forged-steel (non-welded) type.

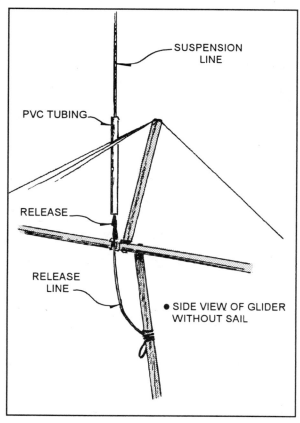

Figure 11-11: Balloon Drop Release

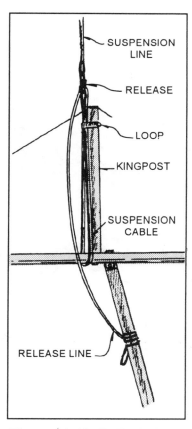

Figure 11-12: Balloon Drop Release

There are two ways to hook up the release to your glider. the first is with a webbing around the keel only as shown in figure 11-11. The result will usually be a nose down hanging position since the lifting force will occur in back of your hang point. This isn't a bad release position, but you must hold yourself behind the control bar on the ascent. With this release system there is a danger of the suspension line entangling the upper rigging, so a short length of PVC tubing should be placed over the rope as shown in the figure.

The second system involves using webbing or aircraft cable to route down the kingpost, around the keel and back up the kingpost with a loop at the top as shown in figure 11-12. It is held close to the kingpost with a loop at the top: With this system the glider will remain level. Never pull directly off the kingpost.

The release chord in any system should be routed *loosely* to a control bar upright with the end rolled up and taped within easy reach. It should be out of the way so you cannot accidentally release on the ascent.

BALLOON DROP PROCEDURES

At low altitudes you are completely at the mercy of the balloonist. Don't pick a hot-shot. Try the guy in the tophat.

It is extremely important to associate with a competent and safety-minded balloonist. Talk to your chosen balloon pilot to find out if he or she understands how your life is at stake. The most dangerous part of the entire stunt is while you're within several hundred feet of the ground. A premature release there could kill you. Also, a drifting balloon could drag you through trees or power lines—not a way to spend a pleasant morning. For this reasons it is necessary to have the balloon lift you to safety altitude (500 to 1,000 feet) as quickly as possible.

✓ The Launch

While the balloon is inflating you should be setting up, preflighting and donning your harness. Position your glider upwind of the basket so the balloon doesn't drift over you and destroy your wing when it first inflates. It is best to face away from the balloon to avoid suspension line entanglement. An assistant to hold the line free of the glider is absolutely necessary throughout the whole launch procedure.

As the balloon starts to lift, you should back under the basket until you are in the air. Ground observers should do a last minute check and OK the procedure or have the balloon return you to earth if there's a problem. Once you begin the ascent, remain still to prevent inadvertent release.

Jeff Dunn hitches a ride for altitude.

You can communicate with the balloonist by yelling when the burners aren't running. Using radios is a wise choice. When the predetermined altitude is reached, the balloon should begin a descent. This is very important for it helps reduce the amount you nose down after release but especially prevents a burst balloon envelope when the balloon surges up after it drops your weight. The descent rate should be at least 300 FPM and will take several hundred feet to achieve.

When you are dropping fast enough, the technique John Heiney suggests is to untape the release line, put it in your mouth so you can have both hands on the control bar, hold the bar into your stomach (dive position) and rotate down to release. The glider will dive almost vertically for it will be initially stalled. Once the glider picks up speed, ease the bar out slowly to avoid a whip stall.

Now go have your fun, but watch out for the balloon if it descends with you.

✓ Overview

Generally balloons have to operate in very light winds. That means your balloon drop will take place in very early hours or evening. Chances are you won't get more than a sled ride, but what a view! In light winds with thermals there may be a problem controlling the balloon on launch. Use extreme caution until you know the limits of the system and skill of the balloonist.

Any balloon that can carry two passengers can carry your 250 lbs or so of equipment and body weight. However, we again caution you to fly only with a serious balloonist. As John Heiney writes from his experience in air shows:

You have never gone over the falls like you will when you do a balloon release. Have fun!

Balloon Drop Safety Rules

1. Do not have a premature release.
2. Do not allow the balloonist to drag you through ground obstructions.
3. Always have a clear landing field before lift off.
4. Do not choose a wild man as a balloon pilot.
5. Do not release until the balloon is descending over 300 FPM.

V - SETTING RECORDS

Records are made to be broken.

Most of us have been conscious of setting personal records throughout our flying career. These may be altitude gains, distance or duration records. There are also state or local records, regional records and national records to be set as well as the prestigious international records. Currently many world records have been set in the United States southwest, including Larry Tudor's 303.35 mile distance to a goal, Jim Lee's 121.8 mile triangle, Kari Castle's 210 mile straight distance, and Jim Wills' 34 hr 3 min duration record in Hawaii. Normally we don't condone duration records due to the danger of flying hang gliders at night and without sleep, but Wills' record is notable because it is the overall record for single place aircraft eclipsing the previous record holder, Charles Lindbergh.

Attempting to set records can put pizzazz in your flying. For as record setter Jim Lee says:

"If you ever get bored in the air, try setting a record. You'll find it adds a new element of excitement and keeps your spirit alive. It takes the same amount of planning and preparation as competition but often avoids pressures. Record setting is competition with yourself to do better."

THE PAPERWORK

Sorting out the red tape is almost as daunting as the flight itself.

Setting local and regional records requires no paperwork. Just go and do it with reasonable witnesses and you'll be believed. National records and world records on the other hand require sealed barograph evidence, witnesses and plenty of documentation. Your national club (the USHGA in the USA) should have this documentation available upon request.

These records must be sanctioned and approved to be official. The ultimate sanctioning body is the Federation Aeronautique Internationale (FAI) of which the Commission Internationale de Vol Libre (CIVL) is the hang gliding segment. In the USA the National Aeronautic Association (NAA) is the representing body. Therefore, your records must go through all these organizations with the proper paperwork. Generally all you have to do is contact the hang gliding organization and they do the rest.

✓ Equipment

The main thing you need to set a record is a recording barograph. This is a device that prints out a running account of your altitude. It must be sealed and unsealed by an official witness so no tampering can take place. Traditional barographs are bulky and expensive, but now a number of variometers with memories have been approved by the CIVL for records. These devices plug into a personal computer and print out a whole flight. They are great to use as a log book as well. We suggest you get such a vario instead of a barograph. They are expensive also, but they accompany some of the best features available.

RECORD SETTING POSSIBILITIES

The first thing you should do is decide what records are feasible to set in your area of operation. If you are living in Maui the world distance record might not be too realistic. On the other hand, if you plan to travel and devote some time to record-setting you need to prepare by studying topographic and weather maps. Some places are much more conducive to garnering records than others.

✓ Record-Setting Areas

For straight distance records you seek powerful thermals and an assisting wind. The Owens Valley has long been a record gold mine because the combination of high mountains and desert conditions produces good lift for covering ground. However, changes of wind direction in less than 100 miles can throw out an anchor in this region. The world distance record ultimately moved to the Great Plains of the USA for the south tail wind that is a prominent feature in this area.

The Namib desert in the southwest of Africa has produced numerous records along with the American southwest. Other possibilities include the long mountain chains of South America and the North American plains with a stiff post-cold front tail wind. Then there's the deserts of inland China, the Gobi and the Takla. The Altai Mountains north of the Gobi extend over 600 miles into Mongolia. South of here the Astin Tagh uplands at the north side of the Tibetan plateau extend for over 1,000 miles! There's no roads, but a camel caravan track follows the entire chain. Getting there is half the fun.

For triangles records or out-and-back, good thermals with lighter wind is required. Such conditions often exist in the Alps and parts of the American Southwest which is where these records are currently held.

✓ *Record types*

Quite a number of records are available for attempts by the motivated pilot. There is open distance, distance to a declared goal, out-and-back, dogleg distance (around a turn point with less than a 90° change in heading), triangles (with the shortest leg at least 28% of the total course) and various altitude records. All these records are separate for males and females as well as Class I (weight shift), Class II (aerodynamic controls) and Class III (paragliders), both single place and tandem. If we take all these combinations, there are currently 72 possible world records! Surely there's one waiting for you.

MEASURING DISTANCE

For official records besides all the paperwork, a sealed barograph and an official observer, we must also submit maps pinpointing our exact launch point, our landing and any appropriate turn points. These maps should be large-scale topographic maps from which latitude and longitude can be read. An alternative is maps that exhibit a national grid as in England.

From the latitude and longitude values of our points our official distance is calculated by the *great circle formula*. This formula appears in the Appendix and is necessary since the earth is spherical while maps are flat. If we just measured our distance on the map we would get errors in excess of a couple miles for the very long flights.

GOING FOR IT

To set records you need time, money and assistance. Weather being what it is, you may have to wait many days, weeks, months or more for the ideal day to get your name in the record books. But persistence pays off.

Listen to Kari Castle, multiple World Record holder:

"I believe there are two critical factors that are essential in order to break a world record, The first is the organization part and the second is the mental and physical stamina.

"Being organized by having your paperwork filled out ahead of time and your flight plans and goals in mind allows you to think about the most important thing when the right day comes …flying! Furthermore, you must mentally and physically be able to stay in the air until you have reached your desired goal. If this goal is open distance, it means staying in the air ALL DAY!

"A proper mind set has served me well. When I went for the open distance record I pictured being in the air for 8 to 10 hours. I planned on staying up all day and told myself not to even think about landing until the sun went down. It sure put a whole new perspective on things."

All the work, near misses and washout days are worth it once you have achieved the goal of a lifetime: a World Record.

VI - TRAVELING WITH YOUR GLIDER

*N*o, we don't mean cross-country flying. We are referring to taking your glider along for a vacation, most specifically when you must use airline transport.

FLYING WITH YOUR GLIDER

The most stressful flight you can make with your glider is when it accompanies you on an airliner. Baggage handlers are not accustomed to 80-pound packages with an overall length of 12 feet. Baggage is generally treated roughly and oversize packages can bring out the beast in mankind, especially if key individuals have had a taxing day.

There is a thick book that sets standards for international flights. All airlines must use this book as a starting point but also may add their own rules. For instance Continental Airlines has a rule disallowing hang gliders as baggage. Other airlines allow gliders, but charge varying amounts to haul them. Normally you can get by with one unit excess baggage which costs $60 to $70 each way. In truth, this should be two units, one for overweight and one for overlength. However, check-in personnel are usually unaware of such details and will normally settle for one unit if you volunteer information in a neat package such as: "Well, one unit is what I've been charged before."

On busy international flights, a supervisor is often assisting operations. Unfortunately, supervisors are a bit more knowledgeable and can be anything from very helpful to autocratic. We have had supervisors help us load gliders and wish us bon voyage, while others would only allow the gliders on as air freight. The latter situation is the worst case, since the glider must then go through customs at your destination (and may take hours or days to clear), is not guaranteed to be on the same plane and costs hundreds of dollars to transport—each way.

Foreign soaring is a great adventure, but...transporting a hang glider doubles your travel arrangement considerations.

The best policy for maneuvering through all such obstacles is to call the airlines (they all have 800 numbers) to find out if they transport hang gliders. If they say no, offer a polite thank you and hang up. Then call the next day and ask if they take wind surfers. They'll all say yes. Now magically transform your glider into a wind surfer (that's what you do with it don't you?) and tell the airline employee the dimensions, weight and what flight you'll be taking it on or have your travel agent do this for you. They will double check to make sure that the baggage compartments can accommodate your package and tell you how much it will cost. Also, make sure they put the note that you have excess baggage into the computer and get the name of the person you're talking to. Both of these points are to use as ammunition to argue with a recalcitrant supervisor.

If connecting from one airline to another overseas, prearrange for space and excess baggage charges through your airline or travel agent as discussed above. Otherwise, you may

Another balloon drop underway at the Siskiyou air show.

charges fully twice, have to hassle with claiming your bulky cargo and dragging it through the succeeding airport to be checked in again or both.

Next, arrive two hours early for your international flight (one hour for domestic). This is very important because it gives baggage handlers time to do the special loading required and supervisors are less harried at the beginning of the check-in. Offer to help carry your glider down to the baggage staging area. Generally they'll accept your offer and you'll be able to prevent abuse of the glider for at least one stage of the journey.

I have heard of pilots shipping their gliders full length, but this only increases the chance of damage and airport hassles. Modern gliders break down to 12-13 foot packages quite readily with no tools. Once your glider is broken down, pad it generously and judiciously. The tubing ends tend to be most vulnerable so protect them well. Perfectly fitting dowels inside the ends are the ideal fix. We suggest you pull your mylar out and roll it in a tight cylinder held with a rubber band, otherwise it may be badly wrinkled. This mylar cylinder is also a fine tubing end protector.

Here are a few additional notes to make your passage more trouble-free:

▶1. If you travel with your glider often, get a ballistic bag for its protection. Several manufacturers make a good one with handles and padding at each end. It will set you back more than $100.

▶2. Be conversant with airline terms so it sounds like you know what you're doing. The key words are *excess baggage* and *one unit overweight*. Remember, you're allowed two bags of 85 pounds each. If you have only one bag but it's over 85 pounds, it will cost you more than you can believe, so use two bags.

▶3. Fly the airlines of the country to which you're heading if possible. We had trouble once on Air France, but the Greek, Brazilian and Costa Rican airlines were more than happy to take our gliders, sometimes for no charge. Be aware that these national airlines don't always have good deals, so shop around and look for charters.

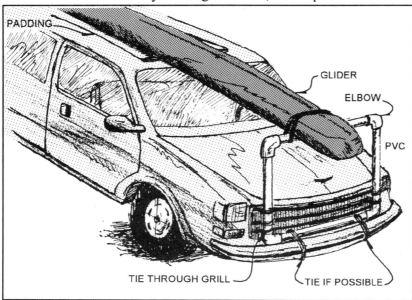

Figure 11-13: Rental Car Glider Rack

▶4. If you pass your glider off as a wind surfer, be familiar with that sport since people will ask you what's in your long package, then want to talk about it. Hopefully you will avoid the fate of a friend, who once shipped his glider as a batch of pole vaults only to find the check-in clerk was an ex-pole-vaulter. Our friend spent several nervous minutes inventing his highest vault, jumping style and pole design. Finally, if passing off your glider as something else, do not wear or display, hang gliding logos.

✓ *Ground Transportation*

When you get to your destination you need to get around. Since you have a glider, public transportation is out. You have to rent a car which is generally more expensive than in the USA even in poorer countries. Some pilots take along ski racks for the car roof although generally you can get away with resting the gliders on the carefully padded roof as long as you only carry two gliders. For the front rack the best idea we have seen yet is to buy some 2 inch PVC tubing (about 15 feet with four elbows), some glue, cheap rope and a hacksaw blade and make a rectangle as shown in figure 11-13. Rest the rack on the front bumper and tie it through the grille and you're in business.

SUMMARY

*H*ang gliding has a tendency to sustain our interest because each day exhibits slightly different conditions. However, we can get in a rut flying the same old site on the same old glider. There is nothing like new equipment, of course, to put punch in our flying. But if you can't afford such luxuries because the kids need new shoes (remember priorities, priorities), you can always branch into new endeavors. Naturally we discourage taking up aerobatics, but the other endeavors mentioned here plus aerial photography and instructing can greatly add to our enjoyment. All the new learning makes for more happy hours in the air.

CHAPTER 12

Design Concepts

A spectacular soaring eagle does not have the slightest idea of how its flying machine is put together. All it knows is a sensation of flight and freedom.

We too can enjoy the thrill and thrall of the air without knowing too much about how our wings do their stuff. However, the eagle's maker had unlimited energy and time to improve the design while we are strapped to a system that evolved in only a couple of decades. *Our* flying machine is not yet perfected. The more we know about how our wings work, the better we are able to understand how to maximize their performance. Consequently we offer this summary of the hows and whys of hang gliding design.

I - DESIGNING FOR PERFORMANCE

First we will look at many of the factors that determine a glider's performance and what design tricks can be used to enhance sink rate, glide and speed.

AN OVERVIEW

A designer is like a diplomat, using compromise and calculation to coax the desired results.

Like any sport hang gliding has seen a great improvement in equipment since its inception. The improvement has been a slow process for several reasons: First, much of hang gliding design was a pioneering effort since flexible wings with slow-speed airfoils were a big unknown. Secondly, aviation requires a conservative approach for testing new ideas is hard on test pilots. Finally, the relatively small size of hang gliding companies dictated by the small potential market means research and development must be limited to what can be paid off in a couple year's worth of sales.

At any rate, from the original standard Rogallo to today's gliders is a great leap in safety and performance. We added battens first to stop the sail from flapping, then found they could define our airfoil. We added a little double surface to fair in the leading edge then found we could bury the crossbar. We added a keel pocket to free the sail and found out we could do the same thing by freeing the crossbar. We started getting better pitch stability with little defined tips and found out that reflex bridles can do the trick. We gradually learned that we could widen the nose and remove twist and still maintain control. New sail material and Mylar leading edge inserts complete the major changes that have given us our current awesome... well, reasonably good performance.

All aircraft tell a tale of compromises. These include the trade-offs of weight, slow performance, fast performance, handling, stability, complexity, longevity, versatility, portability, cost and weight. Yes, weight is in there twice because ultimately any trick you want to pull to improve any of the other items generally adds weight. That's compromise. An example of one compromise made to achieve the ultimate foot-launched performance is the fixed wing Swift. Its weight and portability are certainly less desirable than that of a flexible wing, but the payoff is matchless performance.

Let's review a passion play entitled "The Designer's Dilemma."

*A typical high performance hang glider
—the Merger by Kamron Blevins*

THE DESIGNER'S CHOICE

The most important number to indicate a glider's performance is it's effective aspect ratio.

For a flexible wing, weight-shift glider format, the designer really has only three major things to choose: the planform (this is the shape when viewed from above and includes the size and span), the nose angle and the airfoil. All the other matters are important, but are generally dictated by the current configuration (swept, twisted, tailless gliders). The reason the designer has so little to work with is that only four things determine performance in any aircraft:

- ▶ 1. Effective aspect ratio
- ▶ 2. Lift distribution
- ▶ 3. Drag
- ▶ 4. Wing loading

We do not consider the airfoil here because its contribution is accounted for in the drag factor. The performance equations in the Appendix show how these four items determine all performance factors. Let's look at each and see how they come out on a hang glider.

EFFECTIVE ASPECT RATIO

Design milestones:
- **Taras Kichunak** *—Icarus II and Icarus V ca 1974*
- **Roy Haggard,** *first fixed tip glider —Dragonfly, 1974*
- **Don Mitchell** *—Mitchell wing (fixed wing), 1976*
- **Klaus Hill**—*fixed wing Fledgling, 197 (continued...)*

Aspect ratio is a comparison of a glider's span to its chord (front to rear measurement). A high aspect ratio glider is long and thin like a sailplane. Why this is good is shown in figure 12-1. Here we see two wings loaded the same. To produce the same amount of lift, the lower aspect ratio wing disturbs a shorter width of air but must deflect it more vigorously. As a result the tip area experiences larger losses in the form of swirls as shown in the figure. We call these swirls wing tip vortices and identify the losses they represent as induced drag.

The reason these vortices are losses is that the wing must expend energy—that is, fall an extra bit since our energy comes from gravity—to produce them. Imagine connecting a couple fans big enough to make 30 foot swirls in the air (that's about the size of your glider's vortices) to your car engine and you will see how extra energy will be required. You can also view wing tip vortices on a glider by watching one land in a light mist or with streamers on

- **Terry Sweeney,** *first double surface and fixed airfoil on a flex wing —Kestrel, 1975*
- **Dick Boone,** *first radial tip—Phoenix 6B, 1976, first shifting crossbar (in US)—Mariah, 1978*
- **Bob Trapenau,** *first curved tip on a flex wing—Sensor 210, 1977*
- **Brightstar Aviation Team** *—fixed wing Swift, 1991*

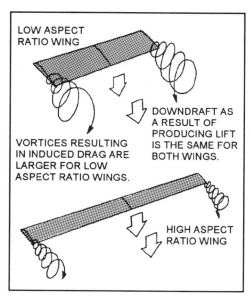

Figure 12-1: Aspect Ratio Effects 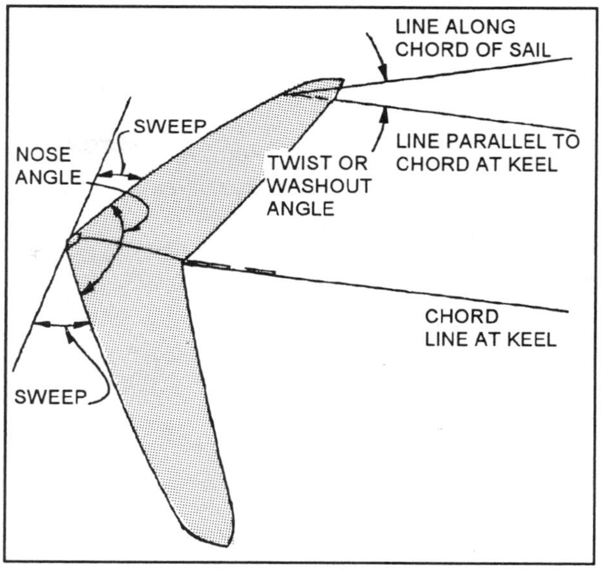   **Figure 12-2: Sweep and Twist on a Glider**

its tips. Simpler yet, plane your hand slowly across water and you will see a vortex formed at the end of your fingers.

✓ *Washout and Sweep*

The operative word in our discussion of aspect ratio relative to hang gliders is *effective*. A hang glider has twist or washout and also sweep. Washout is a twisting of the wing from the root (center) to the tip as shown in figure 12-2. Sweep is the angling back of the leading edges as indicated. The more sweep, the narrower the nose angle. Washout and sweep both reduce the *effective* aspect ratio because they alter the flow pattern and lift distribution on a wing.

The effective aspect ratio is nearly the same on most hang gliders.

It is interesting to note that the current flock of high performance designs vary from 7.2 to 8.1 aspect ratio, yet they all perform similarly. The reason is their effective aspect ratios are about the same. The higher aspect ratio gliders are washed out more because it is harder to keep the twist out of the sail on a long narrow wing.

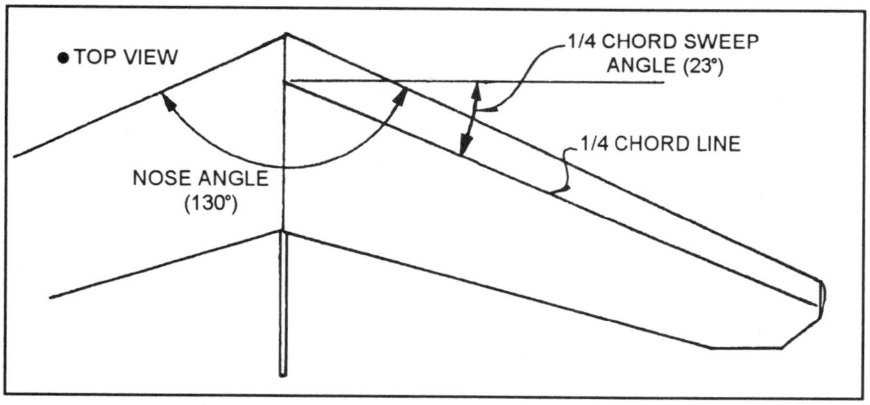

Figure 12-3: Finding Washout

Some years ago an optimistic designer decided to devastate the competition by marketing a glider with an aspect ratio of 11, appropriately named the Elite. Unfortunately, it did not perform as well as other state-of-the-art gliders of the time with aspect ratios of around 6.5. The Elite was too washed out and fell victim to that same old demon: effective aspect ratio.

We can think of this whole matter as efficiency. The higher the effective aspect ratio, the more efficient. Washout and sweep reduce the efficiency approximately 12% for every 15 degrees of washout and 5% for every 10 degrees of 1/4 chord sweep. We use the 1/4 chord line as shown in figure 12-3 because we can assume the sum of all the lift forces on an airfoil are at the 1/4 chord point. Typically, a hang glider with a 130° nose angle will have a 1/4 chord sweep between 23 and 25°. Since a typical glider will have up to 15° of washout (depending on the

VG setting) we can expect a total of 22% loss of efficiency due to washout and sweep (12% from washout and over 10% from sweep).

✓ Finding Washout

It is seemingly very difficult to determine in-flight washout of a glider. However, a simple trick makes it easy. First, beg, bribe or bully someone into taking a photograph of your glider from below looking straight on. This assistant can shoot the picture on landing or while you're soaring above takeoff (the closer the better). Next, measure the chord (leading edge to trailing edge) of your glider at the root (measurement A) and at the place where you wish to determine the washout (measurement B). Make sure your measurements are parallel to the keel. Now measure your *photograph* at the root (measurement C) and same spanwise point (measurement D). The washout angle θ will be given by the formula:

$$Cos\ \theta = \frac{A \times D}{B \times C}$$

We can find the washout graphically as well. In figure 12-4 we lay off the C and D measurements along a line (we assume these are smaller values) using any suitable scale. Next draw perpendicular lines up from the ends of these measurements and draw in the A measurement at whatever slant necessary to fit exactly within the outside vertical lines. Finally, draw in the B measurement at a slant between the vertical lines at the ends of the D measurement. The angle of washout θ is the angle between A and B. As mentioned, this method works for finding washout at any station along the span and it is not necessary for the photograph to be taken looking perpendicular to the sail, just straight along the keel.

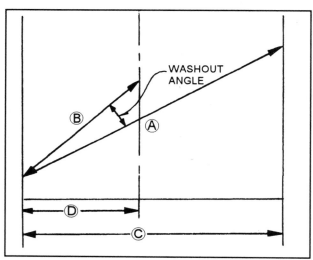

Figure 12-4: Finding Washout

A dramatic photo showing washout in a glider's tips.

LIFT DISTRIBUTION

If we look at a wing from the rear we can imagine the relative lift produced at each point along the span. It was discovered in the 20s by a German professor of fluid flow with the impossible name Prandtl that the ideal lift distribution is an elliptical shape as shown in figure 12-5. We see the lift is greatest in the center and tapers to zero at the tips with the dashed line being half an ellipse. Such a lift distribution results in the least amount of tip losses and 100% effective aspect ratios.

The typical lift distribution on a hang glider is shown in the figure as well. It is far from elliptical due to washout, sweep and planform irregularities. Because of washout, our lift pattern changes with angle of attack, but in general the center of our wing is working the hardest.

✓ Achieving the Elliptical

How can we gain more elliptical perfection? It has been found that having an elliptical planform with no washout will give you an elliptical lift distribution. This of course means no 1/4 chord sweep as well as shown in figure 12-6. Recent research with powerful computers has altered Prandtl's work to show that a circular leading edge still retaining the elliptical lift distribution results in slightly better performance (see the figure). New sailplane designs are simulating this shape.

Early airplanes used elliptical planforms, but these are too hard to build in mass production with compound curves in the wing surfaces. A good compromise is to use a tapered wing with the tip chord ideally 0.4 times the length of the root chord. How do hang gliders match up? Most use a tapered wing with too much taper. Rounded wing tips help simulate an elliptical planform, but of course sweep and washout destroy this effect somewhat. In general, all hang gliders are too narrow in the midspan area to have an elliptical area and thus lift distribution.

At this point we can see where flex-wing hang gliders can be improved. Get rid of some sweep and washout and make things more elliptical. We'll see later why this may be difficult.

The perfect figure: an ellipse—the aerodynamicist's dream.

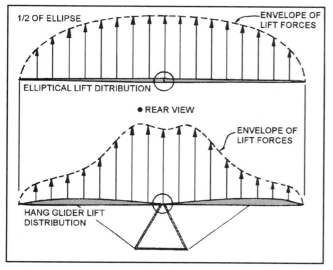

Figure 12-5: Lift Distribution on a Wing

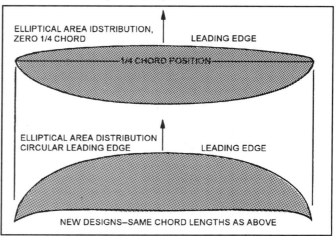

Figure 12-6: Ideal Planforms

THE DRAG STORY

Most of us know drag on our wings is a real drag. It obviously hurts our performance so we should investigate how to reduce it. Take a stroll with an air molecule. It usually goes jitterbugging along until it hits something solid—like your nose—and gets the bounce. As it ricochets away it leaves your beak with a little bit of its kinetic energy, slowing you down and sending it speeding in another direction. Now one little molecule doesn't make much difference, but since you hit billions of them every second, you get significant drag.

This same process happens all over the wing. We call such drag *parasitic* drag and it can be broken down into several types. A chart of drag types is presented in the side bar.

Every ounce of drag constantly erodes our store of altitude.

Drag Types	
INDUCED DRAG	**PARASITIC DRAG**
Caused by losses at	Form drag
the tips as discuss-	Profile drag
ed previously.	Interference drag

✓ Parasitic Drag Types

FORM DRAG — is caused by solid, non-lifting items in the airstream. Your body, control bar, cables, kingpost and instruments are the main items of concern. Of all these factors your body is the greatest source of drag.

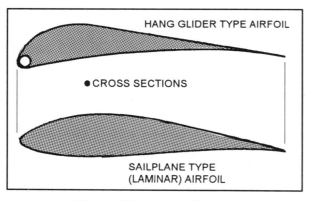

Figure 12-7: Airfoil Drag

PROFILE DRAG — Is that caused by the lifting surfaces—the wing. It consists of skin friction and drag like form drag at the leading edge. This is the airfoil contribution. A larger area wing and a more blunt leading edge will increase this type of drag, as will a thicker or irregular airfoil. Figure 12-7 shows two airfoils of roughly the same size. The lower one is much more streamlined and therefore exhibits less drag.

INTERFERENCE DRAG — is a matter of losses occurring when flow around parts of an aircraft interferes with another. This is not a major factor on a hang glider, but we can classify the losses due to the air escaping out of the kingpost hole as interference drag.

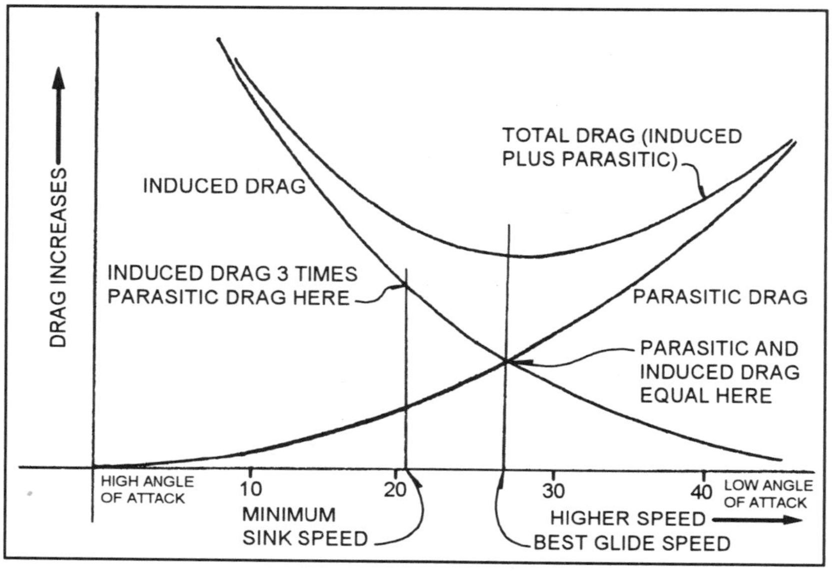

✔ Total Drag

As it turns out, induced drag is greatest the slower we go since vortices are worse at high angles of attack (think of it as pushing more air). You can witness this by planing your hand in the water at different angles of attack. Parasitic drag is worse the faster we go since the air molecules are hitting us harder. We can look at this graphically as in figure 12-8.

Here we see induced and parasitic drag separated. The total drag is the sum of the two at any given airspeed. The point of lowest total drag is that of maximum L/D (best glide) and it occurs where induced and parasitic drag equal one another as shown. As a point of interest, minimum sink occurs where parasitic drag is 1/3 the value of induced drag.

Figure 12-8: Total Drag on an Aircraft

The chart below indicates where the drag comes from on a typical glider with faired downtubes and a pilot in a pod at best glide speed.

How can we reduce the total drag of our gliders? Getting rid of things plowing through the airstream is the first answer. If we can't scrap the pilot we can at least request as streamlined a harness and hang straps as possible. Getting rid of the kingpost and upper rigging will also be a boon. Using faired or streamlined shaped downtubes is in order. Ideally they should be about 3.5 times as wide as they are thick, but since we yaw so much in flight they produce less overall drag if they are more narrow.

We may be able to improve airfoils somewhat, but smooth (laminar) flow will probably always elude us as long as we use a foldable, flexible surface. The efficiency of our airfoils is also limited by the demands of pitch stability. (Without stable airfoils we would create tremendous drag as we tumbled out of the sky.)

With the pilot in the breeze we will never achieve the slipperiness of a sailplane—but then we get to constantly savor the air.

Drag Sources	
Pilot	13%
Wing (induced)	50%
Wing (parasitic)	17.8%
Downtubes (faired)	1.0%
Base tube	6%
Cables	6%
Luff lines	1.5%
Kingpost (airfoil)	0.3%
Fittings	1.4%
Interference drag	3%

In summation, drag is with us to stay. Anything short of altering our configuration (for example, using a different structure to get rid of external bracing) will not make any great strides in drag reduction. However, we can defeat drag in tiny battles. Getting rid of defined tips, using faired downtubes and faired instruments are some examples.

WING LOADING

Wing loading changes more than just airspeed because of our flexible wings.

We all know that the heavier we load our glider, the faster we fly. In fact, the speed goes up with the square root of the weight ratio (see the Appendix). If we add 10 pounds, our speed increases about 1/2 mph at every angle of attack. Our sink rate also increases although our maximum glide ratio remains the same. In Chapter 7 we discussed wing loading in respect to performance.

We can alter our wing loading somewhat with the use of ballast. A designer does it for the flying public by selecting glider sizes. Obviously only a few sizes can be offered, so wing loading is a semi-fixed factor in our performance equation, especially since we prefer to launch and land on our feet.

We should note that because our wings are flexible, weight changes do more than move a glider polar. More washout and dihedral occurs when more weight is added. This may reduce straight ahead performance but help the glider slow down and produce a smaller diameter turn when banked. The camber of the sail also bows up more with heavier wing loading. This too may improve sink rate though the effect is difficult to measure.

OVERALL PERFORMANCE

Polars are performance maps illustrating the effects of design changes.

Now let's turn our attention to the specifics of sink rate, glide and handling and see how the above four factors (effective aspect ratio, lift distribution, drag and wing loading) affect these individual marks of performance. We can best do this with pictures. Specifically if we draw a glider's polar (see Chapter 7) and display how it changes as we change design factors we can see what it does to performance.

In figure 12-9 we see the affect of increasing aspect ratio. This is also the same affect we get when we improve lift distribution, for better (more nearly elliptical) efficiency results which is the same as saying we have a higher effective aspect ratio. In Figure 12-10 we see the affects of reducing our drag. In figure 12-11 we see the changes due to increasing our wing loading.

From these graphs we can note that for better minimum sink rate we need a higher effective aspect ratio and a lighter wing loading (figures 12-9 and 12-11). Airfoil selection

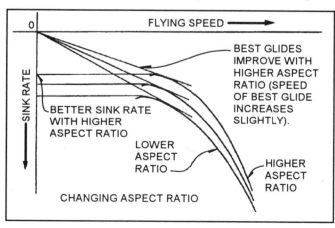

Figure 12-9: Performance Effects of Changing Aspect Ratio

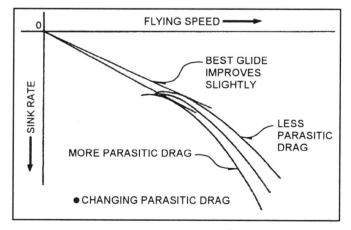

Figure 12-10: Performance Effects of Changing Parasitic Drag

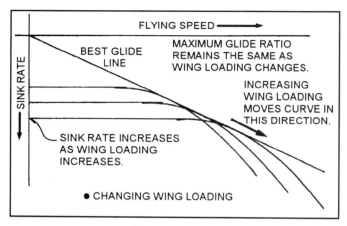

Figure 12-11: Performance Effects of Changing Wing Loading

is also a factor for it determines how slow we can go and is partially responsible for the original shape of the polar curve by helping determine the drag at each angle of attack or airspeed.

For better maximum glide, we need to increase our effective aspect ratio and decrease our drag, especially parasitic (figures 12-9 and 12-10). For high speed performance we need to reduce drag and (or) increase our wing loading (figures 12-10 and 12-11). Increased wing loading also helps improve handling as do other factors as we see in the next part.

In closing we should mention how aspect ratio mainly affects slower speed performance while parasitic drag affects higher speed performance. This is clearly indicated in figures 12-9 and 12-10. We can deduce this by looking at figure 12-8 and from the fact that higher aspect ratio reduces induced drag. We should also note how the polar curve flattens somewhat at higher wing loadings.

II - DESIGNING FOR HANDLING

*W*e all want to be able to turn on a nickel, drive effortlessly through chop and weave a sinuous path through a confused public gaggle. However, the ideal handling is often compromised—out of choice or default—for pure performance. Let us see where it comes from (and where it goes).

THE SOURCES OF GOOD HANDLING

A good handling will make up for a sink rate deficiency in rowdy, elusive or iffy lift.

When a weight-shift glider turns it flexes and pushes air as the pilot unloads one side and loads up the other with a roll control. The less flexible it is, the more it must push air out of the way as it banks. So we can say immediately that the more flexible a wing is, the easier the turn initiation will be.

In the same vein, the smaller a glider is, the less air and wing inertia it has to overcome when rolling. Two other items, airframe geometry and stall characteristics also help determine handling. Let us briefly look at each of these factors.

GLIDER FLEXIBILITY

We often think of our glider as having two major parts: the airframe and the sail. Each affects flexibility.

✓ Airframe Flex

If we use stiff leading edges we can tighten the sail more, achieve less washout and thus better performance. Our handling will suffer. On the other hand, flexible leading edges will let the glider react to a turn input as shown in exaggerated form in figure 12-12. Such flexibility will hurt performance ultimately so what can be done? In the early years we had deflexors (like outriggers) to keep the wings stiff even though we used 1 1/2 inch leading edges. We don't suggest going back to drag producing deflexors, but it is possible to alter the leading edges by ovalling them or using a tube with an internal webbing (this is currently available) to make the leading edge stiff in the direction of sail tension, but flexible up and down so it bows during roll initiation.

Designer's ideal: a leading edge flexible in the vertical direction and stiff in the horizontal.

✓ *Sail Flex*

In Chapter 4 we reviewed the choices of sail material and made the general statement that the lighter the material, the easier the handling. This holds true with the added factor that leading edge flex is also responsible for how much the sail can give. In addition, batten tension, flexibility, amount of camber and arrangement affects glider flexibility. It should be clear that the designer has to choose carefully to balance the airframe with the sail to produce the desirable balance of pure performance and handling.

Small gliders are often more difficult to perfect due to material stiffness, Reynolds number effects and the large size of test pilots.

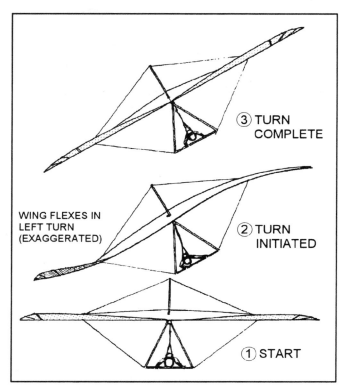

Figure 12-12: Effect of Wing Flexibility

GLIDER SIZE

Glider size determines wing loading which we have seen helps determine performance. We also know that it helps determine handling. A smaller glider has less tip inertia and pushes less air when rolling. However, simply scaling down a glider doesn't necessarily create a proportional improvement in handling. The reason for this is that stiffness of materials does not change at the same rate as length, weight or volume.

Figure 12-13: Scaling Effect on Flexibility

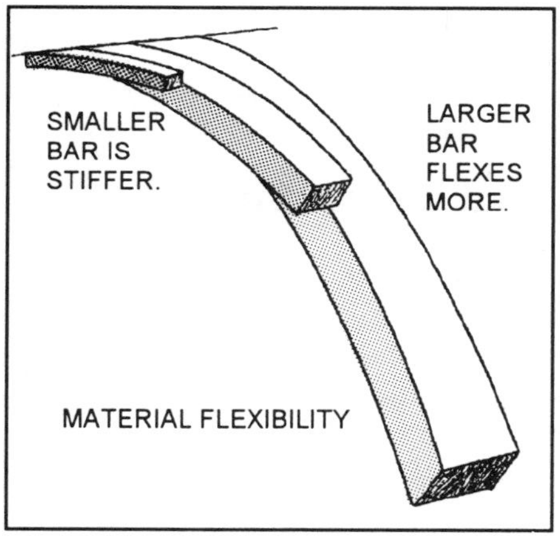

To see this look at figure 12-13. Here we have a three-dimensional picture of three semi-flexible bars of the same material. Each one is an exact replica of the next size up only 1/2 size in all dimensions. The flexibility of each bar is much less than that of the next larger size, even though is exactly proportional. (For reference, the area changes with respect to the square of the length, the volume and weight by the cube of the length and the stiffness by the fourth power.)

We can't expect to get a change in handling commensurate to the change in performance as we change glider sizes. This is borne out by experience whereby some smaller models of a design don't handle much better than the larger size with the same pilot.

AIRFRAME GEOMETRY

The shape of the airframe affects handling because it determines the sweep, dihedral and amount of crossbar shift. Sweep is the major factor determining yaw stability. With more sweep we have less adverse yaw, less hesitation and therefore have to hold a roll control for a shorter time. The result: less arm fatigue. (We have already seen the negative affects on performance that sweep causes, however.)

Dihedral is the angling up or down of our wings as viewed directly from the front.

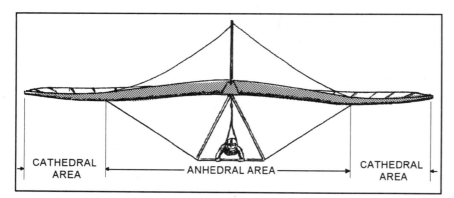

Figure 12-14: Dihedral Balance in a Wing

Anhedral is downward angling, cathedral is upward angling although this is widely assumed to be dihedral. The more anhedral we have in the airframe, the more our wing will want to roll into a turn. The result will be easier roll initiation, but more difficult coordination (high siding will be necessary) and rollout. One trick is to use lots of airframe anhedral but a relatively loose sail which adds cathedral. The result is a good performing, good handling glider. The original Kiss and Foil Gliders employed this trick and they were both influenced by Australian designer Mark Mitzos. As figure 12-14 shows, a flexible airframe has both anhedral and cathedral in the wing so the designer must find the right balance for the intended wing loading.

Different weight pilots change the dihedral balance of a glider resulting in different handling.

✔ Shifting Crossbar/Keel

When we move weight to the side we unbalance the forces on our glider so that we pull the keel to one side as shown in figure 12-15. This action, in effect, exaggerates our weight shift for a given side force and simulates power steering. This control aid can only take place if the crossbar is free from the keel by being attached to a tether. The longer this tether is (ideally behind the kingpost) the easier the shifting will be. It is also necessary to have somewhat slack side cables to allow for a changing geometry, or the effect will not be as free. That's why you have to put up with sloppy side wires on launch.

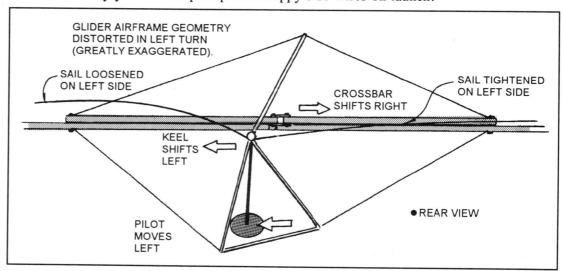

Figure 12-15: The Action of a Floating Crossbar in Turn

STALL EFFECTS _____

Most of us know either from rude experience or the admonition of a drill master instructor how control goes out the window when we perpetrate a stall. Let us see where our gliders stall.

Previously in figure 12-1, we saw vortices created but we also can see the air flowing outward under the wing and inward on top. This is called spanwise flow and it results in greater loading toward the tip area which results in a stall there first. Increased sweep and taper make this worse. Our gliders would always stall at the tips in their current configuration and thus spin readily except for the abundant washout (twist in the wing to lower the tip angle of attack) they have. Imagine scratching close to the hill with a spin-prone glider. If we didn't have sweep and taper in the wing we could get by with 3° or less of washout.

Because of washout, the point that stalls first on our wings moves inboard to about where indicated in figure 12-16. You can witness this by taping tufts of yarn about 3 inches long on the top of your wing. On a sunny day you can see them through the sail. When they reverse direction a stall is in effect.

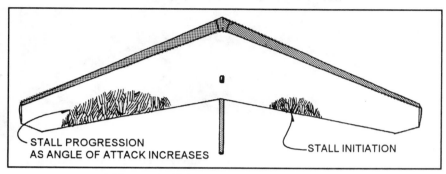

STALL PROGRESSION
AS ANGLE OF ATTACK INCREASES

STALL INITIATION

Figure 12-16: Stall Initiation on a Hang Glider

✓ Turn Limitation Due to Stall

The stall limits our turning in two ways. First when we initiate a turn we increase the angle of attack on the downward moving wing. Thus if we try to turn vigorously when flying very slowly we stall that wing and it usually drops making the whole maneuver inefficient.

In addition, as we saw previously in Chapter 3, the inside wing is always going slower than the outside wing in a turn. It therefore limits how much we can slow down while banked. It stands to reason that the more washout on the inside wing, the more we can slow our turn. However, with too much overall washout the outside wing, which is already at a lower angle of attack, will not be working much at all, so performance is not necessarily enhanced.

It should be clear that the designer has to strike a careful balance between planform sweep, taper, washout and airfoil shape to allow proper handling yet still deliver performance equal to the rest of the flock.

III - STABILITY CONSIDERATIONS

*A*nyone who has flown in raging thermal conditions is grateful for every once of pitch stability designed into our gliders. The lessons of pitch stability were learned the hard way: we added stability devices until gliders stopped entering terminal dives or pitching over. Here we investigate these pitch stability tricks.

HANG GLIDER STABILITY

The several factors that make up our pitch stability package are pendulum effect, sweep and washout, reflex bridles along with defined tips and airfoil shape. Here is a few words on each:

The most important design feature of any glider is (or should be) its stability.

✓ Pendulum Effect

A hang glider has a type of stability known as artificial stability. Our wing tips which are behind the center of gravity serves as our tail. But instead of giving a net downward force like the tail of an airplane, our wing tips lift.

To see the difference, look at figure 12-17. With the airplane, the downward force of the total weight and the tail are balanced by the lift on the wing. Because of this balance, the lift force is applied behind the weight (center of gravity). As a result, when an airplane flies into an updraft, the increase in lift acting against the inertia of the weight causes a nose down pitch reaction and a relieving of the load.

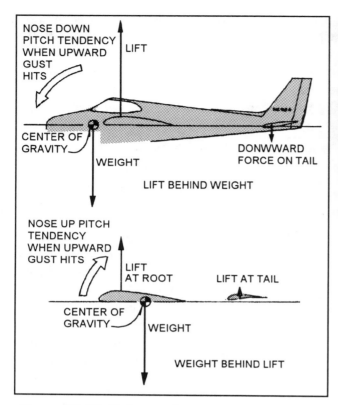

Figure 12-17: **Balance of Forces on an Airplane and a Hang Glider**

A Moyes XS equipped with tip fins for yaw stability.

On the other hand, the hang glider with its lifting "tail" has the main source of lift in front of the total weight or the center of gravity (CG). When an updraft hits, it increases the lift which tries to raise the nose, increasing the angle of attack. That's why you feel the bar pull away from you when entering a strong thermal. We get away with this state of affairs because the center of gravity of the system is considerably below the wing for a pendulum effect which dampens the motion. If we let go of the bar in varying air we experience wild porpoising.

✔ Sweep and Washout

With sweep and washout we are assured that our tips are behind us and that static stability exists. *Static pitch stability* is when a glider tends to remain at one trim speed. If we pull in, our tips unload more than the root (center) so more lift remains in front of our CG and the nose tends to pull up. If we push out from trim the tips lift more and tend to rotate the nose down. It should be clear that we can move our trim point simply by moving our CG which is what we do when we move our hang strap fore and aft.

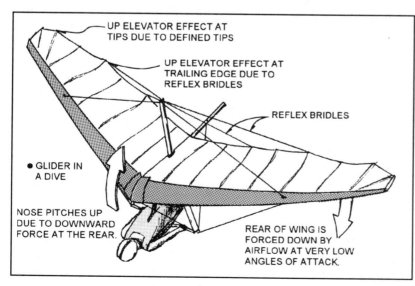

Figure 12-18: **Dive Recovery on a Hang Glider**

✔ Reflex Bridles and Defined Tips

Besides static stability there is also a stability in a dynamic (changing) situation. This stability takes effect when a glider is changing angle of attack rapidly. When a glider is disturbed from trim angle of attack, how it returns to trim is dependent on its dynamic stability response. Pendulum effects, sweep and washout along with a statically stable airfoil (one that wants to remain at one angle of attack) provide static stability and some dynamic stability, but the real contributors to pitch stability when we get knocked around or spit out in a "dynamic" situation are reflex bridles and defined tips. Figure 12-18 shows how both reflex bridles and defined tips hold up the trailing edge and wing tips to create a powerful nose-up effect. Usually flexible battens are used with bridles to increase this effect.

Defined tips when used are now internal for low drag and articulate upward as the sail varies washout but are limited in downward motion so they can do their stuff when things go negative. Reflex bridles also are out of play in normal flight. With a VG system the bridles have to be loosened as the sail is tightened or they kick in too soon and limit speed. This is the reason we have bridle compensators—the bridles are effectively shortened at loose VG settings and lengthened at tight settings.

A Sensor sporting a tail fin for yaw stability in slips.

Pitch changes can be felt at different VG settings. These are differences in pressures and trim position. We would expect that tightening the VG would reduce washout, make the tips fly better and result in pitch down. However, often the opposite takes place, for tightening the VG takes out more mid-span than tip washout and it moves the weight of the crossbar backward so most gliders pitch up at tighter settings.

We should note that any glider will tumble given the right type of ugly air, no matter how stable it is. Imagine a very long boat with a deep keel. If it heads into a breaking wave as large as it is long, over it will go, head first as shown in figure 12-19. Similarly, in the air we can encounter a mammoth vortex—often on the borders of a missile-like thermal—that can tumble us.

Bruce Goldsmith of the English team was racing in front of a gaggle in the 1992 Owens meet when he suddenly tumbled several times. Other pilots behind him witnessed the whole affair then reported hitting horrendous turbulence themselves, but no tumbling threats. Bruce unluckily found the one mean swirl carrying a grudge against Englishmen. Just to show his mettle, Bruce went on to finish with the first group at goal.

Despite such stories, tumbles are extremely rare because designers have paid attention to statistics and put enough stability in our glider to handle 99.99% of what's lurking in the sky.

Figure 12-19: Overwhelming Natural Forces

✓ *Airfoil Shape*

Our airfoils (batten shape) greatly influence pitch stability. In general, our airfoils with their forward high point and flat or reflexed rear are very stable. However, too much camber can reduce this stability which is why we must check our batten pattern occasionally. We learn more about airfoils next.

IV - THE HANG GLIDER AIRFOIL

AIRFOIL HISTORY

The evolution of the airfoil used in hang gliders is a story itself. The first solid battens were used in fixed wings like the Quicksilver and were not tried in flex-wings until the Sky Sports Kestrel appeared in 1975. It took another couple years before a fully battened sail using a fixed airfoil appeared with the Sky Sports Sirocco and the Seedwings Sensor 210. The airfoil used was one Terry Sweeny, designer for Sky Sports, developed from the mean camber of a Liebeck* airfoil. This airfoil was later sold to other companies (notably Wills Wing and Ultralite Products) and became the standard in most gliders until the late 1980s.

One other airfoil was developed by Jean-Michel Bernasconi in 1979 for use on the Atlas and later the Moyes Mega. This airfoil was curved abruptly at the front end and remained straight for the remainder (see figure 12-20). It was good for sink rate but not at higher speeds.

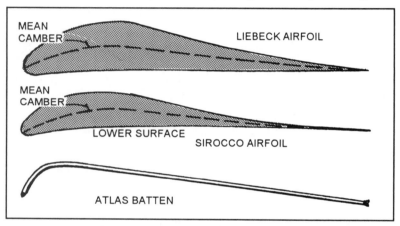

Figure 12-20: Hang Glider Airfoil Origins

Today many airfoils are being designed by computers and a variety of curved shapes are being used. It is interesting to note that, according to the designer Christof Kratzner, twenty eight different airfoils were tried in the German Firebird Lazer glider.

Figure 12-21 shows the typical airfoil curves of a number of current high performance gliders. These were all taken from the batten patterns using battens of similar length. It should be clear that a variety of airfoils work in our wings, but the particular shape must be wedded to the wing to maintain stability and handling.

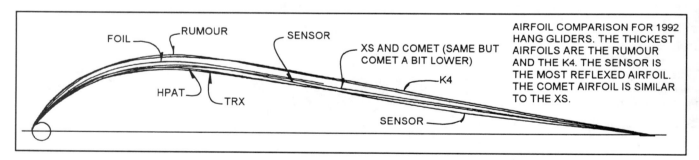

Figure 12-21: Hang Glider Airfoil Patterns

THE AIRFOIL JOB—EFFICIENT DEFLECTION

Hang glider airfoils have been undergoing more refinement with the advent of computer airfoil design techniques.

The main duty of an airfoil is to deflect air. It is supposed to do this with as little drag as possible, hopefully be stable and accept a high angle of attack. Let's see how this is done.

A flat plate will serve as a wing. It deflects air downward as it is pushed along and thereby produces lift (see figure 12-22). Although a flat plate is stable, it also produces a lot of drag. We can alter this somewhat by curving the plate. The figure shows that the deflection of air is smoother, lift is maximized and drag is reduced.

* The Liebeck airfoil was designed with aid of a computer to produce high lift at low speeds while remaining stable.

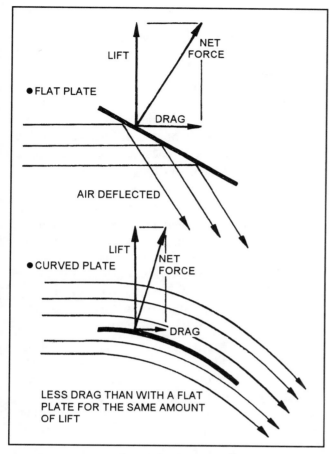

Figure 12-22: Flat and Curved Plate Characteristics

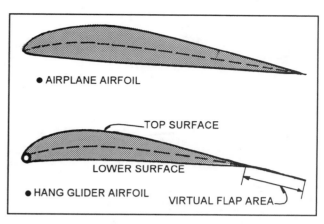

Figure 12-23: Streamlining an Airfoil

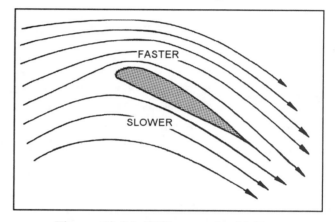

Figure 12-24: Difference in Airflow Around an Airfoil

Such a curved airfoil is a high lifting one but it is only good at a limited angle of attack range and is not stable. (this single-surface airfoil is similar to that on some early gliders.) We can fix this state of affair by adding a top and bottom to the airfoil and get what appears in figure 12-23 as the modern hang glider airfoil or that of an airplane.

When an airfoil moves along it pushes air out of the way in front and deflects it downward behind. Much of the air in front gets pushed over the top so that the air is accelerated above the wing and is slowed below as shown in figure 12-24. That's why the airspeed measured below your glider is up to a few miles per hour slower than the actual flying speed. This effect is increased the higher the angle of attack. You can see this work by moving your hand like an airfoil in water just below the surface.

The amount of deflection of the air's path is determined by the curvature of the airfoil's surface at any point. In turn this deflection combined with the speed of airflow determines how much force the air exerts on the airfoil. Because the curvature and flow are greater on top of a wing, about 2/3 of the lift is produced there as shown in figure 12-25.

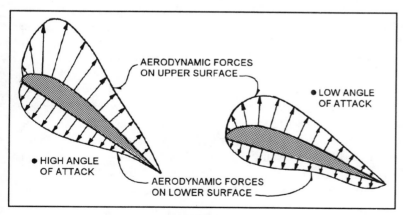

Figure 12-25: Pattern of Aerodynamic Forces Around an Airfoil

AIRFOIL SHAPES

We define the airfoil in our glider with our batten shapes. Several things determine the ideal shape of an airfoil for a particular job. These are the angle of attack range and speed at which it is expected to operate, its necessary stability and its lifting capabilities. The things we change to get these properties are the entry curve, the maximum camber (thickness), the high point position, the amount of double surface and the reflex or recovery area (see figure 12-26). We look at each in turn.

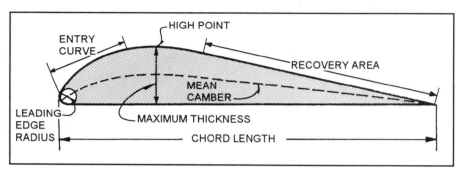

Figure 12-26: Identifying Airfoil Characteristics

In general, the more cambered or curved a double surface airfoil is, the wider the efficient range of angle of attack. As mentioned earlier, a single surface airfoil is efficient over a much more limited angle of attack (such is the case with beginner gliders). The leading edge radius and entry curve also affect the range of efficiency. A very sharp leading edge like on the wing of a jet is the lowest drag, but works well at only one angle of attack. For our purposes, a leading edge radius near 3% of the chord length is ideal.

The airfoil's job is to slip through the air efficiently and kick passing parcels downwind.

Mean camber is the curve of the line drawn exactly between the upper and lower surface as shown in the figure. The greater this camber is, the more potential lift the airfoil can develop, but it may pay a drag penalty. Moving the high point back and easing the entry curve will reduce this drag, but usually hurts stability. Adding thickness and undercambering to the lower surface will increase the mean camber, but again this is at the expense of stability as well as high speed performance.

An airfoil's shape is its whole essence. Keep yours in shape by frequent checking against the pattern.

More double surface will also reduce drag, but it can also reduce mean camber. Look at the camber of the single surface curve of figure 12-22 and compare it with that in 12-26. Hang gliders have been built with 100% double surface but they suffered in sink rate.

The recovery area from the high point back is where the accelerated air on the top surface must slow to the speed of the main airstream. Usually the curve here is gentle to avoid premature separation (stall). Also, this area is most important in terms of airfoil stability.

✓ Airfoil Measurements

We conveniently express all measurements on an airfoil as a percent of the chord length. These measurements such as leading edge radius, maximum thickness, high point position and amount of mean camber help define an airfoil. The chord length is the measurement from the leading to the trailing edges as shown in figure 12-26. Typically, on a high performance hang glider our airfoils are from 11% to 13% thick. High points are relatively far forward for stability—around 20%—compared to sailplanes which are back as much as 35%.

AIRFOIL STABILITY

A stable airfoil—just as a stable glider—has a tendency to return to a particular angle of attack when disturbed. A highly cambered airfoil as in figure 12-27 is unstable because it will want to nose down more when it is lowered in angle of attack since more lift is created toward the rear. Conversely it wants to nose up more when the angle of attack is raised since more lift is created up in front. The stable airfoil on the other hand does just the opposite. It creates more lift up front in a dive and more lift rearward in a climb.

The way we achieve this stability is to use long, straight recovery tails on our battens with

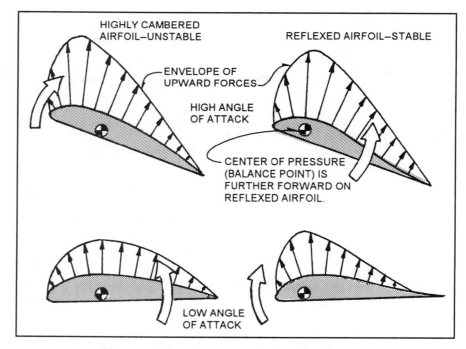

Using a stable
airfoil requires less
application of
other stability
devices.

Figure 12-27: Stable and Unstable Airfoils

far forward high points, or reflex (upward bowing of the batten as shown). The effect of a double surface ending before the trailing edge is to create a flap which destabilizes the airfoil as can be seen in figure 12-23. The addition of reflex or moving the high point forward can combat this effect.

AIRFOIL DECISIONS

Batten density: To
maintain the ideal
airfoil along the
entire wing it is
desirable to have as
many battens as
possible. However,
this is detrimental
to weight and
prolongs the agony
of setup.

It is obvious that a designer must choose an airfoil wisely to balance all the aspects of performance and stability. If more camber is added, more washout may be required to maintain stability. Obviously too much camber adversely affects performance. Higher camber in the outboard areas can help reduce washout because the sail tension working over the higher curve holds down the trailing edge.

If we look back on our discussion of lift distribution we see that the ideal elliptical distribution is defeated by sweep and washout. We can overcome some of these affects by using airfoils with a greater degree of camber out at the tips. In general, a different airfoil should be used at each station along the span because each point flies at a different angle of attack. One trick is to use a progressively further forward high point towards the tips which simulates slightly less sweep. A problem with some of these techniques is that anything that improves the lift distribution makes the outboard area fly better and the glider become harder to weight shift without other tricks.

REYNOLDS NUMBER

Some time ago a British physicist named Osborne Reynolds discovered that the air reacts differently at different densities or when small or slow objects move through it. He worked out a way to compare these effects and we know this as the Reynolds number.

The Reynolds number relates to inertia to the viscous forces in the air. Viscosity is how "sticky" the air feels to an object. Obviously to us it doesn't feel sticky at all. However, to a bumblebee or a dandelion seed viscosity is the main factor in determining their reaction with the air. At high Reynolds numbers we are dealing mainly with the *inertial* forces of the air. At low Reynolds numbers the *viscous* forces are more important.

The Meaning of Reynolds Number

$$Re = \frac{Vl}{\nu}$$

where: V = velocity through the air (in feet per second)

l = characteristic length. Typically we use the chord length (in feet)

ν = (Greek letter *nu*) the kinetic viscosity at our altitude of interest (.0001564 ft²/sec at sea level)

✓ *Reynolds Number Transition*

The problem that Reynolds number presents is the smaller it is, the greater percentage of drag is present for an airfoil or other solid moving through the air. If this wasn't bad enough, there is a transition area near a Reynolds number of 100,000 where the drag jumps up considerably (see figure 12-28). It is very desirable to stay above this transition area and maintain as high a Reynolds number as possible—over a million is preferred.

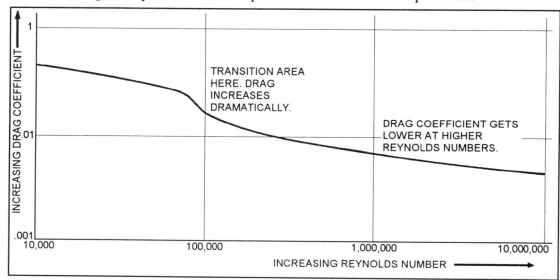

Figure 12-28: Reynolds Number Effects

The smaller our chord, the slower we fly and the higher we are (kinematic viscosity increases with increased altitude) the lower the Reynolds number. To see where we stand, a hang glider with a root chord of 5 1/2 feet and a tip chord of 2 feet flying near stall at sea level has a Reynolds number of 1,023,689 at the root and 372,250 at the tip. At 10,000 feet these numbers are 800,662 and 291,150 respectively.

We can see that we are quite close to the transition area in our tip area. Also it should be clear that our performance decreases some at higher altitudes. As a rule of thumb, we can roughly estimate Reynolds number at sea level by multiplying 6,400 × chord (in feet) × airspeed (in feet per second).

BOUNDARY LAYER

Much of what is important on an airfoil happens very close to the surface. This is where the air must change from practically zero flow right at the microscopic surface (even at supersonic speeds) to the free stream velocity. The layer in which this change takes place is called the *boundary layer*.

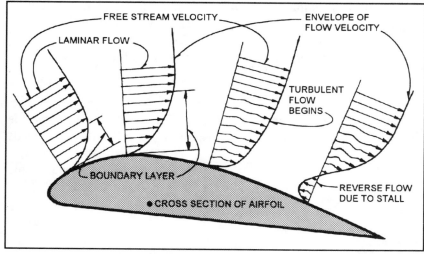

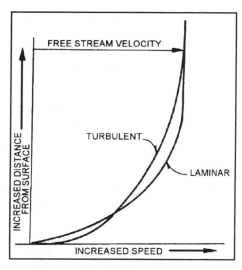

Figure 12-29: Boundary Layer Changes

Figure 12-30: Laminar and Turbulent Flow

In figure 12-29 we see how a boundary layer changes as it moves along the airfoil from front to back. It starts out small and smooth (laminar) then thickens and develops wrinkles (turbulence) and possibly reverses at the rear if a stall occurs. Laminar flow exists only in the first part of our wings, because of surface roughness and imperfections such as seams.

Laminar flow is desirable, since it reduces drag, especially at higher airspeeds. However, laminar airfoils are unstable because they require a very rearward high point and only a fixed wing hang glider can retain the smooth surface required for laminar flow.

Due to boundary layer effects, a rough surface helps at slow speeds and hurts at high speeds.

While laminar flow is good for high speeds, turbulent flow is better for the lower speeds because it spreads the change out more gradually so stall doesn't occur as soon. Figure 12-30 shows a comparison of the laminar and turbulent flow gradients. A good laminar airfoil will produce laminar flow back as far as possible than use a carefully placed increase in curvature to produce turbulent flow. Sometimes airplanes will use vertical stall fences on top of the wing to activate the boundary layer with turbulence to allow slower flight. The important point for hang glider design is that with our airfoils a stall bubbles often appears just behind the high point, so a turbulent boundary layer needs to be established by that time. This may be the advantage of a rough leading edge.

V- THE AIRFRAME

The bones that form our wings are hollow and fold just like a bird's. But theirs is where the analogy ends, for our structure is man-made. Let's learn a little about its design.

AIRFRAME BACKGROUND

The triangle is the most rigid geometric figure. Note all the triangles in your airframe—at least 14.

The basic structure we have with a keel, two leading edges, a crossbar, a control bar and a kingpost have been with us from almost the beginning of the sport because they make sense. Most of the parts of this structure are truss systems—a spar supported by cables—which is the lightest possible structure for a given required strength.

With the removal of deflexor cables to support the leading edges, the part beyond the crossbar became a cantilevered (supported only by its internal strength) piece which requires more weight but produces less drag. It is interesting to note that several designers intend to build totally cantilevered gliders: no lower or upper rigging. These will most likely perform better but be 10 or more pounds heavier than current gliders. This configuration will be the first departure from the original hang glider format since the removal of deflexors.

STRESS IN FLIGHT

Our airframes undergo various types of loads in normal flight. Since it is almost impossible to determine the exact lift distribution on our wings, it is difficult to calculate the exact loads on each element. However, a strain gauge on a side cable lets us make estimates.

In figure 12-31 we see a typical airframe denuded of sail with the in-flight loads indicated. Arrows pointing in together indicate compression. Arrows pointing in opposite directions indicate tension. Broad arrows indicate bending. The larger the arrows the higher the force. Note that the keel has very light forces on it which is why it is so small in diameter—it only takes a pounding if you pound. The downtubes have high compression loads but they are short so they too can be small. It is easy to see why the crossbars are so big in diameter. Here are typical loads on different frame parts:

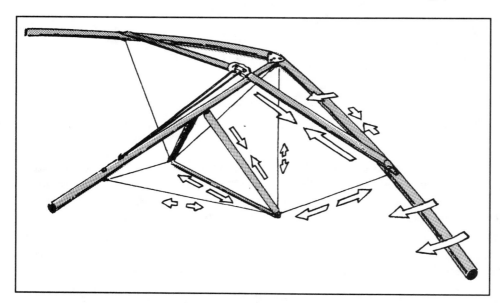

Figure 12-31: Forces on a Glider Airframe

Airframe Loading	
Part	
Crossbar	250 to 300 lbs compression
Downtube	100 lbs compression
Leading edge (fore part)	290 ft-lbs bending plus some compression loads
Leading edge (aft part)	55 ft-lbs bending (approx.)
Keel	30 lbs compression plus bending loads
Base tube	134 lbs tension
Side cable	125 lbs tension
Front to rear cables	20 to 25 lbs tension

Highly loaded members should be inspected regularly and kept in pristine condition.

These forces are under one G conditions as indicated. During maneuvers or turbulence they go up. For example in a 60° coordinated bank we pull 2Gs so all forces are doubled. The more a crossbar is swept back at the outboard ends, the greater the compression load. With a typical VG system the sail loosens as we sweep the crossbar more so we avoid trouble. It should be clear from the amount of loading on our downtubes why we must not fly with bent downtubes.

The base tube is another matter. It is in tension in flight so it could actually be a cable. A curved "belly bar" base tube is safest with an internal cable since the tube flexes at the bends in turbulence or in ground handling. Note the kingpost is absent in our chart since it only has a load on the ground.

A Pacific Airwave glider undergoing a -30° pitching test. Note the rear area held by the reflex bridles.

✓ Strength Standards

All certified gliders are tested for strength. Essentially they have to withstand a positive load (at 30° angle of attack), a negative load (at −30° angle of attack) and a rearward load (−150° angle of attack). the rearward load is the most difficult to pass because the glider is run backwards into the wind with the tail down. As the leading edges bow down the sail scoops more air which increases the loading. When a glider fails in this mode, the leading edges bust near the crossbar. When a glider fails in the positive mode the crossbars usually break in the middle of their span. No wonder these are the heaviest parts on our gliders.

AIRFRAME MATERIAL

✓ AN Parts

The material used in hang gliders has proven itself with umpteen hours (literally tens of millions) of air-time.

Most of our structure is made out of aircraft quality parts. The bolts are designated as AN bolts which stands for Army Number. They are made of a tough high grade steel with a yellow cadmium plating. The bolts can be bent in half without breaking. The plating helps prevent corrosion between the steel bolt and aluminum tubing. Any bolt with the plating worn off should be replaced. When removing bolts, twist the nut—not the bolt—or you will wear away the plating.

➤ **Pro Tip:** Replace Nylock nuts when they no longer require two wrenches to fasten or unfasten.

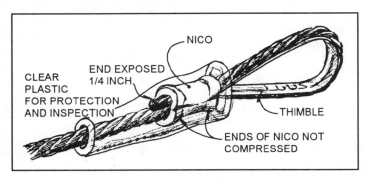

CLEAR PLASTIC FOR PROTECTION AND INSPECTION
NICO
END EXPOSED 1/4 INCH
THIMBLE
ENDS OF NICO NOT COMPRESSED

Figure 12-32: Proper Nico Fitting Application

✓ Nico Fittings

Our cables are stainless steel and designed for aircraft. The method of attaching them was invented for the telegraph industry and adopted for aviation because it works so well. The only approved method is shown in figure 12-32. Note that only one Nico press fitting is used and the end of the cables protrudes. Clear plastic covers the fitting for protection and inspection.

Crimping the end of the Nico creates a fulcrum which can break the cable as can crimping the cable end inside. The latter mistake is the problem with most two Nicos systems. As many as 20 extra Nicos are required when using double Nicos which can add more than a pound to a glider's weight. All Nicos must be crimped to a specific tolerance to be safe. A properly made fitting should be as strong as the original cable which is close to 1,000 pounds for 3/32 inch stainless steel cable.

✓ Aluminum Tubes

Aluminum comes in many grades and alloys. Those typical to hang gliding are 6061-T6 and 7075-T3. Other alloys used in the past are 6063 (not good) and 2024 (great). The numbers refer to the alloy and heat treatment.

The 6061 vs 7075 debate has quieted for both alloys have proved their worth. 6061 is much less expensive while 7075 is stronger. To realize lighter weight, 7075 is used in thinner walls. This results in a bit more flexibility so a 6061 airframe glider tends to retain high speed performance better since the wings don't bow back as much. The 7075 alloy is a bit more susceptible to corrosion and should be inspected more often.

✓ Carbon Graphite Airframes

Carbon graphite has made a welcome entry into our sport (on a modern glider) with the TRX designed by Terry Reynolds. Carbon Graphite is stronger and stiffer than aluminum and can be laid up in almost any shape. Oval tubes and other shapes for cantilevering a wing are just around the corner. Carbon graphite has made a big impact in many other facets of aviation and should surely be a boon to our light weight requirements.

Graphite, unlike aluminum, doesn't bend but splinters when it is impacted or bent beyond tolerance. The damage appears on the inside of the tube as imperfections. You must remove tubes and sight their insides for splintered fibers or protrusions. There is almost no way to quantify this damage, so any tube showing such imperfections should be replaced. This can be expensive if your landings are frequently dramatic. Currently graphite tubes are laid up individually which contributes to their cost. Hopefully they'll see more use in the future so we can all enjoy their benefits.

Carbon graphite has revolutionized the aerospace industry. It is slow to capture hang gliding because the market potential is low, but the performance potential is high.

A K4 and an HP in the midst of the torturous -150° tests.

V - THE ONCE AND FUTURE WING

New designs have always been in demand. The Wright Brothers sold their 1908 design to the Army Signal Corp. for $25,000. That's over 1 million in today's money!

Pete Brock, the owner of Ultralight Products who brought us the Comet in 1980 predicted at the time that it was the end of all design work. Fortunately Pete was wrong. Today our glider are faster, sink and glide much better and handle easier than the ground breaking Comet.

We have reached a plateau in design at the present time and new models are improving hardware, setup and ease of handling more than performance. This is because of the natural limits imposed by our weight-shift-body-in-the-breeze desires. But new designs are just around the corner. The jaded pilot won't have to wait long to get a shot of pure performance. Let's see what's in the offing.

FIXED WINGS

The future is here. Various designs are being built or currently available. Most notable is the Swift. It offers about 50% better glide, 15% better sink rate and an untold amount of speed better than the best flex wing. It is heavier (10 to 40 pounds more than a flex wing, if we count our harness), less convenient (the package is larger and longer to rig) and more costly (about twice as much) but oh do they fly! In the 1992 Pre World Meet Eric Beckman and Brian Porter were at goal and broken down before the first flex wing arrived almost every day. We covered fixed wings flying in Chapter 11.

Here a Moyes XS passes the +30° load test.

Another potential winner is the German Experience which folds like a flex wing, weight shifts for pitch and rolls using spoilers. Finally we must point out Danny Howell's long standing efforts to produce the portable Cirrus (see photos in Chapter 11). This wing can be transported much like a conventional glider and is relatively light. These designs are omens of a renewed interest in Class II designs.

CANTILEVERED WINGS

Class II gliders will see a resurgence in popularity when they prove their performance and popularity.

A design with a crossbar and leading edge center junction strong enough to support the wings along with downtubes held rigidly to the structure can eliminate all upper and lower cables as well as the kingpost. The use of carbon graphite will minimize the added weight. the problem will be to maintain stability without reflex bridles. This will happen with reintroduced defined tips and a large tip area.

Such a design shouldn't be too long in coming, for more than one designer has approached the problem. We should expect 10% gains from this format.

FLAPS AND WASHOUT CONTROL

Flaps on an airplane increase the airfoil camber and allow it to slow its forward and vertical speed. On a hang glider they would allow us to take off, land and thermal at current speeds yet fly a much smaller glider. The result would be a wider speed range, more versatility and enhanced cross-country potential.

The limit of hang glider performance is weight, but new technology and techniques are still to come.

The drawbacks of flaps are they destabilize the wing and add complexity. We may be able to make a simple flap system since after all we have a flexible membrane wing. However, we may have to wait until we get a tail before we can solve the stability problem. One bright hope is that flaps are used on the Swift with no great stability problem because they are close to the system's center of gravity.

Another promising design is a control of washout using the torsional rigidity of the leading edge rather than sail tension. Such a system coupled from one side to the other could reduce washout yet allow easier handling.

OTHER CONFIGURATIONS

Canard designs (with a little wing in front) do not work for soaring wings because they are hard to control in thermals and they do not allow the main wing to reach maximum angle of attack. What does work? Thousands of sailplanes prove that a conventional shape—main wing in front, tail in back—is the best possible for performance. Michael Sanolin has been experimenting with this configuration on class II designs (fixed wings) for quite some time.

With such a configuration we can open up the nose angle and get rid of all washout as well as the upper rigging for a real jump in performance (see figure 12-33). The tail must be close enough to allow a proper flare and large enough for yaw stability so that weight shift can control the glider. With this design flaps, washout control and unlimited aspect ratios are possible. Tom Peghiny designed and flew a prototype like this called the Jaguar in the late 1970s. With today's technology reasonable performance gains should be possible. At least one such project is in progress.

The Sky Puppy from Michel Sandlin takes to the sky.

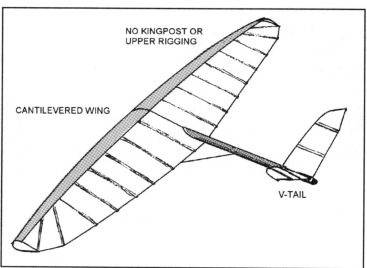

Figure 12-33: Possible Future Hang Gliding Configuration

SUMMARY

*H*ang gliding has changed the world of aircraft design. More than one aerospace engineer has marvelled at how much performance we have wrung out of rags, earwax and tubes. Our principle method of design has been cut and try. A hang glider lends itself wonderfully to this method since the planform can be changed with scissors and the airfoil changed with a good bending knee.

We are unique in our foot-launched capabilities, our flexible airframes and airfoils, our asymmetrical wings in turns and our convenient breakdown. All design progress has been true innovation, pulling inspiration out of the blue. The designers that brought us to where we are deserve our admiration and appreciation. Those that will take us further deserve our encouragement with just a dash of impatience...we can't wait!

CHAPTER 13

Aeromedical Factors

Hooking your mammalian body to a pair of wings and imitating the avians in the air can create some unexpected medical consequences equal to those discovered when we first went undersea exploring. Both of these environments—the air and the sea—are somewhat hostile to humankind and therein lies their allure.

If we are going to comfortably remain in an unnatural environment we should understand our body's demands and limitations in that environment. In this chapter we explain how your body and mind behave in the flying milieu and what you can do to maximize its performance and thus your enjoyment.

I - THE SENSES

We most likely fly for the sensory pleasure. While this pleasure may not be as intense as with some other form of activity, it lasts longer. All our senses come into play in making our flights consistent and safe. Let's look at what can go wrong and how to correct it to insure pleasure rather than pain.

VERTIGO AND BALANCE

We spend our lives engaged mostly in two-dimensional motion—forward and back, side to side. Various sensory organs provide data to our central nervous system (CNS) which then calculates our position and motion. From birth to maturation we develop a data base from the CNS to make these calculations.

When we take to the air we mostly engage in two-dimensional motion. Only when we perform turns or aerobatics do we start to get beyond the limits of our CNS's experience. Then we can have problems or at the very least have to update our data banks. The problem can be disorientation, dizziness or nausea all of which we'll place under the heading of vertigo. Each one of us have different degrees of susceptibility. This may be partially due to how much disorienting practice you had as a child on swings, merry-go-rounds, carnival rides, underwater and the like.

✓ The Balance Sensors

To summarize the senses that help orient us: we have the inner ear, the eye and certain muscles called the *proprioceptors*. The inner ear sensors consist of a chamber called the *utricle* that has little elves inside sensing G forces and linear acceleration. Another organ called the *semicircular canals* consist of three half circular tubes filled with fluid and tiny hairs that detect circular motion in any of the three axis relating to pitch, yaw and roll.

The eye is a marvelous organ that gives us orientation information by fixating on the horizon or an object outside the glider. If we are still and the object is moving (another glider perhaps) or we are moving and the object is still or both are moving, our eyes can fixate on the object and remain there through all types of motion.

Vertigo is a personal reaction to a conflict of input signals.

If we are turning, the eyes will automatically jump to a new fixation point once they have reached their lateral limit. The only problem is, it takes the eye time to initiate fixation so if we're spinning too fast we see nothing but a blur. The eye is sensitive to the inner ear vestibular apparatus so that when we move our head the eye moves in the opposite direction.

Finally, the muscles in our neck provide feedback to the CNS as to the orientation of our head through the action of gravity. All of these senses work together until we confuse them.

✓ What Goes Wrong

The first problem we encounter is that the inner ear can only sense accelerations. After about 20 seconds the fluid in these organs settles down and if no new acceleration takes place they report a rest situation. If we are in a continuous coordinated turn our eyes and muscles say something entirely different. This conflict with the senses is what causes confusion in the CNS and a sensation of vertigo. In shallow banked turns the problem occurs after two 360s. In steeper banked turns it takes about 2 1/2 complete circles, but the higher G forces and rate of turn create more confusion. Beginners are warned to practice 360s one at a time with shallow banks for this reason.

Alice Englehardt launches over a bed of poppies.

If your head is not oriented with the axis of the aircraft and you make a sudden head movement additional disorientation can occur as the semicircular canals put out a wrong signal. One of the quickest ways to create vertigo is to turn your head rapidly while in a tight high-G turn. This effect is worse once you have been in a constant rate turn over 20 seconds so that your motion sensing inner ear has reached equilibrium. Conversely, the best way to prevent vertigo in maneuvers is to keep your head steady and look to the horizon or ground toward the inside wing. Learn to do all maneuvers gradually so you build up experience in your CNS. Note that sudden pull-ins or pushouts can also be disorienting until you gain experience.

To avoid dangerous disorientation: Learn new maneuvers gently and gradually.

The second problem occurs when vision, our most reliable orientation sense is lost. This most commonly occurs in a cloud. The inner ear cannot tell you for sure if you are turning or not. Control inputs can become very confusing and seem to conflict with the muscle inputs (proprioceptors). If you wish to experience this effect, get yourself plenty of clearance from the hill and traffic and close your eyes as you do a turn or two. You can do this more extensively by having a friend on the radio monitor you for safety.

Often when we are lost in a cloud we can experience instant vertigo and nausea as we exit the cloud for we are confused by the relative motion and we don't recognize our orientation.

Vertigo of any sort can be dangerous, especially when low. Several pilots have augered right into the ground when trying their first rapid 360s. All maneuvers should be learned gradually.

✓ Nausea

Airsickness is not uncommon in a hang glider and indeed plagues some very experienced pilots. Nausea can be partially brought on by anxiety, stress and physical discomfort as well as vertigo. Being too hot or too cold can lead to airsickness.

When it comes to a battle of senses, "the eyes have it."

I recall the 1984 US Nationals at Crestline, California where I was bundled up for altitude but ended up wrestling in the foothills with cranky thermals. The sweat poured off me and I felt sicker than a steerage class immigrant on a tuna boat until I got high again. This statement from Mark Bennett confirms a suspicion I had about the site: "Crestline is the only place I have competed at where I consistently get airsick with nausea and a sharp pain in the diaphragm area...maybe due by the putrid air quality!"

To best prevent nausea, wear clothing that can be adjusted for temperature changes, then avoid rapid head movements and glider gyrations. If all else fails, there are over-the-counter motion sickness remedies that do work. We suggest Bonin or Scopolamine patches and discourage the use of Dramamine because it causes drowsiness.

THE EYE IN THE AIR

We have seen above one facet of the important role of our eyes in flight. They also help us perceive the dangers and benefits in the air. Here's how we can help them do their job.

✓ The Right Input

The light that reaches our eyes is scattered by the atmosphere and reflected from surfaces in different ways according to their color. One component, blue light, is the first problem. Blue light is greatly scattered by air molecules and thus produces less sharp images. Furthermore, within the eye it scatters in the fluid and doesn't focus exactly on the retina as shown in figure 13-1. In fact, there are fewer blue receptors than green or red in the foveal area where most focusing takes place.

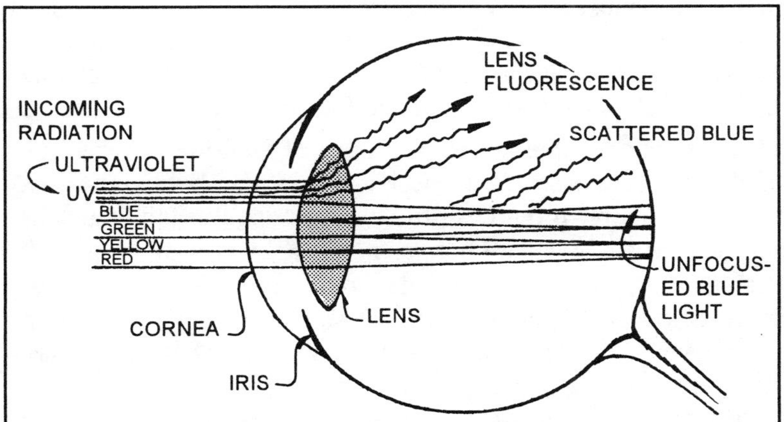

Figure 13-1: Blue Light Scattering in the Eye

Another type of radiation beyond the visual range but equally debilitating is ultraviolet radiation (UV). This form of radiation is not only damaging to our eyesight, but also fluoresces in the lens to further blur vision. Finally, glare from direct or reflected light can greatly attenuate our vision. For example, glare arriving at 40° to our line of sight can reduce visual effectiveness by as much as 40%. At 5° above our line of sight, glare can cause a loss up to 85%.

We can cure all of these problems with proper sunglasses. The lenses should be blue-blocking yellow-amber with an ultraviolet filter. NASA scientists have developed such lenses using organic dye technology to simulate the filtering effect found in the eyes of eagles. We human eagles may encounter 40% more blue light and 75% more UV when aloft when compared to sea level, but a proper pair of sunglasses can block 98% of the blue and 100% of the UV.

Not all sunglasses are created equal. Cheap sunglasses may be fashionable, but they are best used only to attract admirerers. Bad sunglasses stop the natural squinting reaction that reduces UV in the eye and can lead to damage. A perfect pair of sunglasses stops fluorescence, scattering, chromatic aberration and damage as shown in figure 13-2.

Protect your eyes with sunglasses for they are the guidance of you the auto-pilot.

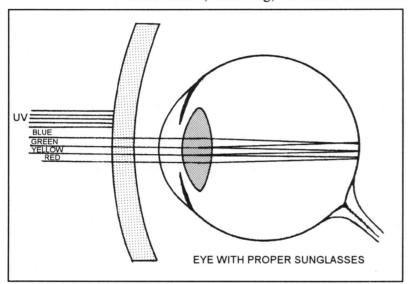

Figure 13-2: UV and Blue Blocking Effect of Proper Sunglasses

The proper type of sunglasses will appear yellow to brown, will be dark enough to stop glare and have enough wrap to provide a wide field of vision. Be especially sure to have good upward range because you need to spot clouds and gliders while gliding. An added bonus: sunglasses will prevent that red-eyed look acquired by running your eyes for hours through the airstream.

✓ Perception Problems

Flying at dusk has its own vision problems. It takes over 30 minutes for the eyes to acquire their maximum night vision capacity. Also depth perception is seriously hampered as the light fails. At 5,000 ft (1,600 m), there is a 6% loss in image sharpness over that at sea level, even on a bright day. Also at this altitude, night vision becomes hampered due to lower oxygen supply to the retina. On top of a very high mountain, stars actually appear dimmer due to this effect. Cigarettes, alcohol and other drugs also reduce night vision dramatically.

Due to the makeup of the retina you detect movement and can see in dim light better a little to the side of your direct line of sight. Use this knowledge by not looking exactly at what you want to discern in dim conditions.

One of the important function of vision during flight is avoiding other air traffic. Anything that adversely affects our vision compromises our safety when other air traffic is around. Some of these factors are: dust, fatigue, emotion, germs, age, optical illusions, oxygen supply, accelerations, glare, heat, drugs and psychological effects. The eyes only see what our mind lets us see. A daydreaming pilot is a prime candidate for an in-flight collision.

One problem that occurs when looking for other air traffic is that of focusing. It takes one or two seconds for the eye to change focus from far to near and this may be a significant delay if a collision is imminent. Furthermore, if there is little to focus on at infinity (such as above a haze), our eyes do not focus at all. We stare but see nothing, even if other aircraft enter our field of vision. Backlighting and the effects of another aircraft moving over cluttered ground can also prevent detection of that aircraft. We should further note that an aircraft on a collision course with you will appear to remain stationary (whether you are converging head on or from the side) without growing significantly in size. A fast moving aircraft will suddenly appear larger as it gets near—this is known as the looming or blossom effect.

✓ Scanning for Traffic

Clearly we need some technique for using our eye effectively. The following scan method is suggested as being perhaps the most effective.

In normal flight, scan from 90° to either side and 30° up and down. Also clear the area behind and to the side of you before making a turn. Be sure to perform clearing turns to scout out an entire area before performing a series of extended turns.

To scan the area outlined above, divide the area into vertical segments of 10 to 15° wide. This corresponds to the normal focusing field of vision. Now you have twelve or more segments from one side to the other. Start in the middle segment and scan it for about 3 seconds (up and down). Move left to the next segments and repeat. Follow this procedure until you have cleared all the way to the left, then return to center and scan to the right.

Obviously, this takes a bit more time to cover the entire area, so repeat this scan procedure often and keep track of any air traffic you see. Occasionally, check behind you (a bit of heading change is helpful) for airplanes can sneak up from the rear and your size may make you nearly invisible. Keep your eyes in good shape, remain alert, scan carefully and avoid other traffic.

✓ The Blind Spot

The human eye has a blind spot where the optic nerve passes through the retina. We can see this by closing the *left* eye and staring at the *left* dot in figure 13-3. Now, move the paper forward or back until the middle dot disappears. The figure will be about seven inches from your eyeball. Now, move a little further away and the middle dot will reappear while the right hand dot will disappear. This is due to your blind spot.

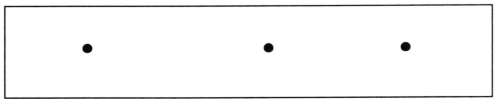

Figure 13-3: Finding your Blind Spot

By looking a little to the side of the dot you are staring at, it is possible to get an idea of the extent of your blind spot. It is surprisingly large. With both eyes open, the blind spot in one eye is taken care of by the other eye. However, one-eyed pilots and those who wear certain types of glasses may have the inside vision of each eye blocked so the blind spot is indeed blind. The blind spot is located approximately 16° to the outside of each eye's line of sight. Obviously, being aware of your blind spot is important so that you know to double check for traffic when other aircraft are in the vicinity.

EAR PROBLEMS

We detect our airspeed largely by listening. If we change helmets so that our hearing perception is altered, we must be careful to monitor the situation until our new perceptions are formed.

Other problems with ears mainly consist of ear discomfort due to pain when changing altitudes. Usually this results from congestion of the sinus passages. Chewing gum and swallowing are the standard ways to clear your ears. What you are trying to do is equalize pressure on both sides of the eardrum.

Note that pressure effects can upset the inner ear balancing system, so do not fly if ear pain persists. In addition, consult a physician if ear pain does not go away soon after landing. Beware of flying when suffering from a cold.

I once got on a ski lift with a blocked sinus. On the way up I began to experience intense pain that wasn't relieved until I skied back down. Upon consulting a doctor I found I had burst an eardrum. Fortunately these membranes are about the best healing part of the whole body.

II - EXTERNAL FACTORS

$\mathcal{M}$any factors that we subject our body to before or during flight can have grave effects on our performance. Some of these are obvious and others less so. We review them here.

HYPOXIA

We live and breathe at the bottom of an ocean of air. For most of mankind's history not much thought was given to the structure of that air as we sucked it in, blew it out and borrowed a few molecules. But in the last century we have taken to the sky on manufactured wings. There, new properties of the air were discovered, one of which was the depletion of oxygen with altitude.

Hang glider pilots in desert conditions regularly reach altitudes where oxygen reduction presents real hazards in terms of health and safety. Oxygen is the most critical raw element that fuels the processes of our bodies, for while you can perhaps live years without sex, weeks without food, and days without water, you can only survive a few minutes without oxygen.

You will not have your full complement of wits above 10,000 ft without supplemental oxygen.

The effect of lowered oxygen is called *hypoxia*. Since oxygen fuels the brain, many of the symptoms of hypoxia are mental. Some of the common symptoms of hypoxia are in the side bar below.

The symptoms each pilot experiences depends on the individual. It has been found, however, that one tends to exhibit the same pattern of symptoms every time hypoxia occurs.

One of the real problems with hypoxia is that the pilot suffering from lowered oxygen supply often experiences a state of inebriation in which he or she is no longer able to judge whether or not the symptoms are in evidence. Many pilots have been known to be hypoxic by their ground crews talking to them on the radio, yet the pilots could not or would not acknowledge the fact. Other pilots have landed in a daze from hypoxia, and a few have even lost consciousness aloft, only to come down under canopy or wake up in a dive at lower altitude.

Hypoxia Signs
1. Increased breathing rate
2. Light-headed or dizzy sensation
3. Tingling or warm sensation
4. Cold extremities
5. Tunnel vision
6. Loss of night vision
7. Sweating and nausea
8. Sleepiness
9. Blue coloring of skin, fingernails and lips
10. Behavior changes such as euphoria or belligerence

While losing consciousness is an extreme result for a pilot, hypoxia also affects your ability to make safe judgements and wise decisions. Hypoxia creeps up slowly and gets worse the longer you spend at altitude, and the higher you go. Consequently, for safety and performance reasons, no pilot can risk hypoxia in flight.

The average individual begins to lose night vision above 5,000 feet MSL. By 8,000 feet as much as 25% of night vision is lost. This process continues with increasing altitude. Of course, hang glider pilots rarely fly at night, but this factor indicates at what low altitudes the effects of hypoxia begin.

Pilots in general aviation are advised to use supplemental oxygen above 5,000 feet at night and 10,000 feet during the day. Above 12,500 feet it is mandatory for all flights lasting over 30 minutes, and above 14,000 feet it is required at all times. These rules are for the USA, but similar rules apply in all regulated countries.

Aaron Swepston flies the high Sierra, an area demanding oxygen.

At what altitude hang glider pilots should begin to use supplemental oxygen is open to discussion. We usually use more strength when controlling our gliders in thermal turbulence than do sailplane pilots, for example, so our oxygen requirements would seem to be higher. However, our prone flying position gives our brains good circulation so the more severe effects are somewhat delayed. In addition, each individual has a different susceptibility to hypoxia, determined by his or her age, physical conditioning and body efficiency. Personal habits such as smoking, drinking alcohol and the use of drugs can result in greater susceptibility to hypoxia.

In any case all pilots should consider the use of supplemental oxygen above 12,500 feet. Flying above 15,000 feet for any extended period of time should absolutely be done with supplemental oxygen. Pilots have gone much higher than this without oxygen, of course, but they *were* suffering from hypoxia effects whether they knew it or not. If you are fun flying at such altitudes hypoxia is compromising your safety. If you are competing you are not making the best decisions of which you are capable if you are hypoxic.

Finally, we should know that while the symptoms of hypoxia often go away in 30 minutes or so (except for nausea), brain damage can occur every time you are hypoxic. This damage is irreversible.

One other breathing problem is breathing fast and shallow or hyperventilation. This occurs most often when fear or lack of oxygen addles our brain. Hyperventilation upsets the carbon dioxide/oxygen balance in our body and can worsen the effects of hypoxia and lead to dizziness. To control this and reestablish the balance, force yourself to take deep regular breaths until the natural balance is restored.

HYPOTHERMIA

Extreme changes of temperature— typically 50° or more in high desert flying in a matter of minutes—cause stress to body and mind that should be understood.

When the body temperature drops below its normal level the result is hypothermia. This condition is particularly of concern to hang glider pilots, since even on a warm summer day temperatures can be freezing cold aloft. Most hang glider pilots fly dangling in the wind. For this reason, all bare body parts should be covered during high or long flights. If you find yourself getting cold, come down to a warmer altitude or land, dress warmer and go back up. The rule of thumb is: if you are not sweating at launch you are not dressed warmly enough for altitude.

The body is designed to protect the vital organs at the expense of other parts in dire situations. In the case of lowered body temperature, the capillaries in the hands and feet will constrict so as to reserve more blood and warmth to the brain. Thus, the best way to keep your hands and feet warm is to keep your head and neck warm. This is especially pertinent since a large part of the body's heat loss is from the head and neck in windy conditions. The silk scarf, leather helmet and goggles worn by the open cockpit pilots of yesteryear were for a very good reason. They knew that hypothermia results in reduced efficiency. Note: the use of caffeine in sodas or coffee as well as nicotine constricts the capillaries and produces cold extremities.

ALCOHOL AND DRUGS

We are not decrying the use of these substances since we recognize many of them are a part of modern life and we believe that each person has a right to choose their own vice. However, we are saying that they do not mix with flying.

Since flying any aircraft requires so much judgement and motor coordination, any substance that impairs these items is dangerous. The case against alcohol is well documented. The loss of flying ability goes up with the amount of alcohol consumed. The more drinks under the belt, the longer the effects last. For example, it takes about three hours for one ounce of alcohol to wear off. Only time will reduce alcohol effects, not coffee, exercise or sleep. In addition, altitude worsens the effect of alcohol since lowering oxygen supply to the brain is exactly how alcohol works. For example. if you have ever had a drink on a commercial airlines you may notice its strong effect since the cabins are pressurized for up to 9,000 feet. Then, when you return to sea level you sober right up.

Drugs are extremely dangerous since they can blur the senses, cause confusion and act in unpredictable ways at altitude. This includes seemingly harmless non-prescription drugs. Antibiotics, antihistamines, tranquilizers, barbiturates, anaesthetics, sulfa drugs, reducing drugs and even aspirin have been implicated in flying accidents. Each of these drugs require a 12 to 48 hours waiting period before flying can be considered safe.

Remember, you are flying for enjoyment, so don't risk ruining your fun permanently by using questionable substances before your flights. There is plenty of time to fly tomorrow if your system is not in shape today. If you enjoy flying in the present, fly with the utmost caution and you will enjoy flying far into the future.

CARBON MONOXIDE

Carbon monoxide can impair your ability to use oxygen (one of the problems with smoking), thereby inducing hypoxia at lower altitudes than normally. It can also cause disorientation and eventually death. The effects of carbon monoxide poisoning can last for days, so make sure you aren't breathing fumes from a poorly placed exhaust on your way to launch. Although carbon monoxide is odorless, it is usually accompanied by other exhaust fumes. If you smell exhaust, make some changes to get fresh air.

DECOMPRESSION

Under normal conditions, nitrogen is always present in the blood and other body fluids. At higher altitudes this nitrogen comes out of solution and forms little bubbles that can block blood vessels and cause headache, pain, and other more serious symptoms including death. Other gases in the body may expand at altitude causing pain in the ear, sinus, teeth or intestines. In general, hang glider pilots don't climb high enough to suffer decompression effects. However, if a scuba diver attempts to fly soon after diving below 30 ft (10 m) the ceiling on the onset of decompression sickness is lowered dramatically. Since scuba diving introduces more nitrogen into the blood stream than normal, the simple rule to follow is wait for 24 hours after diving before flying.

III - HUMAN FACTORS

There are several physical and psychological factors that come into play in our flying performance. Most of these are directly controllable by us by adopting the right habits.

PHYSICAL FITNESS

The better shape we are in, the better we are able to combat the effects of fatigue, hypoxia and stress. It goes without saying that a good working heart and mind are prerequisites for safety. While hang gliding isn't as demanding physically as say soccer or good sex, physical conditioning to strengthen the upper body as well as aerobic exercises can increase our comfort and endurance in the air. We recommend running, bicycling, swimming cross-country skiing for aerobics and the specific exercise shown in figure 13-4 for creating turning power in the air.

As the flying community greys, the pilots that stay in shape are the ones that will enjoy the sport when they have the time— after they retire.

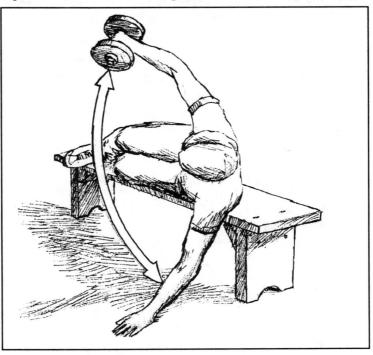

Figure 13-4: Hang Gliding Pilot's Exercise

FATIGUE AND OTHER FACTORS

Fear will increase the heart rate more than exercising will.

Physical fitness goes a long way to preventing fatigue, but there are other factors that must be considered. Obviously, sleep must be ample or mental fatigue is unavoidable. Fatigue lowers our resistance to stress and hypoxia so it must be controlled for safe flying.

It has been shown that experiencing continuously varying G forces can add to fatigue and stress. In the course of a flight we accumulate plenty of increased G time, especially in strong conditions. Remember, it's important to relax in the air when possible.

The affects of stress are additive—keep a straw count.

We have witnessed two dramatic and debilitating accidents which can be directly attributed to fatigue. In both cases the pilots plowed back into the hill soon after launching. One was hurt badly and one was unscathed. After the event both pilots admitted they had a sleep deficit and were not flying with crisply breaking brain waves. One pilot said he knew he should make a turn away from the hill but his mind was on vacation and the signal didn't make it out of the shop.

DEHYDRATION AND DIURETICS

Desert flying can leave you feeling dry as a horned toad. The threat of dehydration can be dangerous in the air and deadly on the ground if you land away from a quick rescue. Many pilots fly with water usable in the air in such conditions. Sensible pilots at least have a minimum of a quart of water retrievable upon landing.

Dehydration can impair your decision-making and visual judgement as well as produce dizziness. The sad thing to note is that caffeine-containing drinks and alcohol, including that ever-so-popular post-landing beer, can dehydrate you. If you use these beverages, be sure to include plenty of good old H_2O in your daily consumption.

Beer, caffeine-containing drinks and grapefruit juice are all diuretics. That means they make you urinate (which is one reason they dehydrate you). If you plan a long flight it is unwise to drink these beverages beforehand. Some pilots with weak bladders have a problem with long flights no matter what they drink. The solution adopted by the serious ones is to use a urinary device for invalids available at drugstores or medical supply houses. Some very experienced pilots also use adult diapers.

NUTRITION

We aren't about to tell you to change your lifetime eating habits, but when it comes to flying, irregular meals can wreak havoc on blood sugar levels which can be dangerous in the air. We strongly suggest a good breakfast (no, not poptarts) and a consumption of carbohydrates in the form of starches rather than candy bars (including granola bars) or other sweets for lasting energy.

PSYCHOLOGICAL FACTORS

Fear is one of our worst enemies. If you have excessive fears, reread the section on fear in Chapter 1, go back to work on the basics and have an instructor watch your technique to correct possible mistakes and teach you confidence building procedures.

Emotional stresses are very common causes of accidents. If you are upset by a job situation, family problems, love complications, a missed soap opera episode or any other psychological stress, you are not operating at 100% and should not be flying. Anger and anxiety impairs our ability to make wise judgements. Good physical health can contribute to good mental health. Allowing peer pressure to affect our judgement is one sign of lack of maturity. We alone are responsible for our decisions and we alone suffer the most severe consequences of bad decisions.

SUMMARY

Our minds and bodies sure like the sensation of flight, so we must be doing something right. However, we can run into complications if we break the laws of physics or good health. Of course, we all have our little shortcomings, peccadillos and personal problems that prevent us from being perfect, but we need to leave these on the ground so we are superhumans in the air. Flight may not solve all our problems, but it certainly is a good excuse to get our earthbound house in order so we can spend more time airborne and unbounded.

APPENDIX

Many matters of glider performance can best be described with formulas. For the reader wishing to know more about how their wings work or interested in doing their own performance calculation we offer the theory here. We have divided this appendix into sections relating to specific references in the text as indicated by the page numbers next to the section titles.

TURN PERFORMANCE (page 56)

When we enter a coordinated turn our glider experiences a change in performance due to the increase in the apparent weight as G forces build up and the fact that the lifting forces are no longer vertical as shown in the figure.

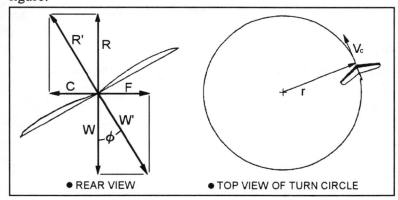

● REAR VIEW   ● TOP VIEW OF TURN CIRCLE

where:

C	=	centrifugal (inward) force
R	=	net aerodynamic force in level flight
R′	=	net aerodynamic force in a bank
W	=	overall weight
W′	=	apparent weight due to the addition of centrifugal force
m	=	mass
r	=	radius of turn
t	=	time to complete one 360
V_C	=	circling flying velocity
ϕ	=	bank angle

From these diagrams we can define three basic equations:

$$\tan \phi = \frac{F}{W}$$
so $F = W \tan\phi$
but $W = mg$
so $F = mg \tan\phi \quad (1)$

Circumference of the turn equals $2\pi r$ and $2\pi r = V_c t$ since the distance traveled equals rate multiplied by time.

So $r = \frac{t\, V_c}{2}\pi \quad (2)$

In any physics text we can find the formula for centripetal (or centrifugal) force:

$$C = F = \frac{m V_c^2}{r} \quad (3)$$

✓ Velocity in Turn

Using (3) and (1), we have
$$\frac{m V_c^2}{r} = mg \tan\phi$$
$$\text{so } V_c^2 = rg \tan\phi$$

Using equation (2) to substitute for r we have: $V_c = \frac{tg}{2\pi}\tan\phi \quad (4)$

This gives the flying velocity if we know the bank angle and time to complete one 360 (complete circle). It is easy to note a glider's bank angle sighting with a protractor that has a plumb line suspended at the vertex as shown. By timing the glider's circle we can calculate speed which is the best possible way to calibrate an airspeed indicator.

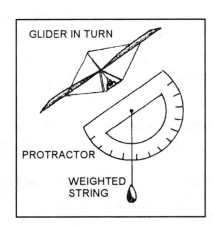

GLIDER IN TURN

PROTRACTOR

WEIGHTED STRING

✓ Minimum Airspeed Turn

The velocity we found above is faster than for straight flight at any given angle of attack because of the increase in apparent weight. We can find the relationship between level and turning flight airspeeds by noting:

$$\frac{V_s^2}{V_c^2} = \frac{W}{W'}$$ (this equation is derived in the WING LOADING section)   but $W' = \dfrac{W}{\cos\phi}$

so $V_s = V_c \sqrt{\cos\phi}$

so $V_c = \dfrac{V_s}{\sqrt{\cos\phi}}$ (5)

where: V_s = velocity in straight flight
V_c = velocity in circling flight
W = weight
W' = apparent weight in turn
Note: W'/W = G loading

For example, if we use our straight flight stall speed for V_s, we can find our circling flight stall speed from equation (5). Since our stall speed is the slowest we can go whether we are flying straight or turning, we can use this speed to give us our minimum turning radius. Replacing V_s with V_{LS} (level flight stall speed) and substituting (5) into (4), we have:

$V_{LS} = \dfrac{tg}{2\pi} \tan\phi \sqrt{\cos\phi}$ We can solve this for t to find our minimum time for one 360: $t = \dfrac{2\pi V_{LS}}{g\tan\phi \sqrt{\cos\phi}}$

✓ Minimum Turn Radius

If we fly at minimum possible airspeed in a turn we can easily find our minimum radius of turn using equation (3).

Turning radius, $r = \dfrac{m V_c^2}{F} = \dfrac{m}{F}\left(\dfrac{V_{LS}}{\sqrt{\cos\phi}}\right)^2$ from (5)

Applying equation (1): $r = \dfrac{W\left(\dfrac{V_{LS}}{\sqrt{\cos\phi}}\right)^2}{gW\tan\phi} = \dfrac{V_{LS}{}^2}{g\cos\phi\tan\phi}$

but $\tan\phi = \dfrac{\sin\phi}{\cos\phi}$ (basic rule of trigonometry) so: $r = \dfrac{V_{LS}^2}{g\sin\phi}$ (6)

This equation gives our minimum turning radius possible at any chosen bank angle. Such a calculation is important to analyze thermaling flight. Note that the slower we can fly, the smaller our radius is. Weight or wing loading does not appear in the equation but is included in V_{LS}, for the heavier the wing loading, the higher our stall speed.

It is also apparent from the equation that the greater our bank angle, the smaller our radius. However, greater bank angles increase our sink rate dramatically as well as our stall speed due to the added G loading. So we find a limit to our circling radius and an ideal bank angle for each thermal as explained in Chapter 3.

✓ Weight Effects

Just as G loading in the turn increases our speed, so does actually adding weight (ballast or a heavier pilot) to the system. This increase in speed increases the minimum radius of turns as follows:

$\dfrac{V_N{}^2}{V_O{}^2} = \dfrac{W_N}{W_O}$, so $V_N = V_O \sqrt{\dfrac{W_N}{W_O}}$

where: V_N = new velocity
V_O = original velocity
W_N = new weight
W_O = original weight

substituting in (6): $r = \dfrac{\dfrac{W_N}{W_O} V_O{}^2}{g\sin\phi}$

WING LOADING (page 305) ———————————————————————

The aerodynamic force that any object, including a wing moving through the air, produces is given by the formula: $F = \tfrac{1}{2} C_F \rho S V^2$

where: F = aerodynamic force
C_F = coefficient relating to the shape of the body
ρ = air density (.00238 slugs at sea level)
S = surface area of the wing
V = velocity or airspeed

> NOTE: If we are looking at lift or drag we replace F with L or D and get our lift and drag equations.

In steady gliding flight, the net upward aerodynamic forces must equal the weight, so F = W. Thus we have $W = 1/2\ C_F\ \rho\ S\ V^2$. If we consider two different weights on the same wing in the same conditions we can form the ratio:

$$\frac{W_1}{W_2} = \frac{1/2\,C_F\rho S V_1^2}{1/2\,C_F\rho S V_2^2} \qquad so \qquad \frac{W_1}{W_2} = \frac{V_1^2}{V_2^2} \qquad and \qquad V_1 = V_2\sqrt{\frac{W_1}{W_2}}$$

This equation says that if we are given an original flying velocity and weight, V_2 and W_2 and we have a new weight, W_1, we can find the new velocity, V_1. For example, assume our original stall speed is 20 mph, our original weight is 250 lbs and our new weight is 270 lbs. We then have for our new stall speed:

$$V_{NEW} = 20\sqrt{\frac{270}{250}} = 20.8\ mph$$

THE SPEED POLAR (page 188)

We can derive the speed polar mathematically from the observation that a polar closely follows a parabola above best glide speeds. With the mathematical expression we can then draw a complete polar from only a few data points and also calculate speed ring values and best average speeds.

We start with the quadratic equation: $W_s = aV^2 + bV + c$ where W_s is the sink rate and V is the airspeed. To find a, b and c we need to know three data points which are three airspeeds and the related sink (in still air). For maximum accuracy, we suggest using best glide speed, a speed with the bar below your waist and a speed halfway in between these two.

We now can write three equations with the three points:

$$W_{s1} = aV_1^2 + bV_1 + c$$
$$W_{s2} = aV_2^2 + bV_2 + c$$
$$W_{s3} = aV_3^2 + bV_3 + c$$

By subtracting one equation from the other we can eliminate all but one of the unknowns (a, b and c) to get:

$$a = \frac{(V_2 - V_3)\,(W_{s1} - W_{s3}) + (V_3 - V_1)\,(W_{s2} - W_{s3})}{V_1^2(V_2 - V_3) + V_2^2(V_3 - V_1) + V_3^2(V_1 - V_2)}$$

$$b = \frac{W_{s2} - W_{s3} - a(V_2^2 - V_3^2)}{V_2 - V_3}$$

$$c = W_{s3} - aV_3^2 - bV_3$$

For the polars used in Chapter 7, the values are :
a = −0.608
b = +26.198
c = −461.970

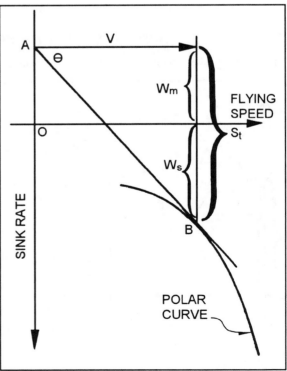

The signs and size of these coefficients are typical for hang gliders if V is expressed in miles per hour resulting in W_s in feet per minute. If, for example, we use a V of 35 mph we have: $W_s = -.608\ (35)^2 + 26.2\ (35) - 462 = 290\ FPM$

CALCULATING A SPEED RING (page 168)

If we know our polar graph we can graphically determine value pairs for our speed ring. Likewise, if we know our polar formula (see above) we can calculate the value pairs.

As shown in the figure, the air mass sink between thermals W_m moves the axis from O to A where we draw a tangent to the polar. The best speed-to-fly is then V and our total sink is S_t which is the sum of W_m and W_s, the glider's sink rate. For every given W_m our polar will give a V and S_t pair which we use for our speed ring.

We shall derive formulas for finding V and S_t with two methods:

METHOD I

$$S_t = W_s + W_m$$
and $$W_s = aV^2 + bV + c$$
so $$S_t = aV^2 + bV + c + W_m$$

dividing by V: $$\frac{S_t}{V} = aV + b + \frac{c + W_m}{V}$$

Now $\frac{S_t}{V}$ defines the slope of the tangent line AB. We can differentiate this slope and set it equal to zero to find the minimum angle θ. Thus:

$$\frac{d\, S_t/V}{d\, V} = a - \frac{c + W_m}{V^2}$$

so $$0 = a - \frac{c + W_m}{V^2}$$

Solving for V: $$V = \sqrt{\frac{c + W_m}{a}}$$

Once we know V we can find S_t from:
$$S_t = aV^2 + bV + c + W_m$$

METHOD II

The slope of the tangent AB equals $\frac{S_t}{V} = \frac{W_s + W_m}{V}$

This slope also equals $\frac{d\, W_s}{d\, V}$ (from calculus).

Since $W_s = aV^2 + bV + c$,

$$\frac{d\, W_s}{d\, V} = 2aV + b = \frac{W_s + W_m}{V}$$

so $$2aV + b = \frac{aV^2 + bV + c + W_m}{V}$$

$$2aV^2 + bV = aV^2 + bV + c + W_m$$
$$aV^2 = c + W_m$$

so $$V = \sqrt{\frac{c + W_m}{a}}$$

S_t is again found from the equation in method I.

When using these equations it is important to preserve the sign of the values. For instance, W_m can be negative (sink) or positive (lift). Once you have your polar coefficients (a, b, c) as found in the previous section you can get as many V and S_t pairs as you require. Here's an actual example using the polar from before:

Assume the air is sinking 425 FPM, then our optimum flying speed V is: $V = \sqrt{\frac{c + W_m}{a}} = \sqrt{\frac{-462 - 445}{-.608}}$

$$V = \sqrt{1458.9} = 38.2 \text{ mph}$$
Then $$S_t = -.608 (38.2)^2 + 26.2 (38.2) - 462 - 425$$
$$S_t = -887 + 1000.7 - 887 = -773.3 \text{ FPM}$$
So $V = 38.2$ mph and $S_t = -773.3$ FPM is one value pair we could mark on our speed ring.

AVERAGE SPEED-TO-FLY CALCULATION (page 189)

Previously we choose to optimize our speed through lifting or sinking air without considering an expected climb. Here we add an expected climb and find a new optimized average speed.

✔ Speed Ring Pairs

Proceeding as above, we can define a net sink S_n as the sum of air mass sink W_m and glider sink W_s minus the expected climb rate C_l.

So $$S_n = W_s + W_m - C_l$$

Since $W_s = aV^2 + bV + c$, $\quad S_n = aV^2 + bV + c + W_m - C_l \quad$ (1)

Using the same method as before we can find V, the optimum airspeed:

$$V = \sqrt{\frac{c + W_m - C_l}{a}} \quad (2)$$

Then using equations (1) and (2) we can find S_n and V to make a new speed ring. However, since we see our S_n equation is similar to previously except for the added C_l term, we realize that we can simply turn our speed ring an amount equal to C_l to increase our flying speeds proportionally. This is the basis of a movable speed ring. Note that since a is negative in equation (2), an increase in C_l or a negative value of W_m increases our optimum flying speed V.

✓ *Finding Optimum Average Speed*

From the figure we see a relationship from similar triangles where: $\dfrac{V_{AVE}}{V} = \dfrac{C_1}{C_1 + (-S_t)} = \dfrac{C_1}{C_1 - S_t}$

Let us find this mathematically by assuming that during a glide we lose altitude h and cover a distance d. Our average speed will then be $V_{AVE} = \dfrac{d}{t}$ where t is the total time. But $t = t_g + t_c$ where t_g is gliding time and t_c is climbing time. Our altitude lost is: $-h = t_g \times S_t$ where $S_t = W_m + W_s$. Our altitude gained while climbing is: $h = t_c \times C_1$. Relating the two h equations, we have:

$$-t_g \times S_t = t_c \times C_1 \;\text{ so }\; t_c = -t_g \frac{S_t}{C_1}. \text{ But } t_g = \frac{d}{V}, \text{ so }\; t_c = \frac{-dS_t}{VC_1}.$$

Then $\;\; t = t_g + t_c = \dfrac{d}{V} - \dfrac{dS_t}{VC_1} = \dfrac{d}{V}\left(1 - \dfrac{S_t}{C_1}\right). \text{ But } V_{AVE} = \dfrac{d}{t}, \text{ so } \dfrac{d}{V_{AVE}} = \dfrac{d}{V}\left(1 - \dfrac{S_t}{C_1}\right)$

Rearranging we have: $\dfrac{V_{AVE}}{V} = \dfrac{C_1}{C_1 - S_t} = \dfrac{C_1}{C_1 - W_s - W_m}$ (1)

Now we can get rid of V and W_s in equation (1) so we can calculate V_{AVE} for any given air mass sink W_m and expected climb rate C_1 if we know our polar equation. Multiplying (1) by V we have:

$$V_{AVE} = \frac{C_1 V}{C_1 - W_s - W_m}, \;\text{ so }\; V_{AVE} = \frac{C_1 V}{C_1 - W_m - aV^2 - bV - c} \;\text{ but }\; V = \sqrt{\frac{c + W_m - C_1}{a}} \;\text{ for optimum average speed.}$$

$$\text{So }\; V_{AVE\,(OPTIMUM)} = \frac{C_1 \sqrt{\dfrac{c + W_m - C_1}{a}}}{C_1 - W_m - (c + W_m - C_1) - b\sqrt{\dfrac{c + W_m - C_1}{a}} - c}$$

$$\text{and }\; V_{AVE\,(OPTIMUM)} = \frac{C_1 \sqrt{\dfrac{c + W_m - C_1}{a}}}{2C_1 - 2W_m - 2c - b\sqrt{\dfrac{c + W_m - C_1}{a}}}$$

PERFORMANCE FORMULAS (page 300)

Using the formulas for induces and parasitic drag, it is possible to derive a more accurate equation for a glider's polar. Such a derivation is beyond the scope of this book, but we can use the equation to solve for various cardinal points such as minimum sink and best glide using only our glider's parameters. We provide the equations here related to the accompanying polar.

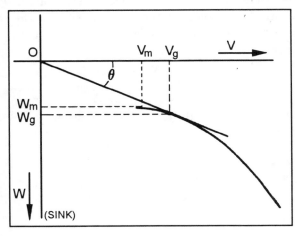

■ BEST GLIDE $= \dfrac{1}{\tan\theta} = \sqrt{\dfrac{\pi\,AR}{4K\,C_{DO}}}$

■ SPEED AT BEST GLIDE $= V_G = \sqrt[4]{\dfrac{4K}{\pi\,AR\,C_{DO}\,\rho_0^2}}\sqrt{\omega}$

■ SINK AT BEST GLIDE $= W_G = \sqrt[4]{\dfrac{4^3 K^3 C_{DO}}{\pi^3 AR^3 \rho_0^2}}\sqrt{\omega}$

■ SPEED AT MINIMUM SPEED $= V_m = \sqrt[4]{\dfrac{4K}{3\pi\,AR\,C_{DO}\,\rho_0^2}}\sqrt{\omega}$

■ MINIMUM SINK $= W_m = 4\sqrt[4]{\dfrac{4K^3 C_{DO}}{27\pi^3 AR^3 \rho_0^2}}\sqrt{\omega}$

where: AR = Aspect ratio
θ = Glide angle
C_{DO} = Drag coefficient at zero lift
ω = Wing Loading = $\dfrac{weight}{wing\ area}$
ρ_0 = Air density at sea level = .00238 slugs
K = Span efficiency factor

The span efficiency factor is necessary because the formulas are derived for an elliptical, non-swept, non-twisted wing. The efficiency factor can be combined with aspect ratio to give an effective aspect ratio. However, it is simpler to use K as a separate entity and calculate it.

The above equations show that our glider's performance depends on our wing loading (ω), our parasitic drag (C_{DO}), our aspect ratio (AR) and the efficiency factor. We can readily figure our wing loading and aspect ratio, but C_{DO} and K are more difficult. However, if we have data points for minimum sink or best glide we can use two of our equations to find K and C_{DO}.

For example, assume: aspect ratio = AR = 7.5   wing loading $\dfrac{W}{S} = \omega = 1.6$ lbs/sq.ft.

and best glide is 11.5 at 27 mph (39.6 FPS)

Using the first two equations above gives: $11.5 = \sqrt{\dfrac{\pi\,7.5}{4K\,C_{DO}}}$ and $39.6 = \sqrt[4]{\dfrac{4K}{\pi\,7.5\,C_{DO}\,\rho_0^2}}\sqrt{\omega}$

Solving for K in one equation and inserting it in the other gives: K = 1.19, so C_{DO} = .037.

The drag coefficient found here is close to that found in wind tunnels. The reciprocal of K is the efficiency. So 1/K = .84 which means our glider is 84% efficient. This is the upper end of a flex wing glider and indicates we pay a 16% loss of performance penalty for our sweep and twist. If our aspect ratio is 7.5, our *effective* aspect ratio is 84% of 7.5 or 6.3.

GREAT CIRCLE DISTANCE (page 222 and 296)

Because we live on a roughly spherical earth, we cannot measure exact distances on a flat map. In fact, a line drawn on a globe representing the shortest "great circle distance" between two points would appear as a curved line on a flat map.

To find a, the distance between two points in nautical miles we use the formula:

a = 60 arc cos (sin b · sin c + cos b · cos c · cos A), where: b = latitude of location 1 (takeoff for example), c = latitude of location 2 (landing for example) and A = absolute value of longitude 1 − longitude 2.

The official value for a nautical mile is 1.50779 statute miles and 1.851999 kilometers. A nautical mile is one minute of arc on a great circle and there are 60 minutes in a degree which is why the multiplier 60 is in the equation.

METRIC CONVERSIONS

We recognize the metric system as making more sense from the mathematical viewpoint. However, cultural inertia results in the continued use of the "English" system in the United States even though the rest of the world has adopted the easier metric system. We have included the metric measurements in the text where it was deemed important. Here are the conversion factors for the reader's convenience.

DISTANCE
1 inch (in) = 2.54 centimeters (cm)
1 meter (m) = 39.37 inches = 3.28 feet
1 foot (ft) = 30.48 centimeters (cm)
1 mile = 1.61 kilometers (km)

WEIGHT
1 pound (lb) = .45 kilograms (kg)
1 kilogram = 2.2 lbs

SPEED
1 mile per hour (mph) = 1.61 km/h
1 km/h = .62 mph
200 feet per minute (FPM) ≈ 1 meter per second (approximately)

AREA
1 square foot (sq.ft.) = .0929 square meter (m²)
1 square meter = 10.764 sq.ft.

WING LOADING
Combining the weight and area conversion factors we can find the equivalent wing loadings:
1.3 pounds per square foot (lbs/ft²) = 6.3 kg/m²
1.4 lbs/ft² = 6.78 kg/m²
1.5 lbs/ft² = 7.26 kg/m²
1.6 lbs/ft² = 7.75 kg/m²
1.7 lbs/ft² = 8.23 kg/m²

GLOSSARY

ADVERSE YAW — The yawing of a glider in the opposite direction of the control input (pilot rolls left, glider yaws right, for example).

AEROBATICS — Performing maneuvers beyond the normal tested envelope of a glider.

AERODYNAMIC CONTROLS — Movable surfaces on a wing to effect turns or angle of attack changes.

AEROTOWING — See AIR-TO-AIR TOWING

AIRFOIL — The curved shape of a wing cross section intended to produce lift and minimum drag.

AIR-TO-AIR TOWING — Towing a hang glider aloft with an ultralight.

ANHEDRAL — A downward angling of the wings from the root (center) to the tips.

ASPECT RATIO — A measure of how long and narrow a wing is. The ratio of the span to the chord.

ATOL — Abbreviation for Airtime of Lubbock, the company that first developed payout winch towing.

BALLAST — Additional weight carried by a pilot to achieve faster speeds on cross-country flights.

BEST AVERAGE SPEED — The speed to fly between thermals to provide the fastest flight over a given distance considering both gliding and climbing time.

BLUE HOLE — A clear area in an otherwise cloud-studded sky.

BLUE STREET — A thermal street without clouds.

BLUE THERMAL — A thermal that is not producing a cloud due to an inversion layer or very dry air.

BRIDLE — PARACHUTE — The leader from the pilot's harness to the parachute lines.

      — TOWING — The webbing or rope attachment from a towline to the pilot's harness.

CAMBER — The curve of an airfoil.

CANTILEVERED WING — A wing unsupported by cables or struts, holding itself rigid by its internal strength.

CENTERING — Finding and remaining in the perfect center of a thermal core.

CENTER-OF-MASS TOWING — Towing from the CG of the pilot/glider combination.

CG — Abbreviation for center of gravity. Where all the mass of a solid body can be considered to lie for purposes of understanding forces on that body.

CHORD — The measure of an airfoil or wing from the leading edge to the trailing edge.

CLASS I GLIDER — A flex wing hang glider controlled purely by weight shift.

CLASS II GLIDER — A fixed wing hang glider controlled all or partially by aerodynamic control.

CLOUD STREET — Clouds lined up with the wind indicating a line of thermals.

CLOUD SUCK — Strong lift below a cloud that may pull a pilot into the cloud.

CONVERGENCE — A flowing together of air masses resulting in an upwelling or lift.

CRABBING — Angling into the wind that is crossing a desired flight path so that the path can be maintained.

CROSS-COUNTRY — Flying a distance over the ground beyond a glider normal gliding ability by using natural lift.

DIHEDRAL — An angling up of a glider's wings from the root (center) to the tips.

DIVING TURN — A slipping or spiraling turn produced by pulling in on the control bar and moving to one side.

DOLPHIN FLYING — Speeding up in sink and slowing in lift to maximize flying speed.

DRAG — Losses in flight due to swirls produced in the air by solid forms on our gliders or the wings themselves.

DROGUE CHUTE — A small parachute on a towline or glider to produce drag.

DUST DEVIL — A swirl of air created by a thermal in strong conditions that picks up dust.

DYNAMIC STABILITY — The tendency of a glider to settle to trim speed when it is pitched rapidly up or down.

FINAL — The last leg of a landing approach that ends with a flare.

FINAL GLIDE — The last glide on an open distance X-C flight after lift is depleted. The last racing glide on a speed course after sufficient height is achieved to reach goal.

FIXED WING — See CLASS II GLIDER

FLAT TURN — A turn made with a minimum bank angle, usually used in very light lift.

FLIGHT PATH — The ground track you describe when flying from one place to another.

FLIGHT BANDS — Imaginary layers in the sky that a pilot uses to determine strategy.

GAGGLE — A group of pilots in one thermal.

G FORCE — Gravity force. G forces can be more than one gravity in turns and other accelerations.

GLORY — A pilot's halo produced by the shadow effects on a cloud.

GREAT CIRCLE — The shortest line drawn between two points on a globe of the earth. This is an accurate measurement of a cross-country flight. It always is a curved line on a flat map and so must be found mathematically.

HAZE DOME — A lifting of an inversion layer in a localized area due to a penetrating thermal.

HEADING COMPASS — A compass with a movable ball (rather than a needle) which points in the direction you are heading.

HIGH PERFORMANCE GLIDER — A glider that provides state-of-the-art performance.

HIGH SIDING — Moving to the outside (high side) of the control bar in a banked turn.

HYPOXIA — Lowered oxygen in the bloodstream (due to altitude effects in our case).

INDUCED DRAG — Drag caused as a result of the wings producing lift and thereby disturbing the airflow.

INVERSION — A layer of stable air. Near the ground an inversion can prevent thermals from forming. Higher up it can stop thermals from climbing.

LAPSE RATE — The change in the air's temperature with altitude. The greater the lapse rate (change) the more unstable the air is.

LEAD GAGGLE — The first group of pilots along a contest course.

LIFT — The sum of the aerodynamic forces perpendicular to the flight path of a wing.

LIFT DISTRIBUTION — The profile of the lift forces along a wing when viewed from the front or rear.

LOCKOUT — A problem during towing whereby a glider is displaced to one side of the tow line of force. A lockout may automatically worsen if a correction isn't made.

MEAN CAMBER — The curve of the line drawn midway between the upper and the lower surface of an airfoil.

MSL — An Abbreviation for Mean Sea Level. Used to refer to height above sea level.

OUT-AND-BACK — A form of cross-country flight that consists of flying to a goal then back to the start point.

OVERDEVELOPMENT — An atmosphere condition whereby the sky gets overcast because so much moisture exists aloft that cumulus clouds don't dry out. Also the condition where strong updrafts with associated moisture build into thunderstorms.

PARASITIC DRAG — That part of drag caused by solids disrupting the air flow. Parasitic drag plus induced drag equals total drag on an aircraft.

PAYOUT WINCH — A winch that moves and feeds out line as a glider climbs.

PERFORMANCE MAP — See POLAR

PITCH — A nose up or down control.

PITOT TUBE — A tube pointing directly into the air flow to measure dynamic pressure and thus airspeed.

POLAR — A graph of a glider's performance which gives the sink rate at each flying speed.

POSITION RING — A ring on a variometer dial indicating the proper bar positions for various amounts of indicated sink.

POSITIONS-TO-FLY — A system of selecting the proper control bar position for any given air movement encountered in order to maximize performance.

PULLED DOWN APEX — A parachute design whereby the center is pulled down which expands the skirt and creates more drag.

REFLEX BRIDLES — Thin cables running from the kingpost to a sail's trailing edge whose purpose is to hold reflex in the sail (simulating up elevator on an airplane) in low or negative angle of attack situations in order to provide pitch stability.

RELEASE — A device to separate a glider from a towline or a balloon tether.

REYNOLDS NUMBER — A comparison of the inertial to the viscous effects of the air. The higher the Reynolds number the lower the drag is at any given airspeed.

ROLL — A control action whereby the wings move up or down.

ROOT — The center of a wing (the keel position on a hang glider).

ROTOR — An organized swirl of air behind a large obstruction to the wind (mountain e.g.) or beneath an atmospheric wave.

SKID — Sliding to the outside of a turn.

SKYTING — A term devised to indicate a special combination of ideal towing practices and equipment configurations.

SLIP — Sliding to the inside of a turn. A slip can result in lots of acquired speed and be dangerous if uncontrolled near the ground.

SPEED RING — A ring on a variometer dial indicating the proper speeds-to-fly for different amounts of indicated sink.

SPEEDS-TO-FLY — A system of selecting the proper flying speed for any given air movement encountered in order to maximize performance.

SPIN — A normally uncontrolled turn during which the inside wing is stalled. Flex wings gliders are very resistant to spins.

SPIRAL — A diving turn which is coordinated (no slippage) and pulls high Gs.

STATIC LINE — A type of towing where the tow rope remains one length behind a vehicle (as opposed to a payout winch system).

STATIC STABILITY — The tendency of a glider to return to trim position when the bar is held in or out from this position.

STATIC WINCH — A stationary winch that reels in a towline and thus pulls a glider aloft.

STALL — Disrupted flow on a wing's surface due to too high an angle of attack.

STEP TOWING — Gaining altitude in steps by climbing under tow then flying away from the winch to pull out line and repeat the process.

STREETS — Lines of thermals or clouds usually appearing as a series of parallel lines.

SUPINE — A flying position whereby the pilot lies reclining as in an easy chair.

SWEEP — An angling back of a glider's wings.

THERMAL — A rising bubble of air.

THERMAL STREET — A line of thermals.

THUNDERSTORM — Overdeveloped thermal lift that results in large, fast cloud build-up with possible lightning, precipitation, strong winds and turbulence.

TOTAL ENERGY COMPENSATION — A variometer rigged to factor out a glider's climb or sink due to pitch control changes and thus report only the air's vertical movement.

TRIM — The angle of attack or bar position that a stable glider settles on hands off. Hopefully this is between stall speed and best glide speed.

TUMBLING — The action of a glider flipping head over keels.

TURBULENCE — Random or organized (as in a rotor) movement of the air.

TURN POINT — A ground location that defines a dogleg or point to round in a competition course.

TURN POLAR — A glider's performance map or sink rate to flying speed comparison when in a bank.

TWIST — See WASHOUT.

UV — Abbreviation for ultraviolet radiation.

VARIATION (COMPASS) — The amount that magnetic north varies from true north in a given location.

VARIOMETER — A sensitive rate of climb indicator pointing out sink and lift.

VERTIGO — Loss of spatial orientation due to conflicting signals from the sense organs.

VG — Abbreviation for variable geometry. A system on a glider for expanding a crossbar and tightening a sail in flight.

VOX — Abbreviation for voice activated microphone.

WANG — A term coined to describe a rollover maneuver on a hang glider since these craft can't perform true wingovers.

WASHOUT — A lowering of the angle of attack of a wing as it progresses from root to tip. A twisting of the wing.

WAVE LIFT — Lift due to a waving or a rippling action of the air downwind from a mountain.

WEAK LINK — A loop on a towline designed to break at a specified force and thus limit loads on the glider.

WING LOADING — The weight per unit area (lbs per square feet) a glider carries.

WING TIP VORTICES — Swirls of air at a glider wing tips due to spanwise flow above and below a wing.

X-C — Abbreviation for cross-country.

YAW — A control or glider action whereby one wing goes forward or back.

YAW TURN — Turning a glider with a strong yaw input along with the usual roll.

INDEX